The Wars Against Saddam

JOHN SIMPSON is the BBC's World Affairs Editor. He has twice been the Royal Television Society's Journalist of the Year. He has also won three BAFTAs and the News and Current Affairs award in 2000 for his coverage, with the BBC News team, of the Kosovo conflict. His reporting of the 2001 war in Afghanistan received many awards, including an international Emmy, and there were more for his coverage of the invasion of Iraq in 2003. After the first Gulf War in 1991 he was made a CBE. He has written several books, including his three volumes of autobiography, *Strange Places, Questionable People, A Mad World, My Masters* and *News From No Man's Land*.

Also by John Simpson

Strange Places, Questionable People

A Mad World, My Masters

News From No Man's Land

JOHN SIMPSON

The Wars Against Saddam

Taking the Hard Road to Baghdad

PAN BOOKS

First published 2003 by Macmillan

This edition published 2004 by Pan Books
an imprint of Pan Macmillan Ltd
Pan Macmillan, 20 New Wharf Road, London N1 9RR
Basingstoke and Oxford
Associated companies throughout the world
www.panmacmillan.com

ISBN 0 330 41890 4

A CIP catalogue record for this book is available from
the British Library.

Typeset by SetSystems Ltd, Saffron Walden, Essex
Printed and bound in Great Britain by
Mackays of Chatham plc, Chatham, Kent

To the reporters, cameramen, photographers
and translators who died during the Iraq War of 2003:
good friends and good colleagues, whose memory
the rest of us have a duty to keep alive.

Photographs courtesy of:

Abdullah Zaheerudin: 19, 22, 24, 26, 27, 31
AP Photo Archive: 23
Al-Arabiya TV: 3
BBC News: 1, 4, 5, 6, 7, 8, 9, 10, 11, 12, 13, 14, 15, 16, 17, 28
Hulton Getty: 2, 18, 20, 21, 32, 33
Tom Giles: 25, 29, 30

PREFACE

Several months after the American and British overthrow of Saddam Hussein in April 2003, I went back to northern Iraq from where I had covered the war for the BBC. It was late summer, and the grass which had been fresh and green when I was there in the spring was dying, and the yellow flowers which showed gaily in every camera shot were long since dried and withered to brown stalks. The bare, open landscape, with the ancient mounds of long-dead civilizations, showed no sign whatever of the fighting that had taken place. The larks sang high above my head. They had done that on the morning of Sunday 6 April, I remembered, in the instant of silence between the shattering noise of the exploding American missile, and the screaming of dying men.

Even at the crossroads where my colleagues and I had been mistakenly attacked and eighteen people killed, the ground had healed over like a wound. Someone had filled in the crater where the missile had landed, and the places where the vehicles had burned and blown up, and people had burned to death, were just enigmatic stains on the roadway. We marvelled yet again that we ourselves should have survived when we were only ten or twelve yards from the place where the missile landed, and we paid our respects at the place where our translator had been mortally injured.

As I write this, it has been exactly twelve months since that moment: twelve months of putting my life back together, of getting used to the constant, low-level pain in my leg and coming to terms with deafness. I've long since ceased to be bitter about what happened to me; after all, if someone had come to me a minute before and asked me to choose between being burned to death myself or going round with a bit of a limp and not hearing terribly well, I would have gone down on my knees begging for the limp and the deafness. But I confess to feeling angry: angry that our translator's young life, and the lives of seventeen other people, were thrown away through the actions of an American pilot and navigator who, we learned, had not been trained for air-to-ground operations.

Yet we cannot prove this because the results of the official investigation, if there has been one, have not so far been made public. Only two hours after the incident, a senior American officer, deeply shocked, confided to us in considerable detail what had gone wrong; yet what took him a few minutes to find out has so far taken American officialdom a year to mull over. There has been no formal outcome, no question of anyone being court martialled, and certainly no apology, a year after Kamaran Abdurrazak Mohammed's life was cut short at the age of twenty-five.

During the only contact I myself have had with top American military officials about this, I was left with the feeling that it was, somehow, my own fault: the US forces had made it possible for journalists to be embedded with them, so my team and I had no business being out in the open where we could be attacked. A bus-driver who drove onto a crowded pavement and killed eighteen people would have been tried and sentenced by now; if you are a pilot flying off the USS *Harry S. Truman* in an antiquated F-14 armed with Maverick missiles, it seems that you have special protection if you make a mistake. There is certainly no method of seeking redress through the American courts; the US military are specifically protected from legal action in time of war.

When you have been involved in something like this, the memory never really leaves you. But the world in general quickly forgets, just as the scars on the ground fade. The first thing that vanishes is our sense of the atmosphere in which these events took place. Though the facts are clear enough, the feeling of the time is impossibly hard to recapture afterwards: especially in the case of the two wars which the Americans and British waged against Saddam Hussein. Over the past ten years, war has succeeded war with depressing frequency. Who now remembers the war in Bosnia, or the NATO bombing of Serbia and Kosovo in 1999? Even the memory of the war against the Taliban in Afghanistan in 2001 is beginning to fade. This is how British public opinion must have responded to the welter of small colonial wars in the last part of the nineteenth century: they came and went too fast to recall.

For a quarter of a century I have been involved in reporting and writing about Saddam Hussein and the wars he fought. That is why, in writing this book, it seemed to me that no account of this last war, the most divisive the United States has been involved in since Vietnam, could possibly be complete without looking at the other conflicts

Saddam was involved in: his invasions of Iran and Kuwait, and the war to dislodge his forces from there. If you grow old in the job of writing and reporting you don't assume (as tyro journalists and US administrations sometimes seem to do) that each new event in the world is sui generis, something entirely without precedent. In Saddam Hussein's case, the precedents go back to the time when he first emerged as a political force in Iraq; indeed, they may go back even further to the British Mandate of 1920–32, which had to be curtailed hurriedly because of the ferocious opposition in Iraq to British rule. That is a precedent which the planners in the Pentagon seem not to have considered.

I didn't want to write a formal history of Saddam and his wars, because it is far too soon for that. Instead, I wanted to write an account of how things seemed at the time: something that historians, however good, cannot always manage to achieve. In this book, therefore, I have trawled through much of my past journalism, as well as some of my past books, in search of the things I wrote at the time about Saddam Hussein and Iraq's wars. I wanted to recreate the atmosphere as we observed it at the time, rather than as we see it now, with hindsight. But of course, as well as the battered old notebooks and the yellowed cuttings from magazines and newspapers, and the extracts from elderly books of mine which now belong firmly on the five-pence shelf outside charity shops, I have had more up-to-date help. There are various important sources in this book who have either asked to remain anonymous, or who would probably be better advised to stay that way. As a result, I shan't thank any of my informants by name here, but they know who they are and I am grateful to them. The BBC's chief Middle East researcher, Louisa Brooke, provided me with some excellent research material and went through the manuscript for me, catching some egregious errors; any lingering faults are mine, not hers. Louise Coletta, the presiding deity of the World Affairs Unit at Television Centre, was as helpful and pleasant as ever in digging out the illustrations. At Macmillan, Georgina Morley stayed calm and relaxed in spite of a horribly tight schedule for this book, and stood me a comforting lunch at a critical moment when my injuries were starting to hold me back; and Philippa McEwan, as ever, made the prospect of publication and promotion of the book something positively to look forward to.

My colleagues at the BBC, Richard Sambrook, Mark Damazer, Adrian van Klaveren, Jonathan Baker and Malcolm Downing, were all remarkably supportive and understanding; as were Dominic Lawson and his excellent new foreign editor Topaz Amoore. Tom Giles, the BBC producer who went through all the difficult experiences of the war in Iraq with me, was a great help; every time I needed information, or a bit of moral support, or even just the chance to laugh about someone or something, he was always there at the other end of the phone line.

My life was, as ever, held together during the months of writing by my PA, Gina Nelthorpe-Cowne, who sorted everything out magically in her usual easy, charming manner; and her husband Mark, who has now started to work with me in strange and difficult places as a photographer, performed all sorts of technological wonders in getting the illustrations selected and sent, and went through some of the manuscript for me. My wife and producer Dee would normally have come with me on this trip, but for various family reasons had to stay behind. Afterwards I was profoundly glad she had; but I missed her companionship in Iraq more than I can say. That, finally, is what keeps me going.

The Wars Against Saddam

AFTERMATH

'It will run away with him, just as it ran away with me.' So predicted ex-Kaiser Wilhelm II in 1939, when Adolf Hitler began the Second World War by invading Poland. Experience shows that wars rarely end in the way those who start them expect, and it is one of the great mysteries of human existence why anyone should deliberately choose to provoke them.

Yet all three of the wars which this book deals with were started as a matter of policy. Firstly, Saddam Hussein chose to invade the new Islamic Republic of Iran in 1980, confident he would be victorious within a matter of days; instead, he had provoked one of the longest-running wars of the century. Then, only two years after his war with Iran ended in 1988, he invaded Kuwait and overplayed his hand to such an extent that he suffered the most humiliating of defeats in the first Gulf War. Thirdly, after twelve years of appallingly destructive sanctions, sponsored by the United States and Britain, President George W. Bush decided on an invasion of Iraq which would overthrow Saddam Hussein. This, in its turn, duly ran away with him.

The war itself was well-planned and quickly over; though since the Iraqi army's weapons were outdated, its morale rock-bottom and its expectation of defeat total, and given that it possessed no air cover and no faith whatever in its leaders, the outcome was never remotely in doubt. The only real question was how many Iraqis would be killed as a result of the Coalition's overwhelming superiority in weapons and manpower.

Yet after the capture of Baghdad and the flight of Saddam Hussein, those who had planned and approved the war were continually taken by surprise. They didn't find any of the weapons of mass destruction whose supposed existence had provided part of the war's rationale. But they did find that, contrary to everything they had been promised, the Coalition forces were not generally welcomed as liberators. They were increasingly seen as an unwelcome occupying force, and the hostility towards them grew stronger and stronger.

A year later, in April 2004, the security situation in Iraq had

degenerated badly. There were dozens of attacks on the Coalition
forces and their Iraqi supporters every day. More American soldiers
were killed in two weeks than during the entire invasion of Iraq the
previous year. Car-bombs exploded, armoured columns were attacked
and foreigners were kidnapped daily. There was powerful and growing
resentment against the US forces among both Sunnis and Shi'ites.

No one could be certain whether the violence would grow or
subside. The Americans and British maintained, probably correctly,
that only 20 per cent of the population was actively hostile to them;
but successful revolutions are usually carried out by a minority of
activists, who are often unpopular with the majority. It is only after
the revolution has taken hold that their version of events becomes the
orthodox one.

The fall of Baghdad was dated to the moment when an exultant
crowd, almost entirely composed of Shi'ites, gathered in Ferdows
Square in the south-eastern part of the city centre, and tried to pull
down the big statue of Saddam Hussein which had stood there since
the 1980s. When they failed, the US army brought in an armoured
vehicle to do the job for them. The crowd jumped onto the statue,
beating it with their fists and shoes. Because the incident took place
beside the Palestine Hotel, where most of the world's press were based
at the time, it received maximum publicity.

The entire business was regarded by many of the journalists
entirely at face value, as so much of the invasion of Iraq had been.
Most of the television cameramen, concentrating on the activities of
the crowd, failed to notice how few people had actually turned up
for the occasion: a few dozen at most. Broadcast around the world,
the pictures tended to give the impression that the entire nation of Iraq
was celebrating, instead of just fifty or sixty individuals.

Every opinion poll taken later in Iraq was to show that the vast
majority of people were delighted to be rid of Saddam Hussein.
But they did not necessarily regard the Americans and British as liberators. In some respects, opinion was fairly evenly divided. A properly
conducted poll, carried out in April 2004 for the BBC and a number
of other international broadcasters, indicated that while 46 per cent of
Arabs thought the invasion had been wrong, almost as many – 40 per
cent – thought it had been right. After that, though, the differential
increased; 48 per cent thought the invasion had humiliated Iraq,

33 per cent thought it had been a liberation; 60 per cent opposed the presence of Coalition forces, while 30 per cent supported their presence. Interestingly, though, 74 per cent thought it was unacceptable to attack the Coalition's soldiers, while only 21 per cent thought it acceptable; perhaps the American and British estimate of 20 per cent for their opponents' strength was accurate.

On the first anniversary of the fall of Saddam's statue, the scene in Ferdows Square could scarcely have been more different. Saddam had been replaced by an uninteresting piece of abstract sculture; and on this someone had tied a small green Islamic flag, and pasted a portrait of the Shi'ite religious leader who had recently emerged to challenge the Americans: Moqtada al-Sadr, wagging his forefinger defiantly.

Friday prayers were being held in the large and beautiful Shi'ite mosque which dominated the square; loudspeakers relayed the sermon, which combined a veiled denunciation of the Coalition with appeals for supplies of blood and medical supplies for the people of the Sunni town of Falujah, west of Baghdad, which was in open revolt against the Americans. The square itself was entirely empty; and when a couple of television crews came there to film they were turned away rudely by three nervous American soldiers.

In the meantime, an armoured vehicle drove round and round the square, broadcasting a taped warning to the worshippers inside the mosque, and anyone else, that anyone seen carrying a weapon would be shot. The raucous voice on the tape mingled with the exhortations of the preacher in the mosque, and the two streams of sound echoed back from the surrounding buildings.

Finally, the American armoured vehicle left the square and drove up and down a nearby avenue, where large numbers of Shi'ite squatters had taken over the privileged blocks of flats where Saddam Hussein had once housed his secret policemen. Directly Friday prayers were over, the vehicle started playing rock music at ear-splitting levels (by, suitably enough, the band Guns N' Roses), taunting the inhabitants of the flats. Even the westernized, relatively pro-Coalition translators who worked for the American television networks were scandalized as they watched all this from the roof of the Palestine Hotel.

On the outskirts of Baghdad, and especially on the road to the airport, the insurgents were learning how to attack American convoys. Again and again they hit oil tankers and trucks carrying supplies. They also hit a number of tanks. It angered the British soldiers in Baghdad, who insisted that if the Americans had only carried out properly organized foot patrols on either side of the road they would have been able to break up the ambushes along the way. Instead, the Americans relied on speed, and the machine-guns on their tanks and armoured personnel carriers. The burned-out wrecks by the roadside showed that this was scarcely an effective defence.

Elsewhere, a new tactic had suddenly become popular: the taking of foreign hostages. The kidnapping of Iraqis had been going on for months, but the international press had shown little interest until the same thing happened to a number of Japanese, Italians, Czechs and other nationalities (including a Briton, who was fortunate enough to be released, and two Americans). At one point, forty-four foreigners were held. A French television reporter who was released told a disturbing story, which was reminiscent of the kidnappings in Lebanon in the 1980s: he was picked up by a group who seemed relatively well-disposed, and simply wanted to check him out. Soon, though, he was passed on from one group to another, each more extreme than the last. He was incredibly lucky that one of his captors was sensible enough to realize that France had refused to take part in the invasion of Iraq, and soon afterwards he was released.

A terrible precedent was set when a group of fanatics murdered an Italian hostage, and videoed the gory business to show what they had done. Not long afterwards the two other Italians who had been kidnapped with him were quietly freed: the newspapers suggested that the Italian government had paid a ransom for them. If so, that was a disturbing precedent too.

There was terrible loss of life in the town of Falujah in April. It followed an ugly incident when four American security contractors were attacked and killed in their car. Their bodies were ripped apart by the wildly angry crowd, and displayed on the town's bridges. A little over a week later, on 5 March, United States troops began an operation to 'pacify' the town. Some senior Iraqi politicians, although closely allied with the Americans, complained angrily that the American operation amounted to collective punishment for the population of Falujah. Seven hundred people were killed: ten times the number of American deaths.

The US forces insisted that the operation was 'humane', and said they had done everything possible to protect non-combatants. But the head of a European humanitarian agency reported that two of his ambulances had been fired on by American soldiers. One had been hit three times. An Iraqi doctor described how an ambulance had been hit in an area of Falujah controlled by the Americans. A doctor and a paramedic were injured, he said. Although other members of his team tried four times during the next two days to reach the ambulance, they were fired on each time by American soldiers. The injured civilians stranded in the back of the ambulance died from loss of blood.

Lt. Gen. Ricardo Sanchez, the commander of US forces in Iraq, denied that troops were firing on ambulances. 'If we're shooting vehicles, it's because those vehicles have shot at us,' he said. Other American officials maintained that a gunman had escaped in an ambulance. According to the Coalition's military spokesman, Brigadier-General Mark Kimmit, 'There have been a lot of people running around the city with blankets on their vehicles asserting that they are ambulances.'

There was evidence that civilians, some of them elderly, had been shot by American soldiers. A British aid worker said she had seen an elderly woman, still clutching a white flag, who had been shot in the stomach. The woman's son insisted the Americans had shot her. Fewer people would have died if US soldiers had not blocked access to the main hospital in Falujah by occupying the bridge which led to it.

Stories like these increased the feeling of alienation felt by British soldiers, right up to the most senior levels. Often the relationship between individual groups of British and American soldiers was good, but there was a widespread contempt among the British contingent for the way the Americans behaved in Iraq. With occasional exceptions, the British-controlled sector of southern Iraq, centred on Basra, was peaceful, and there was strong emphasis on getting things working again so that they could be handed back to the Iraqi people. If you talked to ordinary Iraqis in Basra you would find that they usually felt the British soldiers were doing a good job, even though most people wanted them to leave as soon as it was done.

Spain's decision in April 2004 to withdraw its troops after a terrorist attack and a subsequent change of government in Madrid was a further sign of the erosion of international support for the Iraq operation. This was more important for what it represented than for what it was, since there were only 1,300 Spanish troops in Iraq. Increasingly, Europeans regarded the war and its aftermath as symptoms of the perceived extremism of the Bush administration.

It became commonplace to accuse the Pentagon, which had controlled the entire Iraqi enterprise, of having underestimated the number of soldiers needed to police the country after the invasion. Donald Rumsfeld, the US Defense Secretary, was so certain his troops would be greeted as liberators that he had insisted on sending as few of them as possible. It became a ruling principle within the Pentagon that the Vietnam War had been lost in part because of the huge, unwieldy forces that were sent there.

But too few troops can create as much of a problem as too many; and as the towns and cities of Saddam Hussein's Iraq fell to the invading forces there were not enough soldiers to restore order and prevent the extraordinary wave of looting in which virtually everything to do with the Iraqi state was trashed and destroyed. The sudden lawlessness which erupted then never entirely subsided, and it became the basis of the violent hostility towards the Coalition forces later.

The decision to disband the Iraqi army was a mistake of equally serious proportions. It meant that there was no one on the Iraqi side who could prevent the security vacuum after the fall of Saddam – and, in particular, no one to guard the country's borders from the hundreds of foreign volunteers who wanted to join in the attacks on American troops. The demobilized Iraqi soldiers took their weapons home with them, and thereby ensured that the resistance movement would always be well armed.

So Donald Rumsfeld and his deputy, Paul Wolfowitz, were the authors of their own misfortunes. They micro-managed the war and its aftermath from thousands of miles away, they were insufficiently questioning about their own doctrines, and they had no alternative plan to fall back on when Plan A showed signs of inadequacy. In April 2004, the unfortunate American troops, who had already been in Iraq for a year, were told by Mr Rumsfeld that their tour of duty was being arbitrarily extended for another three months. The effect on morale was serious. Soldiers who were already deeply tired and often frightened had to face a major uprising just as they reached their lowest point in terms of morale. According to Senator Edward Kennedy, Iraq had become President George W. Bush's Vietnam.

The Vietnam analogy was an inevitable one, but that didn't necessarily make it correct. It was always going to be easier for George W. Bush to get out of Iraq than it had been for Lyndon Johnson or Richard Nixon to get out of Vietnam.

There was no opposition to negotiate with, no super-power to confront, no major upsurge in hostility on the streets of American cities. The American phase of the Vietnam War lasted more than twelve years; the invasion of Iraq and its aftermath has, so far, lasted less than two. It was always going to be relatively easy for the Bush administration to create a government from the Iraqi diaspora, push and prod it into position, and then let it sort out itself, and the country, as best it could. It was Vietnam the cheap way.

But there was a heavy price to pay, all the same. Part of it was paid in American prestige, which suffered across the world as a result of the invasion of Iraq. A large part of it was paid by Iraqi civilians, who died or were injured at a rate ten times greater than that of the Coalition forces. And American troops themselves paid a price too.

Bill Clinton, as president, felt unable to send in ground troops during his various wars and expeditions around the globe, for fear that he would be accused of risking the lives of Americans when he himself had carefully avoided fighting in Vietnam. George W. Bush effectively avoided service in Vietnam as well, but Republican presidents seem better protected against such charges than Democratic ones. Nevertheless, the White House made it clear right from the start that the return of American servicemen's bodies from Iraq would be carried out in the greatest secrecy, at night, with no photographers or cameramen present. Nor would the president attend their funerals, as Bill Clinton had.

This tactic worked for an entire year. Then a peace activist, using the Freedom of Information Act, succeeded in obtaining a number of pictures taken by official army photographers of the flag-draped coffins of dead soldiers at an American air force base. The sight of twenty coffins, lined up in rows in the back of a cargo plane, had a force which the mere repetition in print of the day's casualties never could. It was probably true, as critics of the war maintained, that twenty American coffins had a far greater effect on US public opinion than two hundred coffins of Iraqis killed by Americans. Perhaps that is only to be expected. But it says something about the way the war was fought, all the same.

1. CHECKMATE

The ultimate betrayer can sometimes be the most faithful of followers.

Mohammed al-Musslit was regarded as the best of Saddam Hussein's bodyguards: the most loyal, the toughest. He guarded him in the last days of fighting before Baghdad fell, and they escaped together up the Tikrit road in a white Oldsmobile as the Americans secured the city on 9 April 2003.

He often travelled with Saddam after that, and he knew most of the hideouts which had been prepared for this eventuality long before. It was rumoured that the men who dug the secret holes in which Saddam hid were all executed to make sure they wouldn't talk.

The Americans found al-Musslit through intelligent, painstaking police work. They traced as many people as they could who might know where Saddam was, and eventually they found him. Al-Musslit was a strong man, and a tough one; his nickname, 'the fat one', did not indicate any softness. The Americans probably didn't torture him physically. There is no real point: people will make up any story simply to make the pain stop. On the other hand, the strongest and most resilient person will break under sleep deprivation and clever interrogation. It was just before 10.50 on the morning of Sunday 15 December 2003 that Mohammed al-Musslit finally gave in and told his interrogators where Saddam had been hiding. He was, according to one of the American officers involved in the search for Saddam, 'a middle-aged man who went pear-shaped'.

The Americans flew al-Musslit to the town of Tikrit, the place which had always been Saddam's power base; and they made him show them the two places outside Tikrit where, he said, Saddam had hidden in the past. Then they called in six hundred troops from the 4th Infantry Division to examine the sites; they called them 'Wolverine 1' and 'Wolverine 2'. It was six o'clock in the evening when the troops arrived. Darkness had fallen. For two and a half hours the soldiers searched by the light of powerful arc-lamps and torches, and they found nothing.

One of the places they looked was a small, unremarkable compound close to the River Tigris. The Americans had searched it before, but had found nothing suspicious. This time one thing was different: an old orange and white taxi was parked outside, of the kind you see everywhere in Iraq. In the barricade of reeds which surrounded it, a couple of local men were sitting. They seemed stupid and frightened, and couldn't answer questions rationally. Inside the small compound was a lean-to with two beds in it, and a few clothes and basic toiletries. Next door was an open makeshift kitchen and a toilet. I visited the place three days later and would never have believed that Saddam Hussein might have been there.

The beaten earth outside was strewn with rubbish, including a bit of carpeting. As the soldiers were reluctantly deciding to give up the search, one of them glanced at this again, then bent down to look closer. There seemed to be something a little strange about the piece of carpet: it looked almost as though it had been arranged. The soldier pulled it, and it came away. Underneath was a piece of polystyrene, smeared with mud. And under the polystyrene was a square hole.

In the first moment of surprise, a soldier pulled out a hand grenade and was going to throw it down the hole. One of the others stopped him: and that made the difference between capturing an exploded legend who surrendered meekly and killing a martyr whose legend might have united and inspired millions of Muslims across the world.

Two hands appeared in the light of the soldiers' torches: the man in the hole was surrendering. Then came a head, dirty and bearded.

'My name is Saddam Hussein,' said the figure in the hole, with as much dignity as it was possible to muster at such a time and in such a position. 'I am the president of Iraq, and I want to negotiate.'

'Regards from President Bush,' replied one of the soldiers, and the others laughed. The time was eight thirty-six.

Saddam had a pistol with him in the hole, but he left it behind when he stood up. He had no intention of resisting; yet it was typical of his extraordinary self-belief that even at this stage he could have thought there might be something to negotiate about.

It was his two hundred and fiftieth day on the run. Afterwards his captors wondered who had been in charge, Saddam or his minders? The hole was 1.8 metres deep at its shallow end, shelving to 2.4 metres at its deepest. A heavy man in his sixties could not have climbed out of it unaided, and it was impossible to lift the polystyrene lid from the inside. If the two men who looked after him had been taken away by the Americans and not allowed back, Saddam might have starved to death. But he would not have died of asphyxiation, because an extractor fan had been built into the hole with a cleverly hidden air vent.

There was no communications equipment at the site; not even a mobile phone. Saddam and his men knew that the Americans would be listening for the faintest suggestion of a call from him and would be able to trace him immediately. The soldiers found $750,000 in cash, two AK-47 assault rifles and a briefcase full of extremely sensitive documents.

It was hard for people to accept that this man, who had been so careless of other people's lives and so willing to take risks for the honour of Iraq, should give up so easily. Journalists across the Arab world would soon maintain that Saddam had been drugged, and some of them tried to suggest that his capture must have happened long before. A branch with dates on it was hanging from a tree beside to the hole in the ground, and many people managed to convince themselves that the condition of the dates showed they were very old. I looked at the dates when I went there: they were recent.

Saddam's favourite daughter Raghad, interviewed in Jordan, agreed that he must have been drugged. A lion, she said, was still a lion, even when it was shackled. But after the first shock of his capture had passed, no one seemed to regard him as a lion any more. Saddam had demanded the ultimate price from so many others, yet at the critical moment he had not been prepared to pay it himself. Even Saddam's two sons, the hated Uday and his younger brother Qusay, had resisted the Americans and died fighting. Saddam's own life had always been one of conflict and confrontation. Now, as a result of his tame surrender, he had lost everything. He was finished.

Mohammed al-Musslit, in betraying him, had lost everything too: honour, self-respect, pride. For the rest of his life he would be vulnerable to anyone who might choose to take revenge on him. He could not even claim any share of the twenty-five million dollars offered by the Americans for information leading to Saddam Hussein's arrest, because he had not divulged it willingly. In one way or another, Saddam destroyed the lives of almost everyone who worked for him; but Mohammed al-Musslit's life was destroyed more completely, more savagely, than the rest. He was a dead man who had kept on living.

2. VISAS

Ever since July 1979, when Saddam Hussein elbowed his way to supreme power in Iraq, much of my career has been spent reporting on the remarkable twists and turns his life has taken. I recorded his gangsterish beginnings, and the years when the British and American governments regarded him as their bulwark against revolutionary Islam, and finally the time when they decided he himself represented a threat to them and would have to be stamped out. One of the advantages of being in the job as long as I have been is to be able to watch a shooting star like Saddam all the way from the first moment he appeared in the firmament to the time when he passed out of our sight.

This book is a record of that extraordinary trajectory of his, and of my experiences in reporting it. The pattern has never been smooth, and has certainly not been predictable. After the first Gulf War I wrote that it was like reporting on a football match from a position behind one of the goals: when the action was down at my end I had a superb vantage-point, but when the players streamed away to the far end of the pitch it was hard to see what was going on. After that, it was as though I left the ground altogether: for twelve years the Iraqi authorities refused to allow me back to Baghdad. But I finally returned in 2003, and found myself a seat in a different part of the stadium.

After the first Gulf War, when I spent more time in Baghdad before, during and after the fighting than any other Western journalist had done, I decided to write a book about my experiences. As I sat at my desk and planned it out, I knew I would have to face one very difficult question: how honest was I prepared to be? If I were happy to leave out quite a few things I knew, and cover up some of the others, I would never have any problem getting a visa back to Iraq. But the things I would have to leave out were the things that were most important: for instance, that the vast majority of Iraqis, including Saddam's own officials, were desperately anxious to see the end of him. It was an important point. People in the outside world often assumed that because so many Iraqis paraded up and down the streets chanting Saddam's praises, he must be popular with them.

In the end I wrote it all. Other writers on Iraq – Alexander Cockburn, Said Aburish and Dilip Hiro, for instance – have faced the same problem with Saddam Hussein's Iraq and have taken the same decision. There are, after all, more important things than visas. But I seemed to attract a particular degree of hostility from within the Iraqi government. Black-market copies of my book changed hands at greatly inflated prices, though with no profit to me, of course.

The first time I wanted to return to Baghdad was in March 1991. I asked a clever and very attractive friend of mine in Amman to see if she could persuade the Iraqi ambassador to give me a visa. She got her father to invite him to dinner, made sure she sat beside him, put her hand on his knee and leant very close.

'You will give poor John Simpson a visa, won't you? He so wants to go back to Iraq.'

It worked just that one time. Afterwards the word was always 'no'. I wrote personal letters to ministers; I asked every senior BBC person who went to Baghdad to put my case; I even came perilously close to apologizing for anything I might have said to offend them. Still no.

'The time is not yet right for John to return,' said the man in charge of the information ministry.

I seized on that word 'yet' – but, as things turned out, it meant nothing.

And then, at the beginning of 2002, the BBC asked me to make a documentary about Saddam Hussein. I knew it was likely to cause me more grief with the Iraqis, but I agreed; since I regarded myself as something of a specialist in the life and times of Saddam it seemed unreasonable to say no.

It was a good documentary; too good for comfort, in some ways. I asked if it could be kept off BBC World so that Saddam wouldn't see it himself, and for a time it wasn't shown internationally. Then it was aired, at the worst possible moment, and Saddam saw it. He didn't, apparently, like it.

The crisis wore on, and by the end of 2002 I was asked to update the documentary. I did, and this time we revealed, by carrying out a careful comparison of different video-clips of Saddam Hussein, measuring them precisely, and then matching them with pictures that were unquestionably of him, that he had had at least four doubles over the years.

Saddam watched this one too. A few days later, when a foreign visitor came to see him, he grinned.

'Look,' he said, pulling his cheek, 'it really is me, not a double like they say on the BBC.'

Great, I thought when I heard that; at least it shows he's got a sense of humour. He can take a joke against himself.

But he couldn't. I tried to get a visa soon afterwards, and failed. Another attempt; this time I was told by the information ministry never to bother again. Still, I felt unable to leave it there. As the second Gulf War drew near, my options for reporting on it were becoming very narrow. I was determined to be a free agent, away from the big public relations machines; that meant I couldn't base myself with the Americans or the British. My instinct was to be an independent, out in the open, but I knew the murderous possibilities only too well. No man's land in a war like that would be the most dangerous place imaginable, filled with angry, resentful Iraqi soldiers who would be only too happy to steal everything we had and kill us; and the chances of being attacked by the American forces were, I knew, very high. The Americans were probably more dangerous than the Iraqis, I thought.

Baghdad was the only remotely safe option for me. Of course, it wouldn't be really safe; the Americans and British would bomb it with particular force, and there was always the possibility of being taken hostage or killed by the Iraqi government. But I believed it would be safer on balance to be in Baghdad, and events proved me right. Being out in the open cost the lives of four good and valued colleagues of mine, everyone in my own team was injured, and I was left with a limp and permanent deafness in one ear.

So, with only three or four weeks to go before the war broke out, I asked someone to approach a particular Arab government on my behalf. Its leader had always been friendly to me, and I thought he might help. He did. A message was sent to the Iraqi information minister, Mohammed Saeed al-Sahhaf, asking him as a personal favour to let me in. By this time it was February 2003, and I was in Istanbul on my way to northern Iraq; the Kurdish part, which was out of Saddam's control.

We were gathering our gear together to fly to the Iraqi border when the call came through on my mobile phone.

'Congratulations, John. You have your visa to Baghdad.'

I was overwhelmed: it was the answer to all my problems. I couldn't pull out of the Kurdish trip immediately, because we were too far committed, but I decided to stay there for as short a time as I could. I wouldn't do any broadcasting so as not to offend the Iraqi government, which became furious when foreign journalists reported from the Kurdish area. We settled down in the northern Iraqi town of Arbil, meeting people, interviewing them, working out our options, but all the time thinking that we would slip out again and get our visas to Baghdad soon.

A week later there was another call.

'I don't know how to say this, John, but they aren't going to give you a visa after all. Al-Sahhaf says he doesn't want you there.'

I was angry and humiliated and depressed, and more than a little nervous. Now my war would be fought out in the open, with no protection from either side. The last chance was gone.

By a ludicrous synchronicity at the very end of the war, three days before the Americans entered Baghdad, al-Sahhaf relented. It was the afternoon of the day when my team and I were nearly killed by an American air-to-ground missile. I stumbled into my hotel room in Arbil, my clothes torn and bloodstained. My mobile phone rang.

'Al-Sahhaf says you can go to Baghdad any time you want now.'

By then it was, of course, far too late to get there.

A couple of months later, still deaf, still limping, I was back in London. Baghdad had long since fallen, Saddam Hussein was in hiding, his two sons were still alive, and nothing had been heard from al-Sahhaf since he had vanished at the end of the war. He had become a figure of absurdity because he had denied the obvious advance of the Americans until the very last moment; 'Comical Ali', the British press called him.

I was invited to a restaurant in London to meet my friend, the man who had acted as a go-between to try to get me a visa to Baghdad. The place was dark and noisy, and I had difficulty hearing his voice in the ambient noise.

'Al-Sahhaf wants you to help him.'

I explained what al-Sahhaf could do. But the go-between was

insistent: al-Sahhaf had done me a real favour, he said. I should just listen, and then I would agree.

The story he told me was as follows. The officials in the Ministry of Information had indeed disliked me for years, and were worried that if I were allowed back to Baghdad I would write another book which might get them into trouble. But they were prepared to overlook this if necessary, because they realized that the BBC had to be catered for in some way. The trouble was, Saddam himself was angry with me. He had seen both the documentaries I had made about him, and felt that I had insulted him and his two sons. Uday Hussein, the elder and nastier son, also seems to have seen the broadcasts. In the second documentary I called him a serial rapist: undeniably true, but not necessarily the kind of thing you like to see broadcast about yourself.

Nevertheless, when al-Sahhaf received the message from the leader of the friendly Arab government he had felt that politeness obliged him to do what was asked of him. That was why I was told that the visa had been agreed, as I was passing through Turkey. Then al-Sahhaf had second thoughts; perhaps, he reflected, it would be a good idea to check it out with the boss. At his next audience with Saddam, a few days later, he mentioned that he had given me a visa.

Saddam, according to al-Sahhaf, went wild and called me a long and inventive variety of names. He seemed to have full recall of entire passages from the documentaries. You should never have promised him a visa, he stormed; cancel it at once. The man has insulted me, Saddam Hussein, your President.

Al-Sahhaf apologized long and hard. He was extremely nervous. Then there was a pause. The tone of Saddam's voice changed from angry to thoughtful and cunning.

'Maybe on second thoughts you should give him a visa. Let him come, and we can deal with him here.'

Al-Sahhaf knew trouble when he saw it. He agreed humbly and apologized again several times, but it sounded to him as though Saddam would have me killed once I got to Baghdad. Who knew what vengeance the BBC or the British government might take then? There are many places in the world where the BBC is credited with extraordinary powers, and Iraq is one of them. The fact is, of course, that if I had been murdered the BBC would have complained noisily and the British government rather more quietly, and that would have been that. The British government has about as much affection for me as Saddam Hussein did.

Al-Sahhaf didn't understand this. Maybe he was genuinely concerned for my welfare; I had certainly always found him a pleasant, chirpy little man. For whatever reason, he told the Arab leader's intermediary that it wouldn't after all be possible to accept me in Baghdad. As a result, the quiet voice in the dark restaurant in London told me, I owed al-Sahhaf a favour. He had saved my life, so I should get him political asylum in Britain.

Over the next couple of weeks I genuinely tried hard to do it. The British government weren't interested.

'There's nothing in it for us,' a senior official said.

Then I tried to get him smuggled quietly out of Iraq; that didn't work either. The most I could promise him was that I would go with him to the British embassy in Baghdad, let him hand himself over, and try to make sure the Americans didn't mistreat him. Like most Iraqis, he much preferred the British: he thought they understood Iraqis better, and perhaps he was right. But the best I could do for him wasn't what he wanted or needed, and he had to look elsewhere for help.

It was a shame; I think there is a genuine possibility that I owe my life to al-Sahhaf. If he had done what Saddam Hussein wanted, and let me go back to Baghdad, I would certainly have wandered around in the city as much as I could; it would have been easy for someone to bundle me into a car and dispose of me. Much better to limp around with a chunk of shrapnel in my hip and a damaged ear than to be lying at the bottom of some hole covered with quicklime, being slowly forgotten – just somebody else Saddam Hussein had got even with.

3. THE GENERAL

Mosul, Monday 14 April 2003

Yesterday he had been a general in Saddam Hussein's Republican Guard. Today he had come over to the side of Saddam's enemies, and was trusted by them. He had, our Kurdish host told us, often intervened to save the lives of Kurds during the worst times of Saddam Hussein's repression, even though he wasn't himself Kurdish.

It was Wednesday 14 April 2003. General Ali al-Jajjawi sat now in a darkened room in a suburb of the newly liberated city of Mosul, a good-looking man in his early fifties, trim and with a black moustache which had so far resisted the greyness that was beginning to show in his hair. We talked about the war, and about his former master. He had been in charge of the defence of Mosul against the American and Kurdish troops; had his units been armed with the weapons of mass destruction we had heard so much about? He smiled.

'If we'd had them, we would have used them. That's all.'

'So you didn't have them?'

'No, we certainly didn't have them.'

'Why not?'

'How can I answer that? Saddam didn't want us to have them, that's all.'

'But even if you didn't have them, maybe some of his other generals did.'

'We didn't have them.'

I turned the conversation to Saddam Hussein himself; was he still alive?

'Yes, I'm certain he is. He wouldn't kill himself, and he would never surrender: he's not that type at all. He wasn't killed by the bombs the Americans dropped. We know that.'

'But he's on the run now? He's in hiding somewhere?'

'This, you must remember, is his background: he knows what it is to be hunted.'

'When did he escape from Baghdad?'

'I don't think he did escape from Baghdad. I think he has been spending most of his time there. He was there when the Americans entered the city.'

And then he started to tell me the story as he had heard it from an Iraqi general who was in Baghdad with Saddam at the time. When the first American tanks entered the city, and came up against the barricades the Iraqis had placed there, Saddam himself hurried to the spot and ordered a soldier to give him an RPG-7 grenade launcher. He took careful aim at the lead tank, and the grenade hit its armour but didn't stop it. He fired two more grenades at the tanks, then turned to his faithful bodyguard.

'That's it,' Saddam said. 'We've done what we had to do.'

'So he's a brave man?' I asked the general.

'Oh yes. We hated him and we were very afraid of him, but we always respected his courage. He did some crazy things. He ruined the country. He was a terrible man. But no one could deny he was very brave.'

'Did you respect him?'

He paused for a moment before answering. Now that Saddam had been overthrown, there was absolutely no value in praising him in any way; on the contrary, it might harm him with his new friends, the Kurds. But the general was a truthful man.

'I have to say I did. Perhaps I shouldn't have, but I did. He was terrible, of course, but at the same time he was great and powerful. He destroyed our country, but we will always remember him in our history with a little bit of pride, because he stood up to the whole world.'

4. THE DAUGHTER

Saddam Hussein was, for a time, the most interesting man on earth. How many other people are there whose fate could bring everyone in every city in every country across the globe crowding round a television set?

Without him the world would have been a different place, and history would have taken a different course. Millions of lives which he disrupted would have been more peaceful. The comparisons are invariably on a grand scale, and are often made to denigrate him: Napoleon, Stalin, Hitler, Mao Zedong. In reality, they show his stature. We may not like him, but that is the company he keeps.

For those of us who saw what he did at the height of his power, Saddam can never be a hero; but it would be stupid to deny that there was much that was heroic about him. For a poor, neglected boy from a poverty-stricken village on the banks of the Tigris to dominate a country almost the size of France and then proceed to take on the world's only hyperpower is an achievement on the heroic scale. Of course he lost; who wouldn't have? But even his failure was heroic, in its way.

As for his successes, they were mostly based on violence and cruelty – the ethic of the *mafioso*. But Saddam Hussein had a grander strategy in mind than any Mafia boss could have aspired to. He wanted to challenge the way the world was ordered; and although he could never have succeeded, the fact that he attempted it at all sheds a kind of ugly magnificence on him. He will be the man to whom the impatient, the angry, the violent, will look for a long time to come: Saddam Hussein is the saint of the poor and the dispossessed.

So this is the story of how a small-time gangster, a bandit, rose to confront the world, and fell by doing so. There are no real lessons to be drawn, no morals to be pointed up. His life was all about power: gaining it, keeping it, using it, losing it. Stripped of the power, he went back to being a small-time gangster again: this time on the run.

And yet all the evidence now shows that the months after his fall in 2003 were a period of remarkable freedom for him. He grew a beard and allowed it to go its natural grey colour, even though he continued to dye his hair black. He often wrapped a *k'fir* round his head and face, like a Bedouin, and spent his time in the area between the Tigris River and the desert to the north-west of Baghdad. Sometimes he drove a truck, with a lone bodyguard beside him; sometimes he was a passenger in a taxi. The responsibilities of office, the incompetence of his followers, were left behind. He was a free man again, taking risks, chancing his life on every turning of the road.

He had done it once before, when the Coalition forces were attacking Baghdad in January and early February 1991. His head of military intelligence, General Samara'i, told me afterwards how Saddam had driven around in a red Volkswagen Passat with his bodyguard, meeting his Cabinet ministers and his generals in villages outside Baghdad at the shortest possible notice.

'I had the impression he was really enjoying himself,' Samara'i said.

This, therefore, is the true matter of folk-tale and legend: a humble bandit rises to become president and eats off golden plates in palaces, and then at the end of his life goes back to being a humble outlaw once again. Napoleon died in miserable exile; Hitler declined to a quivering shadow and shot himself, or was shot, in the ruins of his capital; Stalin and Mao died in their beds. Saddam Hussein, by contrast, liberated himself until the moment he surrendered. That destroyed his legend forever.

He is not a man to admire. He brought such misery and despair to the Iraqi people that his own secret policemen fired in the air with joy in 1991 when they thought he was about to be overthrown. He kept the torture chambers and the execution yards of two dozen major prisons busy; in Baghdad, the hangmen and firing squads had to work a twenty-four-hour rota to be able to keep up with the work he gave them.

He himself wanted to be regarded, like Nasser, as a liberator of the Arab people. Yet his methods had not moved on since Nasser: the secret police, the truncheon, the state structures which controlled the masses rather than freeing their potential. Nasser was a dictator whose people loved him; Saddam was a dictator whose people were forced to pretend they loved him. He could survive only by keeping his generals and politicians continually occupied. As a result he started wars against Iran and Kuwait, and from 1990 to 2003 ensured that Iraq confronted the United States and its allies. All this was Saddam Hussein's policy; his propaganda maintained that these crises were forced upon him, but only the credulous believed it.

The world was a worse place for his being in it. Yet for reasons that people in the West find hard to understand, his popularity outside Iraq while he was in power was second only to his popularity once he had been overthrown. It is a fundamental human instinct to prefer the victim to the victor; and although for much of his life he behaved like a victor and his victims were in the tens of millions, large numbers of people in the poorer countries of the world saw him as someone who fought the fight they themselves would have liked to fight against the rich countries of the world, and was crushed for it.

Saddam Hussein was what his name proclaimed: the one who confronts. It was this propensity which won him power, which made him fight his wars, and which eventually brought him down into the dust. It also made him a hero to hundreds of millions who were too weak to do the confronting themselves.

In private, Saddam Hussein was a remarkably rounded man: a human being, not a monster. There were sides to him which many people found attractive. I once interviewed Latif Yahia, the man who had acted as double to Saddam's appalling son Uday; his life had been wrecked, he had lived in fear for years, and he bore the visible scars of his experiences (though he was honest enough to explain that some of them had been left by an angry wife). He loathed Uday, who had once been his friend at school and who had, he said, stolen his life and his very appearance. But when I asked about the parties he used to attend with Uday and Saddam, his face took on another look altogether.

'Saddam was always polite and pleasant to me,' Latif Yahia said. 'You should have seen him, going around on the carpet on all fours giving his grandchildren rides on his back. Then when he was finished he would stand up and laugh and be very happy, and everyone around him would laugh with him.'

These were the grandchildren whose fathers he allowed to be killed after they defected to Jordan; and yet the children's mothers continued to adore him even after he made widows of them. Saddam Hussein, in other words, was a good deal more complicated than the British tabloid press or American tabloid television news could imagine.

On 1 August 2003 al-Arabiya Television, one of the new twenty-four-hour Arabic news stations, which, alongside al-Jazeera TV and the Lebanon Broadcasting Company, have begun a profound process of change in the Arab world, broadcast an interview with Saddam Hussein's eldest daughter, Raghad. The Western press reported on a few of the more sensational aspects of the interview, but a great deal that was of interest about Saddam and his family was ignored. Two presenters from al-Arabiya, Sa'd al-Silawi and Wa-il Isam, conducted the interview in Amman, where King Abdullah II had given Raghad and her children asylum.

Al-Silawi asked her about the last time she saw her father, five days before the outbreak of the war.

'I cannot forget how he looked,' she said. 'He is always known for his elegance. When he entered the place, his visit looked like a farewell visit. He was in control and confident. You know my father as a very courageous person. I am thirty-five years old. I have never felt that he was afraid. Throughout my life, I have never seen him experiencing a moment of fear. As usual, he was in control, strong and fully confident that everything was in great shape.

'I do not recall his last words. But the children, the grandsons, all of them, sat around him. May God watch over them, there were many kids. They pulled up the chairs and sat around him.'

'Was the meeting held at the house or at the palace?'

'The meeting was held at my mother's house in al-Jadiriyah. It did not last for more than an hour.'

'Was the house a small one?'

'No, it was not a small one: a presidential palace. He was very nice. When he left the house, I felt that I had drawn some strength from him, and that my fears might have been exaggerated. But my fears appear to have been justified. I was the only person who expected what was to come. He was very nice with us and with the children. He closely and clearly watched the way I walked and sat. This was because there was a special spiritual link between us.

'Before 1995, I was known as the closest child to him. They always said that even my looks and habits were the closest to his. My mother always said that I was as stubborn as my father.'

In 1995 she had accompanied her husband when he defected to Jordan. The interviewer returned to the subject of their last meeting just before the war, and how Saddam had behaved towards her.

'He watched my movements whenever I stood or sat. I asked myself why he was staring at me so much that day. I thought that he, as a father, might have wanted to see more of me. He was very normal and highly elegant. He was nice to the kids. When he left, he sent them sweets. We did not even discuss the details as to where we would be heading. Not at all.'

'If President Saddam had the chance to see his eldest daughter Raghad speak,' one of the interviewers asked finally, 'what would you say at the end of this interview through al-Arabiya Television to the President, who could be anywhere?'

'I would tell him: I miss you, Dad. I miss you very much.' At this point she broke down into tears. 'May God give him strength to face his current circumstances. This is the only thing I can say now.'

It is a remarkable interview, about a real family. Yet we can never quite forget that Saddam Hussein was essentially a *mafioso*, and that his sons and daughters were not just part of the family, they were inextricably involved in the general gangsterism of their closest relatives. Raghad's own husband betrayed Saddam, and forced her to defect with him to Jordan. When he returned, he was killed – and

Saddam must have approved of the killing. Then, less than eight years later, Raghad escaped to Jordan again in April 2003, just as Baghdad was about to fall to the Americans.

'After noon, my father dispatched special security vehicles to us and asked us to leave. Qusay's wife and the children were with us. [Qusay was the younger of her two brothers, regarded as more reliable and sensible than Saddam's elder son, Uday.] The farewell moments were horrible. The children began to hug each other and cry. We left Baghdad.

'A few hours later, we met my mother. I also met Hala [her younger sister]. They gathered us at a house located on the outskirts of Baghdad. But we were almost cut off from my father and brothers. This is because things got out of control. I saw with my eyes the army withdrawing and the Iraqi soldiers, regrettably, retreating panic-stricken, running and looking sideways.

'Missiles were falling on our right and left sides. I can tell you that they were less than fifty or a hundred metres from us. Due to the intensity of the bombardment, the house where we were staying was shaken. We got into small cars. I had my weapon on me. I left my weapon on my lap and chest.'

One of the interviewers asked if she knew how to use it.

'As a matter of fact, to a certain extent, I do. I am not a "professional"' – she used the English word – 'but to a certain extent I do. This was because the fate to which we were heading was unknown. I was afraid of the driver who was driving the vehicle, of the road and of what might come after we had travelled some distance.'

Al-Silawi: Was there a driver with you or was a family member doing the driving?

Raghad: No, he was not a family member. He was a driver. But this driver was not mine. I –

Al-Silawi: Did you observe that his treatment of you had undergone any change?

Raghad: Not at all. He was highly sympathetic. But one makes all possible calculations . . .

Al-Silawi: Of course.

Raghad: One takes the worst possible calculations into consideration. We stayed with Mother for one night. When

the sun set the following day, I spoke to my mother, telling
her: I think that it is all over. She answered: I also have the
same feeling.

We were a group of women. We had to decide the next
step. She said: Daughter, disperse. Each and every one of you
must find a place to hide pending a possible reunion.

Al-Silawi: And you parted?

Raghad: Yes, since then, we have spread out. I have not heard
anything about them, nor . . .

Her voice trailed away. It was quite affecting – until you recalled that
Raghad had had a gun on her lap, had known how to use it, and
had been perfectly prepared to shoot the driver if he had done anything to arouse her suspicions. She was unquestionably her father's
daughter.

5. DOUBLES

Assassination had always been a real danger for Saddam Hussein, just
as it was for his son Uday; and, like Uday, he used doubles to protect
himself. He had more than one, though the White House, the Pentagon
and the Downing Street press machine all encouraged journalists
to believe he used them more than he actually did. When Saddam
made his final public appearance on the streets of Baghdad, walking
round the streets of a working-class suburb of the city while the
Americans were on its very outskirts, this was dismissed as the work
of a double. Yet careful examination of his features reveals that it
was certainly Saddam; apart from anything else, his son Qusay was
with him, looking anxiously around to check that there was no sign
of the Americans. The appearance was as characteristic of Saddam as
the reports of his last-ditch demonstration of resistance by firing at the
American tanks as they entered his city.

There were always suggestions, particularly in the West, that some
of Saddam's most famous exploits were the work of doubles; particularly the swim he took in the waters of the Tigris at a time when

he was trying to persuade his ministers, and the entire nation, that everyone should be fitter. His daughter Raghad, in her interview with al-Arabiyah Television, poured scorn on the idea that someone else might have carried out the swim in Saddam's place.

'I can identify my father among a million men. I can identify his way of laughing, his voice, eye and look. No matter how this person resembles you, the expressions on his face and his features cannot be you. When he swam across the river, they said that this was his double because his muscles and body were strong. My father is very strong. He is over sixty-four years old, but when he walks you can tell that he is strong. He can easily swim across the river. He comes from the countryside and he is very strong. It is known that men from the country are stronger and braver than city people. It is not difficult for a brave man to cross a river.'

Yet the doubles unquestionably existed. A friend of mine, after saying goodbye to Saddam, went into an outer room where people were waiting for limousines to take them somewhere, and found Saddam sitting there in a line with the others; only when he looked more closely he realized it wasn't Saddam, merely a man who looked and dressed like him. An habitué of Saddam's court told me the double was a pleasant, rather melancholy man. Presumably he lived a life of some grandeur, but no one who knew who he was had any interest in him.

In this case, his job was merely to leave the building when Saddam did, in a line of vehicles like Saddam's, and take a different route. Saddam had been the target of wayside attacks more than once, and Uday had been paralysed and almost killed by the male members of a Baghdad family whose daughter he had raped; they hung around a crossroads which they knew his car would pass, and fired at it with automatic weapons.

So for Saddam to have a double increased the odds for any would-be assassins. Naturally, the double had to look very like him, and sometimes it was necessary to make a few alterations with plastic surgery.

Late in 2002 I worked on the BBC documentary about Saddam which he saw and joked about. It caught the public imagination remarkably. We brought over a forensic scientist from Germany, Dr Dieter Buhmann, whose speciality was reconstructing faces of murder victims from their skulls. To lighten things a little after a long day at the morgue, his hobby was to examine all the known video of Saddam Hussein and work out if it really was the man himself. He had a system of measuring the key points of a face and using this as a template to check the other images of Saddam.

Dr Buhmann's view, after several years of study, was that Saddam had had four different look-alikes over the years. It was difficult to be certain how many there were at any one time, though a leading figure who knew him told me there was only one at the end. The double never made a speech for Saddam; that would have been unthinkable. But it does seem that sometimes, when Saddam was extremely busy, the double would stand in for him at official meetings with visitors who were not on the A-list.

Dr Buhmann insisted, for instance, that Jorg Haider, the extreme right-wing Austrian leader, was only given an audience with the double when he came to Baghdad. This was an accusation which brought Haider a good deal of ridicule when it appeared. I asked Dr Buhmann to look very carefully at the video of the meeting between Saddam – supposedly – and George Galloway, the British Labour MP who often visited Baghdad and was something of an apologist for Saddam. He did all the measurements, from the mole on Saddam's cheek to the corners of his eyes, the line of his eyebrows, the distance from his lips to the tip of his chin.

'Well? What do you think?'

'This is Saddam.'

George Galloway can be a difficult man; he refused to help me get an interview with Saddam in the run-up to the war at a time when a word from him would have achieved it, on the (accurate) grounds that he himself had been unfairly dealt with by a freelance, working for the BBC. This man had given Galloway the impression he was going to make a serious programme about him when all along he was planning to show him in a bad light. I couldn't blame Galloway for refusing to help the BBC again; I would have taken the same decision myself. Nor did he keep his support for Saddam Hussein a secret. Whatever Galloway was, he wasn't a yes-man.

But Saddam's doubles have confused and undermined all sorts of reportage. If you know what to look for, you can see their faces in television documentaries, in newspaper photographs, on posters, even sometimes on postcards in the Arab world. The general appearance of the face is somehow subtly different. The pebble-hard, obsidian eyes are less piercing, the lines of the face a little softer, a little more self-indulgent.

In the run-up to the war I went into a bookshop in Washington DC and came across a fat, pompous volume called *The Iraq War Reader*, which proclaimed that it contained 'Everything You Need to Know About the War with Iraq'. There was scarcely anything by real live Iraqis in it, and not much by Arabs of any kind. What it did contain was enormous quantities of journo-guff: opinions by writers and journalists, mostly American, for and against the idea of invading Iraq. I used Dr Buhmann's measuring techniques to examine the photograph of Saddam Hussein on the cover. It was a double, of course.

6. THE EGOIST

Absolute power sometimes has the same effect as enormous wealth; it can lead its possessor to hide from the world. Stalin lived in a couple of rooms in the Kremlin, or else in his small dacha. Ceausescu indulged himself and his family hugely, but they were insulated from Romania's poverty by a particularly nasty secret police force which had its own links with Saddam's Mukhabarat. Kim Il Sung lived the life of a total recluse in North Korea.

This wasn't Saddam Hussein's way. He was an extrovert who wanted people to see him. Not necessarily in the flesh: he knew how many Iraqis had reason to kill him, and he increasingly kept away from them as the years went past. But he believed in his own popularity, and he kept his face before his people to an extent that no one except the leaders of North Korea has emulated.

It was partly because he was vain. He regarded himself as a ladies' man, and it was always one of the clichés of what passed for political life in Iraq that women supported him because of his virile good looks. His son Uday was different, with his buck teeth and his taste for kidnapping women and raping them. Saddam was no rapist; he behaved himself, for the most part.

He thought he looked good, and he wanted everyone to see him – at least in pictures. In the late 1980s he ordered the entire nation to diet and exercise, and his ministers had orders to keep their stomachs as trim as his. The newspapers published their weight (though not his) every week; it humiliated them, and he liked that. He was a young man by the standard of international politics, and he made sure his public portraits were a few years younger than the original. Every day he personally selected the photographs of himself which would appear in the next day's press.

Throughout his twenty-four-year reign, most of those photographs were taken by one man: Hussein Mohammed Ali, a large, gloomy figure with a Clark Gable moustache and a taste for double-breasted suits with plenty of shoulder-padding. Every afternoon he would spread out the day's contact sheets, and Saddam would go through them with him. If by some chance the President hadn't appeared in public or met anyone worth photographing, the newspapers would have to choose a shot from their extensive libraries of him. At times of major crisis the same picture could be used day after day. There was only one rule: no newspaper could ever appear without a photograph of the President on the front page. As well as being inordinately vain, Saddam was also a role-player, an actor. Iraq's long history gave him a number of incarnations to adopt, from Hammurabi the Law-giver to Saladin (who was born in Tikrit, his home power-base) and King Faisal I, whose statue, on horseback, he had placed in the redeveloped centre of Baghdad. He rebuilt Babylon to his own design, and the Iraqi archaeologists had to pretend to like it.

'From Nebuchadnezzar to Saddam Hussein,' proclaimed a poster in the Babylon gift shop, 'Babylon invokes its glories.'

The southern palace, where the Hanging Gardens had once been, was completely rebuilt in the 1980s and 90s. The place was entirely empty of structures, just yellow brick walls twenty-five feet high, crowned by fantastic machicolations which Saddam himself had selected from a list of archaeological possibilities. During the various crises which Iraq had to undergo, the place was usually empty. The work was carried on only fitfully, and whenever I went there the workmen all seemed to have vanished. An occasional group of Vietnamese nurses would giggle as they took each other's photographs beside the statue of a lion straddling a prone victim: a representation of the curiously sexual power of ancient Babylon. *Agents provocateurs* would dart forward, trying to persuade the unwary to buy a Babylonian clay cylinder-seal – a real crime, which would render the buyer liable for heavy blackmail, or several years in gaol.

There was, I thought, something not quite right about the brickwork at the base of one of the walls. I went over and looked: the three courses at the base of the wall were irregular and crude. They turned out to be the original mud-brick walls of Babylon, and the tidy new brickwork above it was Saddam Hussein's work. It requires a special brand of self-belief to take one of the world's great archaeological sites and make it look like an unfinished hypermarket; but Saddam Hussein never lacked confidence. Lines of inscribed bricks were built into the new walls:

> In the Name of the Victorious Saddam Hussein, President of the Republic, Protector of the Great Iraq and the Renewer of its Civilization, this Palace – built by King Nebuchadnezzar II, who reigned from 605 to 563 before the modern era – has been rebuilt at different stages, the second ending in 1986.

On a hill overlooking the site of Babylon, Saddam built himself a palace that was bigger in conception than anything Nebuchadnezzar could have dreamed of. It was supposed to be the grandest of all his various palaces, but in the end he decided he didn't like it as much as some of the others, and he rarely went there.

If his architectural ideas were based on those of the ancient Babylonian kings, he constructed his self-image along the lines of an early Abbasid caliph. Just as al-Mansour and Haroun al-Rashid had held open court where their subjects could seek redress for injustice, so Saddam nurtured the romantic idea that anyone could approach him. In the early 1980s an American journalist visited Baghdad and was given an interview with Saddam. With a certain necessary caution, he broached the question of Iraq's human rights record. Wasn't it true that people lived in considerable fear in Iraq?

Saddam was visibly annoyed. Where had the journalist heard this? From Amnesty International, he answered, greatly daring. There was an explosion of rage, and the correspondent thought he was a dead man.

'Come with me. I want to show you something,' Saddam shouted.

He grabbed the American correspondent by the arm and pulled him into the palace courtyard. Several Range Rovers were parked there, with various of Saddam's bodyguards standing around. The correspondent was certain now that he was going to be shot, but Saddam yelled at the bystanders and jumped into the driving seat of one of the Range Rovers. The correspondent got in beside him.

Behind them, the bodyguards threw themselves into other vehicles and tried to catch up with Saddam as he roared out of the court-yard, tyres screaming. They drove at high speed towards the centre of Baghdad, while cars, horse-drawn carts and frightened policemen leaped out of the way.

Eventually the motorcade fetched up in Rashid Street, and the Range Rover screeched to a halt. The other cars stopped suddenly behind him, and the bodyguards threw themselves out again and gathered around. He pushed them impatiently aside and lunged into the crowd of passers-by. Most of them were too shocked to make their escape. The American correspondent watched him single out one unfortunate, and poke him in the chest with his swagger-stick.

'This foreign journalist thinks I'm unpopular in Iraq. What do you say to that?'

The man said everything he could possibly think of, and more: how everyone loved and respected Saddam, how he was the only leader who could keep the country together, how he had made everyone wealthy. Saddam listened, nodding his approval. Finally he took the swagger-stick out of the man's chest.

'You see? Of course the people love me!'

He laughed uproariously and jumped into the Range Rover again. They went back and finished the interview.

Just as Haroun al-Rashid secretly wandered the *souqs* of Baghdad to listen to and act upon the complaints of his subjects, Saddam Hussein took a delight in descending on towns and villages without warning to show himself to his people.

On the spur of the moment – partly for security reasons and partly because that was how he did everything anyhow – he would head out into the countryside. Often the local Mukhabarat would only have half an hour's warning.

I saw the video of one such visit. Saddam descended on the house of a half-blind villager who had once been a soldier in the days of the old royal family. The poor old man realized what he had to do: he pretended not to know who this visitor was who had arrived with an army of bodyguards, a fleet of Mercedes and Range Rovers, a couple of armoured personnel carriers, and two fully equipped camera crews wearing military uniform. Saddam squatted down in front of the old man as he sat on a bed in the porch.

> *Saddam:* Is your old age pension big enough for your needs?
> *Old man:* Yes, thank you, sir. Nowadays it's much bigger than it used to be, and we count ourselves very lucky.
> *Saddam:* Who was it that raised the level of your pension? Who do you have to thank for that?
> *Old man:* Why, our leader, President Saddam Hussein, of course. We're very grateful indeed for everything he's done for us, I can tell you.
> *Wife (appearing suddenly from house and ululating with joy):* Look who it is, husband! Don't you recognize him?
> *Old man (startled):* Me? No! Who is it?
> *Wife:* It's our wonderful President, Saddam Hussein himself, that's who!
> *Old man (shouting and crying):* O God! Let me kiss your hand, sir!

And so on for a very long time. That was the lead story on the night's television news bulletin, which naturally had to be extended to an hour and three-quarters to take it all in.

Throughout his entire time in supreme power, from 1979 to 2003, Saddam Hussein's activities always were the lead item on the daily television news; and since no one wanted to edit anything the President said or did, the reports tended to last a very long time. The news itself began with what was known as the 'Saddam Song':

> Saddam, our victorious
> Saddam, our beloved,
> In your eyes you carry
> The nation's dawn.
>
> Saddam, everything is good with you.
>
> Allah, we are happy.
> Saddam lights our days.

Requiring this embarrassing doggerel to be sung every night, and watching it himself, took an unusually high degree of self-regard. Stalin used to think the excessive homage of his followers was absurd, and sometimes used to force them to show more, merely in order to punish them for their grovelling behaviour. Saddam, by contrast, was never known to object. He would watch television with a smile on his face, which would turn to a frown if the adulation wasn't quite sufficient. He thought, in other words, that he deserved it.

Saddam's officials were all privately aware that the emphasis on him was grossly overdone, even embarrassing, but they would explain it by stressing that a complex country like Iraq, with so many different ethnic and religious groups, required a strong, clearly defined leadership to hold it together. Since Iraq's population was still largely backward and composed of peasants, everything had to be kept simple.

Yet no matter how simple and uneducated most Iraqis might be, they had a natural sense of self-protection. They knew perfectly well that if Saddam suddenly descended on them, as he had on the old man and his wife, they should play to his lead with all the apparent sincerity they could muster.

The true reason for all the grotesque emphasis on Saddam's personality, all the lengthy news reports, all the portraits of him in the streets and shops and houses, was that he wanted it like this. It wasn't merely policy: he enjoyed it. At the same time he was a realist, and a highly suspicious and well-informed one at that. He knew perfectly well he wasn't loved, so he ordered the creation of a façade of love and worship which would provide much the same effect.

In 1982, during the Iran–Iraq War Ayatollah Khomeini issued a direct, personal challenge to Saddam Hussein's political legitimacy. He pointed out that whereas the President of Iran was elected by a majority of the people in what was a highly restricted yet genuine vote, Saddam was completely unelected. Saddam's response was characteristic: he didn't, of course, organize elections, but he announced a Day of Allegiance. On 11 November the secret police and the Ba'ath Party exerted all their efforts to get the people out, and eleven million took to the streets to show their love for the leader.

After that, Saddam wanted to see daily evidence of this love. As a result, Iraqi television introduced a new entertainment programme, broadcast every night. It consisted of crooners singing his praises, and poets declaiming verses in his honour.

> All evil people fear your sword, Saddam.
> It has already been tested.
> You are the Father of good things,
> And with you we will challenge
> All the aggressors who have built up their power.
> We beg God to keep you well and happy,
> And to maintain your appearance
> Shining on us all the time,
> So that we can have pride in you
> Above all others.

The newspapers had their laureates too. One of the last editions of the newspaper *Babylon*, an appallingly badly produced rag, printed a large photograph on the back page of its edition of Wednesday 19 March 2003, showing Saddam flanked by his two sons. Uday, tall and gawky, looks at the camera in his usual aggressive way, as though he is about to pick a fight with the reader. The sleeves of his shapeless overcoat are too long for his arms, and he has a large handgun tucked into the waistband of his trousers.

Beside him, smiling his usual smile and dressed as beautifully as ever, is Saddam himself, his teeth showing slightly above his lower lip. On the right is Qusay, a carbon copy of his father right down to the haircut, the moustache, the expression, and the posture, hands hanging by his sides, fists lightly clenched. They look like a group of extortionists, as indeed they were.

The headline in red over the picture says in shaky English: 'This is Saddam the help in need And this is Saddam the optimum generous.' Below, in this same odd style, with a caesura in every line, is a poem: no title, just the words 'The poet Abdul Minim Hamden' and the following, mostly meaningless piece of sycophancy:

Your Iraq keeps its glory

　　　　　　　　　　　And your light its covering

Your patience has generated

　　　　　　　　　　　Mountains which are loudly crying

The victory morning is blossomed

Joyful not rare for yearning

Crowned with glorious Jihad

Guarded by fighters all around

Ye [sic] Saddam his sight we love

And every word of his wisdom

His glitering [sic] shine appears
    in light

In his presence the crescent falls
    asleep

This people your iron people

As strong as never has an equal

For victory is eminent in his eyes

As victory may witness rallies and
    fete

He retrieved glory and hopes

Cause the dreams provided with
    dawn and kindles

Every tale tells host

Every poem followed by hospitality

We loved him in the path of God

From his eyes, always beauty
    pours

You don't have to be able to understand a word of this to realize that
it is grovelling of a fairly high order.

There was, of course, no minister, no relative powerful enough to
suggest to Saddam Hussein that his personality cult might be a little
over the top. This was the greatest weakness of his system. When a
crisis arose, there was no one who could be contacted quietly, and no
channel through which messages could be passed. Saddam Hussein
was President of the Republic, chairman of the Revolutionary Command Council, prime minister, secretary-general of the Ba'ath Party
and commander-in-chief of the armed forces. He had no advisers,
because no one could give him advice.

He did occasionally listen to criticism: he once visited a village and
heard the local people complain about the creation of a local cooperative. Then and there he declared the cooperative abolished. It was
typical of his entire way of behaving. He did things for effect, and he

did them at once; there was no time for reflection, no discussion with officials or experts, no concern about the consequences.

To question what he did or said was extraordinarily dangerous. In 1983, during the Iran–Iraq War, two of his most senior generals decided that his personal conduct of the war was becoming disastrous, and might end in Iraq's defeat. They talked to each other and decided that it was their patriotic duty to confront him with the facts. He listened, and saw the force of their argument. As a result, he played less of a part in planning military operations. The generals were both arrested, as they had known they would be, and only one of them seems to have survived.

The Revolutionary Command Council of the Ba'ath Party was the highest governing body in Iraq. Each time it met, Saddam's personal cameramen would film the occasion without recording the sound. The pictures would be dubbed with music by Vivaldi or Bach and broadcast that night on television. When the rest of the members had settled themselves, the doors at the end of the room would open and Saddam would stand for a moment or two in the doorway as everyone stood up to greet him. He, and they, would all be dressed in their olive-green Ba'athist uniforms. Saddam was always perfectly turned out, and his valets were important men in their own right.

Half the high-backed chairs around the long table were always empty. The Revolutionary Command Council had had seven members after the 1968 coup, and the number had slowly risen to twelve. Then, accidents – or what appeared to be accidents – befell some of its members, while others were eased out, so the number fell again. Yet the absentees' chairs remained, each of them as accusingly empty as Banquo's place at Macbeth's feast.

In earlier times, violent things had happened at Revolutionary Command Council meetings. In 1970, when Saddam was vice-president, he and the defence minister, Hardan al-Tikriti, pulled their guns on one another during an argument about Iraq's failure to help the Palestinians during the Black September violence in Jordan. Soon after he became President in 1979, Saddam held the families of several members of the RCC hostage to ensure that a vote was passed and the necessary documents signed. Some of the RCC members and their families were reportedly shot.

After that, the Council became entirely subservient to Saddam's will, and its sole function was to work out how to put his wishes into effect. The leading Council members were an odd group: Saddam's deputy, the tall and painfully thin Izzat Ibrahim, with his shock of bright red hair and his grim, undertaker's manner; Taha Yasin Ramadan, a close associate of Saddam's since the 1960s; Tariq Aziz, foreign minister and later deputy prime minister, a Christian and a profound nationalist whose jovial appearance belied a fearsome temper. Only Ramadan appeared to have the personality to be a leader rather than a follower; and since that was the most dangerous characteristic to possess in Saddam's Iraq, he obeyed orders as slavishly as the rest.

New evidence about Joseph Stalin shows him to have been a much more complex figure than the brutal, two-dimensional despot we have always imagined. He was, it turns out, witty, intellectual, nervous, self-deprecating as well as being savagely suspicious, violent and cruel. By contrast it doesn't seem likely that we will have to rethink our views of Saddam Hussein so much when all the evidence about him is finally available. In private, he may well have been more attractive than he seemed on the surface. But his enthusiasm for the cult of personality which he created around himself does not argue any kind of sensitivity in his make-up. He was what he had made himself: the *capo di tutti capi*, head of the biggest mafia family on earth, as cruel and violent as Stalin but without the more complex characteristics. Stalin was a gangster who became a politician. Saddam Hussein was always a gangster, from first to last.

7. TURBULENCE

Spring comes and goes so fast in Iraq that everything has changed before you properly notice it. Sometimes it lasts only a few days, and then you realize that the annual change has happened, the leaves and flowers are out, and the country is swept up towards the ferocious heat of summer. There is no compromise in Iraq, no mild uncertainty. The climate, the countryside and the people are as forthright as each other. The very name 'Iraq', which emerged around the time of the country's conversion to Islam in the seventh century of the Christian era, means 'the country which is firmly rooted'. It is a land of mountains, of deserts and marshes, as tough and determined as its people have to be in order to get a living from it.

There is a wildness about it, too. In the hottest months, from June to August, when even the flies disappear because of the heat, the country is racked by dust storms, while the prevailing northerly wind, the *shamal*, sweeps across and dries out the atmosphere, laying bare the land and the people to the blistering heat.

At other times of the year, particularly from March to May, flooding is common. The legends of Sumer and Akkad speak of the great inundations of prehistory; in the *Epic of Gilgamesh*, which is thought to have been written around 3000 BC, the gods notice the goodness and wisdom of Ut-Napishtim and warn him that a flood is coming:

> Pull this house down, build a ship,
> And take on board the seed of every living creature!

The Jews who endured captivity in Babylon picked up the story and made it their own: an account of a great flood which only Noah, his family and selected pairs of animals survived. When the Jews eventually returned to their own country, where flooding on any large scale is rare, they incorporated it into their accounts of their early history.

The most important natural features of Iraq are its two great rivers, Tigris and Euphrates, which flow south-eastwards from Turkey. At first they are separated by 250 miles of harsh mountainous land, but they draw closer and closer until they are only twenty miles apart. Then they turn away again before draining into the Shatt al-Arab and the Persian Gulf through the marshlands and swamps at Qurnah, which people have claimed as the site of the Garden of Eden. The rivers too have helped to form Iraq's character. The great civilizations of Mesopotamia (Greek for 'the land between the rivers') are dotted along their course.

But the Tigris and Euphrates are not predictable and reassuring like the Nile, which floods year after year, century after century, millennium after millennium, replenishing the earth and providing the inhabitants with a reliable livelihood. Egypt's civilization was supremely placid for three thousand years, and there was scarcely any real social evolution during that time; for the most part sons succeeded their fathers as scribes, labourers, soldiers, peasant farmers, neither rising nor falling in the great scheme of things. As a result the Egyptians' universe was unchanging and eternal, and each succeeding pharaoh represented the triumph of this immutable order.

Not so the fierce civilizations of Mesopotamia, which emerged fast, burned brightly and died away, leaving around them the wreckage of other civilizations they had destroyed. Throughout the vast extent of Iraqi history there runs a continuous thread of the deepest pessimism. No achievement lasts long; political disaster and collapse are as close as destruction by the frequent catastrophic flooding of the two rivers. The kings and chief priests of Mesopotamia had the task of placating the inexplicable violence of the gods, and trying to turn it to their own advantage. The universe could only be so hostile, so impossible to predict, because the gods themselves were hostile and unpredictable. And yet the function of a king was not merely to work out ways of propitiating them; it was to imitate them.

This was a land formed by fear and by ferocious power. You have only to compare the restless, vibrant, aggressive reliefs of Nimrud or Nineveh with the calmness of Egyptian tomb art, unchanged for millennia, to get some idea of the way in which the unpredictability of the Iraqi climate and the toughness of the landscape affected its people.

In its earliest stages Mesopotamia was not a single, unified kingdom like Egypt. Instead, it was a collection of small, independent, often mutually hostile city-states. They started off as small farming settlements on the banks of the two rivers and ended up as the core of great aggressive empires, swallowing up the cities and kingdoms round about them, and usually plagued with internal dissension. The political history of city-states such as Ur, Kish, Nippur and Uruk was an immensely complex business. They joined together in brief alliances which were always directed against other states, then betrayed them and created new groupings. War and conquest were the life-blood of the civilizations which grew up between the rivers.

They were civilizations of a high order. Arbil, in Iraqi Kurdistan, claims that its citadel, perched 100 feet high on a vast mound of earlier settlements, is the oldest continuously occupied city in the world, with a recorded history going back at least to 5000 BC; yet there are plenty of other contestants for the title in Iraq. The culture, the discoveries, the worship of the Mesopotamian city-states, play a clear part in our own civilization. If you drive through the Zagros mountains of north-eastern Iraq in the summer you can see wild wheat, barley and oats growing like weeds by the roadside. These were the plants which at some impossibly distant time were domesticated in Mesopotamia and turned into the staples of everyday food.

Writing began very early in Mesopotamia: perhaps, though this is always a matter of controversy, earlier than in Egypt. The people of the two rivers believed it originated in the city of Uruk, modern Warka, near the southern city of Samawa. Certainly the habits of bureaucracy seem to have begun there, and at some point in the fourth millennium BC cylinder-seals were produced there, capable of transfer-ring images permanently onto damp clay.

After that the scribes of Uruk began to make their own marks on the clay, registering allocations of goods, receipts, the ownership of property and all the other things a thriving bureaucracy needs in order to flourish and to remember the debts and obligations of its people. The settlements along the two rivers had expanded hugely, and some may have contained as many as 100,000 people.

The signs and pictograms became simplified and standardized. Later, elsewhere in Mesopotamia, they were adapted to record speech. The marks were made on the clay with wedge-shaped (or 'cuneiform') sticks, and when the tablets were baked in ovens or dried by the sun they were capable of lasting indefinitely.

The technology for building palaces, temples and ziggurats 150 feet high was developed relatively early. By 2500 BC the craftsmen of Mesopotamia had learned to make glass. The arts were just as sophis-ticated in the towns and cities of Mesopotamia as they were in contemporary Egypt.

These elaborate, complex, increasingly sophisticated societies required proper planning and organization. In the city of Ur, for example, a general called Ur-Nammu came to power in 2113 BC by means of a coup. He created a union with Sumer which produced a remarkable new civilization, and he formulated a complex legal code to govern this new political force.

Three hundred years later Hammurabi became the sixth king of Babylon and in 1780 BC, not for the first time, Mesopotamia was united. He updated the legal system, and set up an eight-foot stele, or monument, on which 282 laws were set out in full. These were often surprisingly liberal: women were as free as men to own property and go to law, and even slaves were allowed to trade on their own account and buy their freedom. Many of the cuneiform tablets which have survived from this period are records of court cases, usually involving property.

The pattern of cultural and social advancement combined with violent political upheaval continued until the eleventh century BC, when the Assyrians under the terrible Tiglath-Pileser I began to dominate Mesopotamia and expanded their power to the Mediterranean. Later kings ruled an empire which stretched to Egypt and the Caucasus mountains. The Assyrians' chief weapons were discipline and ferocity. They slaughtered the male inhabitants of every town and city they captured in an empire which stretched 1,000 miles. Tiglath-Pileser III created a standing army, which, if it was not necessarily the first in the ancient world, was certainly the best organized. The conquests and the killing were all done in the name of the Assyrian sun-god Ashur: the king's enemies were Ashur's, and vice versa.

In the end the Assyrians' ferocity and their forcible deportations of different peoples across the face of the empire brought about the inevitable reaction. A new combination of forces came to the fore: the Babylonians, the Elamites and the Medes, who were the ancestors of today's Kurds, came together in 612 BC to attack the Assyrian capital Nineveh and destroy the empire.

Babylon was the dominant power of the fifth century BC. Under Nebuchadnezzar II it was a city of a quarter of a million people; perhaps the largest the world had seen at that period. The surrounding walls were ten miles long, wide enough for two chariots drawn by four horses each. There were more than 1,000 temples, and the dominant feature was the Tower of Babel, a ziggurat 300 feet high.

The 40,000 Jews who were taken to Babylon as slaves after the capture of their country saw the Tower with the eyes of people from a far less advanced society: they assumed it was intended to reach heaven, and they explained the wide range of languages spoken in the capital of the Babylonian empire as God's revenge on those who had the temerity to build their human structures so high.

The Jews were profoundly influenced by their exile in Babylon, and through them modern Western society still retains some of the faint echoes of Babylonian beliefs: the observance of a weekly day of rest, for instance. The Babylonians, who divided the month into periods of seven days associated with the phases of the moon, ended each week with an 'evil day', which required specially enforced ceremonies if the gods were to be propitiated. The day of the full moon, which required particular sacrifices and ceremonies, was known by the Babylonian word *shabbatum*.

Around 500 BC the Babylonians developed the theory of the zodiac, the belt round the earth which supposedly contained the sun, moon and stars. The Babylonian astronomers then divided the zodiac, and by extension any circle, into 360 degrees, the figures 12, 24 and 60 having particular significance for them. We divide our week into seven days, our days into twenty-four hours, and our circles into 360 degrees, as a direct result of Babylonian science; and each week we have one day of rest, or holy day, as a result of Babylonian religion.

After the Persian conquest of Babylon in 538 BC the Jews were allowed to go home. Yet many of them stayed and became a powerful and wealthy community over the centuries, until Saddam Hussein, the latter-day Tiglath-Pileser, began arresting and executing Jews on the grounds that they were agents of Israel, and eventually threw them out of the country entirely.

As for the Assyrians, the collapse of their 1,000-year empire left them a small and highly vulnerable tribe scattered over the whole extent of their former possessions. They converted to Christianity very early, in the decades which followed after the crucifixion of Jesus, and as a result were persecuted ever afterwards. The twentieth century almost destroyed them as a people: there were massacres by the Turks and by Arabs, and as with the Kurds, British promises to give them a homeland were never kept.

An estimated quarter of a million Assyrians threw in their lot with the Kurds in the uprising against Saddam in 1991 and had to flee Iraq altogether. Some returned, and during the 1990s the Assyrians were allowed to rebuild their churches and worship openly: partly, perhaps, because of the influence of Tariq Aziz, Saddam's deputy prime minister, who came from an Assyrian family though he himself was an Assyrian Christian.

8. GLORY AND DECAY

Mesopotamia remained a Persian possession until Alexander the Great destroyed the Persian empire in 331 BC, then died in Babylon, possibly of malaria, eight years later. The glory of the land between the rivers seemed to have drained away for ever; for 1,000 years its fate was decided elsewhere.

And then, in the years after the death of the Prophet Mohammed in AD 632, came the irresistible explosion of military and intellectual force represented by Islam. Within a century, from its capital in Damascus the empire of the Umayyads covered a swathe of territory 3,000 miles across, from France and Spain to India. For the most part the conquering Arabs, though they were backward and illiterate themselves, were remarkably respectful of the civilizations they controlled. Destruction and persecution were relatively rare, and the invaders quickly adopted the culture of their new subjects.

Politics was a different matter. The ninety-year rule of the Umayyads saw endless plots, murders and divisions within Islam: especially the schism between the Sunnis and Shi'ites over the critical question of who should rule the Islamic community as caliph after the death of the Prophet Mohammed. Some believed the new ruler should come from the Qaraysh, the Prophet's own tribe, others that Ali ibn Abu Talib, the Prophet's son-in-law, should succeed him. Ali, essentially a peacemaker, suggested a compromise; Muawiyah, his rival, pretended to accept Ali's proposal, then had him murdered.

Ali's body was tied to the back of a camel, which wandered through the desert until it reached Najaf, in Iraq, where one of the two greatest shrines of Shi'ite Islam was later built to commemorate him. Muawaiyah's son Yazid succeeded his father as caliph, and Ali's son Hussein set out to reclaim what he regarded as his rightful inheritance. Near Kerbala in Iraq, Hussein and his seventy-two followers were massacred by Yazid's force of 4,000.

His martyr's death changed the course of Islamic history. The followers of Ali and Hussein formed themselves into a separate party ('shi'a'), and their shrines at Najaf and Kerbala became the centre of a separate sect, which tended to become the religion of the down-trodden and the poor, and often identified itself with their interests. Today, of the billion or more Muslims, something like 190 million are Shi'ite. In Iraq Shi'ites make up somewhere between 55 per cent and 65 per cent of the population, most of them descended from Sunni Muslims who converted to Shi'ism during the nineteenth century.

In AD 750 the Umayyads were driven from power by another Sunni dynasty, the Abbasids; they were the descendants of Abbas, the Prophet Mohammed's uncle. Abu'l Abbas, his great-great-grandson, who called himself the Shedder of Blood, seized power and lived up to his name. Yet in the ninety years which followed, the Abbasid Caliphs lifted the Islamic world to a new plane of intellectual, artistic and scientific glory – and Baghdad was their capital. Mansour (754–75), Haroun al-Rashid (786–809) and Mamum (813–33) were enlightened rulers who created a civilization which was the most advanced in the world. It took Western Europe at least another 500 years to match the Abbasids' achievements.

Caliph al-Mansour shifted the capital of the Muslim world to Baghdad, and he gave it a revolutionary design. It was entirely circular, and was made up of three concentric enclosures: his, naturally, was the central one. According to a ninth-century Arab scholar, Ya'qubi, the city in its heyday had 10,000 bath-houses; the population has been variously estimated between 100,000 and a third of a million. The teahouses and restaurants were far too many to count; at this period coffee became the most popular drink in the city.

The houses of the rich were known for their decorated balconies, and when the heat of the day lessened, the inhabitants would sit on a raised and carpeted platform (known as a *dukkan*) by their front doors; one writer describes a visit to a friend who was sitting on a *dukkan* of teakwood, inset with poems inscribed in letters of inlaid lapis lazuli.

During the ninth and tenth centuries Baghdad and Constantinople were the two greatest centres of commerce in the world. Caliph al-Mansour is supposed to have pointed to the river which flowed past his circular city, and to have said, 'Because of the Tigris, there is no barrier between us and China. Every ship can use it to come here.' That, certainly, was true. Baghdad imported silk and porcelain from China, together with goods from India, East Africa, Central Asia,

Russia and Northern Europe. A coin from Samarkand, excavated in York and now on display in its archaeological museum, may well have reached Saxon England via Baghdad.

The arts and sciences flourished. Ibn Sina (979–1037), whose empirical methods were as influential as his conclusions, was one of the greatest medieval physicians; Western Europe knew him as Avicenna, and his works were still circulating in France, Germany and England in the sixteenth century. A Baghdad mathematician, Muhammed Ibn Musa al-Khwarizmi, wrote the first book on algebra. Philosophy, politics and history were subjects for which the university of Baghdad, built near the observatory, was particularly famous. Translations of many classical European texts were available there, as well as manuscripts from India and China.

The Caliph governed his huge empire from the heart of Baghdad's circle, and could meet merchants from every part of the known world there. Haroun al-Rashid was said to wander the streets in disguise at night-time, accompanied only by his chief minister and his public executioner, checking on the public mood and the things that were being said about him. This is how he enters the *Thousand and One Nights* in Sir Richard Burton's translation of 'The Porter and the Three Ladies of Baghdad':

> . . . the Caliph, Haroun al-Rashid, had gone forth from the palace, as was his wont now and then, to solace himself in the city that night, and to see and hear what new thing was stirring; he was in merchant's gear, and he was attended by Ja'afar, his Wazir, and by Masrur, his Sworder of Vengeance. As they walked about the city, their way led them towards the house of the three ladies; where they heard the loud noise of musical instruments and singing and merriment; so quoth the Caliph to Ja'afar, 'I long to enter this house and hear those songs and see who sings them.'

And so begins another adventure.

But the Caliphs, including Haroun al-Rashid himself, became a little too concerned with their own pleasures and diversions, and ceased to take a controlling part in the business of state. Haroun was absurdly extravagant; the story is told that he mistakenly promised a peasant in whose hut he had sheltered 500,000 dirhams instead of the 500 he was asked for, and he insisted that the treasury pay up. Ja'afar and his other ministers took an increasing part in government. Caliph al-Mutasim (AD 822–42) gave his Turkish bodyguards greater and greater powers, until under later rulers the Turkish military leaders effectively ran the country and the Caliphs became mere ciphers, allowed to indulge themselves to the maximum but prevented from having any real say in administration or politics. By the eleventh century the Seljuk Turks had made themselves the formal rulers of the caliphate.

Baghdad's position as one of the world's great cities was finally destroyed 200 years later. The Mongol army, led by Genghis Khan's grandson, Hulagu, swept across from Central Asia, destroying every town and city they conquered and murdering most of the inhabitants. It was said you could smell the advancing horde a mile away.

On 10 February 1258 Baghdad fell to them. According to the chroniclers three-quarters of a million people were slaughtered. Everything of value to the Mongols was looted; the libraries for which Baghdad was famous throughout the civilized world, being useless to them, were burned, and the books thrown into the Tigris.

The Mongols then set about destroying every sign that the city had ever existed. They pulled down the buildings and destroyed their foundations; when the city was painfully rebuilt, it was further to the south and along the banks of the river. Nowadays almost nothing remains of the city which al-Mansour constructed; much of where it stood is a public park, and the outline is traceable only as a circle of dotted lines on the map of the modern city.

The Abbasid caliphate slipped into oblivion in 1517, and its former capital, Baghdad, took several hundred years to recover fully from its destruction. In 1534 Suleiman the Magnificent took the city without a battle, and over the next two centuries it passed backwards and forwards between the Turks and the Persians. By the eighteenth century Iraq as a territory was beginning to re-establish itself as an important economic centre. The Turks allowed the British East India Company to establish a trading agency at Basra.

The climate which had made the lives of the Assyrians and Babylonians so unstable had not improved. In 1831, during a visitation of bubonic plague in Baghdad, the Tigris burst its banks and flooded the city. Its population fell by two-thirds, to a mere 50,000. Turkish rule during the nineteenth century was more enlightened than anything the country had experienced before, but Iraq suffered as a result of the general decay of the Ottoman Empire. Nationalists grew in power accordingly, but their hopes of independence were disappointed when Turkey was on the losing side in the First World War and the victorious powers agreed that the territory which became Iraq should be mandated to the British, along the lines of the secret Sykes–Picot Agreement between Britain and France.

9. REBIRTH

The mandate came into force in 1920. As a result of it Iraq was incomparably better governed than it had been, but the new governors were disliked by most Iraqis: British rule was seen as Christian rule, and the administrators' determination to uphold the law was never properly understood. The so-called Great Iraqi Revolution of 1920 united most elements in the newly formed country against the British, and was put down with considerable harshness. At Winston Churchill's suggestion, the RAF used tear gas against the rebellious Kurds.

The British at last repaid Hussein ibn Ali, the Sharif of Mecca, for joining them during the Arab Revolt against the Turks in 1916 by putting his son Faisal on the throne of Iraq in 1921; though they first had to ensure that he won a nationwide referendum. But it was clear to the British within a few months that they were not wanted in Iraq, and that they would not be able to govern it for long. The first negotiated treaty for ending the Mandate was signed in 1922, and the process was complete by 1932, when the British marched out. They were, however, determined to remain the real power behind the Hashemite throne. Iraq's oil riches were too great to give up.

Britain spent as little money as it could on Iraq. Still, during the twelve years of the Mandate the foundations of modern Iraq were laid; manufacturing, the roads and railways, schools, universities, social services, hospitals, the law courts and, most important of all, the oil industry all owed their later strength and importance to the period of British rule. Iraq entered its independence free of debt, and with a sizeable income from oil.

The 1930s were a time of almost constant plotting by the military to take power or overthrow those who had it. Coup followed coup without regard for the national interest. Between 1937 and 1941 there were seven, ending with the pro-Nazi, anti-British regime of Rashid Ali Kailani. The British, who were faced at the time with the real possibility of defeat in the Middle East, landed a military force which captured Basra and occupied the country once more. For the next seventeen years, until 1958, the country was run by the pro-British Nuri Said. In 1955 Iraq became a member of the Baghdad Pact, a defence treaty which eventually included Turkey, Iran, Pakistan and Britain.

But the British link remained unpopular, and two major uprisings, in 1948 and 1952, were both directed against it in one way or another. Nuri Said, who was always regarded as a British stooge, eventually paid a heavy price for maintaining it. The government became increasingly isolated and corrupt; the subject of land reform, which was becoming a serious necessity, was largely ignored.

On 14 July 1958 a group of military men under Abdul-karim Kassem organized a coup of particular savagery. The young king, Faisal II, was brutally murdered, together with several members of his family. Nuri Said escaped at first, but was recognized and caught. He too was murdered, and his body was paraded through the streets and grotesquely abused. Iraq had always had a reputation for political instability, but from now it would be seen across the world – unfairly, perhaps, yet understandably – as a country where violence and cruelty were endemic.

Many Iraqis were repelled by the excesses carried out against the members and supporters of the old regime, yet there was a general sense that major change was required. The Suez débâcle two years earlier had united feeling across the Arab world, and Gamal Abdel Nasser of Egypt was now the dominant figure in the region: a man to be admired and emulated.

Iraqis had always known that their country was so disparate and divided that it was in permanent danger of falling apart; and the conclusion they drew from this was that it could be held together only by strong, fierce and at times brutal government. This was the price people were prepared to pay for stability and continuity. The monarchy had been perpetually weak; now that it had been overthrown, there was a demand for strong, effective power which would be exerted in the interests of the country and of Arab unity.

The time had come to deal with the power of the great land-owning elite, and to give the people of the big cities, particularly Baghdad and Basra, their proper due. It was time, too, for a complete switch in Iraq's international alignment. The British were finished as a Middle Eastern power, and the mood of the time seemed to require an opening to the Soviet Union. The long-repressed Iraqi Communist Party was legalized, and Communists began to take positions of real power in the new regime.

Yet Kassem's government was as insecure as the one it had overthrown. Ultra-nationalists and conservatives were both outraged by its new closeness to Moscow. There was outright war with the Kurds, whose hopes of self-government were once again betrayed, and trouble from various smaller ethnic minorities. No one really wanted Kassem as President, and his basic method of government was to play off all his various enemies and critics against one another. After five years and a number of usually violent efforts to get rid of him, he was overthrown in February 1963.

For the next nine months the Ba'athists ran the country. Their party ('Ba'ath' means 'renaissance') was founded on the belief that Arabs constituted one nation, and that it was everyone's duty to work for eventual union. At the same time they were narrowly nationalistic. The years of personal rule by Saddam Hussein have obscured the true ideology of the Iraqi Ba'ath Party; but it was more a grouping of the radical right than the radical left, created by resentment at the activities of the old European colonial powers in the Arab world, and by distaste for American efforts to thrust their way into the gap which Britain and France had left behind them.

The coup which got rid of the Ba'athists in November 1963 was carried out by army officers. Much of the new regime's time and effort was taken up with fighting the Kurds. It decided to limit its partici-pation in the 1967 war against Israel (though it did send one com-pletely inadequate brigade) and this destroyed what little support the regime had left in the country. There was a coup within the coup, and the Ba'athists took advantage of it. They assumed full power, and elbowed the military men aside.

The new regime was powerful and determined, and it had learned from its previous mistakes. Power, the Ba'athists realized, mattered far more than ideology; and the youngest but toughest member of the new government, Saddam Hussein, understood it better than anyone.

10. THE VILLAGE

If you didn't know the significance of the village of al-Awja, five miles south of Tikrit on the road to Baghdad, you certainly wouldn't give it a second glance. It lies to the left of the road, a collection of perhaps 100 dwellings. None of them has any pretension to wealth or grandeur; al-Awja has always been poor, and for most of its existence has been justifiably ignored. The older houses are made of mud-brick, but there are fewer and fewer of those remaining. The rest are of concrete, grey, small and unremarkable. One or two dogs, suffering from sores, wander down the little garbage-strewn lanes between the buildings, jumping nervously at every loud noise. From one house, a radio is blasting out music by an Iraqi singer. It is hot, and scarcely anyone is around.

The nearby town of Tikrit, by contrast, has been largely rebuilt since the first Gulf War; there are electronics and clothes shops, the remains of a vast, grandiose marble museum to Saddam Hussein and his rule, now bombed by the Americans, and the palace complex on the hill overlooking the Tigris. Al-Awja is as dirt-poor now as it always has been. Which is odd, since it is the place where Saddam Hussein was born.

Al-Awja means 'the bend', and it stands on the western bank of the Tigris, where the river takes a wide turn to avoid some slightly higher ground. This part of central Iraq is flat and characterless. The mountains of the north have petered out, and although the land is rich, the climate is not hot enough to support the magnificent date-palms which adorn southern Iraq.

Joseph Stalin allowed his slavish officials to build a ludicrous marble temple around the small wooden house where he was born, in the little Georgian town of Gori. Saddam, though he made Stalin his hero in many other ways, did not follow him in this. He spoke with pride of his humble origins, and never lost his harsh peasant accent in Arabic; but he hated al-Awja, and – it is said – used pointedly to look out of the opposite window when his convoy of vehicles passed it.

He was born in a small mud-brick hut, out of sight of the road. 'My birth was not a joyful occasion,' Saddam said bitterly to Amir Iskandar, one of his official biographers, in 1981. 'No roses or sweet-smelling herbs bedecked my cradle.' His mother, Subha Tulfah, a tough, ugly, strong-minded woman with a reputation locally of being able to read the future, called him 'the one who confronts'; we might perhaps shorten it to 'the fighter'. He was her first child. The birth supposedly took place on 28 April 1937, and this would one day become a national holiday in Iraq; yet Saddam Hussein's passport later gave 1 July 1939 as his date of birth. There are several possible reasons for the discrepancy, one of which is that during his time in the Ba'athist underground he adopted a different date to confuse the authorities. But it is also possible that Saddam wanted to take on a little more gravitas when he became a leading figure in the Ba'ath Party at a particularly young age.

Saddam's father was Subha's second cousin, Hussein al-Majid. It seems unlikely that they were married, though they had a second child together, Saddam's sister Siham. (In keeping with the aggressive names Subha Tulfah presciently chose for her children, 'Siham' means 'spear'.) After that, al-Majid disappeared. Other children in al-Awja taunted the young Saddam with being illegitimate, and various political opponents picked this up and used it against him later in life. At the last meeting between Saddam Hussein and a Kuwaiti delegation before the invasion of Kuwait on 2 August 1990, the Kuwaiti prime minister shouted across the table that if Iraqis were poor enough to need Kuwait's oil money, they should send their wives and mothers onto the streets to earn money for them. Saddam's impulsive decision to invade Kuwait was the direct result.

For the most part, Saddam's life at al-Awja was miserable. Subha married another of her cousins, Hassan al-Ibrahim, a school caretaker who had been sacked for drunkenness. The villagers tell how al-Ibrahim abused the young Saddam, beat him brutally, and sometimes threw him out of the house. Curiously, although Saddam scarcely mentioned al-Ibrahim in later life and must have loathed him, he stayed on good terms with his three half-brothers, Barzan, Sabawi and Watban, who were all given highly lucrative jobs in Saddam's administration.

The savage mistreatment Saddam received from al-Ibrahim affected his entire life. His later patterns of behaviour were all established during his violent, unhappy childhood: the delight in compensatory violence, the feeling (often justified, of course) that he couldn't trust anyone, however close, the constant need to reassure himself that in spite of everything he had undergone in his formative years, he was braver, better, tougher, more intelligent than everyone around him.

Dr Jerrold Post, an American clinical psychiatrist retained by the CIA to create a psychological profile of Saddam Hussein in the run-up to the first Gulf War, reached the conclusion that Saddam was exhibiting the behavioural condition known as malignant narcissism. The symptoms of this include an almost total self-absorption, a paranoid approach to those around him, a complete lack of interest or awareness of the suffering of others, and the absence of anything that might be called conscience in the pursuit of his own drives and compulsions.

None of this involves what the layman might think of as insanity, even though it became commonplace among politicians and journalists after the invasion of Kuwait to accuse Saddam Hussein of being 'mad'. Yet someone who shows the signs of malignant narcissism is not wild or irrational. The condition can be highly dangerous, but it does not necessarily involve any loss of control. On the contrary, it often brings a high degree of control and rationality, but in pursuit of paranoid ends.

Saddam Hussein in person was serious and thoughtful, and could be mildly jovial. Yet his eyes were hard and cold; they locked on to yours in a way that was distinctly unnerving. There was no personal interaction between you, however, because the moment he started to talk, his gaze would begin to dart around the room. Perhaps this was a way of enabling him to sort out his thoughts, but it gave the strong impression that he was suspicious of everyone. Still, Western visitors to Saddam over the years, aware that they were stirring up criticism back home, usually tried to stress Saddam's statesmanlike qualities. Sir Edward Heath, the former British prime minister, said after seeing him in 1990, 'The whole of our conversation was conducted in an atmosphere of the utmost calm ... I was very impressed by the extraordinarily detailed knowledge he showed on the subjects we were discussing.'

A brutal upbringing doesn't necessarily result in a deranged personality, of course, but it always has some noticeable effect later in life. In Saddam Hussein's case the violent treatment he received from his stepfather produced some of the classic symptoms of paranoia. Yet unlike most sufferers Saddam put these symptoms into the service of a cause; and from his earliest years he knew that the cause would be Iraqi nationalism.

In a society which is often still remarkably tribal, the al-Majids belonged to the al-Bejat clan, a small and insignificant sept of a group which was relatively important in the region round Tikrit: the al-Bu Nasr tribe. Tribal influences helped Saddam's uncle, Khairullah Tulfah, to get a commission in the Iraqi army in the late 1930s. As an officer, he was a man of some importance; and he was to play a considerable part in the young Saddam's life.

Saddam told one of his biographers that his mother, Subha, had recounted stories about Khairullah's involvement in the pro-Nazi uprising in 1941 against the British presence in Iraq. According to Subha, several members of the family had been killed by the British, and their houses burned down. There was a tradition of nationalist resistance in the family; some of Saddam's ancestors had been involved in rebellions against Turkish rule. It seems likely, too, that Subha told him stories about Saladin, the greatest warrior of the medieval Arab world, who had defeated the Third Crusade. Saladin was born in Tikrit in 1138 – almost exactly 800 years before Saddam's own birth. Saladin featured heavily in Saddam's speeches, though he never seems to have mentioned that Saladin was a Kurd. So Saddam's head was filled with grandiose notions of courage and resistance, and his official biographies give the impression that very early on he had a sense of personal destiny which was only enhanced by his stepfather's savagery and contempt for him.

Khairullah Tulfah's son Adnan, Saddam's cousin, was sent to school in Tikrit. He boasted to Saddam about his ability to read and write. (Forty years later, Adnan became a noticeably effective and popular defence minister, but immediately after a row with Saddam he died when a bomb blew his helicopter out of the sky.) Saddam, who was only eight, insisted on learning to read and write too; and when his stepfather objected, he ran away to Khairullah's house. Khairullah sent him to school by car with Adnan, and (according to Saddam's own account) gave him a gun. That, in the hands of an eight-year-old, meant that no one would taunt him to his face with being a bastard again.

A year later Khairullah Tulfah settled in Baghdad, and took Adnan and Saddam with him. At school there, Saddam's violent streak began to show itself, and he started to compensate for the cruelty and shame he had experienced in Tikrit. He seems to have relinquished the gun (which may of course have been a figment of his later imagination), but took to carrying an iron bar around with him. According to a fellow-pupil, Dr Ali al-Hakim, who eventually escaped from Iraq to live in exile, the headmaster wanted to expel Saddam.

'When Saddam heard about this he came to the headmaster's office and threatened him with death. He said, "I will kill you if you don't withdraw your threat." Why did the headmaster want to expel him? Because he was troublesome at school.'

Saddam wasn't expelled, of course. It was a lesson in the effectiveness of brute force which must have been as important as anything else he learned while he was at school.

He lived with Khairullah and his family in a poor area of Baghdad called Tikirte, after all the people from Tikrit who had settled there. Nowadays it has lost its connection with the town, and is just another run-down suburb with grimy, single-storey grey brick buildings draped with electrical cables and heaps of rubbish by every lamppost. But in the 1950s it was a natural home for small-time crooks and thugs, and there must have been every reason to assume that the young Saddam would simply grow up as one of them. Hassan al-Alawi, who was his press secretary from 1975 to 1980 (after which he fled the country), says the future President's penchant for cruelty was obvious even while he was growing up.

'He used to collect firewood and burn it. Then he would put an iron bar on the fire and make it red hot, and when he saw an animal passing he would run out and stab it in the stomach. I believe this story is true. Saddam grew up thinking that only his iron stick would protect him.'

According to several biographers of Saddam, his uncle Khairullah sent him back to Tikrit in 1956 to kill an enemy of his, a relative who had insulted him. Saddam performed the task to Khairullah's satisfaction. He would have been somewhere between sixteen and eighteen at the time: a precocious gangster.

The following year, having shown something of his abilities, he was recruited into the Ba'ath Party. The savage revolution of 14 July 1958, when the prime minister and virtually the entire royal family were massacred, fed Saddam's enthusiasm for violence and bloodshed; but as a Ba'athist he had no sympathy for Brigadier Abd el-Karim Qassem, who led the *coup d'état*. The Ba'athists regarded Qassem, who wanted to create strong links with the Soviet Union, as little better than the royal family who had made Iraq dependent on Britain; and Saddam was particularly exercised by this.

A former Iraqi diplomat, Mustapha Karadaghi, met him soon after the revolution. 'He was very aggressive,' Karadaghi said. 'He kept talking about how to overthrow the Qassem regime, and shoot everybody, wipe them out, and make the streets of Baghdad a lake of blood. He used that phrase, a lake of blood, a lot.'

11. POWER

The Ba'ath Party was founded in Damascus in 1944 by a group of eight young Arab nationalists, including Michel Aflaq, a Christian Syrian schoolmaster. They based their ideology on two beliefs: that all Arabs belonged to a single nation, which must be united politically, and that only radical social change could free the Arab lands from colonial power. The first Ba'athist organization in Baghdad was set up secretly in 1951.

Although it was strongly anti-Marxist, and only allied itself with the Communists occasionally and for tactical reasons, Ba'athism gave a strong Stalinist tone to Arab nationalism. It aimed, just as the early Soviet Union had done, to create a 'new man'. This new man was to be a dedicated servant of the Arab state, a willing sacrifice for the future of the wider nation. He was to have no feelings other than love for his leader and for the political entity of which he was a citizen.

He was a tiny component of the Arab masses, a Muslim perhaps but first and foremost a political and cultural conformist, obedient to the vision of the Ba'athist founders. It is hard to think of any society less suited to this fascistic dogma than the individualistic, family-conscious Iraqis, with thousands of years of sophisticated urban existence behind them. But some Iraqis, rootless and embittered nationalists, found the notion of the 'new man' distinctly attractive. The young Saddam Hussein was one of them.

He moved slowly up the Party structure, starting off as just a hard man, an enforcer, but receiving more responsibility as his very considerable abilities became clear. At each stage he, like every other Ba'ath Party worker, was carefully vetted. The Party was at heart an underground movement, and it trusted no one. At this stage there was no reason to think that it was more likely than any of the other radical nationalist movements in the Arab world to be in a position to take power; but like Hitler in the small, ineffectual National Socialist Party of the early 1920s, or Stalin in the faction-ridden Social Democratic Party before the First World War, Saddam Hussein had backed an unexpected winner.

The Ba'athists had originally supported the 1958 coup which destroyed the royal family, on the grounds that it would get rid of British influence. But the new President, Brigadier Qassem, was not a serious pan-Arabist, nor did he show any signs of introducing the kind of radical social change the Ba'athists demanded. The Party decided to go underground again, in order to challenge the new regime.

When the coup came, Saddam was at Baghdad University, studying law. A few months later he had orders to go back to Tikrit to murder a senior government official there. The murder was duly carried out, though in later years it was always regarded as unacceptable to mention Saddam Hussein's responsibility for it; by that time Saddam had become respectable. Nevertheless, he was arrested and gaoled for it. The murder was an important part of his apprenticeship, and when the Party leadership decided to assassinate President Qassem, Saddam was asked if he would take part. He jumped at the chance, of course.

The official account of the assassination attempt, which took place on 7 October 1959, gives Saddam pride of place in the action. It might not be acceptable to say that he had carried out the squalid murder of a local official, but there was a kind of glamour about the notion that

Saddam had been part of an attempted *coup d'état*. A museum was dedicated to the incident, though even at the height of Saddam's power only a few groups of schoolchildren seemed to visit it, and the caretaker was quite annoyed to be asked to open it up without a prior appointment.

In the exhibits and paintings contained in the museum, Saddam was the key figure, the light of youth and idealism shining from his features as he stood beside the dictator's car and blazed away at it with his gun. The reality was that Saddam was a bit-part player, whose sole task was to give covering fire to those who had been selected for the assassination itself. Dissident Ba'athists maintained afterwards that the attempt failed because Saddam opened fire without waiting for the signal, and according to this version of the story, he fled before finding out whether Qassem was dead or alive. But it sounds unlikely. Saddam was a man with a notable degree of self-control, and he never lacked personal courage.

He was slightly wounded in the attack, having been struck in the shin by a spent bullet which had lodged under the skin. Saddam cut it out himself with a razor-blade, and a noted Ba'athist, Dr Tahsin Muallah, cleaned and dressed the wound. Like so many people who came into contact with Saddam in these earlier years, he later went into exile. Although the official account turned Saddam's flight into an epic of self-sacrifice and suffering, Dr Muallah knew better: he maintained it was all pretty small-time stuff.

Saddam spent the next three years, from 1958 to 1961, in exile in Cairo. There he became a figure of some consequence, because of the Iraqi Ba'ath Party's strong loyalty to President Gamal Abdel Nasser. Yet according to Hussein Magid, the owner of the café he frequented, the violent streak still showed itself.

'He was rowdy with the customers and the waiters. He would sit by the pavement and tease the girls who passed. Once he had a fight with some Yemenis, and he hit one of them with an axe. When I called the police they sided with him, because he was under Nasser's protection.'

Saddam was a hoodlum; but he was always more than that as well, and his political ambitions were now beginning to show themselves. In February 1963 the Ba'athists succeeded at last in killing Qassem. This too was a gangland execution, and the grisly pictures showing the bodies of the President and his entourage were shown again and again on national television to prove he was really dead. The pictures always ended with the same sequence: the camera followed a soldier as he walked over to Qassem's body, pulled the head up by the hair, and spat full in the dead face. Ba'athism was never known for its sensitivity, and this announced as forcefully as anything could that a new regime had taken power.

For Saddam, it was the height of good fortune. The new President was Ahmad Hasan al-Bakr, an ex-officer who had been a member of Qassem's government. Al-Bakr came from Tikrit, and was a distant relative of Saddam's mother. The clan politics of Iraq ensured that Saddam would be given a job. He had a post at the Central Office of Agriculture, but this was merely a cover; his real task was to head al-Bakr's security department. Other Tikritis were brought in to join him. It was the start of a new dynasty.

Saddam's talents for violence and political manoeuvring made him indispensable to his new boss. Saddam also had the personal support of the most prominent of the Ba'ath Party's founders, Michel Aflaq, who recommended him for a place on the Party's Command Council in Iraq even though he was still only about twenty-six.

But the Party was bitterly divided between its moderate and radical factions. The army backed the moderates, Saddam backed the radicals, and al-Bakr hovered nervously in the middle. Saddam's solution to the problem was a characteristic one. According to his own official biography, he planned to gather the leadership together. He was to have entered the conference room, where the civilian and military leaders were meeting, and machine-gunned them all. But the moderate leaders got wind of it, and Saddam was arrested. Although many of the other prisoners who were rounded up at this time were tortured during their time in gaol, Saddam was treated leniently. It was suggested later that this was because he had established links with the CIA. The links remained at least until 1968.

The Ba'athists had been driven out by the Iraqi military after a mere six months in power. Saddam, however, used the period of his imprisonment to finish his political education. During this time his interest in Stalin and Stalinist methods became serious. According to other prisoners, Saddam had a shelf of books on Stalin in his cell, and read them as political manuals, working out ways in which a determined leader could deal with his enemies and prevent unrest. Eventually he and his closest associates escaped from gaol, and played their part in the 1968 coup which brought the Ba'athists back into government.

Al-Bakr now made Saddam deputy general secretary of the Party – he was still only about twenty-nine – and gave him responsibility for national security. Immediately Saddam initiated a clamp-down on Iraqi Jews, accusing them of being agents of Israel. Hundreds of people were arrested and tortured, and several dozen were executed publicly in Independence Square. Between 1968 and 1971, 2,000 political prisoners were executed or disappeared.

It was at this time that Saddam spoke revealingly to Sami Ali, a journalist who later took refuge in London.

'We are different from the former regime. We are going to clean Iraq of all the weak people, all the people we don't want. We have a plan, and we are going to do it.'

Although the Ba'athists were determined not to allow themselves to fall under Soviet influence, they were happy to accept help in the task of governing the country in their new fashion. Saddam asked the KGB for assistance in reorganizing Iraq's intelligence services, and this was done along much the same lines as the Soviet Union had followed. There would eventually be an absurd and dangerous proliferation of intelligence agencies in Iraq, often little more than private armies; but for the time being there were four main departments: the Mukhabarat, or Ba'ath Party intelligence, which was much the most powerful and the most feared; the Amn, or internal security; the Estikhabarat, or foreign intelligence; and conventional military intelligence.

The KGB helped Saddam establish a standard Marxist-Leninist system, in which Party officials supervised the activities of everyone in their apartment block or street. Benefits of any kind, from education to food aid for the poor, were entirely dependent on loyalty to the system; anyone suspected of disloyalty went without. Every citizen was expected to tell the Mukhabarat of the slightest murmur of complaint or criticism, and the smallest sign of nonconformity. Anyone who failed to do so was regarded as sharing the guilt of the person they should have turned in.

Children were used to inform on their parents, as was standard under Marxism-Leninism, but there was an evangelical tone to this

particular tactic in Iraq. Teachers were under the strictest instructions
to question the children in class, in order to uncover any irregularity
about their parents' lives. It became something of an obsession with
Saddam, and in 1977 he spoke publicly of the value to the government
of children as spies in the home. As often happened when he turned to
the subject of children, there was an unctuousness of tone which
contrasted powerfully with the underlying cynicism of the exercise:

> To prevent the father and mother dominating the household with
> backwardness, we must make the little one radiate internally to
> expel it. Some fathers have slipped away from us for various
> reasons, but the small boy is still in our hands and we must
> transform him into an interactive radiating centre inside the family
> through all the hours he spends with his parents . . .
>
> You must place in every corner a son of the revolution, with a
> trustworthy eye and a firm mind that receives its instructions from
> the responsible centre of the revolution.

As a result of all this, 'Uncle Saddam' was not universally popular in
the home, and there were always large numbers of Iraqis who couldn't
bear to watch the almost undiluted diet of programmes about Saddam
Hussein on Iraqi television. Many children made this clear when they
were questioned about it at school. If the teacher was decent, he or she
would warn the parents privately rather than report them to the
authorities, though this put the teachers in some danger as well, since
the pupils or the parents themselves would then be in a position to
inform on them.

In Ba'athist Iraq, you could not trust anyone, and you could never
be frank. A story, which may or may not have been literally true, went
the rounds in Baghdad and was generally believed: Saddam, on one of
his frequent unscheduled trips round the country, stops at a village
and takes a child on his knee.

'Do you know who I am?' he asks jovially.

'Yes,' says the child. 'Every time you come on television my father
spits on the ground and switches it off.'

According to the story the entire family disappeared – including
the child.

Iraq was a country where children had to become old and responsible long before their time; where you could say nothing without

thinking over the consequences in advance; where only your closest family and friends could be trusted, and even they might betray you to protect themselves. Under Saddam, the Ba'athist Party did its best to weaken the natural links between parents and children, brothers and sisters, husbands and wives. There must be nowhere for hostility to the Party and the Leader to take root and grow. The Ba'athist new man's only loyalty was to the state, and his greatest love was for Saddam.

Take, for instance, the case of Naji al-Haddithi Sabri, who was to become minister of information and finally, before Saddam's overthrow, his foreign minister. I always liked Naji; he was clever, highly amusing, and a confirmed anglophile. It was he who allowed me to stay in Baghdad for six months before, during and after the first Gulf War; something for which I shall always be grateful. He was also the one who prevented my going back after the war, but no doubt he had good reasons for that.

Naji spent seven years in London as press attaché at the Iraqi embassy, and enjoyed himself greatly. But he was always a Ba'athist by personal conviction; and when he was suddenly recalled to Baghdad he did not ask the British for political asylum, as might have been prudent; he went back. It turned out that his brother had been implicated, rightly or wrongly, in a plot against Saddam. The *Mukharabat* questioned Naji long and hard to see if he was somehow implicated, and when they finally decided he wasn't, they demanded that he should write a letter condemning his brother and alleging that he had always been evil and disloyal from his childhood up.

Iraqis are traditionally stubborn; hence, perhaps, the extreme lengths Saddam and his colleagues had to go to in order to make them conform. Naji, however, was faced with the collapse of all his ambitions, and with the possibility of imprisonment or death. So he wrote the letter. His reward was that he was the only male member of the family who wasn't forced to join the firing squad which killed his brother. The father, the uncles, the cousins were all made to stand in line and given guns, and armed security policemen stood behind each of them, with orders to kill anyone who deliberately aimed away from the target.

But his brother's sins meant that Naji too was unclean. He was dismissed from the foreign service and sent to a country school in the farthest reaches of Iraq, where he worked as a teacher for many years. At last he was allowed back to Baghdad, and worked in the Ministry of Information. It was he who, with considerable courage, convinced Saddam to allow large numbers of foreign journalists to come to Iraq in the run-up to the 1991 war, on the basis that it was likely to generate more international support for Iraq than continuing to keep the country closed would achieve.

That experiment proved to be a considerable success, but Naji still wasn't entirely safe. A vicious colleague within the department tried to undermine him, and perhaps have him arrested as a traitor. I tried to help him leave the country, but my efforts came to nothing. Naji survived anyway, and eventually rose to become minister of information. He wrote a handbook in 1998 on Iraq's thirty years under the Ba'athist regime, which described the Leader in grovelling terms, praised the political plurality and respect for human rights which he claimed existed under Saddam, and insisted that the 1991 war had been a remarkable victory for Iraq. When I reached Baghdad in April 2003, soon after the city had fallen to the Americans, I found dozens of copies of Naji's handbook strewn around on the floor of the wrecked Ministry of Information building. The looters who had taken anything which might remotely be of value had left them where they lay.

Naji's success as minister of information led to a further promotion not long before the war of 2003 swept Ba'athism out of Iraq: he was made foreign minister, and took the name Naji Sabri. Naji was an excellent ambassador for his country, suave, intelligent, amusing, and highly articulate in English. Much of Iraq's diplomatic success in the run-up to the war was due to his skill.

Nevertheless I once saw how Naji behaved when he was in Saddam's presence. A meeting of the government and the Ba'ath Party's general council had been summoned for an audience with the President. When the audience sat down, Naji was the last to sit. When the audience applauded, Naji was the first to start clapping; afterwards, he was the last to stop. When Saddam spoke, Naji never dared to raise his eyes; instead, he kept them on the floor, as though he was not worthy even to look at his leader. In normal life he was a man of considerable spirit and charm, and he had a natural air of authority. In the presence of Saddam, though, he took on the demeanour of a servant who had been soundly whipped. It was the authentic behaviour of the new man in Saddam Hussein's Iraq.

Fear and suspicion were, right from the moment the Ba'athists seized control of the state, the characteristic emotions in Iraqi politics and society. This, according to Hassan al-Alawi, Saddam Hussein's press spokesman in the late 1970s, was the direct result of Saddam's own character and behaviour.

> The curious thing [he said in an interview], is that when the Ba'ath Party came to power, its secret organizations remained secret even though they no longer needed to be. One wonders why the Party needed to remain secret when it was in power. Here we should take into account the psychology of Saddam Hussein – a man who is afraid of society, who doesn't trust his neighbours.
>
> These features have left their mark on Iraq since the Ba'ath Party came to power. The state doesn't trust its neighbours, the Ba'ath Party doesn't trust its members, the government doesn't trust its ministers. All this reflects the atmosphere of fear and terror in which Saddam Hussein has always lived.

The new President, Ahmad Hasan al-Bakr, was a colourless, uninspiring character. He soon seemed distinctly in awe of his young cousin whenever they appeared at big public occasions, eventually deferring to him openly. Al-Bakr was stooped and elderly; Saddam, by contrast, was energetic, good-looking and self-confident. He was still only in his early thirties, yet he was the force behind the regime and everyone including the President knew it. At this stage, though, Saddam was not concerned with elbowing al-Bakr aside; his aim was to build up the Ba'ath Party and ensure it would remain in power permanently.

Remembering the lessons of Stalin's Russia, Saddam knew he could not trust the Iraqi army and immediately set about purging it. At first he got rid of senior officers who were not members of the Ba'ath Party; then he turned his attention to generals and colonels whose loyalty was to al-Bakr. The purge was not a large one: only thirty-five men altogether. Among them was the defence minister, Hardan al-Tikriti. He was exiled in October 1970, and Saddam went on board to kiss him goodbye. Within five months he was murdered in Kuwait City, clearly on Saddam's orders.

12. THE PURGE

By the early summer of 1979 Saddam had swept away al-Bakr's last remaining political supporters, and was ready to get rid of al-Bakr himself. As with Hardan al-Tikriti, al-Bakr was given an oleaginous farewell at a specially convened Party meeting on 17 July, the precise anniversary of the coup which had brought the Ba'athists to power in 1968.

'It has never happened before,' Saddam said, looking affectionately at al-Bakr as he spoke, 'that two leaders have been in power for eleven years within one command, without . . . one of them driving the other out.'

Everybody present, including al-Bakr, knew that was precisely what had happened now.

The former President answered in terms that had been carefully prepared for him.

'For some time now I have been telling my comrades, and especially my dear comrade Saddam Hussein, that my state of health no longer permits me to carry out the responsibilities the Command has honoured me with, and I have asked them to relieve me of the responsibility.'

Al-Bakr went into house arrest, which was explained away as convalescence after ill health. Yet the quiet *coup d'état* didn't pass off peacefully. Instead it became the pretext for a murderous purge of the Ba'ath Party's leadership. Six days earlier, the news that al-Bakr would be stepping down was announced at a meeting of the Revolutionary Command Council. The Council secretary, Muhyi Abd al-Hussein al-Mashhadi Rashid, demanded a vote.

'It's inconceivable that you should retire,' he shouted at the helpless al-Bakr. 'If you're ill, why don't you just take a rest?'

Saddam was furious, but the President's resignation was approved. Muhyi Abd al-Hussein Rashid was arrested, and the remaining members of the Command Council unanimously elected Saddam President in al-Bakr's place.

Everyone in Iraqi political life had known for years that Saddam was the real force behind al-Bakr. For the most part he had been relatively discreet. People were afraid of him, yet he had done his best to appear mild and benign, and had rarely intervened to attack his enemies within the Ba'athist Party. Now all this was over. He had a free hand at last, and he proceeded to get rid of everyone he regarded as an enemy. According to his official biography, Saddam 'decided to keep under observation those leaders who had looked worried or distressed after the Regional [i.e. Iraqi] Command had decided that Muhyi Abd al-Hussein Rashid should be taken in for questioning.'

Saddam once told Fuad Matar, the biography's author, 'I know that someone will betray me before they know it themselves.' Stalin would have approved; he said much the same thing himself.

'The participants in the plot tried so hard to act naturally while the questioning of Muhyi Abd al-Hussein was going on,' Fuad Matar wrote, 'that they made themselves conspicuous . . . Muhammed Ayesh behaved in an increasingly guilty manner, and he was arrested on 16 July. Ghanem Abd al-Jalil's behaviour was also suspicious, although he had not been investigated . . .'

Saddam asked everyone present at the meeting to write a detailed report on any meetings they had had with the supposed plotters. This put everyone in the most exquisitely difficult position, since none of them knew what the men who had been arrested and were presumably now being tortured by Saddam's thugs would say about them; should they tell the truth, or should they hide any criticisms they might have made of Saddam in the past?

Ten days after Saddam's coup in forcing al-Bakr aside and getting himself voted in as his replacement, Saddam was ready for the first purge of his presidency. The interrogations had been completed, and Saddam knew exactly who he would keep and who he would get rid of. No one else, not even his closest associates, could be certain what was going to happen.

An extraordinary conference of the Iraqi Ba'ath Party opened on the morning of 22 July 1979, only eight days after Saddam's take-over of power, at Khald Hall in Baghdad, an unremarkable modern conference centre with an auditorium at its heart much like any other around the world. About 1,000 delegates were present. On Saddam's express instructions the entire proceedings were filmed for the edification of the Party and the country as a whole. It was to be the theatre of terror, and copies of the videotape were sent to Party organizations throughout

Iraq and to Iraqi student groups in Britain, France, Germany and the United States. The film is in black and white, the picture quality is badly degraded because of the number of times it has been copied, and the sound is abysmal. It is, nevertheless, both terrible and fascinating to watch. Most versions have been edited for one reason or another, but the copy which the BBC obtained in 1991 seems to have been complete.

The tape opens with a speech by Taha Yasin Ramadan, one of Saddam's oldest and most loyal supporters, a man with strangely Asiatic features. He announces that a plot has been discovered, and that all the traitors are present in the hall. The shock and consternation in the audience are presumably genuine: for many of them it must be a way of venting their personal terror. Then Muhyi Abd al-Hussein Rashid comes slowly up to the podium. He has obviously been tortured. Speaking with evident difficulty, he makes a lengthy confession in which he condemns himself in grovelling terms and accuses four other members of the leadership, including his closest friend and ally, Mohammed Ayesh, of plotting against the life of Saddam Hussein. The plot, he says, has been sponsored by President Assad of Syria, and its purpose was to unify Iraq and Syria – on Syria's terms. At last he finishes speaking. He looks about him uncertainly for a moment or two, then takes his seat in the audience. It is noticeable that he sits well away from the small group of Saddam loyalists: Ramadan, Tariq Aziz, and Izzat Ibrahim.

Throughout the confession Saddam has been sitting alone at a table on the platform, slumped in his chair and smoking one of the eight-inch Havanas which Fidel Castro sends him by the hundred every year. The smoke wreathes around him as he listens; he is the only relaxed man in the entire auditorium. Whenever the cameras cut away to the audience you can see clearly how disturbed and nervous people are. They shift uncomfortably in their seats, trying to work out how they should relax, dreading the mention of their own names.

Then it is Saddam's turn to speak. He has put out his cigar, and now walks over to the lectern where he stands very straight, hands behind his back, and speaks confidently and without notes in his harsh, ungrammatical peasant Arabic. Long silences punctuate his phrases.

'We could scent the conspiracy before we even gathered the evidence. Nevertheless we were patient. Some of our comrades blamed us for knowing about it, yet doing nothing.'

A voice interrupts: shocking at first, until the delegates in the hall see that it is Saddam's cousin Ali Hassan al-Majid, Chemical Ali, the man who throughout Saddam's presidency was to perform the dirtiest of jobs for him: gassing the Kurds, governing captured Kuwait, suppressing the Shi'ite revolt, overseeing the mass murder of tens of thousands of men, women and children.

'What you have done in the past is good,' he shouts, 'and what you will do in the future is good as well. But there's just one point I want to make: you're being too gentle and merciful now.'

The audience, anxious at first, relaxes: this is not the voice of dissent, it is part of the choreography. Saddam listens to his cousin and frowns, as if considering what he has said. Then he delivers his judgement.

'Yes, that's true. People have criticized me for that. But this time I will show no mercy.'

There is, of course, a storm of applause. Once again, people are relieving the tension by clapping and shouting in near-hysteria. Before it dies away, Saddam announces that everyone he names must stand up, repeat the Party slogan, and leave the hall. Immediately there is silence. Saddam reads out the first name. The supposed conspirator stands up, looking bewildered. There is no question of repeating any slogan; he simply pushes his way past the seated figures beside him, and the camera crash-zooms into a close-up as one of the security men stationed around the sides and rear of the hall moves forward and takes his arm quite gently. Saddam has resumed his cigar now, and the smoke billows around him.

He calls out a second name, and another crash-zoom reveals an elderly man in a light-coloured suit being guided towards the exit. The audience pretends to be enjoying it now: they are clapping and smiling and leaning across to congratulate each other on Saddam's wisdom. Yet the hysteria is still there. Soon individual delegates are standing up and screaming their praises of Saddam. A large man, his face streaked with sweat and his silvery tie crooked, waves his arms in the air.

'Long live the Party!' he shouts. 'Long live the Party! God save Saddam Hussein from the conspirators!'

Saddam keeps on reading out the names: more than sixty of them altogether. A box of tissues has been strategically placed beside him, and when he reaches the name of one of the plotters, Ghanem Abd

al-Jalil, who supposedly behaved suspiciously at the meeting of the
Command Council, tears come to his eyes and he pulls out a tissue,
wiping his face with it and blowing his nose loudly. But his cigar is
still burning in the ashtray, and when he stands up he takes it, and the
tissue, with him.

'We don't need Stalinist methods to deal with traitors here,'
Saddam bellows as he prepares to leave the stage. 'We need Ba'athist
methods!'

The audience claps his words frenziedly. Saddam goes down into
the audience to sit with his most faithful colleagues. Tariq Aziz beams
at him. He sinks into the seat beside the strange, skeletal figure of Izzat
Ibrahim, his hair a shock of red. Saddam is still wiping tears from his
eyes, and Ibrahim comforts him. But he is smiling. So is Saddam.

That same day a special court found fifty-five men guilty. Twenty-
two of them were sentenced to death by 'democratic execution'. This
was apparently a method of Saddam's own devising, and meant that
senior members of the Party had to take part in the firing squads. Like
Naji al-Haddithi's father and brothers, the guilt of association was
expiated by another form of guilt: the shedding of blood. Once that
had been done, there was no going back. The responsibility had been
spread. The purge continued, and by 1 August, when it came to an
end, anything up to 500 senior members of the Ba'athist Party had
been 'democratically' executed. They included Ghanem Abd al-Jalil,
the Shi'ite who was a senior member of the Revolutionary Command
Council and had once been Saddam's close ally; Mohammed Mahjoub,
another RCC member, and Mohammed Ayesh, the head of the labour
unions. Adnan Hamdani, the deputy prime minister, had been arrested
at the airport on his return from Syria a day or two before. He and
General Walid Mahmoud Sirat, Saddam's main opponent in the army,
were quietly executed. General Sirat had been horribly tortured.

Now that Saddam had taken over the presidency, he was determined that everyone should know things would be different from now
on. In the forty-seven years since the British mandate had ended in
1932, there had been thirteen successful coups and an unknown
number of attempted ones. Saddam Hussein planned to construct his
regime by sheer terror. No one would dare to overthrow him now.

13. PRIVATE LIFE, PUBLIC LIFE

Baghdad is not a beautiful place. It probably never has been, since the
day the city of the Abbasids was destroyed by the Mongols. It sprawls
along the banks of the Tigris, dull and grey and flat-roofed, with only
an occasional mosque or office-block to break the monotony. Yet to
those of us who have come to love it, what is important about it is not
the things you see first; it is the things which slowly emerge in their
interest and beauty from the apparent dullness. You have to search
them out from behind the high walls and in the depth of the court-
yards. The people of Baghdad learned from bitter experience that it
was better not to show too much of their wealth and culture to the
outside world. A country with a tradition as violent and angry as
Iraq's is a country where you have to be secretive in order to survive.

Sir Max Mallowan, Agatha Christie's husband and one of the
leading archaeologists of ancient Iraq, maintained that the houses of
Baghdad in the 1960s were built on precisely the same plan as those
he excavated from 2000 BC. In particular, he said, the method the
builders used for constructing the staircases of houses in modern
Baghdad had remained almost identical for forty centuries. These
houses still remain in the side-streets of the capital: from the outside
they are gloomy, unremarkable places with wooden verandas jutting
out over the street, the wood as grey as the mud-brick of the rest of
the building, all of them looking as though they predate Haroun al-
Rashid himself. Not so. Termites, flooding, political violence and a
thousand other causes mean that scarcely any of the houses which
have remained from the pre-Saddam period in Baghdad date much
farther back than the start of the British Mandate in 1920.

Inside, they are remarkably colourful and interesting. The *tarma*, a
colonnaded balcony, runs round the central courtyard, its twelve-foot
upright beams stretching up to capitals which are usually beautifully
carved. In wealthier houses this overlooks the *shithirwan* or fountain
in the middle of the courtyard, which eases the heat and humidity,
sending its gentle, cooling sound echoing through the entire house.
Older, more traditionally minded people tend to live in these houses,

as their families always have. Sir Richard Burton's florid translation of 'The Tale of the Twentieth Night' describes just such a house:

> [T]hey went on till they reached a spacious ground-floor hall built with admirable skill and beautified with all manner of colours and carvings; with upper balconies and groined arches and galleries and cupboards and recesses whose curtains hung before them. In the midst stood a great basin of water surrounding a fine fountain, and at the upper end of the raised dais was a couch of juniper wood set with gems and pearls . . .

I visited several houses like this in Baghdad in 1990 and 1991. It was a difficult business, because people would invite me into their homes out of a sense of duty and hospitality, and unless they were working for one of the intelligence agencies (which was certainly always possible) it put them into a good deal of danger. Foreign journalists were all regarded as spies, so anyone who consorted with them was likely to be seen as an agent. I went because curiosity was as much a duty to me as hospitality was to them, and no one ever seemed to suffer as a result of my visits; not even the delightful Assyrian Christian who was unfailingly generous to me and was inclined to criticize the regime fiercely when he thought no one could hear us. Since he was a taxi driver based at the al-Rashid Hotel, however, he could only have been working for the Mukhabarat.

I placed much more trust in another friend and informant who used to invite me round: a man who knew of my interest in the Mandate, and used to sell me objects and documents from that period. He was Kurdish, and inclined to start on about the wrongs of his people when we were lounging on cushions in the *diwan-khana* or traditionally male section of the house, drinking endless cups of lemon-flavoured tea and talking in low voices. The whole place seemed very silent. In Baghdad the commonest word for this kind of house is *maskan*, which derives from *sikun*, meaning 'quiet'. A house is a place where you can get away from the noise of the streets and contemplate life peacefully.

Apart from places like this, I liked the teahouses best. There, merchants and dealers and hangers-on came to enjoy themselves away from home, meeting their friends and talking guardedly about what was going on in the world. In a country where one person in every three was said to be a spy – that turned out to be a considerable exaggeration when the files of the intelligence agencies were examined, but it was certainly a gauge of what people thought about the society they lived in – there was no one you could entirely trust.

Yet if the teahouse was not a good place to reveal what was on your mind, there were other important things to do there: agree a deal, hear the news, or play one of the various types of backgammon: *adi, mahbous, gulbaha, chesh-besh*. They threw the dice with a tremendous flourish, and passed their hands over the board in movements so fast I was never able to follow them. Behind me, meanwhile, men at other tables were playing dominoes, crashing each piece down on the table as though they had performed some brilliant master-stroke.

Overhead the fans turned slowly, sifting through air which seemed as heavy as molten sugar. The flies settled greedily on patches of spilt sweet tea, the water-pipes were passed around with relish, their apple-flavoured tobacco thickening the atmosphere. The waiter sped between the tables, his metal tray high above his head, replenishing the glasses and taking new orders. The ancient, crippled shoe-cleaner who called everyone 'Lord' bashed away with his brushes in the shade of the courtyard plane-tree outside; behind him as he worked and sweated in the intense heat, the Tigris carried the mud of the fertile Mesopotamian plain sluggishly down, as it had for a million years, towards Basra and the waters of the Gulf.

This Baghdad was very attractive to me. Yet the houses have been knocked down and superseded by modern blocks of flats, which have no discernible element of Iraqi tradition. The new buildings in Baghdad are marked by a total emptiness of design, a mere unimaginative aping of the West. The roads are laid out and built by the kind of city planners who wrecked so many British cities in the 1960s; indeed, some of the same companies carried on their work of cultural eviscer-ation in Iraq at a greater profit than they had once made at home.

In the interests of homogenization, the climate and the habits of the locals were ignored, so that Baghdad has sad beds of dying roses down the middle of its avenues, and ugly, neglected little pedestrian bridges which no one uses arch over them. This is Saddamtown: vast amounts of money were spent, without the slightest sense of what was fitting; there was no understanding of the past, no interest in what the inhabitants might want. At many of the main intersections there were enormous, tasteless statues, portraying figures from Babylonian mythology or the Arabian Nights; Saddamist art was both safe and utterly characterless. Modern Baghdad as Saddam Hussein rebuilt it was precisely the kind of city a dictator likes to see through his limousine window as he drives past at sixty miles an hour.

And everywhere there were exercises in self-celebration. No street, no government building was free of Saddam's image. In portraits ten times life-size he smiled or looked serious, he embraced children, he charged across an open plain on a white horse, he poured out water for farmers, he planted grain, he wore panama hats and dark glasses, he brandished a rifle and fired it in the air, he smoked his eight-inch cigars. Outside the law faculty of Baghdad University he held the scales of justice in one hand and – meaningfully – a sword in the other. There was to be no nonsense in Saddam's Iraq about the supremacy of the law.

'A law,' he once said, 'is a few lines of writing on a piece of paper which we sign "Saddam".'

Hospitals, schools, stadia, barracks, a canal, the main airport and an entire suburb bore his name. He was an inveterate builder of monuments to himself. Just one or two of these monuments are surprisingly tasteful: the Shaheed Memorial to the martyrs who fell in the 1980–88 war with Iran, for example, shows distinctly un-Saddamist qualities of elegance and restraint.

But the most characteristic of all his monuments was the one which celebrated his supposed victory over Iran. For a long time every night's television news was preceded by pictures of Saddam riding a white horse between the two gigantic arches formed by arms (modelled, naturally, on Saddam's own arms) holding aloft enormous scimitars. The arches were designed to be higher than the Arc de Triomphe, and the entire idea was his.

So was the idea of hanging an enormous net, created in the shape of a tassel, from the pommel of each sword, containing hundreds of Iranian helmets gathered from the battlefields of the Iran–Iraq War. When you look closely you can see that most of the helmets have bullet- or shrapnel-holes in them. Not all the helmets are in fact Iranian: the creators of this monument to tastelessness had to make up the numbers with Iraqi helmets. But Saddam wouldn't have noticed. He only drove or rode past the arches; he never walked. When the

Mongol leader Hulagu destroyed Baghdad in 1258 he built a mound
of skulls to celebrate his victory. This monument is Saddam's
mound of skulls; and as if to point up the similarity, he ordered
dozens more helmets to be set in the roadway beneath the arches,
so that he could ride in triumph over the heads of his enemies.

14. INVADING IRAN

Saddam Hussein's most characteristic monument was, however, the
war itself. The decision to invade Iran was the first important act of
his presidency, and at first sight it looked safe enough. Iran had been
seriously weakened by the Islamic revolution nineteen months earlier,
and large numbers of officers in its army, navy and air force had fled
the country when the Shah fell. But Saddam's usual combination of
opportunism and over-confidence led him into serious trouble, as it
always seemed to do. His real skills lay not in taking these big,
irrevocable steps, but in managing to survive afterwards, when everyone was forecasting his imminent downfall. He was a poor strategist,
but a survivor of genius.

On 17 September 1980 he announced the tearing up of the
agreement he had signed with Iran in 1975, settling the demarcation
and use of the Shatt al-Arab waterway. Five days later, on 22 September, Saddam launched a massive series of attacks across the Iranian
border. He promised his generals, who were mostly dubious about the
whole adventure, that a blitzkrieg of four days' duration would achieve
total victory and the collapse of the Islamic revolution in Iran. At a
stroke, he would make Iraq the master of the Gulf, protect his own
large Shi'ite population from Iran's revolutionary contagion, and
delight the West.

There probably wasn't a single government anywhere in the world
which wanted to see Ayatollah Khomeini's Islamic Republic survive.
By comparison, most countries saw Saddam Hussein as just another
unpleasant dictator, who was likely to be overthrown shortly in
another coup of the kind Iraq seemed to specialize in. Saudi Arabia
and the Gulf States were badly frightened by the Iranian revolution,

and the thought that an Arab government was taking action to snuff it out was something which pleased them greatly. Weapons-producing nations like the United States, Britain, France, Russia, South Africa and Sweden were happy at the prospect of two essentially wealthy countries fighting each other. The United States in particular was delighted that Saddam Hussein, whom it regarded as a strong anti-Communist and secularist, seemed likely to sweep the ayatollahs away.

But the Americans did not encourage Saddam Hussein to invade Iran, even if it later became commonplace to suggest they had. Although President Jimmy Carter was personally humiliated when the Iranian revolutionaries took virtually the entire American embassy staff in Tehran hostage and held most of them for 444 days, he was convinced that a war between two of the West's main oil suppliers would be highly dangerous. In the years to come, American involvement with Saddam would become considerable, but it did not start under Carter; it was Ronald Reagan, the victor in the presidential election of November 1980, who gave help to Saddam. It later appeared that Reagan's team had reached a secret agreement with the Islamic revolutionaries in Iran by which the hostages would not be released until Carter had left office and Reagan's presidency had actually begun.

The invasion of Iran did not after all achieve total victory within four days, as Saddam had promised. His troops were not the elite force he had imagined; they had participated in the 1948 Arab–Israeli War, but their involvement in the 1967 and 1973 wars was minimal. As a result, their only serious combat experience had been in fighting the Kurdish rebels of northern Iraq, and burning villages as reprisals. The Iranian troops, after they had recovered from their initial shock, rallied angrily and fought hard to throw the invaders out. As so often happens, even the officers who had no reason to love the Islamic Republic decided that their duty was to defend their country. The Iraqi troops were quickly forced on to the defensive, and their morale was very low.

But Saddam could not afford to sue for peace; he knew that his military commanders would overthrow him the instant the fighting stopped. Instead, he turned to his friends in the outside world. The Soviet Union sent in advisers and military architects to design a huge defensive structure along the entire length of the Iraqi border, composed of walls and fortresses and moats, and diverted rivers so that entire stretches of no man's land could be flooded at the first sign of an attack. Iraq's oil billions were diverted into buying the best weaponry the Russians and the French could provide.

Iran had little more than its superiority in manpower, and its sense of real outrage at being invaded. The United States and Britain, which had supplied the Shah with tanks and aircraft, would not provide the regime which had overthrown him with the spares to keep them going. Iran had to buy its spares and armaments on the black market, and was forced to pay through the nose for them. Yet this encouraged an angry sense of patriotism too. The human-wave attacks which Iran staged against Saddam's defences were regarded in the West as another baffling example of Iran's mindless Islamic fervour; in fact they were nothing of the sort.

Western opinion was often outraged by the fact that young boys ran ahead of the troops through the minefields, showing them the paths to follow. But on the various occasions when I visited the front with Iranian troops, it was always clear that the mullahs serving with the army tried to stop this kind of thing happening. There was a genuine spirit of self-sacrifice in the air, which reminded me of the First World War. An Iranian cameraman I worked with several times took the most extraordinary risks to get good combat footage, and was injured more than once. He was no supporter of the Islamic revolution; on the contrary, he escaped from Iran with his whole family directly the war was over. But while it lasted he felt it was his duty to help his country to the best of his ability.

By June 1982 Saddam Hussein was very close to defeat. He announced a unilateral withdrawal from Iranian territory, in the hope of persuading Iran to call a ceasefire. It was a dangerous move, and might have led to a military coup against him. But the rage of many ordinary Iranians, and the desire for revenge shown by Ayatollah Khomeini, the effective leader in Iran, meant that the ceasefire idea never stood a chance. Khomeini wanted Saddam defeated and destroyed, and he rejected the peace offer with contempt.

It was an historic miscalculation on Khomeini's part, for which Iran was to suffer heavily. Although the United States and its Western allies disliked both sides almost equally, no one wanted to see Iran emerge from the war as the winner. The conventional wisdom was that if this happened, Iran would impose its Islamic revolution on the Shi'ite population of Iraq and other countries, and would soon grow to dominate the entire region. As a result, the United States, the Soviet Union, Britain and France all stepped in to save Saddam Hussein and prevent him being defeated. The result of their intervention was that the war dragged on for another six years, with huge additional loss of life. It suited the big powers: two unpleasant and dangerous regimes were fighting each other to a standstill, and while they did so they were unable to do any damage elsewhere.

As early as March 1982, King Hussein of Jordan sent a message to Washington warning the Reagan administration that Basra, Iraq's second city and a major Shi'ite centre, was in serious danger of falling to the Iranians. The American chargé d'affaires in Baghdad, William Eagleton, agreed. He proposed that the United States should ignore the international embargo on supplying the two warring countries, and should supply Iraq with weapons via other countries. Various senior people in Washington agreed: the Iranians, with their Islamic revolution, were the real enemy, and everything should be done to help Saddam Hussein defeat them. George Bush, Ronald Reagan's vice-president, supported the idea strongly.

But there was a problem. The Arms Export Control Act made it illegal to do this, and it was a federal crime for any individual American citizen to arrange arms sales to a third country if the final destination was a prohibited state. There was no possibility of persuading Congress to lift its embargo on Iraq, because a clear majority was against providing any American support for a country with such an appalling human rights record.

In October 1983 William Eagleton skirted round all this in a cable to the State Department: 'We can selectively lift restrictions on the third party transfers of US licensed military equipment to Iraq.' Normally, any country receiving weapons from the United States would have to sign a formal declaration that they would not be sent on to another country without American agreement. Eagleton proposed that the declaration could be waived for weapons destined for Iraq, and he suggested that Egypt should be the country the arms sales were routed through. (Jordan and Kuwait were also used later.) With strong support from Vice-President Bush, the Reagan administration agreed to Eagleton's plan. It wasn't quite illegal, but it was a clear evasion of the purpose and intention of the Arms Export Control Act. The Reagan administration specialized in getting round laws it disliked.

Washington actively encouraged other countries – particularly Britain, France, Italy and West Germany – to support Saddam Hussein's military machine. West Germany, in particular, supplied the equipment which enabled Iraq to manufacture nerve gases such as sarin. Many of these deals made huge fortunes for the middlemen.

At the same time the United States put heavy pressure on arms-manufacturing countries to stop supplying weapons to Iran. The American diplomat in charge of this effort, Richard Fairbanks, said later, 'It might not have been a one hundred per cent success, but we definitely managed to stop most major weapons systems from reaching Iran from US allies.' Iran had to turn instead to the Soviet bloc for its arms supplies. After stepping down from 'Operation Staunch', Fairbanks became a lobbyist for the Iraqi government in Washington. According to the US Justice Department, Iraq paid a third of a million dollars between 1986 and 1990 for the services of Fairbanks and the law firm he worked for. During the run-up to the 1988 presidential election, Fairbanks worked for the George Bush campaign as a foreign affairs adviser; in other words the president who replaced Ronald Reagan was employing a paid agent of Saddam Hussein.

There were inevitably problems about dealing with a government like Saddam's. In 1982 Iraq bought sixty American helicopters, and signed an agreement that they would be used solely for transporting civilians. It was reported in the United States not long afterwards that many of them were being used to train military pilots, but the Reagan administration did not complain to Baghdad. Two years later, Iraq was allowed to buy another forty-five American helicopters for purposes which were officially described as 'recreation'. The helicopters in question had originally been designed for military purposes, and the Iraqis scarcely hid the fact that that was how they used them. There was no protest from Washington. By the start of 1986 the United States and virtually all the other leading powers were desperate for Saddam Hussein to win his unnecessary war against Iran.

15. THE COUNTER-STROKE

Chance took me back to Iran in February 1986, after I had been barred from returning for seven years. I had agreed to write a book about Iran for my publisher at the time, Robson Books, on the premise that I had a foolproof method of getting back into the country. The method turned out to be proof against me, at any rate, and I rang a friend of mine at the Foreign Office despairingly to ask if he had any ideas. All he could suggest was that I should simply ring up the embassy press office and ask them to let me in. I picked up the phone and dialled.

'Ah, yes, Mr Simpson, you are replying to the invitation we sent to the BBC yesterday. When will you be free to travel to Iran?'

The BBC foreign desk had thrown the invitation away, as being of no great interest. What usually happened on such trips was that an expensive television team would be kept at an hotel in Tehran for a week, then told there was no possibility of going to the front after all. This one turned out to be altogether different.

About a dozen journalists from Europe and the United States had accepted the offer to visit the front, including a large German in a tan suit who looked completely out of place. He was, it transpired, the business manager from the Middle East bureau of a big German news magazine. With the carelessness familiar to anyone who knows Iran well, the information ministry in Tehran had invited him rather than one of the magazine's correspondents; and with the rigidity which is also characteristic they insisted that he, and not one of his reporting colleagues, should take up the invitation.

'Don't worry,' said a Frenchman, 'nothing ever happens on these trips. They always make sure of that.'

The German seemed unconvinced. He was sweating pretty freely in the heat, and his shirt collar seemed much too small for his neck. Poor man: the foolish mistake of an Iranian bureaucrat had condemned him to death.

A Fokker Friendship plane flew us to the city of Ahwaz, only thirty miles from the border with Iraq, and arrived in the early evening.

Ahwaz is an ugly, dun-coloured place, lying along the banks of the sluggish river Karun. The heavy yellowish alluvium of the Karun delta clogs the city streets, so the soles of your shoes are heavy with mud after twenty yards of walking. Although the war was so close, and Ahwaz had often been attacked by the Iraqi air force, all the lights in the city were blazing and the shops were open for business. This was Khuzestan, Iran's Arab province, and as the goldsmiths sat drinking bitter coffee from tiny bowls in the palms of their hands they looked at us and speculated about our origins in Arabic.

At the best hotel in Ahwaz, which was not very good, you had to walk over painted representations of the Stars and Stripes, the Union Jack and the Hammer and Sickle on the floor of the lobby. A large sign depicted an Iranian soldier under what looked like a shower of blood and proclaimed: 'We Are All Warriors And Never Fear From War'. We jammed two or three to a room for the night, and embarrassed each other by snoring.

The next morning we sat and yawned at an early briefing session, as an earnest young man with bad posture and an inadequate tuft of beard under his chin made sketchy, nervous gestures at a large yellow map. It turned out that he had played an important part in the planning of this operation, and his nervousness covered a suppressed pride and excitement about what had happened.

'The enemy were superior in every way,' he announced. 'They never thought that a military force would be able to cross the river here.' He jabbed his stick at the wide wound of the Shatt al-Arab, which cut through the marshes on either side.

'Our aim was to cut off Iraq's access to the Persian Gulf, and in order to do that we had to fool the enemy by staging another operation, further to the north.' He gestured up to somewhere near the ceiling, well off the top of his yellow map. 'As a result of our attack we captured 800 square kilometres of enemy territory and an Iraqi army headquarters. Altogether the Iraqi losses were 15,000 dead and 22,000 captured – mostly men of the special Presidential Guard.'

I have never yet come across a Third World army which did not inflate figures like these, but it was still an important victory: the first involving diversionary tactics on this scale, the first direct assault by Iran on Iraqi territory.

'What is the name of this territory you have captured?'

'It is called Faw: the Faw Peninsula.'

Another officer, this time a thirty-year-old, took his place in front of the map. They both belonged to the Revolutionary Guards, who at that time still had no formal ranks, much like the early Bolshevik army. The hierarchy of command simply emerged. It was pretty surprising that they were capable of capturing anything. The thirty-year-old explained the strategic objective. They planned to establish a large base in the Faw Peninsula in order to capture Basra, the second city of Iraq.

'And when Basra falls, Saddam Hussein will fall.'

I began to see the importance of what had happened here.

At Ahwaz airport we were issued with blue overalls, designed to protect against gas attack. Like every piece of new equipment Iran had, they were bought on the international black market. As a result they were of poor quality, and all of the same size. I am six feet two inches tall, and mine were absurd. The sleeves came halfway up my arms, the trousers halfway up my calves, like plastic plus-fours. I looked inside the square box with a strap attached to it, and found my gas mask. It looked as if it dated from the Second World War. The filter was missing, so I would have to breathe whatever was in the air. I pointed this out to the soldier who had issued it to me. He shrugged. Some arms dealer had obviously made a killing out of the Iranian army, and someone might well make a killing out of me as a result. We tied ourselves up like so many blue parcels, and were led out onto the tarmac.

Several helicopters were waiting for us, elderly American Hueys from the days of the Shah, painted the yellow mud-colour predominant in and around Ahwaz. I crammed into the first one with an American television crew from NBC News, who had promised to help me since I had no crew of my own. Another five people clambered in after me. Altogether there were twice as many people on board as the Huey was supposed to take, but the pilot didn't seem to mind. He, the co-pilot and the engineer were laughing and joking, and they didn't look back to see how many of us there were anyway.

We lifted off clumsily, and the pilot turned round in surprise for the first time. Then the three of them laughed again. For a while we hovered in the air till the other two Hueys had also lifted off, and we headed south-westwards towards Faw. But within a few minutes the pilot shook his head and pointed back to Ahwaz. There was too much early morning fog to make the trip in safety.

I felt a mixture of frustration and a distinct, unworthy relief. We sat in the waiting-room at Ahwaz airport for two hours, drinking sweet Iranian tea and half-hoping the whole thing would be called off. Our anti-gas suits heated up and grew slippery inside with sweat. It was after eleven o'clock when an officer made the sudden announcement that we were going to try again. I glanced at the stout German, who looked even more like a parcel than the rest of us, and saw his face fall. His brief experience of the Huey must have aroused all his worst fears.

This time there were even more people in the lead helicopter: so many that the pilot, a big, unshaven, impressive-looking fellow in his late thirties who spoke good American English, argued for some time with the co-pilot about whether it was safe to take us all. In the end he shrugged like the man who had given me my worthless gas-mask, and started the engine. We were so tightly jammed in, sitting on the floor of the Huey with our chins on our knees, that it took the cooperation of two or three other people to make even quite small movements.

We swooped along in convoy, the three Hueys strung out over a quarter of a mile. The yellow mud-flats were yielding to green palm plantations, and when I could turn my head I could see the flat, oblong buildings on the ground and the river Karun curving round a couple of hundred feet below. It was turning into a beautiful day: much too clear to be flying into a war zone.

In the distance we caught sight of Faw and dropped to seventy or eighty feet. There was great tension. Just as the pilot pointed to the sky immediately above the horizon, columns of white and grey smoke erupted out of the ground in neat lines, eight miles or so away. The Iraqis were dropping bombs over the Iranian front line. The pilot shouted into his radio microphone, and there was shouting back. We were being ordered to go into Faw because it was now too dangerous to go back.

We flew in very low indeed, a few feet above the palm trees. This wasn't just another well-organized press facility, with the dangers neatly ironed out. The pilots were worried, and wanted to put us down as fast as possible so that they could get their valuable helicopters out of danger. Ahead lay the landing-strip with a few gesticulating figures visible on it: a great gold-coloured square, bulldozed out of the surrounding mud and marshland. Before I expected, our helicopter put down with a shuddering jar, and the co-pilot was yelling, 'Out! Out! Out!'

After forty minutes of being jammed together without moving it was difficult to run at first, but I stumbled forward, head down into the hail of dust and mud which the rotors were throwing into my eyes and face. The moment we were away the pilot took off again, and the second Huey came in, filling the air with the racket of its rotor-blades. The third had to stand off, waiting; and while it was still in the air the bombing started.

The Iraqis had known we were coming. They had followed the progress of our Fokker Friendship the previous day, and now they had tracked our helicopters on the radar that morning. Maybe they didn't know we were journalists; they may have thought we were top politicians from Tehran. On the other hand, if a group of foreign journalists died, it would have been an extraordinarily useful way for Iraq to show that the Iranians had not been able to consolidate their positions on the Faw Peninsula. The Iraqi bombers, two miles above us in the brilliant blue sky, had had plenty of time to scramble and attack us as the Hueys ferried us in.

All round us earth and smoke began heaving up into the air in great columns. But the bombs were less frightening than the heart-stopping noise of the Iranian anti-aircraft guns close by as they opened up in an attempt to defend us. It was appallingly disorienting, as we tried to get our bearings out in the open and work out where we were supposed to go.

'Get down! Get down!' I heard the screams and threw myself, elbows first, into some dead bushes by the edge of the landing-zone, in the hope that they would break my fall. They did. I rolled over and managed to get my stills camera out of my shoulder-bag. Taking photographs was a kind of therapy at a time like that. It gave me something to do, stopped me worrying. The columns of earth continued to erupt around us, horribly close. Sometimes, to avoid the blast, I rammed my face down into the loose earth banked up beside the landing-ground.

The third Huey was only now disgorging its tightly packed occupants. I watched them, realizing that the shock and disorientation was twenty times worse for them than it had been for us. It was only now that I started to understand that the loudest explosions were from the anti-aircraft guns, and that they posed no threat whatever to us. The people on the third helicopter didn't have time to work that out.

More shouting: 'Get in the trucks! Get in the trucks!' The trucks were fifty yards away, on the edge of the landing-zone. The drivers were frightened, and were revving up and starting to move. I had to stay with the NBC cameraman, who was coolly filming the chaos around us, standing out in the open. Too much was happening for me to notice what happened to the stout German. He was still wearing his suit and tie under the hot, constricting anti-gas overalls. The heat, the fear, the dreadful noise of the artillery, the great eruptions of earth around us, the fifty-yard dash to the moving trucks all together proved fatal to him. As he lay on the floor of the truck with the bombs still landing and the guns still firing, his heart gave way. He was dead before anyone realized, and although the Iranian doctors tried for two hours to revive him, it was hopeless. Poor man: I admired his courage in coming with us. Plenty of other bureau managers would have refused.

Things became easier once we were bucketing along the pot-holed roads through the shattered remnants of the town of Faw. The green flag of the Islamic revolution flew over the mosque, the only building of any size to have escaped serious damage. Everywhere we were cheered by soldiers in makeshift uniforms, rear-echelon units who guarded the roads and lived in the ruined buildings. All the time the explosions continued, and we could hear the noise of anti-aircraft fire above the grinding noise of our truck's engine.

Soon we came up to the real combatants, exhausted, grey figures, their uniforms thick with dust and dried mud, trudging back for other duties after the bombing they had been receiving that morning. They too managed to raise a cheer for us, and croaked their chants about God and Khomeini. These were the Iranian Revolutionary Guards who had swum the Shatt al-Arab a few days before and captured the Iraqi positions, and had resisted all the Iraqi counter-attacks ever since. Not all the bodies had been buried. Sometimes we saw the huddled bundles of clothes and outstretched limbs which only ever mean one thing. They lay where the bullets or shells had caught them, singly or in enough numbers to fill a trench, their faces frozen and inhuman, their eyes half-closed, the flies at work.

We saw evidence of the kind of weapons Saddam Hussein was using. Our minders spotted a bus full of gas casualties, and encouraged us to climb aboard. We behaved like tourists, snapping and filming the men who lay slouched in their seats, moaning quietly, dribbling, their eyes gummed shut, swaying with the pain, disgustingly big blisters already starting to form on their skin. Others held medicated cloths to their faces. There was a terrible sound of coughing – the kind of cough that tears at the lungs and the throat. At last one of the soldiers who had been less badly gassed than the others realized who we were, and began a feeble chant of 'Allahu Akbar!' Gradually more and more of these damaged men took it up, chanting the words slowly and weakly as if they were talking in their sleep. They waved their fists feebly in time to the chanting. Then the coughing and moaning became stronger and the chanting weaker, and we left the sufferers alone with their pain and their ruined lives. I felt ashamed as well as horrified: ashamed that I should be alive and healthy, while they were slipping into a living death.

The following week a UN team identified the gas the Iraqis were using as yperite, used by the Germans and British in the First World War. The Iraqi planes dropped it, and from the moment we landed at Faw I was aware of a slight irritation which made my eyes water a little. It was the faint, attenuated remainder of mustard gas in the air, and it felt like being at the aftermath of a riot in which CS gas has been used. The Iranian ambassador had complained several times at the United Nations in New York about Iraq's use of poison gas during the war, but the accusation had been ignored. The big countries wanted Iraq to win, and Iran had no friends to take up its case.

Eventually, for less than a year, Iran produced its own mustard gas and used it on the battlefield, but the results were ineffective and the gas often floated back on the wind and affected the Iranian troops it was meant to protect. As a result Iran decided not to deploy chemical weapons any more. There were indications that the Iraqi army would have preferred to give them up as well, but Saddam Hussein himself had decreed that gas should be used as a weapon, and no one wanted to tell him it was not an effective one.

Now, as our trucks bumped across the Passchendaele landscape, a stick of maybe seven or eight Iraqi bombs fell near the landing-strip where our helicopters had set us down. It was about a mile away, and the noise was loud enough to make us shudder. From each explosion a cloud of dirty yellow-white smoke billowed upwards, then seemed to find its own level and hung low over the landscape, heavy and ponderous.

'Now we are going back to the helicopters,' the officer in charge of us said serenely.

This did not seem a good idea, but we were in their hands. We pulled on our gas masks, and tried to see how they worked. I looked round at the others: fifteen or so identical insect faces with long protective snouts, swaying with the movement of the truck. Then the racket of Iraqi planes almost overhead, and the squeal of brakes, and the snouts were peering over the side and jumping down. I jumped with them, burying myself in the mud and sand, my unprotected hands over the back of my unprotected neck, waiting for the huge blisters I had seen bulging out on the necks and hands of the men in the bus. Perhaps I had been more frightened in my life, but I didn't think so.

Then the planes headed on, and there were no explosions. We clambered back into the truck like insects into our nest, and took up our positions again. The Iranians pointed at me, and the noise from behind their masks sounded like laughter. I took my mask off and examined it: whatever was in the air was what I would now be breathing. I smiled as though I thought it was funny too, and kept my useless mask on my lap, my eyes blinking with tears from the residual gas in the atmosphere.

We were back in the ditch twice more, so it was a good hour before we arrived back at the landing-strip. I took my mask off with a certain amount of nervousness, and found that the prickling feeling from the gas seemed no worse there than it had been while we were further out on the peninsula.

'Maybe Saddam was using cyanide gas,' said our escort officer cheerfully.

Cyanide gas kills you stone dead instantly, but unlike mustard gas, which lingers, its effects disappear in a minute or so. After that you can scarcely smell it. As far as I could make out from talking to the Iranians, there was no difference in the colour of the cloud.

Now the Iraqis were back overhead again, but this time a good two miles above us. They bombed us again and again, and it always seemed as though they knew precisely where we were: a common enough delusion of those who are pinned down, out in the open, waiting for a lull that would be long enough for the helicopters to come in and pick us up.

Sometimes the bombers would stay away for as long as twenty minutes at a time, and we would be able to stroll about in the open, interviewing people, filming things. I looked out for any useful spare parts for my gas mask.

But the bombers always came back, and sometimes the explosions were so close that the earth and pebbles they threw up would land on us: painful, but not fatal. Could they keep on missing us, I wondered. I lay on my back at an angle, supported by an eight-foot bank of bulldozed yellow earth, and watched the little silver crosses high up in the perfect blue sky. Each time the anti-aircraft crews would spin round on their guns like kids in an arcade game, trying to get a decent aim and blasting away with ear-splitting inaccuracy.

It occurred to me with uncomfortable clarity that the difference of a thousandth of a second in the bomb-aimer's timing as he pressed the button to release another load of bombs would mean the difference between a direct hit and a near miss. Each time my bag became more mud-stained, as I threw myself to the ground and fished out my camera to take up the photographic therapy again, and at least once I was exactly successful, and caught the yellow upward rush of earth and sand and pebbles as a bomb landed remarkably close to us. But none of us was hurt, and the Iraqis seemed to have stopped using gas on us. Chance is a fine thing, if only you can rely on it.

Eventually someone, somewhere, took a decision: the Iraqi bombers were not going to let up, so we would have to be taken by motorboat across the Shatt al-Arab. From there, trucks could pick us up and take us to an Iranian air base from which we could fly back to Tehran. During the next lull in the bombing we clambered awkwardly into a line of bobbing wooden boats which headed out fast into the middle of the river as soon as they could, with our helpers and guides waving goodbye from the rickety pier.

Just as the last boat pulled away from the shore, the planes returned. We were still only a couple of hundred yards away when a bomb fell on the place where we had been taking refuge. Rocks, mud and splintered wood went up in the air, and yellow-white smoke blossomed out over the landing-strip. No one afterwards was able to tell us how many people had been killed. The lives of all of us seemed to have been miraculously preserved all day – except, that is, for the poor German bureau manager, whose stout body now lay under a sheet in the nearby field hospital.

We flew back to Tehran in an enormous Iranian Hercules, like pencils in an empty box. Our comfortable Fokker Friendship had, we were told, been requisitioned at the last minute so a party of Iranian government officials and politicians could inspect the extraordinary victory at the Faw Peninsula. Our guides insisted that we had been the targets of the day's Iraqi bombing, because they knew it would be the best way to tell the world that Iran's foothold on Iraqi soil was very precarious. The next morning news came that the Fokker Friendship we had been expecting to fly in had been shot down by two Iraqi jets eighteen miles north-east of Ahwaz, as it was returning to Tehran. All forty-four people on board were killed.

16. SAVING SADDAM

The capture of Faw had a sensational effect on Western governments, though it was relatively little reported in the media. Alarm bells rang particularly loudly in London, which still had a strong post-colonial interest in the small states of the Gulf. Iran's stunning victory meant that its troops were only twenty-five miles from Kuwait, with its large Shi'ite community.

I went to Whitehall and saw two grand but rather shy men with superb titles at the Foreign Office. They offered me a cup of tea and asked me a great many questions about what I had seen. Then they told each other how valuable my input had been (the man who used the word put heavy inverted commas round it) but were not at all forthcoming when I started asking them questions about Britain's likely response.

Next, I travelled to Paris and met the man in charge of Middle East policy at the Quai d'Orsay, the French foreign ministry. He was much better dressed and even more charming, and explained with the greatest courtesy that he could only give me twelve minutes. He listened to my story quietly, but exploded directly I finished speaking.

'Impossible! It is the policy of France to support Saddam Hussein.'

It then took him a good twenty-five minutes to explain why I was wrong to think that a small setback – if indeed it was even as much as that – might have altered the balance of the war. I understood then what France's real policy was: that Iran and Iraq should carry on fighting for as long as possible.

In Washington, what was simply a matter of subtle policy in Paris was becoming an American crusade. The White House was inclined to believe the wilder rhetoric of the less important fundamentalist clerics in Tehran and Qom, and thought there was a real danger that Iran might move into Kuwait and begin the 'liberation' of the Gulf states. Even if it did not, the capture of Basra would destroy the regime of Saddam Hussein, which the White House regarded as a bastion of anti-fundamentalism in the region.

Israel, by contrast, made no such mistake. It had long since sorted out its strategic priorities and knew that Saddam represented a much more serious threat than Iran for the next few years. Israeli diplomats and intelligence officers tried to convince their American opposite numbers that Iraq was the real problem. A secret but very logical relationship had built up between the Israelis and Iran ever since Saddam Hussein had invaded Iran six years earlier. Each country knew that if Saddam won, its own safety was at stake. And so Israel skilfully supplied Iran with untraceable weapons, intelligence and training. Israeli jets destroyed Saddam Hussein's nuclear plant at Osirak in June 1981, soon after Iranian jets had failed to knock the plant out. As long as Iran stayed in the war, the Israelis had nothing to fear from Saddam. Now they watched with real anxiety as the Americans decided they must do their best to help him.

Nevertheless, during this time the Reagan administration's policy towards both Iran and Iraq was in a characteristic muddle. Secretly, the United States was negotiating with Iran to buy the freedom of American hostages held by pro-Iranian fundamentalists in Lebanon by supplying the Iranians with missiles for use against Saddam Hussein. For a brief period in the summer of 1986 this deeply cynical approach paid off: a few hostages were released. Robert McFarlane, the President's national security adviser, paid a ludicrously ill-arranged trip to Tehran with Colonel Oliver North, a not very bright adventurer who worked at the White House.

News of the visit came out eventually, of course, as it was always bound to. Why governments ever think they can keep these things secret is hard to imagine. The leak came from a disgruntled source in Lebanon, and shocked public opinion in the United States profoundly. Americans had been so indoctrinated with the idea that fundamentalist Iran was the evil power dominating the Middle East that President Reagan's decision to negotiate secretly with the ayatollahs in Tehran and the religious fanatics in Lebanon seemed like the worst kind of betrayal. Reagan found it hard to give coherent answers to questions about the affair, and never regained the popularity he had enjoyed before the news broke.

But this was all a side-show. The United States was now seriously worried by Iran's victory at Faw, and determined to give extra help to Iraq. And so the relationship between the Reagan administration and Saddam Hussein, which had been fostered with care and enthusiasm by Donald Rumsfeld, the US special envoy in the Middle East, now began to show real practical benefits for Saddam. With Rumsfeld as the intermediary, the US Department of Defense and the CIA began making satellite, radar and signals intelligence available to Iraq in quite large quantities. American intelligence officers plotted the movements of Iranian troops and planes, and passed the information on to Iraqi military intelligence. The United States had become an active, if secret, partner in Saddam Hussein's war against Iran.

It was done selectively and with considerable care. Only images which showed the places where a direct threat to Iraqi positions existed were handed over. Like France and Britain, the United States did not want Iraq to achieve an outright victory, so there was no question at this stage of giving the Iraqis information about the places where Iran was strategically weak. The aim was to help Saddam safeguard himself against defeat at the Faw Peninsula. This, together with some hectic fortification work planned and largely carried out by the Soviet Union, kept Iran at bay. Basra, now defended by a large network of canals and moats, did not fall, and Saddam was saved.

By now the war had taken on a life of its own, just as Siegfried Sassoon believed the First World War did. It existed for itself, with neither side being able finally to destroy the other. The balance was extremely fine: on the Iraqi side, weapons, money, the backing of France and America, and Saddam Hussein's ferocious determination to root out anyone whose nerve seemed to be failing; on the Iranian side, manpower and Ayatollah Khomeini's refusal to accept anything short of total victory.

In the summer of 1987 the entire focus of the war shifted from the Flanders-like battlefield on the Faw Peninsula to the waters of the Gulf. By staging a series of attacks against Iranian ports and oil terminals in the Gulf, Saddam Hussein managed to goad Iran into an act of considerable stupidity; Iranian Revolutionary Guards, using dinghies with powerful outboard motors, were laying mines in the Gulf and attacking the ships of nations which were trading with Iraq.

It was a foolish move on the Iranians' part. In May 1987 an incident had occurred which they might have turned to their advantage. Two US warships, the *Stark* and her sister-ship *Coontz*, had the task of radioing the coordinates of Iranian ships and shore-based targets which American intelligence officers were recommending to the Iraqis. They even guided the Iraqis on to the attack. On 17 May two Exocet missiles from an Iraqi Mirage homed in accidentally on to the radio beam from the *Stark* which was directing the pilot to his target. Following the radio beam downwards, the missiles struck the *Stark* amidships, killing thirty-seven American crewmen and injuring dozens of others.

Saddam Hussein wrote President Reagan a fulsome letter of apology, and ordered his navy and air force to cooperate entirely with a secret American inquiry into the disaster. As for the unfortunate pilot, it was strongly rumoured in Baghdad that he was executed. The Reagan administration did not even ask Saddam for compensation for the deaths and the serious damage to one of its most sophisticated warships. It was fully understood in Washington that the whole thing had been an unfortunate technical accident. Counting perhaps on the American public's lack of interest in the war, the fact that the two warring nations had such similar names, and the American media's tendency to accept without question the official Washington version on the big issues of the day, Reagan issued a strong warning to *Iran* that if there were any further attacks the United States would hit back in the most resolute fashion.

Iran had often accused the United States of siding with the Iraqis and providing them with satellite intelligence. Now it was true, but Iran had made so many wild accusations against the Americans in the past that no one took them seriously.

The Reagan administration also ignored the fact that Iraq had been responsible for the original strikes against shipping in the Gulf. Washington warned that it would use force if necessary to protect itself and its friends from attack, and keep the sea-lanes open; but Saddam Hussein understood from the messages that were sent to him from Washington that he was free to carry on attacking Iranian ships and oil installations as he chose. The United States offered to 're-flag' Kuwaiti tankers and protect them as if they were American. Soon there were more than seventy US ships in the Gulf. The British sent a quarter of the Royal Navy; the French, Italians, Dutch and Belgians all joined them. The Russians dispatched a fleet of their own.

At first things went embarrassingly wrong. The mines which the Iranian Revolutionary Guards laid in the Gulf were ancient Second World War models – the only ones they could buy on the international arms black market. The US Navy, equipped to fight the Third World War, no longer had any minesweepers it could call on. American admirals, it emerged, regarded minesweeping as low-tech and therefore unglamorous, and the ability to build wooden ships of the right size (metal ships set off mines) had died out in American shipyards.

Worse, a 're-flagged' Kuwaiti tanker hit a mine while it was being escorted by the US Navy. The government in Tehran made the most of Washington's embarrassment. It denied having planted the mines, which it said coyly had been 'laid by hidden hands'. For a few days it looked as though an all-out war might erupt between Iran and the United States. But the Americans were not really enthusiastic about it, and Ayatollah Khomeini's main obsession still lay in defeating Saddam Hussein.

By August, the Iranian navy claimed to be destroying the mines rather than laying them. In a maladroit public relations effort, I and a number of other international journalists were invited to see the effort for ourselves. We were flown down to the port of Bandar Abbas, and put on board an American-made Sea Stallion helicopter bought in the days of the Shah. The Americans were using precisely the same helicopters to search for mines not far away in the Gulf.

The temperature in the Sea Stallion was quite appalling. We located the small contingent of Iranian ships which was supposedly on mine-clearing duties, and after circling for a ferocious half-hour so the cameramen on board could get the necessary shots we put down on the deck of a support ship. When we got out and stood on the deck it felt wonderful to get into the cool, fresh air; then the officer of the watch told us that the temperature in this cool, fresh air was actually 119 degrees Fahrenheit.

In the ship's wardroom an Iranian naval captain and his commodore had been delegated to brief us on the mine-lifting operation. They were decent, professional men who had been trained in Britain during the Shah's time, and they were as reluctant as most serving officers to talk to the press. It was almost an act of cruelty to interrupt their prepared lecture and ask who had planted the mines.

'We don't know who planted them,' said the captain. He looked round in desperation at the commodore.

'No, we don't know,' said the commodore.

The captain gave a ghastly smile and tried to continue. But the purpose of the entire public relations exercise had evaporated in the ferocious heat of the wardroom.

Even so, the threat of war slowly ebbed away; neither side had any real interest in fighting. Iran could not resist staging regular provocations against American ships, but they were carried out with greater care in future so as to avoid outright retaliation.

17. HALABJAH

The will to continue the war was starting to fade on both sides. The huge Iranian offensive against Basra at the start of 1987 had been a failure, and more than 100,000 men had been killed or wounded. The Iranian Supreme Defence Council started to put more effort into other theatres of war: the mountains of Kurdistan, for instance, where the Iraqi defences were thinner and the quality of the forces not so high. But the problems of bringing up tanks and artillery through the difficult terrain to exploit a breakthrough were considerable, and the Iraqis were always alerted to the danger by American satellite intelligence. The relationship between the CIA and Saddam Hussein's regime was becoming closer than ever. Iran, meanwhile, was becoming exhausted. The offensives were fewer and farther between, until they resembled the blows from an immensely heavy hammer wielded by a strong but tiring man. Each effort took longer to prepare, and each failure took longer to recover from.

The final phase of the war began with the resumption of Iraqi missile attacks on Tehran and other cities in February 1988. On 20 March I had a sudden invitation from the Iranians to go to Tehran immediately 'for the bombing'. It usually took four hours or more to get through the immigration and customs controls (sometimes the officials wanted to look in detail at every book and every piece of clothing you had brought, and listen to every tape), but this time I was through within an hour. '*Bombaran*', said a notice beside the passport desk; *bombaran* meant bombing. I had been invited in, together with a number of other journalists, to report on the aftermath of an incident which had happened four days earlier on Iran's frontier with Iraqi Kurdistan. The Iranian officials were saying that several thousand people had been killed, but most of us dismissed this as the usual exaggeration of government propaganda.

The next morning we were flown to the border, then taken on by helicopter to the scene of the attack, inside Iraq. It was the town of Halabjah. Kurdish Pesh Merga guerrillas had taken it from Saddam Hussein's forces on 15 March, then handed it over to the Iranians. It had been a remarkable victory: 4,000 prisoners, including more than 100 officers over the rank of major, and several hundred tanks captured. We had not been brought here to witness a victory, though; we were to witness Saddam Hussein's response to his defeat.

Our helicopter headed for twenty-five miles over the mountains along the border, then over the green hills into Iraqi Kurdistan. In the distance lay a lake, and near it a medium-sized town. 'That is Halabjah,' shouted our guide over the noise of the rotor-blades. I was still uncertain of the name, and took the precaution of jotting it down.

The day after the capture of Halabjah, Iraqi planes and artillery had begun attacking it with chemical weapons. The attacks had gone on for most of the day, and then at intervals on the following day. I still assumed at this stage that we would find the number of deaths had been ritually exaggerated. Our helicopter landed on the outskirts of the town, and we walked towards the old centre with its mud-brick walls.

The first thing I noticed, while we were still a few hundred yards away, was the stench. In the fields beside us lay the grossly bloated bodies of sheep and cows, and a few isolated corpses covered with blankets: shepherds who had not yet been buried. But the stench came not so much from any of these, as from the town itself. We turned a corner and entered Halabjah.

The bodies lay in great, appalling heaps, swollen and blackened by the sun. I assumed they had been left for our benefit, but it soon became clear that many more bodies had already been taken away for burial. We turned into a street which was choked with them – so many, you had to stretch your legs to get over them, desperate not to tread on these terrible, bulging, stinking objects which had been human beings until just the other day.

These people had run out of their houses when the bombs started falling. Perhaps they were trying to escape into the fields; perhaps they wanted to get away from the buildings and narrow streets where Saddam's poison gas collected after it had been dropped from the air. Some of the bodies had shrapnel wounds, but it didn't look to me as though the shrapnel had killed them. There was a strange waxiness to their faces, and an almost otherworldly absence of fear and pain. Many of them lay with their eyes open. Even after five days these corpses seemed more human than the usual bundles of dead flesh in old clothes which you see after a massacre.

Close by there was the sound of artillery fire: the Iraqis had not yet given up their efforts to recapture Halabjah. Our Iranian escorts came over, bringing with them an old man in a black and white Kurdish turban. He had witnessed the attack, and seemed to enjoy our attention.

'I heard the planes coming over, and then I saw the bombs starting to fall. White smoke came out of some of them. I was near the concrete shelter, so I went down into it and waited. I was too frightened to come out for a long time. When I did, it seemed as though the whole town was lying dead. People I knew, just lying in the streets or lying in their houses. It was a dead place, this town.'

'How do you know the planes were Iraqi ones? Couldn't they have been Iranian just as well?'

The Iranian officials with us shifted irritably. The old man cackled.

'What, you think the Iranians came and bombed our town the day after their men had come in here? That would be very stupid, wouldn't you say?'

He cackled some more. Later, a younger man identified the planes specifically as Iraqi.

For years afterwards, there was a tendency inside the Department of Defense and the CIA to suggest that Iran had indeed been responsible for the use of chemical weapons at Halabjah, and every now and then the *New York Times* would print an op-ed article proposing the idea. It was foolish, and perhaps it was a deliberate attempt from inside the American intelligence community to rehabilitate Iraq at Iran's expense. In 1988, as before and afterwards, only Saddam Hussein had the capability and the will to use the wide range of chemical weapons that was used against Halabjah: mustard gas, the nerve gas sarin, and cyanide gas. (The presence of the last has been questioned by some experts, but others say the abundant evidence of almost instantaneous death cannot be explained in any other way.)

Nor did Saddam Hussein ever deny that the massacre had taken place. On the contrary, he and his closest henchmen boasted about it; especially Ali Hassan al-Majid, who had been in overall charge of the operation and who from now on was proud of the nickname which the Kurds gave him: Chemical Ali. The people of Halabjah had broken the basic code of loyalty to Saddam by handing their town over to the invading Iranians. They had paid the penalty.

I looked over to a group of bodies lying near me: a young woman, aged perhaps twenty, in a magenta and orange dress, a baby in her arms. Here in the narrow streets the bodies had been almost untouched by the sun, and there was no swelling and bloating. The mother could have been asleep, but the baby's eyes were white and dead. She had tried to protect it with her own life. Their clothes fluttered constantly in the chilly spring wind. Chance had taken them, but left alive the wizened old man with his self-satisfied cackle.

We wandered round the houses. There were bodies in most of them. I walked through one open front door. A missile had struck the roof, and was still lodged in the ceiling of the main living-room. There was a sound of buzzing: the flies were thick on the food which the family had been eating when the attack took place. Six people were slumped around the table; a child had rolled out of his chair and was lying on the floor, face down. A man and a woman were slumped in their seats, side by side. I couldn't see their faces. An older man, the grandfather, lay with the side of his face on the table, his hand to his mouth. His jaw was still clamped on a piece of bread which he had been biting when the missile came down through the roof and filled the room with poison gas. Death must have come within one or two seconds, and it had been very merciful.

As the other journalists and I wandered around, shells began landing close to the town. I threw myself to the ground, and found myself sniffing the air nervously. Mustard gas smells of sewage; the nerve gas sarin apparently has a much more pleasant smell – chocolate, some people have said, or new-mown hay. Cyanide gas supposedly smells like almonds, though a single breath of it will kill you as fast as it killed the old man with his bread, so it is hard to see how anyone knows.

As I lay on the ground I could see another heap of bodies a few yards away. These people had died much harder deaths, killed by sarin. Nerve gas strangles you from the inside, by paralysing the nervous system, and it takes a long time to do it. I already knew the effects of mustard gas: it kills only around 3 per cent of its victims, but it condemns the majority of the others to a dreadful half-life of chest and throat pain, of blisters which can still erupt twenty or thirty years later, of terrible damage to the eyes and nasal passages, of cancers and genetic deformities. Please let it be cyanide, I found myself saying as I waited for the third shell to land. There was another explosion, but this time it was farther away, and no cloud of gas rose from the place where it landed. I never thought I would be so grateful for simple high explosive.

We picked ourselves up and wandered on. More bodies, then an entire truckful: dozens of women in bright-coloured clothes, four or five deep. Dozens of old men and children too. The stench, and the sight, of all those calm, grey-white faces were more than I could bear.

I walked back into the town. A man wailed and ran towards me, arms in the air. He had just come back from a journey and had no idea what had happened.

For the first time, I noticed the dead pigeons on the ground.

On the edge of town there was a terrible, nightmarish moment like something from a drawing by Goya. Three donkeys, two grey and one white, crazed by the latest shelling, galloped insanely across the field beside us, trying to bite each other with their grass-green fangs as they ran. They didn't stop at a pile of bodies laid out in the field. Instead, teeth bared, they trampled heavily over them. The bodies broke out into a horrible farting and belching as the gases were forced out of them. Then they lay twisted and broken as the donkeys charged on, braying, biting and trampling.

Someone, a Belgian doctor, told me he had been counting bodies all that morning. There were around 5,000 of them, he said.

I could see the television cameramen trying to film the bodies in ways that would not offend the delicate sensibilities of the people back home: people who couldn't in their most appalling nightmares imagine what it was like to listen to the brutal eructions from bodies being trampled on by maddened donkeys. Close by, my eyes met those of a small child lying on her back where her mother had dropped her as she herself fell dead.

Afterwards, I couldn't get her face out of my head. The dead, open eyes still held mine even when I tried to sleep. A year later, on the anniversary of Saddam Hussein's attack on Halabjah, a photograph of that child appeared on posters advertising a protest rally in London. One was pasted up on the Victorian-Ionic pillars of an empty house near mine in Kensington, and I used to pass it every day. Over the weeks and months that followed, the poster became more and more tattered. In the end all that remained were those white, empty child-eyes looking out at me, and a few surviving letters of print: 'REMEMBER HALAB . . .' I only wish I could forget it, even now.

18. ENDGAME

The attack on Halabjah helped to bring the war to an end. Although pictures of the massacre were not shown on Iraqi television, people in border areas were sometimes able to see them illicitly. Within a day or two, everyone knew all about what had happened at Halabjah. This naturally reinforced the terror which Saddam liked to create around himself. The town's population had paid a ferocious price for their disloyalty to him, and every Iraqi drew the obvious conclusion: Saddam was strong, and this was not the time to challenge him.

In Iran, the television pictures were shown often and at great length by Iranian television, presumably on the assumption that they would reinforce the national will to resist a dictatorship which was so evil, and encourage a tired population to fight on. In fact, the pictures had precisely the opposite effect. People were terrified that the Iraqi Scud-B missiles which were being fired every day at Tehran would now be converted to deliver chemical warheads instead of high explosive. This fear had a clear effect on Iranian public opinion.

On 17 April 1988, exactly a month after the attack on Halabjah, the Iraqi army staged a massive counter-attack on the Iranian positions on the Faw Peninsula: the scene of Iran's great victory two years before. The Reagan administration played a critical role in this. Iraqi military intelligence had never been particularly good, and it was clear that the generals running the war had very little idea of the strength of Iran's defences at Faw. By contrast, the American analysts who examined the satellite pictures of Faw could see very clearly how thin those defences were. Iran's attention was on the Kurdistan front; Faw was largely forgotten, and the Iranian front line was being defended mostly by reservists and old men – and not very many of them. The satellite pictures were quickly handed over to Saddam Hussein, and the counter-attack was launched. On the night of the attack a US naval force distracted the military planners in Tehran by staging a show of strength farther down the coast of Iran.

Three weeks later the Iraqi army turned its attention to the Iranian positions around Basra, and within seven hours had recaptured territory which had cost Iran 70,000 casualties to win the previous year. Once again, American satellite intelligence had pinpointed Iran's weakness. On 25 June Iraqi troops regained the Majnoon Islands from a weak garrison in only four hours' fighting. A fourth battle took place around Dehloran, which released the final Iranian pressure on Baghdad. Finally Iraqi troops advanced forty miles into Iranian territory near Kermanshah: the first time for years that they had had a foothold on enemy soil. It was a stunning series of reverses, and each time

American satellite intelligence was there to show the weak points in Iran's defences.

On 3 July 1988, with the Iraqi offensive at its height, the USS *Vincennes* shot down an Iranian Airbus which had just taken off from Bandar Abbas on its way to Dubai. All 290 people on board died. It was clearly a mistake – a video camera which was running throughout the incident caught the crew's appalled reaction when the news came through that the plane they had destroyed was not an Iranian fighter, as they had thought – but the Iranians were convinced it had been done deliberately, as a warning. The United States offered compensation, but refused to apologize. Afterwards the Pentagon agreed that the crew of the *Vincennes*, lacking combat experience, had been at fault.

The most powerful politician in Iran, Ali Akbar Hashemi-Rafsanjani, had been looking for a way to end the war with Saddam Hussein, and used the Airbus tragedy to persuade the now failing Ayatollah Khomeini that he must accept peace. Rafsanjani claimed that the United States would soon launch an all-out attack on Iran in alliance with Saddam Hussein. The Islamic Republic itself was now in danger.

Khomeini caved in, and accepted a United Nations ceasefire proposal, though he never forgave Rafsanjani. On 18 July 1988 the UN secretary-general, Javier Perez de Cuellar, received Iran's formal acceptance of Resolution 598. The same day, Khomeini issued a statement which he was too anguished to be able to read in person:

> Happy are those who have departed through martyrdom ... Unhappy am I, that I should still live and have drunk the poisoned cup.

Eleven months later Khomeini was dead.

The Americans had rescued Saddam Hussein from defeat; now he could plausibly claim that he had won a victory. It could never have been achieved without the deliberate help of the United States.

For at least three years the Israelis had been warning the Americans that if Saddam Hussein won his war with Iran he would be a danger to them both, and to the entire region. But the Reagan administration, obsessed with the threat from Iran, paid no attention. The British believed that Iran and its militant fundamentalism were a serious threat to Kuwait and the rest of the Gulf. Between them, they tilted decisively in favour of the one country which really did pose a threat to Kuwait.

19. THE INNOCENT VICTIM

Until August 1988, Saddam Hussein's sole concern had been his war against Iran: the war he could not have won without American help. From the moment the ceasefire came into operation, Iraq became a dominant power in the Muslim world. It was heavily indebted, and still weak from the conflict. But it was potentially enormously wealthy, and its president was inordinately ambitious. Its income from oil, 70 per cent of which had been directed to the war effort, was suddenly liberated for whatever purposes Saddam might choose.

His rhetoric had always included threats against Israel. Yet Iraq had never taken part in any of the wars against Israel, all of which had occurred before Saddam came to power, and Saddam understood that in order to be a major force in the Arab world this was the issue he now had to dominate. In order to outclass Egypt and Syria, he had to build up the notion that Iraq constituted a serious, active threat to Israel, which neither of them did.

After eight years of the fiercest war to have been fought in the last three decades of the century, the people of Iraq longed for a little peace. That, however, was denied to them. Saddam Hussein's position, perhaps his very life, depended on keeping his generals heavily occupied; any let-up, he confided to the Palestinian leader, Yasser Arafat, would quickly lead to a military coup against him.

Now he decided to raise the stakes with Israel. The Scud-B missiles which the Soviet Union had sold him, and which his scientists had carefully modified, were capable of reaching Tel Aviv, as well as Damascus, southern Turkey and northern Saudi Arabia. There were convincing intelligence reports that he had begun a crash programme to develop nuclear warheads capable of being fitted to the Scuds. At some time in late August Israel passed this information to the outgoing Reagan administration. It warned that if the Americans did nothing, Israel would have to take action against Saddam itself, as it had done against the Osirak nuclear plant in 1981. George Bush, the vice-president, and George Shultz, the secretary of state, took the Israeli warnings seriously.

Only a few weeks before, the United States had been supplying Saddam Hussein with first-class military intelligence. Now that he was victorious and newly invigorated, Washington performed one of those remarkable about-faces of which it is capable from time to time, without the slightest warning.

On 8 September 1988 Tariq Aziz, the Iraqi foreign minister, went to Washington for what he assumed would be a friendly and relaxed meeting with George Shultz. Two hours before the meeting took place, Shultz made a speech fiercely condemning a series of attacks which Saddam Hussein's forces had launched against Kurdish rebels in northern Iraq two weeks earlier. The United States had allowed the gas attacks at Halabjah six months earlier to pass with only a mild rebuke, and yet millions of Americans had seen the television pictures of Halabjah for themselves. There were no television pictures of this latest attack, merely eyewitness accounts from Kurdish refugees who had crossed the border into Turkey and told their stories to officials of the American Senate Foreign Relations Committee, who happened to be in the area.

The day after Tariq Aziz had his unexpectedly difficult meeting with George Shultz, the US Senate unanimously voted a series of sanctions against Iraq which the chairman of the Foreign Relations Committee, Claiborne Pell, described as the strongest in decades. (As it happens, though, the sanctions were not imposed. They were appended to a bill which lapsed on a technicality before the House adjourned; and by that time the senators' minds had turned to something else.)

Saddam Hussein was furious. Two days afterwards, on 11 September 1988, more than 100,000 people obediently demonstrated outside the American embassy in Baghdad. It was the largest public demonstration in Iraq for twenty years, and the first against the United States since the Six Day War in 1967. In November the head of the embassy's political section was expelled from Baghdad, and the United States expelled an Iraqi diplomat as a reprisal. Saddam announced that there was an American–Israeli–British plot against his efforts to turn Iraq into a regional superpower. Tariq Aziz later summed up his government's feelings like this:

Israel wants to attack Iraqi industrial and scientific sites to maintain the balance of power, which has changed . . . When an Arab
country achieves [technological advances], then the whole fuss
comes, the comments, suspicions and attempts to discredit the
Arab country.

There was, of course, something in what he said. But from this point
on, Iraq regarded itself as being on a collision course with the West,
and particularly with the United States.

The case of one man, a young Iranian living in Britain, soon
marked this new mood of belligerence. As happened so often with
Saddam Hussein, it made it impossible to return to a quieter, less
confrontational relationship.

I knew him well, and had first met him in 1983, at a diplomatic
reception. He walked over to me, a confident man of twenty-four,
neatly dressed in a blazer and tie. I thought him a little over-eager.

'My name is Farzad Bazoft,' he said. His English was almost free
of any accent.

We talked about Iran for a while, and particularly about the
revolution four years before which had driven him out of the country.
He claimed to have good contacts outside and inside Iran, and asked
if there would be any work for him in the BBC. Not, I thought, in
domestic television, except behind the camera, and he wanted very
much to be in front of the camera. So I said the kind of noncommittal
things one does on these occasions, but because he was an exile, and
young, I didn't want to be too discouraging. If he had any good stories,
I said, he should get in touch with me.

He did, several weeks later. Was I interested in some good, up-to-
date information from Tehran? This was a time when it was next to
impossible for Western journalists to go there, and some fairly disturbing things were going on. I said yes.

The information was quite good; good enough, after being checked
and confirmed and toned down, to be used in a broadcast. I wasn't
able to pay him much; the BBC has never been a good payer. But it
was enough to establish a link between us.

Farzad contacted me fairly regularly after that. The information
didn't get much better, but it was often usable and always interesting.
As we got to know each other better he became noisy and boisterous,

and more than a little boastful. I didn't mind too much. He was young, and had a good deal of anxiety and self-doubt to compensate for. He was also generous-spirited and witty. But he wanted status, and thought the BBC could confer it, and I soon realized that the information he was dishing up to me was often just old Tehran gossip, some of which I had already heard from other sources. He promised me on two occasions that Ayatollah Khomeini had died – this was in 1983 and 1984 – and when I said I didn't believe it he was offended and refused to contact me for a while.

I grew tired of the connection. When he rang me next time I told him there was only one thing I was interested in now: getting back to Iran. Ever since the revolution I had been put on some kind of blacklist, but I thought the official contacts he often talked to me about might be able to fix it. From the way he agreed to look into it I could tell it wouldn't happen.

Occasionally after that, when the phone rang in my office, the secretary would put it on hold and tell me it was Farzad. I would groan and roll my eyes up, and often ask her to say I was out. It's easy, if you have a secure job with a well-known organization, to be effortlessly cruel to an outsider who wants to make his way in the profession but can never quite manage the breakthrough.

Then he started working for the *Observer* newspaper. He didn't have a staff job there either, but you could tell he was trying to earn one by producing bigger and better exclusives about Iran and the war against Saddam Hussein. Some were good, some seemed to me to be distinctly dubious. He was visiting Baghdad more and more often, and I admired him for that. It was a brave thing for an Iranian who, I knew, only had a temporary British travel document to go to a difficult and suspicious country like Iraq. It wouldn't have been hard to accuse someone like Farzad of being a spy, and I thought it was a sign of some maturity on the part of the Iraqis to allow a man with an undisguised Iranian background to visit their country during a war with Iran.

Between 1987 and 1989 he visited Iraq five times. At that time the Iraqis allowed Western journalists into the country at infrequent intervals and for short periods only. The invitation would be to report on some specific event, which was naturally always something the government wanted the outside world to know about.

In September 1989 Farzad Bazoft arrived in Baghdad for what was to prove his last visit. The occasion was a series of highly restricted and unconvincing local elections in the Kurdish area of northern Iraq. The trick, as ever, was to get into the country using this as a pretext, then to try to do some genuine reporting.

There was no doubt what the subject would be this time. Less than three weeks earlier, on 17 August 1989, a huge explosion had taken place at the weapons manufacturing plant at al-Qa'qa, south of Baghdad. The wilder reports reaching the West claimed that 700 people had been killed. The plant covered several square miles, and was protected by anti-aircraft guns and radar. A British intelligence official I spoke to said it was thought that chemical warheads were assembled at al-Qa'qa, and perhaps even nuclear ones. News of the explosion broke on 6 September: the day before Bazoft and the other Western journalists arrived in Baghdad. All of them had hopes of finding out what had happened.

Al-Qa'qa is situated in a suburb of al-Hilla, sixty miles from Baghdad. The road to al-Hilla runs past the ruins of Babylon, so it was not too difficult to get to. Several other journalists who were on the same press facility as Farzad made the trip down there; among them were three members of a team from the British company Independent Television News. They reached al-Qa'qa and climbed over the wire surrounding the place where they thought the explosion had taken place. They were arrested, their video-cassettes were confiscated, and they were questioned for several hours. Then their equipment – minus the cassettes – was returned to them, and they were allowed to go back to Baghdad.

That night the ITN team met Farzad Bazoft and a British nurse he knew called Daphne Parish, who was working at a hospital in Baghdad. The ITN people made light of the incident. To them, it proved that although going to the plant at al-Qa'qa was difficult and more than a little nerve-racking, it wasn't actually dangerous. The Iraqis would not take serious action against Western journalists. Farzad listened to their story, and decided to try it himself as soon as possible.

The next day he asked Mrs Parish if she would drive him there in her car. He explained that he had asked the Ministry of Information for help in getting to al-Hilla and had not been refused; at one point he had even been told to expect an official car to take him, but it had never turned up. He then approached the deputy foreign minister,

Nizar Hamdoun, an intelligent and cultivated man who spoke perfect English. Hamdoun agreed to put in an official request for him.

Farzad told him he would go anyway. He was confident that if there were any trouble his friends in the Iraqi government, like Nizar Hamdoun, would make sure he didn't come to any harm. As someone who has done a certain amount of this kind of thing myself, I would not have rated the trip as something likely to be particularly dangerous. Farzad Bazoft had a persuasive manner, and Daphne Parish clearly found him attractive. She listened to him, and agreed to drive him to al-Hilla and look for the al-Qa'qa weapons plant.

There was no question of maintaining any secrecy. Farzad telephoned the *Observer* in London, even though he knew perfectly well that the security police would be listening, and explained in some detail what he was planning to do.

Afterwards, all sorts of rumours flew around about the way he had gone about his exploit at al-Qa'qa; journalists are among the least loyal of professional people, and always seem ready to believe invented scandal. There was a persistent story later that he had disguised himself as an Indian doctor, but it wasn't true: he wore a sports shirt and jeans that day. Daphne Parish told the transport office at the hospital where she worked where she was going and the route she would take.

They travelled to al-Hilla in a four-wheel-drive car with the hospital's name on the side. After a good deal of searching they found a place which they assumed to be the weapons plant, and Farzad noticed a pile of ash beside the road. He decided to come back the next day to pick up samples, and Mrs Parish agreed to drive him again.

This time he took a camera, and Mrs Parish gave him two medicine bottles. In full view of the soldiers who were guarding the entrance to the site, Farzad jumped out and scooped up some of the ash and a piece of rock. Then he spotted an old shoe and picked that up as well, to Mrs Parish's annoyance. As they left, he took three photographs: one of the fence, one of the general area, and one of the sign which bore the name of Iskanderia, the suburb of al-Hilla where the al-Qa'qa plant was situated.

It was all rather naïve. Farzad collected his samples because he had heard that a well-known television journalist had done the same thing outside a weapons factory in Kurdistan. A laboratory in London had confirmed the presence of chemicals used in the manufacture of poison gas. Farzad planned to get the *Observer* to have his materials analysed too, in order to prove what kind of explosion had taken place at al-Qa'qa three weeks before.

He was booked on the next morning's flight to London. Together with an Arab journalist, he was driven to the airport with a Ministry of Information minder to help them through the red tape. On the road to the airport their car had a puncture, and Farzad was distinctly nervous when three security men came up and stood beside him. They had obviously been following him in their own car.

Nevertheless he went through passport control and into the departure lounge, having said goodbye to the minder. None of the other journalists who were on the same flight saw what happened to him after that. The assumption is that he was quietly arrested and taken to a small office which the security police used in the departure lounge. Realizing that he had disappeared, one of the journalists had the presence of mind to ring the British embassy from the public telephone in the lounge.

It was days before the Iraqi press began trumpeting the news that Farzad Bazoft was an enemy spy. *Al-Iraq* accused him of working for the British, though when he finally appeared on Iraqi television on 1 November 1989 he confessed to having spied for Israel. He had obviously been tortured. Part of his moustache had been pulled out with pliers – a favourite form of torture in a country where the majority of men wear moustaches – and he had a bruise on his right temple. There were heavy bags under his eyes, caused perhaps by sleep deprivation.

A man in a blue suit asked him questions from what appeared to be a script, and Farzad gave what were presumably the pre-arranged answers.

Q. Did you face any kind of pressure or assault when you were arrested during the investigation?
A. The treatment I have received so far I can say is much better than the treatment one would receive in a detention centre or institution in the UK.

The following year, when I spent a good deal of time in Baghdad, I used to see Farzad's questioner sitting in the lobby of the al-Rashid

Hotel: a pleasant-faced man with studious glasses and an expensive suit. He had been educated in Britain, and used to like practising his English on Western journalists, especially women. I never spoke to him, for fear I might not be able to control my temper.

Daphne Parish was picked up soon afterwards. Her interrogators blindfolded her, and kicked her, pulled her hair and threatened her with a knife in order to make her confess. At other times they tried to tempt her.

'We'll send you back tonight,' they said. 'All you have to do is say you work for the British government. If you're not prepared to say that, just give the name of someone who works at the British embassy.'

She refused to give in. I have often advised my colleagues to follow Daphne Parish's example if they should be arrested and asked to confess to some crime they have not committed. The Soviet writer Isaac Babel once asked a friend of his, a senior figure in Stalin's secret police, the NKVD, what to do in these circumstances.

'Say nothing,' the friend replied, looking round to check that no one could overhear them. 'Don't confess. We can't do anything if you stay quiet.'

Poor Farzad wanted to believe the specious promises his interrogators made to him. At one point they put him and Mrs Parish together so that Farzad could persuade her to confess, as he had done. He told her they had used, or threatened to use, electrical torture on him.

'Look,' he said, 'we'll probably be flying out of here in a day or so if we get these last points sorted out.'

But Daphne Parish was fifty-three, with the maturity and wit to look after herself. She was much too sensible and strong-minded to give in to the threats and occasional ill-treatment of her persecutors. Farzad was thirty-one, and an innocent with a strong desire to please.

It turned out that the Mukharabarat, Iraq's main secret police organization, had been watching Farzad for a long time. After his execution they produced pictures they had taken of him photographing empty shell-cases at the Faw Peninsula; they managed to present this as evidence of his spying activities. After he applied to go to the scene of the explosion at al-Qa'qa they watched him even more closely. They had the evidence of the samples he had picked up there. And they found the name of a former agent of Mossad, the Israeli intelligence agency, in his contacts book.

It hardly seems likely that a real spy would openly carry the name and number of his controller with him like this. Later the *Observer*'s editor, Donald Trelford, explained that he had introduced Farzad to the man, whose name was Jacob Nimrodi, as part of an investigation into Israeli arms sales to Iran. After leaving Mossad, Nimrodi had become an arms dealer. Most journalists involved in this sort of reporting have contacts with people like Nimrodi; it is part of the job. You can make as little or as much of it as you like.

There were campaigns in support of Farzad Bazoft, naturally, but they did little good. One or two of the kind of characters who are drawn to these situations like flies to bad meat turned up and made things mildly worse. Tony Marlow, a British right-wing Conservative MP of strongly anti-European views, went to Baghdad for some reason while Farzad was in prison and wrote an article explaining that Iraq was the victim of a 'vociferous and unrepresentative minority that affects to believe that our way of life and systems of government is [sic] the measure by which all other countries should be measured'.

The Iraqis, emboldened by this kind of response, chose to make Farzad's supposed offence a capital one. Iraqi embassies handed out photocopies of his handwritten confession.

'YES,' said one sentence, written in capital letters to make it easier for non-Westerners to understand, 'I DO WORK AND DEAL WITH ISRAELIS AND BRITISH SPECIAL BRANCH (SECRET POLICE).'

Altogether, his confession was stilted, deeply unconvincing, and full of standard Iraqi phrasing. It referred, for instance, to the Iraqi air force's 'great and glorious role in the liberation fight'.

Around this time in London, someone decided to reveal more about Farzad to the British press. He had, it seemed, come to Britain in 1975 to study at the North Oxfordshire Technical College. He developed a reputation for lavish spending, and in those days of sudden oil wealth his father, a middle-ranking executive in the Iranian oil industry, sent him a generous allowance.

With the revolution in Iran the supply of money dried up. By June 1981 Farzad owed his landlady in Banbury, near Oxford, £260, and had no means of paying her. He walked into the Heart of England building society in the Northamptonshire village of Brackley one morning carrying a parcel which he put on the counter. It was a bomb, he said, and he wanted the contents of the tills. He escaped with £475, and was promptly arrested two streets away. There was, of course, no bomb.

He was gaoled for eighteen months, and the judge recommended that he should be deported after completing his sentence. But a year later the Home Office accepted that his life would be in danger back in Iran, and he was allowed to stay. He lived by selling stories to the Iranian émigré press and occasionally to British newspapers. He also offered information to Scotland Yard, though not, it seems, for money. The things he told them were often absurd: once he claimed to have information about Lord Lucan, who had disappeared some years before. He was an over-enthusiastic, gullible, rather naïve young man, but everyone liked him. And now his over-enthusiasm had put his life in real danger.

The trial of Farzad Bazoft and Daphne Parish was a shameful business. Farzad's Iraqi lawyer, who would never have been allowed to defend him properly anyway, was only shown the details of the prosecution's case a few hours before the trial began. Mrs Parish was not allowed to see her lawyer privately before the trial began.

Now that it was too late, Farzad burst out that his confession had been a fabrication. The judge replied angrily that he wasn't interested. Then he asked Mrs Parish if she pleaded guilty or not guilty.

'Guilty of what?' she answered. 'What is the charge? I haven't been formally charged so far.'

The trial was over very quickly. There was further pointless, cruel confusion at the end: neither of the accused was told what the sentences were. Farzad, who spoke a few words of Arabic, thought the judge had said he was to be hanged; the interpreter laughed encouragingly and told him the judge had said he wouldn't be executed. It was a lie.

Someone even told Mrs Parish she was going to be released. It was only when she was taken to another prison that she discovered she had been sentenced to fifteen years. She spent ten unpleasant months in prison, and then, at the request of the *Observer*'s owner, Tiny Rowland, President Kenneth Kaunda of Zambia succeeded in a plea of clemency to Saddam Hussein.

The announcement of Farzad's death sentence created an international outcry. Several Arab governments tried to intercede for him privately, though they supported Saddam Hussein in public. The press in the Arab world was almost unanimous in supporting an Arab government against a Western journalist. The Kuwaiti press, always a rather low-grade collection of newspapers, was particularly strong in its condemnation. One paper announced that Farzad had been working for an air strike against Iraqi military installations.

It is possible that Saddam Hussein might have spared him if the British had been conciliatory; Saddam often liked to make grand gestures, and show mercy. But he was wary of taking any action that could be interpreted as weakness, and the British tabloid press – which received no encouragement from the British government, though Saddam Hussein could never understand that – made any calm or rational outcome impossible. The *Sun*, the *Daily Mail*, the *Daily Express* and the *Daily Mirror* seemed to vie with one another in inventing new insults to scream at 'The Butcher of Baghdad', a man whose very existence they had scarcely noticed when he was carrying out far worse butchery.

The Foreign Office in London tried at first to point out that no one told the British press what to say; but this meant nothing to a man who believed that the only reason for a newspaper's existence was to say what political leaders wanted. Soon, anyway, the British government adopted the same angry tone. Mrs Thatcher herself had an instinct for the confrontational, and she was as wary of laying herself open to accusations of weakness as Saddam Hussein was. She quickly took the lead in demanding Farzad's release.

The decision to condemn Farzad to death was, everyone knew, Saddam's alone; so it was a personal insult when Mrs Thatcher called it 'an act of barbarism deeply repugnant to all civilized people'.

'I have no doubt in my mind,' said President Kaunda after Daphne Parish had been released at his instigation and had been flown to Zambia, 'that if it had not been for that vicious attack on him and on Iraq by the British authorities and press, that man might have lived, might have been here with Daphne together.'

The blame for Farzad's judicial murder belongs in the first place with Saddam, of course; but the British press and the British government bear a great deal of responsibility too. Iraq's angry anti-Western approach had until now been little more than rhetoric. But from the moment of Farzad's trial and sentencing, Saddam Hussein was on a collision course with the West; and he was encouraged in that by a surprising range of Arab countries which ought to have known better.

On 15 March 1990, five days after the 'trial', the number two at the British embassy, Robin Kealy, was summoned to the Abu Gharaib prison outside Baghdad. It was an appalling place, the worst of Saddam Hussein's political prisons. Tens of thousands of people were tortured and executed there during his years in power, and the executioners were on duty round the clock. Kealy was told that Farzad would be hanged that morning.

A thoughtful, sensitive man, he told me in detail a month later about what had happened. The memory of it still weighed heavily on him. He was shown into the governor's office, where Farzad was waiting, unshaven and looking thin and ill in a dirty white *dishdasha* which the prison had given him.

He started talking anxiously to Kealy about his hope that Saddam would listen to the international appeals to free him. Naïve as ever, he even seemed to think he might be given the chance to put his case to Saddam Hussein in person. Kealy, listening to all this, realized that although the room was full of Iraqi officials none of them had explained to Farzad that directly this meeting was over he would be taken out and hanged.

Kealy told him as best he could. Farzad took the news reasonably well. He asked Kealy to send his love to his parents, his sister and brothers, and to the girlfriend with whom he had broken up shortly before leaving for Baghdad the previous September. He remembered Daphne Parish, too: 'Tell Dee I'm sorry.' He denied once again that he was a spy, or that his confession had been genuine. He asked for forgiveness from anyone he had ever hurt, and he gave Kealy one last message: 'I hope the world will decide, after I'm gone, what kind of person I have really been.'

The meeting was over, and Kealy was told to leave. They took Farzad out a minute or two later and hanged him.

I travelled to Baghdad for the first time soon after the execution. While I was there I interviewed Nizar Hamdoun, the deputy foreign minister. Much of our interview centred on the execution of Farzad Bazoft, and both of us grew heated. Hamdoun insisted again and again that Farzad had been a spy, and that the decision to execute him had been correct and just.

Afterwards, when the camera had been switched off, I could see he wanted to say something else to me. I sat and waited in silence for him to speak.

'It's strange and very sad to think that Farzad Bazoft was sitting exactly where you are, only a few months ago.' His voice was very quiet. 'He came to ask me if I would help him get to the al-Hilla site, where the explosion had been. He said the Ministry of Information was useless – that they kept promising that they would take him, and then never did. And then, of course, after he went to al-Hilla he was arrested.'

I sat forward.

'You mean to say you knew in advance that he wanted to go there?'

Hamdoun nodded and looked down at his folded hands.

'Then he told me he was planning to go by himself if he couldn't get anyone from the ministry to go with him.'

'But you've just been telling me he was a spy. What kind of spy is it that tells a government minister and the Ministry of Information beforehand that he's going spying?'

Hamdoun made no answer. Some days later the British embassy told me that Farzad had tried to have Hamdoun called as a witness at his trial. He did not appear, of course. To have tried to intercede on behalf of someone Saddam Hussein had decided was a spy would have been suicidal. But I felt that Nizar Hamdoun, who was a weak rather than an evil man, somehow wanted forgiveness from me for his cowardice.

Some months later I spoke to another senior Iraqi official about the case; I felt I owed it to Farzad's memory to bring his name up when I talked to anyone in Saddam's government.

'If I'd been here when Farzad was,' I said aggressively, 'I would certainly have gone down to al-Hilla and tried to find out about the explosion. Would you have hanged me too?'

The official shook his head.

'You are British. You would have got ten or fifteen years and been released quietly later. He was Iranian. It's as simple as that.'

At his last meeting with Robin Kealy, minutes before his execution, Farzad had asked that his body should be brought back to England, his adopted country, and buried in Highgate Cemetery. To the very end the insults were still passing back and forth between London and Baghdad.

'Mrs Thatcher wanted him alive,' Saddam's minister of information gloated. 'We gave her the body.'

Farzad lies now in a well-tended grave not far from the massive tomb of Karl Marx. At his funeral, when the coffin had been lowered into the grave, his brother spoke briefly and movingly.

'Remember him as a happy man. Now let him rest in peace.'

No one said he had died because he was not a European.

20. CONFRONTATION

The execution of Farzad Bazoft did not create the confrontation between Saddam Hussein and the West, but it ensured that there was no going back now. Saddam himself saw it, not as a Western response to his own savagery, but as a sign that Britain, like the United States, had decided to turn against him.

'To a mind like Saddam's,' said a perceptive American diplomat in Baghdad at the time, 'everything forms a pattern.'

The pattern had certainly changed. Britain, like France and West Germany, had always been prepared to put financial and trade considerations before moral ones in dealing with Iraq. Suddenly, for the sake of a man who wasn't even British, the entire atmosphere was different. In Saddam Hussein's mind, there had to be something behind it.

Britain bulks large in the Iraqi mind. As the country which effectively ran Iraq until 1958, it is generally seen as having a powerful behind-the-scenes influence. Most Iraqis believe that Britain, the old imperial fox, supplies the knowledge of Arab affairs which America, in their view, conspicuously lacks. To intelligent, supple-minded people who have known nothing but colonialism for centuries, the world seems to work through the pulling of hidden strings. Nothing can be merely what it seems.

The Farzad Bazoft affair came just at the moment when Saddam was starting to exercise the new power which his 'victory' over Iran had given him. Yet Iraq was in financial difficulties, and had been obliged to stall its creditors and mortgage its oil revenues. The Soviet Union, Iraq's chief weapons supplier over the decades, was in a state of collapse. The day before Farzad's execution a leading Russian diplomat, Alexander Golytsin, even declared that human rights rather than strategic issues would be taken into consideration in future dealings with Iraq. Saddam realized he would have to look elsewhere for his weapons; characteristically, he looked for a short cut.

On 28 March 1990, with the bitterness over the execution of Farzad Bazoft still at its height, a joint operation by the American and British Customs trapped a group of Iraqis who were trying to smuggle forty American-made capacitors – high-voltage electrical triggers for detonating nuclear weapons – into Iraq. It may not have been a coincidence. There were signs that the British authorities were hoping to exchange the arrested Iraqis for Daphne Parish. The operation had come too late to save Farzad.

Two weeks later, British Customs seized some high-precision steel pipes made by the British company Sheffield Forgemasters. They were intended for assembly into a long-range weapon designed by a Canadian, Dr Gerald Bull, and christened 'the super-gun' by the British press. At first there was reluctance to believe in such a thing, and the super-gun became the subject of endless jokes in the British and European press.

Yet in the days and weeks which followed, more parts for the gun were discovered in other countries, and its ability to fire large projectiles for great distances – for instance from Baghdad to Tel Aviv – became better known. It was also discovered that Dr Bull had been murdered in a Brussels hotel on 22 March, though at the time his death had been ignored by the international press. Israeli intelligence was instantly blamed, though later it was suggested that the Iraqis themselves might have killed him, either to ensure his silence or to punish him for having tipped off the British about the super-gun plan.

Saddam Hussein certainly wanted to give the impression that he was building an elaborate arsenal of sophisticated weapons. In December 1989 Iraq had announced the launch of a three-stage rocket capable of putting a satellite into space, and said it had successfully tested missiles with a range of 1,200 miles. There was much scepticism about these things, and the scepticism proved to be justified. Nevertheless Israel was particularly worried about Iraq's potential nuclear capability, and tried to convince the United States that this was a real threat. The newspapers in both countries carried reports that Iraq was again close to producing its own nuclear weapons. The Osirak raid of 1981, when Israeli planes had bombed the main Iraqi nuclear plant, had delayed Iraq's nuclear programme rather than stopped it, the articles said.

In fact, the anxieties were groundless. Iraq did not have nuclear weapons in 1990 or 1991, though its nuclear research programmes were well advanced thanks to expertise from France, Germany, Argentina and Brazil. Saddam Hussein himself had indicated his desire for these weapons in a rambling speech made soon after he came to power formally in 1979:

> I do not believe nuclear weapons can be used for peaceful, scientific purposes in an underdeveloped, Bedouin society ... I think that if you ask any person in the world whether he would like to possess a nuclear bomb, he will tell you that he would.

By 1990, though, Saddam's speeches suggested that he had decided to counter Israel's own suspected nuclear capability with 'the poor man's H-bomb', chemical weapons. On 2 April 1990 he told the General Command of the Iraqi armed forces:

> The West is deluding itself if it imagines it can protect Israel if Israel comes and strikes at some metal industry factory of ours. By God, we will devour half of Israel by fire if it tries to do anything against Iraq.

And he added:

> [Foreign agents] used to come every day to ask us, 'Don't you want enriched uranium to make an atomic bomb?' We used to say, 'Leave us alone, keep your evil away from us and take your bags with you ...' We do not need an atomic bomb, because we have sophisticated binary chemical weapons.

The fact is, Saddam Hussein often spoke on these occasions without notes, and he never needed to clear what he said with anyone else, or worry about the responses either of his administration or of Iraqi public opinion. Much of what he said was simply hot air; yet it was hot air which tended to flow in one particular direction, and that was what made his enemies deeply uncomfortable. His basic strategy was to talk up Iraq's potential: there was no need for specifics. Perhaps he believed that if Iraq behaved with the self-confidence of a regional superpower, the reality would follow.

An important element in that self-confidence was Iraq's determination to stand up publicly to the United States and its allies. Saddam knew how well this went down in large parts of the Arab world. Several Arab countries – Jordan, Tunisia and Algeria, among others – were going through a phase of increased democracy, and there was greater support for Saddam Hussein there and in other countries than many Arab governments liked. To challenge the political power of the West and rail against the spread of its culture was proving disturbingly popular in what Western politicians and journalists were already learning to refer to as 'the Arab street'.

At the same time, the United States and Britain were employing a remarkable set of double standards in dealing with Iraq. On the one hand they both regarded Saddam Hussein as a potential threat, but neither of them wanted to see the lucrative contracts which Iraq offered going to other countries. There were moves in both the House of Commons and the US Senate to introduce trade sanctions against Iraq, but the British and American governments did not support them.

On 12 April 1990 Senator Robert Dole and four other American senators met Saddam Hussein at his palace in the northern city of Mosul. They were well aware of the danger represented by Saddam's weapons of mass destruction and his growing hostility, yet at the same time at least two of them seem to have been deeply interested in further profitable grain contracts with Iraq. The transcript of the meeting, which was leaked by the Iraqis, is embarrassing to read. It starts with an exchange in which Senator Dole expresses himself so confusedly that Saddam can scarcely have understood the real state of affairs.

> *President Saddam Hussein:* Daily the Arabs hear scorn directed at them from the West, daily they bear insults. Why? Has the Zionist mentality taken control of you to the point that it has deprived you of your humanity? . . .
>
> *Senator Dole:* There are fundamental differences between our countries. We have free media in the US . . . There is a person

who did not have the authority to say anything about . . .
[your] government. He was a commentator for the VOA (the
Voice of America, which represents the government only) and
this person was removed from it. Please allow me to say that
only twelve hours earlier President Bush had assured me that
he wants better relations, and that the US government wants
better relations with Iraq. We believe – and we are leaders in
the US Congress – that the Congress also does not represent
Bush or the government. I assume that President Bush will
oppose sanctions, and he might veto them, unless something
provocative were to happen, or something of that sort.

After that Senator Alan Simpson spoke. There was a heavy bonhomie
about him which came close to grovelling.

Senator Simpson: I enjoy meeting candid and open people. This
is a trademark of those of us who live in the 'Wild West' . . .
Democracy is a very confusing issue. I believe that your
problems lie with the Western media and not with the US
government. As long as you are isolated from the media, the
press – and it is a haughty and pampered press, they all
consider themselves political geniuses, that is the journalists
do, they are very cynical – what I advise is that you invite
them to come here and see for themselves.

President Saddam Hussein: They are welcome . . . I wonder,
as you may wonder, if governments, for example the US
government, were not behind such reports. How else could all
of this [negative reporting of Iraq] have occurred in such a
short period of time?

Senator Simpson: It's very easy . . . They all live off one another.
Everyone takes from the other. When there is a major news
item on the front page of the *New York Times*, another
journalist takes it and publishes it.

After this lesson in practical democracy, Saddam Hussein can have
been convinced of only one thing: that nothing much mattered to
people like Senator Simpson except the money which valuable contracts brought. He will certainly have noticed that according to the
official transcript there was no mention at any time of the execution of
Farzad Bazoft, which had happened less than a month before.

Britain was no better at speaking to Iraq with a single voice. Six months after calling in the Iraqi ambassador to the Foreign Office to receive the strongest complaint about the chemical attack on Halabjah (according to someone present, the ambassador said in some surprise, 'But they were *our* people'), Britain doubled the trade credits it was making available to Iraq. When Farzad was executed the British ambassador was recalled, and six Iraqis on courses with the Ministry of Defence were sent home. That was all. No economic sanctions, no severing of diplomatic relations. Iraq was too valuable a market for Britain to relinquish.

The United States and Britain were prepared to put up with almost anything Saddam Hussein did, and France, Germany and Italy were happy to sell him the most dangerous technology. Not surprisingly, he was deeply contemptuous of the Western democracies.

'Western governments are only interested in money,' he said in one of his interviews with foreign television companies in the run-up to the Gulf War. 'Everything else is just a slogan.'

When, finally, the Western democracies were serious, he found it hard to believe them.

21. FEAR AND ANGER

I tried to visit Baghdad while Farzad was still a prisoner. Perhaps it was from a sense of solidarity, though I think it was probably just guilt: if I had been more helpful to him, maybe his life wouldn't have taken that particular turning. It didn't matter anyway, because my application was rejected. Saddam Hussein's regime did not want foreign journalists in town at a time like that.

Soon after his execution, I started agitating for a visa again. It finally came through at the start of May, so that I could report on a big international conference of militant Muslims which was to be held in Baghdad to show support for Saddam Hussein in his growing confrontation with the West. It was the first time since the execution that any foreign journalists had been allowed into the country.

By now, clearly, Saddam was committed to his oppositional course.

There were daily demonstrations outside the British and American embassies, protesting about the alliance which, the Iraqi government said, the two countries had struck with Israel against Iraq. As we drove up to the British embassy on the first morning after our arrival, we met the Association of Arab Lawyers marching in the same direction: neat gentlemen in lightweight suits and striped ties, who stopped politely at the embassy gate and handed in a message of complaint.

'In our view,' their spokesman told me in excellent English, 'it is a violation of human rights for Britain to withhold the technology Iraq requires for its development.'

'Oh,' I said, 'what technology is that?'

'The technology to defend ourselves,' answered the spokesman, a trifle uncomfortably.

He was referring to the barrels for the super-gun, which Iraq denied had any military application whatever, and to the capacitors for making a nuclear weapon. At this stage I still thought it was entertaining to force these spokesmen – every conceivable group of professional people had one; it was part of democracy Saddam-style – to explain what they really meant. It was only when I spent more time in Baghdad that I began to realize that the people I was goading were probably as opposed to what was going on as I was; and that they said these things as a matter of sheer self-defence. A failure to sound enthusiastic and confident in contributing a sound-bite in Saddam's defence would have meant a death sentence. Not being interested in blood-sports, I no longer tried to make life difficult for them once I had finally grasped that fairly obvious fact. Instead, I would record what they had to say and leave it there.

That evening our television report was halted while it was being satellited to London, and we were forced to take out a reference I had made in the commentary to the fact that we were being followed everywhere we went. I thought I had been quite mild towards Iraqi security: I didn't mention that when our engineer tried to fix up the telephone for me to transmit a radio report to London from my room in the Ishtar Sheraton Hotel he had found ten different wires in the socket: six of them at least must have gone to different security organizations.

The Ministry of Information minder who went everywhere with us was a nervous little man with a moustache disproportionately large for his small, rodent-like face. He confided to me that he had worked with Farzad Bazoft.

'He was a very bad man who caused a lot of problems.'

'Well, he was a really good friend of mine,' I answered irritably, exaggerating a little for effect.

This made him intensely anxious. His gaze darted in every direction, and he developed the nervous tic of wiping his big moustache as though he had just drunk a pint of beer and was afraid it might have attracted some foam. He kept asking me what we wanted to do next, and to tease him I invented more and more unlikely and dangerous tasks. Poor Ali: he too was just trying to make it through a dangerous life without making waves.

Fear was everywhere. It hung over the city like the stench of burning rubber, so thick you could see it, feel it, breathe it, taste it. When we went to the bazaar to film, nobody would look at us. It wasn't just that they wouldn't meet our eyes; they would look straight through us, as though we didn't exist. For a television crew, the biggest problem in an Arab street is usually the huge crowds that collect, watching you. Not here. We wandered round in a little *cordon sanitaire*, which moved around with us. There was never any danger that someone might bump into us and perhaps have to apologize.

No one tried to get into conversation with us, or ask us where we were from, or offer us goods for sale. We weren't there; we had no objective reality. Everyone knew now that Western journalists weren't just dangerous, they were spies for Israel. It made me feel like the carrier of some unpleasantly conspicuous disease.

Some people wanted to be with us, though. Wherever we went, four or five men would be slouching behind us. They stopped when we stopped, and moved on when we moved on. They didn't meet our eyes either. I assumed we were supposed to know they were there because they never troubled to hide themselves. Even when I went out of the hotel for a walk on my own they were all there. I felt like someone in a Greek play with a Chorus of masked performers sticking close to me so they could comment on my every act.

We came to recognize them all, and waved hello to them in the mornings. That too was a form of cruelty, I suppose, but in their case I didn't feel any guilt. In the hotel lobby, in the street, they were always there. In the privacy of our hotel rooms we could sense their presence.

Sometimes our sheer untouchability worked to our advantage. When we went to the big new conference centre where Saddam Hussein's international Muslim solidarity rally was to be held, we set up our camera in the entrance to film the delegates as they streamed in. The security men were appalled, but no one wanted to speak to us and tell us to clear out. They just watched us instead.

The delegates came streaming up towards the main hall, and we stopped them one by one to ask their views. Algerians, Palestinians, Egyptians, Sudanese, Pakistanis, Malaysians, even some from Western Europe: they all believed the same thing, and told us so.

'The West is trying to punish Iraq, because it has dared to raise its head.'

'The West doesn't want an Islamic, Arab country to be strong. It will do anything to stop it.'

'I am a Maronite Christian from Lebanon, but I want to say I support Iraq in its struggle.'

'Saddam Hussein is fighting a battle for us all. He is doing what every Muslim nation should do: stand up for itself, and attack Zionism. And of course he is suffering for it as a result.'

Some of the delegates were hostile to us, but most were rational and pleasant enough. They had been electrified by Saddam Hussein's threat that if Israel attacked Iraq he would burn half of Israel. This stand of his, in particular, had had a liberating effect on them: someone, at last, was saying the things they had always wanted a political leader to say.

'He is the new Nasser,' said an old, bent figure in spotless white, stopping in front of our camera and leaning on his carved walking-stick as he talked. 'You will see. They destroyed Nasser, but they will not be able to destroy Saddam.'

He flourished his stick at us jovially, and hobbled off into the conference.

When Saddam himself appeared, we were not allowed to be present. We had to watch what happened on Iraqi television, with its awkward moves and its unwillingness to glance away even momentarily from the great man to his audience. Perhaps that would have been an act of disloyalty, but to us it was merely irritating and meant we had no cutaway shots.

Saddam's speech was a bravura performance. He was always an instinctive actor, who enjoyed performing for an audience. Understanding instinctively the emotions the people in his audience felt, he played directly to them, encouraging their anger and their resentment but also making them laugh uproariously. I felt a new respect for the man as I watched him. He might be a gangster and a brute, but he was much more as well.

He roused them to a pitch of anger by talking to them about the campaign against him in Britain and the United States. He went through the elements of this latest campaign, as he saw it: beginning with Farzad Bazoft, as though that was somehow an injury to Iraq, and finishing up with the seizure of the various parts for weapons which Iraq wanted.

Then there was a moment of pure theatre which brought the audience to its feet, clapping, laughing and cheering.

'You see this?' He held a small metal object high in the air. 'This is what they're making all the fuss about. It's one of these things they call a capacitor. [Great applause.] It looks rather like a lighter. [Loud laughter.] They say it can be used for an atomic bomb. [Appreciative noises, some stamping and applause.] This is the American capacitor that they say America has imported. [A pause: no one quite knows whether to cheer or boo.] And this [holding up another smallish object high in the air] – this is one that was made by our students at the technical university in only five days. This is the American one, and this is ours.'

To a storm of laughter and cheering, the imposing, uniformed figure on the platform held the two objects high in the air for them to see. No matter that a nuclear capacitor looked nothing like a cigarette lighter, or that it was way beyond the abilities of a group of students at a Third World technical university to knock one up in five days or in five years; what he was telling his audience was that Iraq and the Muslim world were potentially on a par with the West. All you had to do was to stand up for yourself and not be intimidated.

His speech was, I came to realize, entirely characteristic of the man. It was full of unspecific threats, get-out clauses, non sequiturs, unjustified boasts and claims, empty promises that sounded impressive, mutually exclusive pronouncements. He denied that Iraq had nuclear weapons. He denied that he wanted them. Yet everyone in the hall had the strong impression that he was determined to have them and that Iraq would make them itself if it couldn't get them any other way. A masterful performance, then, with no discernible substance in it.

He spoke for more than two hours altogether.

'We don't like talking too much,' he said with manifest lack of sincerity, 'and we don't want to fight anyone else. But when there's no choice but to lose our Arab land and our rights, then we must fight.'

That brought the loudest cheers of the entire afternoon, of course.

His rhetoric built him up as a champion with the courage to take on the Western powers, but he was already showing signs of going farther than he wanted. This kind of support required a mood of confrontation, and could not do without it. If the mood relaxed, the support would wane and he would be vulnerable. The tension had to be continually wound up, or he was lost. He had become the prisoner of the easy laugh, the vague promise, the uncritical standing ovation; but the time would come when he would have to show some results for all this.

We stayed in Baghdad for a week. We worked hard, and gathered some interesting pictures to take back with us to London and produce a good, if short, documentary on Saddam's growing hostility to the West. Then I made a mistake. I was interviewed from London about the mood in the streets of Baghdad – a phrase I came later to detest for its emptiness – and allowed myself to talk about the surveillance and control which we saw all round us. That too was censored, of course.

'You have been doing bad things,' someone from the Ministry of Information said.

We submitted all our video-cassettes to the Ministry for vetting. The process took a long time, but we were assured it was just an administrative delay. In the end – another serious mistake – we agreed that the rest of the team should leave on the appointed day, and that the producer, whose name was Eamonn Matthews, should stay for another day in order to argue for the release of our pictures. He would catch the following day's plane.

But he wasn't on it. Instead, he rang to say there were problems.

I could hear the tension in his voice. He had realized there was no chance of getting the cassettes out, and had gone to the airport to catch the flight he was booked on. The Mukhabarat had picked him up in the departure lounge, just as they had picked up Farzad Bazoft, and they had taken him to the same small interview room just off it. After some hours of questioning he had been taken to an hotel – different from the big international one where we had stayed. As he was walking into this hotel with his Mukhabarat escort, another group of security men brought out a businessman who travelled on a Swedish passport but was Iraqi by birth. He had been arrested for black-marketeering and was later executed.

The following morning Eamonn was taken back to the airport and interrogated again. They didn't use violence on him but they treated him roughly and were very threatening. They found he had $100 less than he could account for: a minor offence which they were capable of building up into the kind of case they had against the Iraqi Swede. Then, without explanation, they allowed him to board a plane to London. When he arrived, eight hours later, he was still showing obvious signs of the strain he had been under.

We had lost all our cassettes: not just the mildly surreptitious filming we had done in the streets, but the long interviews with impeccably pro-Saddam delegates to the conference, and the full rushes of the interview I had recorded with the Iraqi deputy foreign minister, Nizar Hamdoun. I decided it would be a very long time before I would go back to Iraq. The whole experience had been a great deal too close for comfort.

22. TARGETING KUWAIT

As I was sitting in the coffee shop at the Baghdad Sheraton a few days earlier there was an announcement over the hotel intercom. The people around me, mostly delegates to the Islamic conference, broke into spontaneous applause. What was it, I asked someone sitting nearby. He told me that Saudi Arabia had just announced it would attend the forthcoming meeting of the Arab League which Saddam Hussein had volunteered to host in Baghdad. It seemed to be a clear diplomatic victory for Iraq.

The ostensible purpose of the summit was to condemn the large-scale immigration of Russian Jews to Israel after the collapse of the Berlin Wall. Saddam, however, planned to use the meeting as part of his diplomatic counter-attack against the international conspiracy he believed was building up against him. According to him this consisted of the US, Britain, Israel and the Gulf states, and the aim was to sabotage the Iraqi economy.

In January 1990 Iraq had announced publicly that it would devote $9 billion to reconstruction that year, and between $4 and $5 billion to repaying the debts incurred as a result of the war with Iran. Then the oil price began dropping alarmingly. Kuwait and the United Arab Emirates, both of them closely involved with the United States and Britain, had suddenly begun producing much more than their quotas.

It was a disaster for Iraq. Eight years of war against Iran had done serious damage to the country's economy. In 1989, the first full year after the war had ended, Iraq's earnings from oil were $13 billion. Its expenditure was approximately $24 billion, and its foreign debt was $80 billion. Western economists estimated that even if the entire national oil income were devoted to the task of reconstruction, it would take twenty years to achieve. The war which Saddam had launched on the assumption it would last four or five days now seemed likely to wreck Iraq's entire future.

In 1990, Iraq would not even have enough to import its basic requirements. Saddam's view that the Iraqi economy was being deliberately undermined no longer seemed so outlandish and impossible. The real purpose of the Arab League's Baghdad summit would be to recruit support for Saddam's case, and to put pressure on Kuwait and the UAE to reduce their output.

There was indeed an attempt by Britain and the United States to clip Iraq's wings in this way, though both countries denied it strongly at the time. The problem with Iraq was its oil wealth, which meant that it could exert real influence as a major regional military power. Cut its oil money, and you cut its effectiveness. Nevertheless the United States sent a message to Saddam via its ambassador in Baghdad, April Glaspie, asking him politely to avoid insulting attacks on American policy during the summit. Characteristically, Saddam announced publicly that the Americans had made their request – and then proceeded to attack American policy more loudly than ever. He was by no means isolated.

King Hussein of Jordan was not a fan of Saddam Hussein. He disliked him personally, and had often opposed Iraqi policy in the past. Now, though, there was no real alternative for Jordan except to back Saddam Hussein: something neither the Bush administration nor American public opinion ever seemed able to understand. As the leader of a country with aspirations to becoming a democracy, King Hussein could not refuse to listen to public opinion; and that was heavily in favour of Saddam Hussein and Iraq.

There were other major considerations. Virtually all Jordan's oil came from Iraq at preferential rates, and King Hussein could not afford to lose those supplies. It was also likely that if Israel attacked Iraq, it would do so through Jordanian territory. On both counts, supporting Iraq was a necessary self-protection for Jordan. So when the Baghdad summit opened in May, King Hussein criticized the West for what he called its anti-Iraqi campaign, and he aligned himself firmly with those countries which supported Iraq.

The Palestine Liberation Organization also gave strong backing to Saddam. This was partly a matter of gut instinct on the part of the PLO leadership, and partly policy: it had recently made some concessions to Israel, and was anxious not to be isolated as a result. The stronger the PLO's support for Iraq, the better its defence against criticism from other Arab countries.

When the summit opened, Saddam Hussein, as its host, was able to provide the invective against Israel because that suited the mood of all the delegates. But as chairman of the conference he was obliged to remain quiet about the issue of his own dispute with the United States and other Western countries, since that was highly contentious as far as the pro-Western leaders around the table were concerned.

And so King Hussein took on the role of Iraq's defender. He challenged the Gulf states to help both Iraq and Jordan, now that they were in his estimation facing a serious danger from Israel. The leaders of the Gulf states sat stony-faced and embarrassed, and said nothing. Saddam himself eventually broke cover and joined in. He did not mention that Kuwait had depressed oil prices through its over-production, nor that it had increased its own income by 50 per cent,

nor that it was refusing to offer any help to Iraq; but everyone around
the table understood exactly what he was saying.

'Wars can be started by armies,' Saddam said in his final statement
to the conference, 'and great damage is done through bombing,
through killing, or by attempted coups. But at other times a war can
be launched by economic means. To those countries which do not
really intend to wage war against Iraq, I have to say that this is itself a
kind of war against Iraq.'

Saddam, always intensely sensitive to any disloyalty, believed that
Kuwait had betrayed him personally. He had long since maintained,
and perhaps actually believed, that he had fought his war against
Shi'ite Iran in order to protect countries like Kuwait, with its large
Shi'ite population, against subversion by Iran's brand of fundamentalism. And now this was the thanks he got. Iraq had paid dearly for its
victory over Shi'ism and Islamic extremism, and yet Kuwait was trying
to beggar the country which had saved it.

The dispute continued throughout June, as Iraq waited for Kuwait
to make some offer of help. None came. The Emir, having supported
Iraq during the war itself, was now more concerned with patching up
relations with Iran. Knowing he had the support of Saudi Arabia, the
United States and Britain, he showed no sign of giving in.

In June 1990 Saddam Hussein made his demands specific. Kuwait
should be asked to provide an amount equivalent to the income from
the oil wells at Ratga, the Kuwaiti end of the large Rumailah oilfield
which straddled the border between Iraq and Kuwait. Saddam maintained that the oil from Ratga had been stolen by Kuwait, since by
historic right the entire area belonged to Iraq.

Characteristically, he had done nothing to prepare the ground for
such a claim. The Kuwaiti finance minister was able to point out later
that his country had been taking an average of 10,000 barrels of oil a
day from Ratga for the previous twelve years, and Iraq had never
complained or made any kind of claim to it.

Day by day, hour by hour, Saddam Hussein was making up his
strategy as he went along. Now, the Ratga claim marked a major new
stage in a growing crisis. If Kuwait still refused to give financial help
to Iraq, Saddam Hussein's next logical step (whether he yet realized it
or not) would be to claim land in lieu of money.

On 9 July Iraqi intelligence intercepted a telephone call between

King Fahd of Saudi Arabia and the ruler of Qatar, about the increase in Kuwait's oil production and the damage it was doing to Iraq. The King seemed almost amused by it, and hinted that Saddam Hussein might well experience some internal problems as a result. This, almost certainly, would have been the American and British intention in encouraging Kuwait in its course of action. When Saddam Hussein later made the text of the phone conversation public, he declared that the aim of the Kuwaiti move was to 'disturb the relationship existing between the [Iraqi] people and their leadership'.

Saddam was furious. He instructed his foreign minister, Tariq Aziz, to draw up a specific claim for the loss Iraq had supposedly incurred as a result of Kuwait's increased production. On 16 July Aziz announced that Kuwait's strategy had begun as early as 1981, though he produced no serious evidence for this, and had cost the Arab oil-producing countries $500 billion. He followed this vague claim with a specific one: the proportion of the loss which Iraq had incurred was, he said, $89 billion.

At this stage Iraq's demands from Kuwait were based entirely on the supposed obligations deriving from the war against Iran. Very late on, and with no preparation or forethought, Iraq's old claim that Kuwait should be an Iraqi province was resuscitated, to bolster the wider case. The official handbook *Iraq 1990*, for instance, carried no mention of Iraq's claim to Kuwait, even though great care had obviously gone into researching the historical section. Indeed, the only mention of Kuwait was in the list of independent states which bordered Iraq.

But the handbook had been produced in 1989. In July 1990, with evident signs of haste and carelessness, the Ministry of Information in Baghdad produced a booklet called *Kuwait – Historical Background*, which sought to demonstrate that Kuwait had always been an integral part of Iraq. There had been no time to proof-read the text, which was rambling and inconsequential. The argument, such as it was, was that Turkey had governed Kuwait as part of the rest of what later became Iraq:

In 1876, Major Bride and the British Commissioner said that Kuwait, Qatif and Aqir were Turkish ports on the Gulf.

In 1911, the Ottoman Government honoured Mubarak [al-Sabah, the ruler of Kuwait] with the Majidi medal of the first class.

Moving from one vague assertion to another, missing out points which might have suited Iraq's case better, the booklet then settled down to the easier and more congenial task of attacking the al-Sabahs for their subservience to British interests over the years. Under the heading 'Aggressive Attitudes that Harm Iraqis and the Arabs' it lists the following:

> Mubarak al-Sabah also sent a telegram to the British Government congratulating her [sic] on the advance of British troops on Baghdad in 1917.

To justify an action which would lead to hundreds of thousands of deaths and uproot millions before it was finally over, Saddam Hussein's regime could produce only a medal and a telegram.

Ever since its creation by the British after the First World War, Iraq had always had the feeling – it was rarely much more than that – that Kuwait should have been included in its territory. It was not equivalent to the conviction that lies behind Spain's claim to Gibraltar, or Argentina's to the Falkland Islands, or Jordan's to Jerusalem and the West Bank. But it was there. In fact, Iraq was the victim of the British strategic habit of encouraging the creation of small, independent but malleable states at the mouths of great rivers: it was British influence which brought Belgium into being on the banks of the Rhine, and Uruguay beside the River Plate. Kuwait, at the mouth of the Shatt al-Arab, was part of the same imperial instinct.

In 1961, faced with internal problems, President Qassem of Iraq – the man Saddam Hussein tried to murder – talked angrily about invading Kuwait but was dissuaded by the quick dispatch of British Royal Marines.

Saddam Hussein had never publicly questioned Kuwait's sovereignty; in fact, in an interview in November 1979, he had promised to position Iraqi forces 'against any threat aimed at Bahraini or Kuwaiti sovereignty'. The haste and inattention to detail had all the hallmarks of something done on the spur of the moment: a dictator's whim.

As best one can tell from the evidence, Saddam Hussein had no real thought of invading Kuwait until he came to write his speech for the anniversary of the Ba'athist seizure of power on 17 July 1990. When he appeared on television he took Tariq Aziz's argument of the previous day one crucial stage forward. Iraq would not, he said, put up much longer with this conspiracy between Kuwait on the one hand and imperialism and Zionism on the other. It would be better to be dead than to lose the means of earning a living. Then he made the critical threat:

> If words do not give us sufficient protection, then we will have no option but to take effective action to put things right and ensure that our rights are restored.

This was the first time Saddam or his ministers had made mention of any possible action. Yet even then he does not seem to have envisaged a full-scale invasion of Kuwait. He must have hoped that his vague threat would be enough to make the Kuwaiti Emir give in and agree to help Iraq with its serious economic problems; failing that, it could persuade the other Middle Eastern oil producers to fix a price that would be more favourable for Iraq.

Yet it looks as though an idea was forming in his mind. He could seize Ratga and the rest of the Rumailah oilfield which lay within Kuwait, and send his troops to occupy the northernmost third of the country down to the line of the Mutla Ridge. Perhaps, too, he would take the opportunity of putting his forces onto the islands of Warba and Bubiyan, which Iraq had long claimed. There is no indication whatever that he was thinking at this stage of occupying Kuwait City and the country as a whole.

The Kuwaitis and their backers in Saudi Arabia examined the unspecific threat of action, and decided that it would not be a good moment to try to do a deal with Saddam Hussein; this would look like weakness on Kuwait's part, and Saddam would be able to drive too hard a bargain. With the arrogance for which Kuwaitis have long been famous, the government wrote to the secretary-general of the Arab League rejecting Saddam Hussein's demand:

> The sons of Kuwait, in good times as in bad, are men of principle and integrity. They will not yield to threats or extortion under any circumstances.

This left Saddam with only two options: to back down and accept that he would not get any help from Kuwait, or to press ahead. Everything in his psychology must have urged him to keep going. He was an inveterate political gambler, whose response to every challenge was to raise the stakes. He raised them now. On 21 July he ordered his troops to the border.

Neither Washington nor London took this particularly seriously. They thought they knew what it was all about: influencing the OPEC meeting in Geneva on 27 July. Iraq would use the threat of violence and disruption to win agreement for a higher benchmark price for oil. And indeed when the meeting opened Iraq proposed that the benchmark should be raised from the current level of $18, to which it had been brought by Kuwait's actions, to $25. There were long hours of negotiation, and in the end a compromise was reached: $21, the highest level Saudi Arabia would accept, and a production limit of 22.5 million barrels a day. The crisis appeared to be over. Saddam had got what everyone assumed he had been after all along.

But that ignored his gambling instinct. American satellite pictures showed that the 20,000 troops Saddam had sent to the Kuwaiti border were still there, and had even been reinforced. A higher oil price had clearly not been enough to satisfy Saddam. He wanted redress for the insult which, he maintained, Kuwait had offered him, and only one redress would do: Kuwait must pay the full amount which Tariq Aziz had claimed it owed Iraq.

Saddam Hussein was further encouraged in his hard line by a meeting he had had with the American ambassador to Iraq, April Glaspie, two days before the OPEC meeting. She had been posted to Baghdad two years earlier, but this was the first meeting she had had with Saddam on her own; his usual practice was to harangue foreign diplomats in groups.

Their meeting became part of the folklore of the crisis. In the United States, after the invasion of Kuwait, there was a considerable desire to find someone to blame, and many newspapers and politicians decided that Ms Glaspie had failed to explain fully enough to Saddam the consequences of invading Kuwait. The State Department, perhaps insecure about its entire performance during the crisis, did little to support her.

Ms Glaspie's performance certainly seemed weak and ineffectual, when the transcript of their meeting was made available. She, like the American senators who had gone to see him earlier, seemed anxious to placate Saddam by criticizing reaction to Iraq in the United States. She did not give the impression she was speaking with the full force of

American diplomatic and military power behind her; on the contrary, she was more than a little apologetic.

Yet there were two points in Ms Glaspie's defence which were not made when the matter was heatedly debated in the United States. First, it does not seem that even when the meeting took place, on 25 July, Saddam had decided to invade the whole of Kuwait. He was probably not certain in his own mind what he would do, and he gave her a clear assurance that there would be no invasion. She could perhaps have read him a lecture about the consequences if he did invade, but that would have been insulting.

Second, there was still a great deal of confusion in Washington on the day when Ms Glaspie went to the presidential palace about the extent of the American obligation to defend Kuwait. Some officials argued that the US had no defence commitment to Kuwait, although on 24 July the Department of Defense had announced that there would be a joint military exercise in the Gulf at the request of the United Arab Emirates. The purpose of the exercise was to provide cover for the sending of American surveillance planes to the UAE in the event of an Iraqi attack. April Glaspie had been summoned to the presidential palace because Saddam Hussein wanted an explanation for this.

Altogether, then, Ms Glaspie was on the defensive. Saddam reinforced this by haranguing her non-stop for an hour and a half, mostly about his sense that the United States and its allies were plotting against him. As ever, he rambled.

> It was clear to us that certain parties in the United States – not necessarily the President, I mean, but certain parties who had links with intelligence and with the State Department, and I don't necessarily mean the Secretary of State himself – did not like the fact that we had liberated our land [from Iran]. Some parties began to prepare papers entitled 'Who will take over from Saddam Hussein?' They began to contact Gulf states to make them worried about Iraq, so they wouldn't give economic aid to Iraq. We have evidence of these activities . . .

> We do not accept threats from anyone, because we do not threaten anyone. But we say clearly that we hope the US will not suffer from too many illusions, and that it will look for new friends rather than add to the number of its enemies.

Saddam went on like this for a very long time, and finished by complaining about the things the American media had been saying about him. April Glaspie was an intelligent woman, but not particularly forceful; and she responded to this torrent of words by trying to placate him. It was, certainly, a mistake, both in terms of American relations with Iraq and in terms of her own position.

The Iraqis leaked a selectively edited version of this conversation to the Western press two weeks later. In it, Glaspie sounded extremely weak; especially when she hastened to agree with Saddam over his criticisms of the American press.

> I saw the Diane Sawyer programme [about Saddam Hussein] on ABC. And what happened in that programme was cheap and unjust. And this is a real picture of what happens in the American media – even to American politicians themselves. These are the methods that the Western media employ. I am pleased that you add your voice to the diplomats who stand up to the media.

American journalists take themselves seriously, and allying herself with Saddam Hussein against them did not ensure Glaspie a good press in the United States. Nor did the grovelling tone of some of the other comments she made:

> I admire your extraordinary efforts to rebuild your country. I know you need funds. We understand that, and our opinion is that you should have the opportunity to rebuild your country. But we have no opinion on Arab–Arab conflicts like your border disagreement with Kuwait . . . All we hope is that these issues will be solved quickly.

She was, of course, being a great deal less than honest with Saddam, and he knew it. The United States had encouraged Kuwait to make economic trouble for Iraq, and it sided powerfully with Kuwait against Iraq in the resulting border dispute. But to her critics in the United States, these words sounded like outright weakness. They certainly did not constitute a firm warning that the Americans would meet any move against Kuwait with force.

April Glaspie stayed quiet for months afterwards despite a barrage of criticism. The State Department gave her little support, and the only newspaper interview she gave did little to help her position. When she

1. The young Saddam Hussein with his first wife, Sajida.

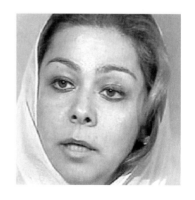

2. *Above*. Saddam and Sajida at a garden party in the grounds of his palace in Baghdad. Sitting on the chair are two of their children, Raghad and Rana.

3. *Right*. Raghad, Saddam's eldest daughter, as she appeared during her television interview in August 2003.

4. In a BBC studio, Dr Dieter Buhmann, a German forensic scientist, shows me which is the real Saddam Hussein and which are the doubles.

5. In both these examples the face on the left is that of the real Saddam. Dr Buhmann's facial measurements show the right-hand pictures cannot be him.

6. *Above.*
Jorg Haider,
the right-wing
Austrian leader,
meets the man he
thinks is Saddam.
He is wrong.

7. *Right.*
The genuine
Saddam with
his elder son,
Uday.

8. Latif Yahia,
Uday's school friend
and later double.

9. Saddam smokes his cigar as he conducts his savage purge of the Ba'ath Party leadership, July 1979.

10. A senior Party figure, named by Saddam, is bundled out by the security guards, probably to execution. Both these images come from a video distributed as a warning to Ba'athist groups throughout the world.

11. The Iran–Iraq War: Iranian soldiers badly affected by Saddam's use of mustard gas are taken to hospital, February 1986.

12. Reporting from the Kurdish town of Halabjah in north-eastern Iraq, soon after the massive gas attack of March 1988. Some of the bodies are lying on the ground behind me.

13. Some of the 5,000 people who died in the attack on Halabjah.

14. Two survivors hold the bodies of their children.

15. Saddam Hussein in his underground bunker during the first Gulf War.

16. Negotiating Iraq's surrender. General Norman Schwarzkopf, on the left,
is about to make the key concession which will allow the Iraqi side, on the right,
to use helicopters and tanks against the rebel Kurds and Shi'ites.

17. The revolt begins. An Iraqi soldier fires at an image of Saddam Hussein in the centre of Basra.

18. Ali Hassan al-Majid, Saddam's enforcer. It was he who led the attack on Halabjah and who destroyed the Shi'ite uprising with extraordinary brutality.

appeared before a sub-committee of the House of Representatives the following March, though, she was at last able to present her side of the story.

She maintained that about a fifth of the transcript which the Iraqis had leaked of her conversation with Saddam Hussein had been distorted, falsified or cut. She had, she said, repeatedly warned him not to use force against Kuwait.

'I told him our policy was that we would defend our vital interests. We did not realize he would be so foolish as to ignore our repeated and crystal-clear warnings.'

She went on to reveal that during their meeting Saddam Hussein had left the room in order to speak to President Hosni Mubarak of Egypt on the phone. Mubarak told him that the Kuwaiti Crown Prince had agreed to meet Saddam's deputy, Izzat Ibrahim, in Saudi Arabia. As far as the Iraqis were concerned, this meant that Kuwait was backing down. There would be no need for Saddam to take action against Kuwait after all.

'He came back,' Glaspie told the sub-committee, 'and in effect said, "We're not going to do it. It's all over."'

'[D]id he say specifically he would not use force . . . or invade Kuwait?' asked a member of the committee.

'Yes, sir,' Glaspie answered.

'And that was not a conditional statement of any kind. It was just a flat, clear, plain statement: we will not invade Kuwait, is that correct?'

'There was certainly no question [of conditionality] about it.'

She added that over the next couple of days two different Iraqi government ministers had told her there would be no military attack against Kuwait.

Saddam thought at this stage that his threats against Kuwait had worked. Not surprisingly, the version of the Saddam–Glaspie meeting which the Iraqis leaked omitted anything which hinted at uncertainty or lack of purpose on Saddam's part. The State Department did not have a transcript of its own, since it had no means of recording the meeting, and it did not trouble to issue its own account because it had no interest in defending April Glaspie, who was regarded as a lost cause.

Yet to blame her for the invasion is foolish. Ms Glaspie certainly played her part in a crisis of misunderstanding and over-confidence, but the key lay where it always did: in Saddam Hussein's own character and his behaviour as a politician. The only way in which the crisis might have been avoided would have been if Kuwait had been milder in its response to Saddam's bullying.

Various intermediaries tried to help. One was the Pakistani prime minister, Benazir Bhutto. Another was the PLO chairman, Yasser Arafat, who, contrary to his reputation in Israel and the United States, was a committed deal-maker. Wherever there was conflict in the Arab world, Yasser Arafat would fly in and try to broker a settlement.

He came close this time. Anxious – rightly, as it turned out – that outright conflict between Iraq and Kuwait would damage the PLO's position and threaten the lives and businesses of tens of thousands of Palestinians, Arafat offered his services as a netotiator. Together with King Hussein of Jordan and the Saudi foreign minister, he flew from capital to capital looking for ways to end the crisis.

His relations with both sides were reasonably good. Saddam Hussein disliked him personally, regarding him as weak and pro-Saudi, but realized he was an ally all the same. Arafat did not get on with the Emir of Kuwait, but he was very friendly with the Crown Prince, Sheikh Sa'ad al-Abdallah al-Salem as-Sabah. In 1970, when King Hussein fought his Black September war against the radical Palestinians, the Crown Prince had saved Yasser Arafat's life by smuggling him out of Amman dressed as a woman, and flying him to Cairo. The Crown Prince was a large, friendly man whose alarmingly staring eyes, the result of an incurable disorder, belied his essentially easy-going nature.

Now, as time was running out, Arafat sat in the Crown Prince's office in Kuwait City and advised him strongly that Kuwait should not say yes or no to Saddam Hussein's demands, but should say it would examine them and see what could be done. Arafat was certain that a peaceful settlement was possible, if Kuwait would only be less aggressive in its responses.

The Crown Prince listened carefully, and Arafat had the feeling that his point had been taken. At that moment, an official came in and whispered in the Crown Prince's ear that there was an important phone call for him in the next room. The Crown Prince left, and stayed away for fifteen minutes or so. When he came back, Arafat could see that something had changed. The Crown Prince explained that the call had been from Margaret Thatcher. She had told him to stand firm and not to yield an inch to Saddam Hussein's demands. Britain and the United States would back Kuwait to the hilt if he did, she said. After that, Arafat believed, there was no serious chance of avoiding war.

A curious lassitude settled over Baghdad in the days before the invasion. Much the same occurred in the days before the start of the first and second Gulf Wars, in 1991 and 2003 respectively. Everyone feared the worst, and no one could do anything about it. Again and again people would shrug their shoulders and say it was nothing to do with them. Iraq at such times reminded me of a plane taken over by hijackers, Saddam, in this case, being the man with the gun in his hand. Scarcely anyone, even among his top officials, wanted to be part of what was going on, yet no one could stop it.

'We expected an American military retaliation from the very beginning,' Tariq Aziz, the foreign minister, told the *New Yorker* magazine some months later. 'We felt fatalistic. That is the mood that governed our judgement here.'

It wasn't true that Saddam's ministers had expected an American attack, but it was certainly true that they were resigned to the worst possible outcome. Only Saddam himself believed this was a confrontation he could win.

In the last days of July he was fairly certain that President Bush would send troops to Kuwait City, to make an Iraqi invasion impossible. The British had sent in the Royal Marines in 1961, when President Qassem threatened an invasion, and the threat had evaporated at once. Saddam knew it would be too dangerous to take action against Kuwait if the US Marines were there. If he were to act, it would have to be fast. Bush's failure to act decisively made the crisis worse.

It no longer looked as though the meeting in Jeddah between Saddam's deputy, Izzat Ibrahim, and the Kuwaitis would achieve anything. The meeting was due to take place on 28 July, but was postponed because the Iraqis issued a statement outlining the 'legitimate demands' they expected Kuwait to address. These were fourfold, and they were very tough: the handing over of part of the Rumailah oilfield, an immediate payment of $2.4 billion, the writing off of Iraq's debts to Kuwait, additional compensation, and a formal promise not to exceed its OPEC quota in future.

The meeting finally took place in Jeddah on 31 July. It changed everything, but not in the way Saddam Hussein had originally assumed. This would not be the forum for a climb-down by Kuwait and a peaceful, lucrative solution to the problem.

The Iraqi team was composed of three men: Izzat Ibrahim, whose daughter was at this time married to Saddam's eldest son, Uday; Sa'doun Hammadi, the deputy prime minister, a quiet and courteous man; and Saddam's cousin Ali Hassan al-Majid, aggressive and violent, who had overseen the attack on Halabjah and had earned the nickname Chemical Ali in consequence. The Kuwaiti side was dominated by the Crown Prince.

From the moment the meeting began it was clear to the Iraqis that Saddam had been wrong. Kuwait was not looking for a way out. They themselves had been instructed to be as flexible as possible, but it was clear that the Crown Prince, with the full support of President Bush and Margaret Thatcher behind him, was not in any way prepared to yield to what he openly called Saddam's blackmail. Ibrahim and Hammadi stayed fairly quiet, but Ali Hassan al-Majid responded with anger and violent words. The meeting lasted all day.

It resumed on the morning of 1 August. The atmosphere was, if anything, more poisonous than ever. Al-Majid shouted across the table that Iraq had defended Kuwait against the threat from Iran, and deserved compensation.

'Why don't you just drink the sea?' the Crown Prince shouted back, his usual relaxed composure completely abandoned.

At that stage things were so bad that it looked as though a fight could break out at any moment, and the security guards stationed outside by the Saudis had to come in and stand between the two men.

Then came the last, unforgivable insult. Al-Majid said that Iraqis were now so impoverished because of the war that they scarcely had enough money to feed themselves. The Crown Prince looked at the Kuwaitis on his side of the table.

'Why don't they send their wives out onto the streets to earn money for them?'

Everyone knew he was referring to the old stories from Tikrit about Saddam's mother and his illegitimacy.

The meeting broke up, and the Iraqi team flew back to Baghdad to report. Saddam was wild with anger when he heard what the Crown

Prince had said. According to a senior Iraqi source, long afterwards, it was at that point that Saddam Hussein gave the order that the Iraqi troops should move into Kuwait, and should not halt at the Rumailah oilfield or the Mutla Ridge, but take the entire country.

That evening, according to another very senior Iraqi source, only four men knew of Saddam's hasty decision: Ali Hassan al-Majid, who would be the governor of Kuwait, Iraq's 'nineteenth province'; Saddam's son-in-law Hussein Kamel al-Majid, the defence industries minister; his half-brother, Sabaawi Ibrahim, the head of the Mukhabarat or secret police; and the commander of the Revolutionary Guard.

The generals commanding the various Revolutionary Guard divisions were under the impression until the last minute that it was just an exercise. But, in the early hours of 2 August 1990, as the tanks crossed into Kuwait, Saddam turned to his four closest associates.

'The Emir will not sleep in his palace tonight,' he said.

23. OCCUPATION

'I suppose it was the tanks I heard first, that horrible, growling, grinding noise they make. I'd never heard a tank in my life before, but I knew there was something very wrong when I heard that noise. I shook my husband and said, "Wake up, Steve, something's going on out there." It certainly was. When we looked out of the window – it was already light – there were dozens of the horrible things coming along the road, past our block of flats.'

Mrs Susan Jenkins and her husband were British expatriates who lived and worked in Kuwait. What they saw that morning was the start of a terrible few months for the Western community of around 8,000, and for half a million others from the rest of the world.

Kuwait City is everything Baghdad is not: neat where Baghdad sprawls, tidy where Baghdad crumbles, extravagantly wealthy where Baghdad's money has been squandered on unnecessary wars and the ego of its president. The people of Baghdad are essentially urban tenement dwellers; Kuwait's inhabitants are by instinct suburban commuters, who live in carefully aligned square houses, two storeys high, each with its garden, its rose bushes, and – where space and money permit – its swimming-pool.

Kuwait's urban motorway system is as sophisticated as anything in Western Europe or the United States. Income per head in Kuwait is at least four times greater than that in Iraq, and perhaps more.

Altogether, though, it is very hard to be fond of Kuwait. It is much disliked in the Middle East, partly because it employs people from all over the region and treats them with equal disdain. Even Saudis – not the humblest and gentlest of people themselves – regard the Kuwaitis as intolerably arrogant.

Kuwait was also a family business. The British MP George Galloway, whose closeness to Saddam Hussein got him into considerable difficulties in 2003, encapsulated the unattractive nature of the state in a House of Commons motion he tabled in January 1991, when the Coalition forces were in the process of driving the Iraqi invaders out of Kuwait:

> That this House notes that British forces are currently fighting, some perchance to die, for the restoration of the legitimate government of Kuwait: and notes that this legitimate government, viz: the Amir Jaber As-Sabah, the Crown Prince Sa'ad As-Sabah, the Prime Minister Sa'ad As-Sabah, the Deputy Prime Minister Sa'bah As-Sabah, the Foreign Minister Sa'bah As-Sabah, the Minister of Amiri Diwan Affairs Khalid As-Sabah, the Minister of Information Jaber As-Sabah, the Minister of the Interior Salim As-Sabah, the Minister of Defence Nawaf As-Sabah, the Minister of Oil Ali As-Sabah, the Governor of Ahmadi Province Al Sabah As-Sabah, the Governor of Jahra Province Ali Abdullah As-Sabah, the Governor of Kuwait Province Jaber As-Sabah, the Governor of Faranawiya Province Ahmad As-Sabah, are an unelected government who appear to be related: further notes that the Kuwaiti National Assembly, which had a limited franchise and even more limited powers, was suspended by the Amir's decree in 1986; and wonders if this war aim of restoration can be justified.

At 2 a.m. on the morning of Thursday 2 August 1990, 100,000 Iraqi troops and 300 tanks rolled into this neatly ordered, highly privileged, unnatural little state. The great majority of the tanks were carrying only minimal supplies of ammunition, in order to be able to reach

Kuwait City without refuelling. Some had no ammunition at all. It didn't matter. Kuwait's armed forces, which numbered only 16,000 men, did nothing to stop the Iraqi forces as they crossed the border.

Yet the Kuwaiti defence ministry achieved one major success. In the two hours which it took for the first Iraqi tanks, driving at their top speed of fifty miles an hour, to reach Kuwait City, the officers on overnight duty alerted the defence minister – another as-Sabah, of course – and he warned the Emir and the rest of the government. They woke up, got their families and their necessaries together, and left for the Saudi border in an immense fleet of Mercedes. It was an immense advantage for Kuwait in the propaganda war that virtually the entire government should have got away intact.

One man stayed. He was the Emir's half-brother, Fahd al-Ahmad as-Sabah, a bluff extrovert very different from his quiet half-brother. Among his various functions he was the manager of Kuwait's national football team. Sheikh Fahd chose not to escape with the rest. He took up position on the steps of the Emir's residence, the Dasman Palace, together with the soldiers who had been detailed to protect it.

The palace was surrounded, and attacked from the air; the defenders stood their ground. It was nearly an hour before the overwhelming odds finally told and the Iraqis charged the building. Sheikh Fahd was last seen standing on the steps of the palace, gun in hand. Then he was shot down where he stood: a genuine Kuwaiti hero.

For the next twelve hours some of the braver inhabitants fought the Iraqis in the streets. Later, most Kuwaitis accused the Palestinians and other foreign workers of collaborating with the invaders *en masse*, but it wasn't true. A British woman I spoke to told me of her experiences that morning.

My children and I were in our kitchen, because that seemed the safest place . . . Then I heard a noise outside the kitchen window and a man was standing out there on the fire escape, trying to attract my attention. I was frightened, but I saw he had a gun, so I thought I'd better let him in . . . I didn't think he was an Iraqi soldier.

He was quite polite and asked if his two friends could come in too. They were all Arabs and they all had guns – goodness knows where they got them from. Then they went into the other room and I could hear them shooting down at the Iraqi tanks . . .

They didn't stay long – maybe ten minutes altogether. I offered them a cup of tea and they laughed, but they didn't say yes. I asked them, 'Who are you?' They wouldn't really say, but one of them said he was a Palestinian and that one of the others was his brother and the other one was an Egyptian friend of theirs. Then they said they had to go and find somewhere else to shoot from, and they climbed out of the window again. Extraordinary, really.

The sound of shooting alerted some people to what was going on. Others had heard as a result of a ludicrous broadcast from Voice of the Masses Radio in Baghdad at 7.10 a.m., Kuwait time:

God has helped the free and honest men of Kuwait to depose the traitor regime in Kuwait, which is involved in Zionist and foreign plots. The free sons of dear Kuwait have appealed to the Iraqi leadership for support to prevent any foreign interference in Kuwait's affairs . . .

Like much of the rest of the operation, the broadcast gave the impression that it had been made up on the spur of the moment. Nothing had been done beforehand to give it even the thinnest veneer of authenticity, and the 'free and honest men' who had supposedly overthrown the Kuwait government never existed.

A station calling itself Radio Kuwait was picked up by BBC Monitoring, broadcasting occasional messages and patriotic music on five short-wave frequencies, probably from the Kabd area, south-west of Kuwait City: 'O citizens,' said the announcer repeatedly, 'defending the homeland is a duty.'

Bad luck, bad timing and a couple of bad decisions brought a British Airways jumbo jet, flight 149 *en route* from Delhi to London, into Kuwait airport well after the invasion had begun. It landed, and was refused permission to take off again. The 301 passengers, many of them Indian, were taken prisoner. So were the crew and the relief crew, seventy-seven in all.

Apart from the airport, all the other key installations – the television station, the power stations, the port – were taken over. The British and American embassies were surrounded. In the first minutes when the Iraqi soldiers arrived there they sprayed the buildings with bullets.

During the day, country after country, from China and the Soviet Union to Britain, France and the United States, condemned the invasion. The United Nations Security Council passed Resolution 660, which by fourteen votes to none demanded an immediate and unconditional withdrawal of Iraqi troops.

The crisis found many key figures away from their desks: April Glaspie, the American ambassador, was on holiday and did not return to Baghdad for the remainder of the crisis. The US Secretary of State, James Baker, was in Outer Mongolia; President Bush was just about to leave for his holiday home at Kennebunkport, and the crisis did not stop him. The British Foreign Secretary Douglas Hurd was on holiday, and so was President François Mitterrand of France. Margaret Thatcher, the British prime minister, rarely took holidays, but she was in the United States in order to give a speech.

No intelligence agency seems to have had any idea that Iraq was going to invade Kuwait. There were stories later that the CIA had known about it and deliberately taken no action, but they seem to have been an exercise in inter-departmental in-fighting. Neither MI6 nor Mossad apparently knew in advance, and the KGB and French intelligence, which were much closer to Iraq, were just as much in the dark. Given the last-minute nature of the invasion, none of this is at all surprising.

The first reaction in Washington was one of shock and anxiety. Six hundred Americans were working in Iraq and 2,500 in Kuwait; they were clearly in danger. There was also an instinctive fear that the attack on Kuwait might just be the first in a more general onslaught against the pro-Western regimes of the region, starting with Saudi Arabia and continuing round the coast of the Gulf to Bahrain, the United Arab Emirates and even Oman. And there was a wider anxiety: that in other pro-Western countries like Egypt and Turkey political radicals would come out onto the streets in support of Saddam Hussein and threaten the stability of the governments.

Even that first day, though, President George Bush and some of his officials realized that the crisis offered opportunities as well as dangers. Saddam Hussein was a disturbing influence in the region and had now put himself clearly in the wrong. The United States would have plenty of international support in any action it chose to take. As vice-president he had seen the way American opinion had rallied round President

Reagan during and after the invasion of Grenada in 1983 – an absurd and rather badly managed affair – and the bombing of Libya three years later. This would be a much larger enterprise than either, and a president who led the country in wartime would receive automatic support and respect at home.

In the wake of the revolutions in Central and Eastern Europe and the virtual collapse of the Soviet Union as a superpower, Bush had spoken presciently of a new world order in which the United States would play the leading role. Now, he felt, this brought the new order closer still.

The American media, with their alarming herd instinct, had made an issue out of what they called 'the wimp factor': a sense that Bush was soft and lacked the killer instinct. It was never anything more than a reaction to his East Coast ways and accent, and his lack of what he himself called 'the vision thing'. George Bush, unlike his son George W. Bush, was a president in the older, recognizably European sense: a politician with experience of government and national administration and a knowledge of the world.

His views were patrician and traditional; when he contested the presidency with Ronald Reagan in 1980 he spoke of Reagan's 'voodoo economics'. Bush had been the head of the CIA and a successful ambassador to China, and as President foreign policy would be as important to him as domestic policy: something which the politicians and journalists of Washington found difficult to swallow.

In Moscow the news came at a time of industrial unrest, with strikes in the Donetsk and Donbass mining areas, continued disturbances in the republics of Central Asia and the Baltic, still at that stage part of the Soviet Union, and nervousness about the possibility that the armed forces might stage a military coup. President Mikhail Gorbachev was by now thoroughly unpopular, both with the people who wanted faster political and economic change and with those who regarded him as a traitor to Marxism-Leninism.

The invasion of Kuwait offered Gorbachev opportunities as well as dangers: he could demonstrate his value as a dependable partner for the West by seeking to exert a moderating influence on Saddam Hussein. At the same time, the Soviet military and security establishment would be deeply offended by any move against Iraq. Saddam Hussein had been a consistently reliable ally for the old, pre-Gorbachev

Soviet Union. Lining up with the United States against Iraq seemed to the old guard in Moscow like the ultimate betrayal of the past. Exactly a year later, on 19 August 1991, the hard-line conservative leadership of the KGB staged a coup against Gorbachev. While it eventually failed, it nevertheless did mortal damage to his political career.

In Britain the invasion came as the governmental system was closing down for its summer break. Britain was bound by its colonial past to help Kuwait, and had anyway become much more deeply involved than it wanted in the bitter dispute with Iraq over Farzad Bazoft's execution and the super-gun affair. At the same time Britain was still Iraq's greatest customer and supplier. More Iraqis were educated at British universities than those of any other country, and there were more British citizens living in Iraq – 700 of them – than those of any other Western country.

This might have been expected to encourage caution. But the prime minister, Margaret Thatcher, had made a political career out of not being cautious. Her main concern was to associate herself as strongly as possible with the United States. She changed her speech to the Aspen Institute in Colorado to take account of the crisis, maintaining that it provided the United Nations with an ideal opportunity to fulfil the role which Franklin D. Roosevelt and Winston Churchill had foreseen for it. The Conservative press in Britain regarded Mrs Thatcher as the real force behind the London–Washington axis, and gleefully reported her press spokesman's account of the conversation she had with the White House by telephone ('Now, George, don't go wobbly on me!').

In fact her words simply raised a smile in the Oval Office, where Bush and his closest advisers were sitting when her imperious call came through. They had considerable respect and some affection for Margaret Thatcher, but enough sense of humour to see that in the tenth year of her premiership she had become something of a parody of herself. Bush had no intention of backsliding, and did not need Margaret Thatcher to keep him up to the mark.

Still, the message was picked up in Baghdad as well as London. The government newspaper *Al-Iraq* reported excitably eight days later:

> This is the lady who is encouraging enemies and vomiting poison like a spotted serpent, attempting by all means to inflict harm on Iraq to make up for the inferiority complex which she has because

of the proud Iraqis and their unique leader, Saddam Hussein, who has dealt the most violent and strongest possible political blows to the ugly British face.

For months to come, the Iraqi government and media found it hard to decide whether Britain was leading the United States ('This disgusting buffoon is urging the United States to use the military option') or vice versa ('What a miserable and lowly role is being played by the circus act and corrupt lady, Thatcher, who is playing into the hands of US politics'). Whichever way it was, they were obsessed by Margaret Thatcher. Even after her tearful fall from power in November, Saddam Hussein and his newspapers were reluctant to give up attacking her.

In France, where the annual holidays were well advanced, there was intense debate within the government about policy towards Iraq. François Mitterrand had followed a more pro-American policy than his predecessors, and was an instinctive supporter of Israel. Nevertheless France, like Britain and Russia, had important economic interests in Iraq. The only time Saddam Hussein visited a Western country was when he went to France in 1975 to negotiate the purchase of the Osirak 70-megawatt nuclear reactor. He praised France's independence from the United States, and even decided that there were links between Ba'athism and Gaullism. (French Socialists were inclined to agree.) France was the second biggest supplier of arms to Iraq, after the Soviet Union.

So there was a division of interests within the French government. The defence minister, Jean-Pierre Chevènement, was a strong advocate for Iraq, and over the next few months would consistently propose solutions which he thought Saddam could accept without humiliation. By contrast, the foreign minister, the short and dashing Roland Dumas, whose eyes always seemed to light up when there were attractive women around, broadly supported the American and British line. Chevènement became more and more isolated, and finally resigned twelve days after the Coalition forces, France's included, had begun their attack on Iraq. But while he remained, France rarely spoke with a single voice.

Germany, by contrast, scarcely spoke at all. It too had supplied weapons to Iraq and had a few large contracts there. But during the 1970s, the period of biggest growth in the links between West

Germany and Israel, it had been hard to enter into too many agreements with Baghdad. Still, a number of German companies had helped supply Iraq with the chemicals it wanted for use against Iran and against elements of its own population.

It was a difficult time for the government of Chancellor Helmut Kohl. He himself was in the process of losing much of the popularity he had gained through the remarkably smooth political union between East and West Germany, because the process of economic union was proving so much more difficult and painful than he or his ministers had expected. For many Germans the crisis in the Middle East was far less important than the revolutionary changes in Central and Eastern Europe.

'You British,' a young woman who worked for the Christian Democratic Party said to me near the newly opened Brandenburg Gate in October 1990, when I was briefly back from Iraq to report on the reunification ceremony, 'you just want to get back to the sands of the desert and wear your solar topees. But that's all in the past, don't you understand? Here, we're trying to think about the future.'

To the British and the Americans, this sounded like selfishness and isolationism. As the crisis in the Middle East deepened and the problems within Germany grew, Chancellor Kohl seemed diminished by it all. West Germany's constitution still forbade the sending of German troops abroad to fight, and his government became mere spectators in the unfolding drama. By the summer of 1991 Germany's standing was nothing like it had been a year before, when reunification made it seem unquestionably the most potent power in Europe.

From the start it was clear that a crisis involving a country as hostile to its neighbours as Iraq would create some new and unlikely alliances. Egypt, Saudi Arabia, and the other Gulf States were obviously going to oppose Saddam. For a few days it looked as though Iran might join them. But President Rafsanjani had a more complex plan in mind: to keep his weakened country out of the conflict, and to use the crisis to reach a formal end to hostilities with Iraq, while strengthening Iran's relations with Western countries (though not with the United States) in order to reconstruct the Iranian economy. Before the crisis was over Iran had achieved each of these objectives, and the radical fundamentalists who wanted to join Iraq in a *jihad* against the United States were badly discredited.

President Assad of Syria ran a regime which was in many ways just as unattractive as Saddam Hussein's. He, however, took a different approach from Iran. The Syrian Ba'ath Party regarded the Iraqi Ba'athists as its natural enemy, though it required a considerable amount of lateral thinking for Assad to align himself with the United States, Egypt and – worst of all – Israel. The dreadful state of the mismanaged Syrian economy, where electricity was often reduced to four hours' supply a day, made it easier, but nothing short of committing troops to the conflict would be enough for the Americans and British to accept Assad as someone with whom they could do business.

King Hussein of Jordan was forced to move in the opposite direction. He knew the invasion of Kuwait was an utter disaster, and he felt a considerable distaste for Saddam Hussein as a man and as a political leader. But he knew that unless he was both careful and very lucky this crisis could pull him down, as his young cousin King Faisal II had been pulled down by the Baghdad mob in 1958. At a dinner-party he gave for a selected group of journalists at his palace in Amman during the conflict he told us frankly that he was very gloomy about the likely outcome, and felt it was more than likely that he would end his days at his stud-farm to the west of London.

The newspapers in Amman and the big public demonstrations in support of Saddam Hussein showed how strong popular feeling was among the majority of Jordanians who were of Palestinian origin. The limited degree of democracy which King Hussein had introduced in Jordan gave ordinary people a new voice in public affairs, and it would have been very hard, and perhaps suicidal, for him to have tried to support the American line. President Bush himself and his secretary of state James Baker understood this, but plenty of people in the administration were bewildered and angry by the line the King took. In the American media, too; 'the flip-flop King' became a commonplace insult among American newspaper columnists.

Palestinians favoured Saddam Hussein because he was so vociferously on their side. In private, many senior figures in the Palestinian leadership realized that it was disastrous to be so close to Saddam, but they were unable to do anything about it. Yasser Arafat, who was himself deeply equivocal and had no great liking for 'my brother Saddam', nevertheless suggested the idea which clinched Palestinian support for Iraq.

On 12 August, ten days after the invasion, Saddam took Arafat's advice and publicly offered to withdraw from Kuwait if Israel would withdraw from the occupied territories, the United States would withdraw from Saudi Arabia and Syria would withdraw from Lebanon. It was probably the cleverest thing – perhaps the only really clever thing – that Saddam Hussein did during the entire course of the crisis. It brought him immense support throughout the Muslim world; not necessarily with governments, but certainly in the streets.

All this, however, lay in the future. On the afternoon of 2 August Iraqi soldiers were taking over the centre of Kuwait City, building by building. In these early stages they had orders to behave politely. It was even possible for people to move around fairly easily, despite the road-blocks. Most stayed indoors, however.

The state radio, which in traditional fashion had been among the first objectives of the Iraqi soldiers, broadcast long rambling statements from what it called the 'Provisional Free Kuwait Government'. Communiqué No. 1 was a self-contradictory, illogical defence of the action which Iraq had taken. It accused the as-Sabahs of gross corruption and of being imposed on the country by Britain. Communiqué No. 2 was more businesslike: it announced a curfew with immediate effect. The people who wrote and broadcast these communiqués were supposedly Kuwaitis, but those who heard them recognized by their accents that they were Iraqis.

> The national forces which rejected tyranny, despotism and corruption and resisted the regime, which is connected with imperialist and Zionist circles, have decided, relying on God, the people's free will, and the good representatives of the people, to assume responsibility and topple the tyrannical, corrupt regime . . .
>
> One of the primary national aims of the Provisional Free Kuwait Government will be to rectify the harm and aggression which the former government carried out against our people and brothers in Iraq.

By late afternoon the shooting which had lasted for the first eight hours of the invasion had died away. Tanks ground their way along the city streets, their tracks cutting deep furrows in tarmac softened by the intense summer heat. The racket of their engines and the thick grey smoke from their exhausts filled the air. Their crews moved them into position at all the main crossroads and outside the main buildings, then switched off their engines. For the first time since dawn that morning the city was quiet.

In London and Paris, all Kuwait's and Iraq's assets were frozen. In Washington the Iraqi ambassador went on television and assured the viewers of the early news programmes that the military operation in Kuwait would last only a few days or weeks. That encouraged the impression that the invasion had been carried out for political effect, and that directly the point had been made the Iraqis would withdraw from Kuwait. In fact the whole affair had been so hectic and unplanned that no one in Baghdad had thought to brief the Iraqi ambassador; lacking any guidance from home, he simply said what he hoped would be the case. But his words influenced American thinking for some time.

Mrs Thatcher, who was still in Aspen, Colorado, issued a joint statement with President Bush calling for a collective international effort to force Iraq out of Kuwait if it did not withdraw its forces voluntarily. It was the first move towards the creation of what would later become a coalition of thirty nations.

In Saudi Arabia the government was so worried that Iraq might continue its attack into Saudi territory that the media were forbidden to report any mention of the invasion of Kuwait until late in the afternoon, as though not reporting it meant it hadn't happened. Members of the Kuwaiti government and the as-Sabah family were gathering in the Saudi city of Dhahran, though characteristically some of them had felt obliged to stop off at their expensive chalets along the Kuwait coast for a siesta before moving on to the Saudi border.

In Kuwait itself one radio station was still broadcasting patriotic songs and messages. A recorded message was sent back to the station by the Crown Prince. Kuwait, he said, was facing a brutal aggression by the enemies of love and peace. He appealed to everyone to rally behind the Emir. The radio station went on broadcasting through the evening and night, but went off the air the following morning after broadcasting an appeal to the outside world to help the people of Kuwait. The last words were 'Hurry to their aid.'

In Iraq the government announced the immediate call-up of the Popular Army, a million or so reservists who had all served in the war against Iran. It also closed Iraq's land borders and airspace. In the welter of statements, condemnation, advice and pleas for help which were being issued from almost every capital in the world, a brief dispatch from the Iraqi News Agency quoting the office of President Saddam Hussein went almost entirely unnoticed.

> The Interior Ministry is empowered to regulate the travel of non-Iraqis in the light of instructions which will be issued later by the Presidential Office.

It was the first indication of one of Saddam Hussein's most serious tactical errors during the entire crisis: the decision to hold foreign citizens hostage in Iraq.

As darkness fell, the 8,000 Westerners and half a million people from other countries who lived and worked in Kuwait sat in their homes and worried about what was going to happen to them. Mrs Susan Jenkins, the British woman who had been woken up that morning by the sound of the Iraqi tanks grinding their way through the streets, felt a sense of desolation and anxiety worse than anything she'd ever experienced before.

> Maybe if we'd had a bit of time to prepare ourselves for the idea of an invasion it would have been different. I was putting the children to bed that night and trying to tell them everything would work out all right and they mustn't worry about it, and I thought, this is exactly what I was doing last night, in every way. And yet everything was incredibly different, and we couldn't think what was going to happen to us.

Outside, she could hear the rattle of gunfire again. The invasion of Kuwait was complete, but resistance was continuing.

24. FIRST RESPONSE

The aircraft carrier USS *Dwight D. Eisenhower*, a fifth of a mile long, elderly, slow, yet immensely powerful, moved with great stateliness under nuclear power down the Suez Canal in the direction of the Gulf. Her upper works shimmered in the intense heat of summer, seeming to melt and liquefy in the ferocious sun. Her radar scanners evaporated into mirage and materialized into reality again every time they turned. On her decks lay her greatest strength: a jumble of folded wings and fuselages which represented sixty of the world's most advanced fighter aircraft. They were parked as close as cars on a cross-Channel ferry.

It was Wednesday 8 August. As the *Eisenhower* moved down the Canal with his full knowledge and permission, President Hosni Mubarak of Egypt was giving a press conference. It was a bravura performance. He waved his arms about energetically, his face taking on a series of exaggerated expressions: alarm, anxiety, reassurance, innocence. There are few more entertaining spectacles than a crafty man showing the world how honest he is. Each time his face registered a new emotion and he emphasized it with his hands, the photographers, crouched in the front row, shot off more stills. His face gleamed in the stark light of their flash bulbs.

It was a difficult moment for Mubarak, and he carried it off impressively. Some Western commentators had already forecast that he would be one of the victims of the crisis: that the people of Cairo and Alexandria, stirred up by the fundamentalists of the Muslim Brotherhood, would come out on to the streets in support of Saddam Hussein and threaten both Mubarak's government and his entire policy of peace with Israel and alignment with the West. He had given the United States various private assurances about sending troops to Saudi Arabia as part of the anti-Saddam coalition, but it did not suit him to be too open about it in public.

As he presented it, his first concern was with Arab unity. He was unwilling to take the lead against Saddam Hussein.

> It shouldn't be assumed that I am on the side of Kuwait, nor that I am going to support Kuwait. We are neutral in this . . . We have a brotherly relationship with Saddam Hussein. I asked him [before the invasion] if any of his troops would move southwards. He said that what was happening was just a routine exercise, sixty or seventy miles from the Kuwaiti border. 'Is it,' I asked, 'your intention to intervene?' 'I have no intention of intervening,' he told me.

Mubarak wanted to establish an alibi for himself, so that he could avoid any accusation that he had lined up with the enemies of an Arab country. If anyone was to blame it was Saddam; Mubarak himself was merely a passive spectator.

I'm afraid that Iraq will be subjected to a very severe threat. Don't think the foreign powers won't act. It's just my opinion, mind you, I haven't heard this from anyone else. But it's obvious to me that there's going to be aggression. It'll be horrible and destructive. The British, the French, the Americans will come here and impose their own solution. Wouldn't it be more honourable for us to solve the problem under an Arab umbrella, without humiliation?

Someone asked him the most important question: was he planning to send Egyptian troops to join the British and Americans in the Saudi desert? There were already reports out of Washington that he had agreed to do so.

People say I already have troops there. I don't have any troops there. I tell you this frankly: I'm not going to join a foreign force.

When a man like President Mubarak tells you something frankly, it's time to listen with very great care to the words he is using.

If Mubarak was cautious, King Fahd of Saudi Arabia was the precise opposite, mastering the nervousness which Saudi statesmen usually show at times of crisis.

'This is the ugliest aggression in human history,' he announced before leaving for an emergency meeting of the Arab League which Mubarak had called in Cairo the following day.

Most of his listeners could have named one or two others which might have stood comparison, but there was no denying the King's new mood of alertness and activity. He maintained that the presence of Western forces on his territory would be purely defensive and temporary; in fact American troops would not announce their withdrawal from Saudi Arabia for another twelve years.

At the conference Yasser Arafat busied himself lobbying the other members of the Arab League in support of a compromise. Now he had settled on the terms of the bargain: a figure should be set for the value of the oil from Rumailah which Kuwait would hand over to Iraq, and there should be an amicable arrangement to cancel a large part of Iraq's debt to Kuwait. Finally, Iraq should give Kuwait a permanent lease on the islands of Bubiyan and Warba. Arafat knew a lot about the islands.

'I've trodden over every centimetre of them when I was a civil engineer in Kuwait,' he told anyone who would listen. 'There's nothing there except sand.'

Eleven days before, such a compromise might just have worked. Now, after the invasion and the murder of the Emir's brother on the steps of the palace, it was unthinkable.

Opening the session, President Mubarak insisted that the summit was not a forum for the apportioning of blame. Then he said it was unacceptable for one country to use force against another. Egyptian television, which was broadcasting the opening session live, cut at this moment to the Iraqi delegation. Taha Yasin Ramadan, Iraq's deputy prime minister, laughed and scratched his nose, and the Egyptian director quickly cut away from him.

There were no pictures of the Emir of Kuwait at all, because the Iraqis had refused to come if he were sitting at the same table; there was no such country as Kuwait any more, they said. So the Emir sat apart from the Kuwaiti delegation, and the Egyptians would not show this on television because they did not want to humiliate him. Soon afterwards he walked out. Mubarak had managed to get everyone together just long enough to show that Iraq was unquestionably in the wrong as far as the other Arab countries were concerned.

The next day, the first contingent of Egyptian troops arrived in Saudi Arabia. Morocco, Bangladesh and Pakistan announced that they would be sending troops to join them. Syria declared that its troops would follow them soon: a diplomatic achievement of the first order for the Bush administration. The USS *Eisenhower* would soon be joined in the Gulf by other American and British ships. Soon France, Canada, Belgium, the Netherlands, Italy, Spain and even Argentina would be sending ships, and many of them also sent their ground troops.

President Mubarak's great achievement had been to make it possible for Arabs and Muslims to ally themselves with a Western force. Partly, of course, it was because no one could easily condone a piece of international savagery like the invasion of Kuwait. But at the time it looked as though George Bush's concept of a new world order was taking firm and assured shape: the well-disposed nations of the world acting together to right wrongs.

25. HOSTAGES

No one, not even the members of the Revolutionary Command Council in Baghdad, seemed to know what Saddam Hussein was planning to do. It is perfectly possible he didn't know himself. The day after the invasion Eduard Shevardnadze, the Soviet foreign minister, received assurances from Iraq's ambassador in Moscow that the troops would be withdrawn from Kuwait soon.

A group of Iraqi journalists, some of them working for Reuters, Associated Press and Agence France Presse, were flown to Kuwait City to observe the withdrawal. They saw large numbers of Iraqi tanks driving off along one of the ring-roads, their crews waving. After that, the tanks took up position somewhere else. Few of the Iraqi journalists had the courage to report honestly on what they had seen. Their reports on this non-event added to the confusion about Saddam's intentions.

The one thing that was absolutely clear was that when he was attacked he would always hit back very hard. It was his gangster instinct. Directly the United Nations Security Council voted on Resolution 661, imposing sanctions on Iraq, the foreign minister in the phantom administration which Iraq had established in Kuwait warned that counter-action would be taken against any country which joined in the sanctions.

His name was Lt-Col. Walid Saud Mohammed Abdullah, and although it had been announced that the military junta running Kuwait was entirely composed of Kuwaiti citizens, Colonel Abdullah was a serving officer in the Iraqi army; as were all the other members of the junta. No genuine Kuwaiti took part in the quisling administration.

'Those governments,' Colonel Abdullah warned the countries involved in the sanctions, 'should remember that they have interests and citizens in Kuwait.'

It was classic gangster-speak: you've got a nice house, a nice wife and nice kids – pity if anything happened to them. The tactic was so obvious that it strengthened the hostility to Saddam Hussein even in countries where it would have been natural to expect support for him. There were tens of thousands of Egyptians in Kuwait, for instance, and the decision to hold them hostage caused a good deal of anger in Egypt. The taking of hostages was strictly contrary to international law, and it gave extra credence to President Bush's attack on Saddam's Iraq as 'international outlaws and renegades'.

At first it was relatively easy to escape from Kuwait. If you could get hold of a vehicle that was up to the journey, there were plenty of Iraqis – including soldiers – who would guide you for a fee. There was often uncertainty at the border crossing-points, and the bolder spirits could take advantage of this and leave with an official stamp in their passports. There was no pattern to it. Sometimes would-be escapers would be allowed to continue on their way; sometimes they would be turned back, or arrested. On one occasion, 11 August, a British man called Douglas Croskery was shot and killed as he tried to escape. As for the Westerners remaining in Kuwait, it was clear that they were now regarded as useful bargaining chips against the United States, Britain and France.

'These countries should not expect us to behave honourably when they are conspiring against us,' said Colonel Walid Abdullah, Kuwait's Iraqi foreign minister, on Baghdad's Voice of the Masses radio station. A threat from Abdullah was a threat from Saddam Hussein himself.

26. OPPORTUNITIES

A heavy palm smote the wall-map of the Middle East again and again: on Iraq, Jordan, Syria, Egypt. Benyamin Netanyahu, Israel's deputy minister for foreign affairs, was thinking aloud about the sudden new possibilities which were opening up for his country. He had a good mind, though he was more than a touch arrogant, and it was like listening to an enthusiastic history lecturer. Then he pointed at our camera.

'Is that thing running?'

It wasn't, since the meeting was off the record. A pity: it would have made excellent television to watch an Israeli minister thinking aloud in the briefing room he and his colleagues used at times of crisis. Maybe he thought it was a pity too; but an agreement is an agreement.

Netanyahu wasn't worried by the events in the Gulf. Far from it: he saw them as offering a new beginning, a chance for the Middle East to break out of its regional stalemate.

'It could bring a new order and a new realism,' he said.

Ten months earlier, in November 1989, the old order had started to break up in Eastern Europe. Now the process seemed to be spreading even farther east. For Netanyahu, it represented a real opportunity. He took it for granted that the United States, Britain and others would destroy Iraq's military potential. After that, he seemed to be saying, Israel would no longer be so isolated and threatened.

Israelis talked endlessly about the parallels with the 1930s, and how important it was to face up to the new Hitler. The expression everyone was suddenly using was 'red line': 'A red line must be drawn in Jordan to ensure that Iraqi troops will not be sent there.' There was a new bustle about Israeli West Jerusalem, I felt: an excitability in the air, a sense of opportunity.

'Maybe this time Israel won't have to fight alone,' said a writer I knew, a large, dishevelled character who despite his appearance always reminded me faintly of Woody Allen. 'I usually feel gloomy about the future. I know things are dangerous, but somehow I don't feel so gloomy now.'

When I went to the Palestinian side I found people were also talking endlessly about historical parallels. But the one they preferred was 1956, and they spoke of Saddam as the new Nasser who was standing up against the West. I wandered round the Arab quarters of the Old City of Jerusalem, talking to people I knew and looking at the slogans which were appearing on the walls: 'Saddam Our Leader', 'United For Action!', 'Arise!' Some of them had been blotted out with black paint. Those were the ones the Israeli soldiers had found most offensive.

It was very quiet in the Arab parts of the Old City. The shops were closed for the latest strike which no shopkeeper really wanted, yet no shopkeeper felt able to break. There was no bustle here, as there was in the Israeli areas, but people seemed to feel that the crisis would somehow work in their favour.

'We have to have pride in ourselves,' said an elderly Palestinian dealer whom I knew quite well. He still had a photograph of King Hussein on his wall and regarded himself as a subject of the King. He certainly had no affection whatever for Saddam Hussein, yet he felt that by standing up to the British and Americans Saddam was asserting the dignity of all Arabs.

I travelled down to Jericho. In the folds and valleys of the wilderness on either side of the road, the Bedouin still pitched their tents and tended their goats, as they always had. But now the hilltops were being colonized by the developed world: blocks of white apartments, like fortified yuppie estates, showed where settlers from the United States and Russia had staked their claim to Eretz Israel. Everything in this country was in the process of change, and the balance of population was shifting in favour of the Jews, not the Palestinians.

For a place so numinous, the Allenby Bridge across the River Jordan, linking Jerusalem with Amman, is remarkably unimpressive. Metal, rickety and surprisingly small, the Allenby's unfixed timbers rattled under our wheels as we crossed a weed-clogged river as narrow as a village stream. Yet it marked a great frontier, not just between Israel and the Arabs but between the First World and the Third World. The no man's land was lined with rusty wire and sown with mines, and the dry limestone hillocks and the empty plain beyond were as delicately coloured as a David Roberts drawing.

Amman, I found, was in a state of high excitement. Saddam's face glared or smiled at me from almost every shop window, the back of every taxi. His offer to withdraw from Kuwait if Israel withdrew from the West Bank had electrified every Palestinian; and Palestinians were the majority in Jordan now.

'This is our opportunity,' said a Palestinian businessman with a heat and excitement I had not previously associated with him.

I asked him how, as a man of honour and decency (which he was), he could think it was possible to build a Palestinian state on the actions of a gangster. Surely, the Kuwaitis had lost their land in something of the way the Palestinians had lost theirs? Wouldn't the very soil of a country gained by such means be tainted for ever? He looked troubled, but told me I was wrong. He didn't explain how.

At first sight it seemed that Jordan agreed with Saddam Hussein wholeheartedly. The columnists in the Amman press had decided to a man (there were no women among them at that stage) that the entire crisis was somehow the fault of Britain and America. Now Britain and America had to act, and act fast, to make up for the wrongs they had done: to Jordan, to the Palestinians, to the children of Iraq, to the Third World in general.

This was not at all the same, of course, as Saddam Hussein was demanding. He wasn't interested in apologies and handouts from the West. He was defying the West, not sitting round waiting for it to do something. The one was the attitude of post-colonial dependence, still looking to the old imperial powers for everything. The other, Saddam's approach, was far more radical and aggressive.

I laboured up the hill to the King's palace in the August heat, and talked to the King's officials. They didn't blame the Americans or the British; they were just extremely glum.

'We all hope His Majesty will come out of this reasonably well,' said a youngish man in a superb double-breasted suit. His tone reminded me of a similarly dressed young man I had talked to in the Shah's palace in Tehran in 1978: 'H.I.M. will, we are sure, lead us out of the present difficulties.' H.I.M. stood for 'His Imperial Majesty', and he was gone in less than six months. No one in the palace seemed to think Saddam Hussein had provided them with an opportunity, or that he had liberated their national sense of themselves.

A day later, Tariq Aziz came to Amman and gave a press conference. Most of the questions related to the position of the hostages. He was distinctly oleaginous.

> First, they are not hostages. I am sorry the President of the United States should have used a wrong word for the situation of these people. We really meant we would like to keep them as guests for a while and live with our own people. And then, living with our people in the places where they live, they might contribute to peace . . .

As he left, I managed to push my way through the crowd and speak to him as he got into his car.

'Would it be possible for the BBC to visit Baghdad?'

Tariq Aziz beamed insincerely as his security men jostled me.

'Why not?'

For once, the standard, noncommittal expression of the Iraqi bureaucrat did not represent a brush-off. My visa to Baghdad came through the next day.

27. RETURNING

It was time to go, and I was intensely nervous. A friend of mine, high up in the Foreign Office, rang me twice from London to urge me not to go. Another friend, who knew Iraq well, was even more insistent. I could, they both said, end up as a hostage myself. Did I have any guarantees that the Iraqis would let me go when I had finished my reporting? No? Then I was crazy to consider it.

I supposed I was, but something that had taken so long to get could not be discarded now that it had arrived. I opened my passport and looked at it for the twentieth time: a green and red sticker on page seven, with a heraldic yet mildly caricatured eagle at its head and a few details which had been carelessly scribbled in with a ballpoint pen:

> *Embassy of the Republic of Iraq in*: AMMAN
> *No*: 2/44/4
> *Date*: 22/8/90
> *Type of visa*: ANTRY
> *Holder is permitted to enter Iraq until*: 3 MONTH
> *Number of journeys*: ONES

Underneath a message had been stamped in blue:

> Visitors who expect to stay in Iraq for more than 30 days should contact the Residence Directorate in Baghdad during their stay. Those who fail to do so will be liable to Prosecution.

I was fortunate in my companions: Ray Gibbon, a witty, quick-minded cameraman and a good friend who wouldn't blame me if things went wrong; Mohammed Amin, whose pictures of the Ethiopian famine of 1984 had touched the conscience of the world when he worked there with the BBC correspondent Michael Buerk; and Dave McDonald, an American who worked for the television agency Visnews.

People shook hands with us with a special intensity as we left the Intercontinental Hotel in Amman. A couple of photographers took snaps of us, just in case. At the airport a cameraman filmed us loading our gear on to baggage trolleys, and a reporter asked us why we were going. I tried to keep my answers as flippant as possible.

A team from CNN was travelling in at the same time, and I got talking with the producer, Robert Wiener. Later he would write the best book about reporting the war, and ensure that CNN's coverage of it was essential viewing around the world. I asked him why he was going to Baghdad.

'I left Saigon before the Viet Cong took over, and spent fifteen years trying to make up for it. I don't want to have to make up for anything again.'

He was, I felt, precisely right.

Because of the UN sanctions, the only way to get to Baghdad by air now was on this one daily flight from Amman. The plane was full of Iraqis flying home to be with their families at a time of crisis. I had half expected that we would have problems with our fellow-passengers; instead, they treated us with politeness, even friendship, as though we were all in the same tumbril, condemned together.

The stewards allowed us off first, and we walked across the tarmac in the enormous heat of early afternoon into the arrivals hall, too quick for the secret policemen who had been standing inside talking. Taken by surprise, they scattered like snooker balls to the outer edges of the hall as we came through the door. Two of them sat near us as we stood waiting for our gear, looking at the wall in front of them with unfocused eyes. A minder from the information ministry met us and ushered our equipment through customs, then melted away. We were on our own again.

We pushed our way through the exit, and the heat wrapped round us again like a hot towel at the barber's. It was, the pilot had told us on the plane, forty-two degrees Centigrade. This, fortunately, was too hot for the flies, which vanish from Baghdad at the height of summer. Less fortunately, it was also too hot for taxis. We stood looking at the empty road for some time. Then a vehicle in the familiar orange and white livery ventured past, and despair made me jump in front of it, waving my arms. The driver took us into town in exchange for large amounts of money.

The motorway from the airport was entirely empty, except for some buses which the driver said were going to the airport to pick up returning prisoners of war just released by Iran. Otherwise nothing: no cars, no trucks, no buses, not even a horse and cart or a bicycle.

'Welcome to Baghdad, Capital of Arab's Saddam,' said a sign by the side of the road. Saddam himself grinned or smirked from half a dozen posters: the most reproduced features of any ruler in the world, I thought, never having been to North Korea.

The temperature inside the taxi was stifling, so I opened the window. The wind burned me like a red-hot poker and I shut it fast, swearing. The driver, a gap-toothed, ill-shaven character, snorted his amusement. He had no interest in any subject except the value of the Iraqi dinar to US dollar. It was, he indicated with a sharp movement of his hand, ruinous. When I had been in Baghdad three months before, it had cost 100 dollars at the official rate to buy three beers, a soft drink and a cup of tea. Now, according to the driver, it would cost three times as much. And if we changed money on the black market? Another hand-movement: the death sentence. Very comforting.

Things had changed in the centre of town. There were two anti-aircraft guns on top of the great gateway leading to Saddam's main palace. The gunners peered down at us because cars were so rare in the streets just now. It was Tuesday afternoon, and the streets of Baghdad should have been full of people. Now they were uneasily quiet. The shops were empty, the teahouses mostly closed and shuttered. An armoured personnel carrier was parked in a side-street, and there were soldiers on every street corner. Saddam was taking no chances; the people of Baghdad were unlikely to rise up against him, but he wanted to make sure.

In the lobby of the empty hotel, where the only other people were security men, a notice at the reception desk warned us not to try paying with credit cards; because of the international situation, it explained. A couple of dark and heavily beautiful Assyrian Christian women were working in the business centre in the hotel, and although their obvious anxiety made me feel like the carrier of a plague bacillus, they smiled and tried to be welcoming. I remembered that Farzad Bazoft had used this office to send his reports to his newspaper; evidence from his phone calls and telexes had been produced at the trial.

'Will things be very bad?' asked one of the women with a touching anxiety. I tried to reassure her.

'Please remember,' she said earnestly, as though I had the power to direct the airstrikes, 'that it isn't our fault.'

A big portrait of Saddam Hussein kept watch over me as I scribbled out my first radio report, about nothing more than our journey into the centre of town. Then he watched me as I read it over the phone to London, uncensored. There were strange noises on the line as I finished, and the line went dead instantly. The girls smiled, but looked at each other in a frightened kind of way.

At the information ministry we were shown into the office of the director-general. A pleasant-looking man who could have been French or British got up from behind his desk and walked over with his hand outstretched.

'Mr Simpson, Mr Simpson,' he said. 'Welcome. I am Naji al-Haddithi.'

I found him charming, and my friendship with him lasted the entire length of the crisis, and into the war which was still five months into the future. Not everyone else shared my liking for him; a *New York Times* reporter was so spooked out by a warning al-Haddithi gave him that he took refuge at the American embassy and slept every night until he left Iraq on the floor of the press attaché's office.

Al-Haddithi reminded me of some witty, feline official trained in Constantinople at the Sublime Porte. Unlike Farzad Bazoft, I never made the mistake of thinking that his friendship would save me if I got into trouble. Under Saddam Hussein, your highly placed, charming friends could do nothing more when trouble came than shrug their shoulders and give a pleasant, apologetic smile.

Now, though, al-Haddithi took me by the arm and led me into a large room with a sofa and chairs in one corner and an Iraqi flag behind them. We were about to meet another stock figure of my time in Iraq, Latif Nsayef Jassim, the minister of culture and information. It was Jassim who had said of Farzad, 'Mrs Thatcher wanted him alive. We gave her the body.' It was Jassim, too, who had opened an international television film festival in Baghdad with the announcement that to celebrate this auspicious moment a dozen Scud missiles had been fired at Tehran. Most of the Arabs in the audience stood up and applauded.

Jassim was a dapper little man in his tailored olive-green Ba'ath Party uniform, with a display handkerchief in the top pocket: a

revolutionary travelling business class. He was undoubtedly close to
Saddam Hussein. On the walls of the corridor which linked the lifts
with the interview room there were photographs of the two of them
with their arms round each other. It was dangerous to touch Saddam
physically unless he really trusted you; he would want to know why
you were doing it.

Now Jassim, the man whom Saddam trusted, started explaining to
me that there was no reason to worry about the Western hostages.
They were the guests of Iraq, and no harm would come to them. Why
must we keep on calling them hostages, anyway? It was very offensive.
By now he himself had used the word half a dozen times.

On the television set the news was beginning. Saddam Hussein was
visiting a camp where British hostages were being held. Children were
playing chess, or kicking a football around. Indoors, Saddam sat down
and asked questions of a group of nervous-looking British people
who were standing up. Saddam beckoned to a boy of about ten, who
walked unwillingly over to him. His name was Stewart, he said.
Saddam draped his arm over Stewart's shoulder in a way that set my
teeth on edge.

'Are you getting your milk, Stewart? And your cornflakes too?'

Stewart, standing very stiff and embarrassed, as though he could
scarcely bear the touch, said he was.

'I don't think all Iraqi kids can get cornflakes now. So please
forgive us, because we, like you, have our own children, like Stewart
and Ian [Stewart's brother], and we have our own women like you,
and our own families. We know how you feel, but we are trying to
prevent a war from happening.'

There was something very wrong with this exchange. Yet it wasn't
what most Westerners might have assumed. In Iraq it is regarded as
perfectly normal for a man to touch children who are not his own; in
most Western societies it is emphatically not. Stewart's evident awk-
wardness made it seem a great deal worse.

But the real unpleasantness behind the episode was the menace
that underlay Saddam's apparent bonhomie. He was reminding Iraqi
viewers that their children were going short of milk while these British
children, whose government was cutting off their milk supply, were
enjoying the best of everything. So the arm round Stewart's shoulders
wasn't really avuncular at all: it was threatening and unnatural. The

outside world misread the exact meaning of the body language between the two, and yet it was not all that wrong, after all.

Saddam rambled on at length to the British adults, and when he discovered that one boy in the group was merely visiting a friend in Iraq he gave orders that he should be allowed to go home.

Jassim, the information minister, was not a very clever man, and afterwards he seemed delighted by the whole spectacle, as though Saddam had scored some major propaganda victory and shown himself in a sympathetic light. On the contrary: his willingness to release one foreign child on a whim demonstrated clearly that he could release all the hostages if he chose. When we broadcast the pictures of Saddam's meeting with the families that night the reaction was a strong one. The British government called it sickening, and it was roundly condemned in the United States, Russia, France and Germany.

On 25 August, two days after we arrived, the Austrian President Kurt Waldheim flew into Baghdad to meet Saddam Hussein. Waldheim had been a dull and plodding secretary-general of the United Nations, and revelations about his unpleasant Nazi war record during the presidential election had ruined his reputation (except, that is, in Austria, where he was elected by an enthusiastic majority). He had come now to plead for the release of the eighty or so Austrian hostages in Kuwait and Iraq, and thereby set a precedent for other politicians whose careers were over or in trouble to try the same trick.

It was clear even to Saddam that the hostages were becoming a serious political liability. He dealt with the problem in his usual impulsive fashion. On 28 August he met a group of British, Japanese and American hostages, and chatted with them on camera. He displayed all the ersatz sincerity of a chat-show host.

'I'm told we've got one little lady here with a birthday. Happy birthday, Rachel!'

On the spur of the moment, he said that Rachel and her mother could leave. Then, as some of the British women started asking him how long the rest of them would have to stay, he told them abruptly that all women and children were free to go. They were: but no planning was in place for an exodus which would involve several hundred people.

28. THE REAL IRAQ

The changes that were taking place in Baghdad were obvious. When
we first arrived, Saddam Hussein seemed to be expecting that the
Americans and British would start bombing Baghdad imminently; he
even told Yasser Arafat he thought there might be a nuclear attack.
The great architectural treasures were taken from the museums and
stored in safe places: the Assyrian bulls, the Sumerian jewellery, the
Akkadian cuneiform texts. And, Saddam being Saddam, he included in
the great national treasures a huge archive of pictures of himself, taken
by his personal photographer, Hussein Mohammed Ali. The entire
Saddam Art Centre was emptied and closed down, so that posterity
might be assured of having enough representations of the great man.

Then the first sense of fear and tension melted away. It was
replaced in most people's minds with a feeling that some compromise
must surely be achieved. Everyone I spoke to in Baghdad, from the
most slavishly loyal of officials to the Kurdish woman who told me
much too loudly of her contempt and hatred of Saddam, forecast a
settlement under which Western forces would withdraw from Saudi
Arabia, Iraqi forces would withdraw from Kuwait, and the way would
be open to solve the Palestinian problem along the lines of Saddam's
offer of 12 August.

By the beginning of September, therefore, there was a new and
easier atmosphere in Baghdad. More Western news organizations were
being allowed into the country, so we were less isolated. We even
noticed that the security surveillance of us was becoming lighter. With
so many foreign journalists arriving, the Mukhabarat must have been
stretched as never before.

Until now, Iraq had been nothing more to me than an extremely
unpleasant governmental system run by people who might easily kill
me if I put a foot wrong. Slowly, I was coming to a rather different
view. It bore no resemblance to the hysterical picture of Iraq that was
presented in the downmarket British and American press. One day we
filmed at the offices of the British Council. There were at least a dozen
people there, reading quietly in the library or drinking tea in the café.

The staff, British and Iraqi, said they had had no problems: no threats, no attacks, no demonstrations. On the contrary, the man in charge said, more and more people were coming in to thank them for staying open during the crisis. I was struck, too, by the general absence of hostility towards us as we walked through the streets. The Iraqi newspapers were full of bitter condemnation of the crimes that Britain and the West in general were supposed to be committing against Iraqis; and yet I never found anyone who, in private, justified the invasion of Kuwait. People might be frightened; they weren't hostile.

One evening, after satelliting our report for the night, we drove along the east bank of the Tigris, past all the cafés and restaurants. Rationing had already been introduced, though apart from occasional queues at the bread shops and rumours of a rice shortage there were no serious problems. Soon the government would close down most of the restaurants, but for the moment they were doing good business. On one side of the road people were eating kebabs and rice; on the other side, along the river bank, they were eating the Baghdad speciality *mazgouf*: a large river fish barbecued in front of a large fire in traditional style. There was plenty of alcohol: Iraq had never been a strict Muslim society, and Saddam's increasingly religious rhetoric would not turn it into one. The appetizing smell of wood smoke and cooked fish swirled around them, and the diners sat back and enjoyed themselves.

At our hotel, too, a strange transformation had taken place. For a few hours the gloom gave way to something more endearing. There was a skirl of trumpets, and a woman in a white wedding-dress came in on the arm of a man in a white dinner-jacket. Both were sweating in the evening heat. I saw them a few hours later, walking shyly down a hotel corridor hand in hand, wearing more sensible clothes. Downstairs, meanwhile, there were sudden bursts of ululation as other pairs of newly-weds headed for the Semiramis Lounge or the Scheherazade Room for their reception. Wars are good for the wedding industry.

That night, as I listened to the faint noise of revelry downstairs, I found my ideas of this country changing. For a moment the atmosphere of threat and anxiety had receded. I had caught a glimpse of something timeless, and much more sympathetic than the angry speeches of Saddam Hussein.

29. CRIMES

It was a quiet day in Baghdad: no press conferences, no threats, no sign of war, just a demonstration in the heat of the day by school-children. They were carrying heart-shaped cardboard placards with a wide selection of slogans:

Iraqi Children Love Their Leader Because
He Cares for Childhood

The Evil Forces Do Not Love Saddam Hussein Because
He Loves Peace

Mr Bush, Do Not Flex Your Muscles on Iraqi Children

Children of the World, Prevent Your Fathers Killing Us

Saddam, We Are Yours Forever

There was, of course, nothing remotely spontaneous about this demonstration, any more than there was about the rest of the daily parades of people in the streets of Baghdad with placards. The security police would tell a school or a factory or a particular union that its members would be expected to turn out at such and such a time, and that the following would be the slogans they should carry and the words they should chant. No excuses were accepted for absence except the most serious illness. Anyone who simply stayed away would be investigated for anti-state activities and might well be imprisoned or even killed.

Nothing about this demonstration was genuine; it was just another of Saddam's entirely cynical ways of attracting international support for his cause. Still, as the years went past I came to believe that Iraqi children were indeed dying through the policy of UN sanctions, for which the United States and Britain were largely responsible. It seemed to me that it was of the greatest importance to lift them, even though it was often Saddam Hussein's manipulation that led to the deaths of the children, rather than the deliberate will of the British and Americans. But I didn't, of course, allow these feelings to show in my broadcast. It was enough to state the facts, and allow people to make their own minds up.

I didn't campaign about this, because I don't think it is right for BBC journalists to be campaigners for contentious causes, no matter how good they might be; to do so weakens the objectivity of the organization.

In September 1990, these sanctions were in their very early stages, and it is unlikely that they were yet having much effect on the health of Iraqi children; but as time went on they had a very serious effect. The United States and Britain might not specifically have intended to target Iraqi children with their sanctions, but that was the result; and Saddam Hussein used the suffering of children, and did nothing to stop it, precisely in order to strengthen his own political position. Between the two sides, a great many children and adults would suffer and die over the next dozen years. And because neither side was innocent of the accusations of the other, ordinary well-intentioned people caught in the middle found it difficult to know what to think.

At the children's demonstration a fat boy was making Mussolini-like gestures and attacking the United States and its allies for singling out the children of Iraq for their special hatred. A little girl shouted out a message in English:

'Yes, yes to peace – no, no to war.'

She did it with great earnestness, beating her fists on the lectern for emphasis.

Beside me as we filmed all this was an American cameraman, a pleasant, thoughtful man. He was troubled by what he saw and heard.

'Guess they really mean all this peace stuff. Makes you think, hey, suppose they're right and we're wrong?'

He shook his head in decent puzzlement. 'I mean, like everybody wants peace. And who wants to kill these kids? I sure don't.'

On these big international issues we all long for a clarity of understanding which usually eludes us. In the United States and Britain, in particular, the governments trimmed off the moral complexities and presented Iraq's invasion of Kuwait as a clear-cut matter of good and evil; it is hard to make democracies fight for anything else. The result was that the war became a matter of sloganeering, of quick short cuts to moral certainty. The tabloids which supported the US/British line screamed in their headlines about 'evil' Saddam; always an adjective to make the wise ponder what is really being said.

At the same time, those who were opposed to a war with Iraq were starting to say it was 'all about oil', as though that somehow meant that no one had to worry any more about the ethics of allowing dictators to invade their neighbours. It was like reading a newspaper story of a robbery and saying, 'Oh, it's all just about money.' Other people maintained that since the United States, Britain and France had supported Saddam in his war with Iran, this meant that none of them had any right to question his later crimes.

All these approaches represented a sloughing-off of the necessity to examine what was really happening and to decide which of several flawed possibilities was the best. Many of the tactics used by Britain and the United States, in particular, were deeply questionable, and some were actively wrong. Yet this did not somehow wash Saddam Hussein clean from the guilt of what he had done. The choices were much more complicated than that.

To accept at their face value the slogans which the children at that day's demonstration were ordered to display was equally naïve. Did Saddam really care about childhood? What about the dead children of Halabjah, attacked with poison gas by Saddam's own men? Did Saddam really love peace? If so, why had he attacked his neighbours, Iran and Kuwait, virtually on a whim?

There was a distinctly unwholesome contrast all the way round between the simple, easy slogans and the nasty complexity of real life – and between the allegations and what really happened. When President Bush's vice-president, Dan Quayle – a man not overloaded with intellect – quoted the American wife of a Kuwaiti as saying she had watched Iraqi soldiers bayoneting a pregnant woman, plenty of people remembered the British and French propaganda of the First World War about German troops bayoneting babies. Nothing more was ever heard about the case quoted by Dan Quayle, and it seems likely it was just a silly fabrication.

Yet there were cases which were equally ugly. I talked to two leading businessmen who had got to Baghdad from Kuwait, an Irishman and a Dutchman. They were not excitable men, and they had both lived in Kuwait for years. They had spent the previous few weeks recording every case of murder and looting by the Iraqi troops that they came across. They showed me the documents they had brought out with them, and asked me to help them get the papers through the airport. In return, they recorded a long interview with me; dangerous for them in itself, since we assumed that our rooms in the hotel were bugged. Fortunately, though, it seems that the secret policemen who had the job of listening to our conversation were thoroughly overstretched by the large number of foreign journalists staying in the hotel.

The two men checked each other's stories carefully and corrected the details where necessary, referring constantly to the notes they had smuggled out. I sat and listened to the conversation, as the tape-recorder turned.

'I happened,' the Irishman said, 'to be looking out of the window when a car with [Iraqi] soldiers in it crashed into another car. Maybe it was their fault, maybe it was the Kuwaiti's; I don't know. Anyway, they pulled him out of the car and started beating him up. Then one of them ran over to a roadworker who was standing there and took his shovel off him, and swung it at this poor fellow's leg. And he almost cut it off with one swipe. He just lay there in a pool of blood with his leg hanging off, and they got in the car and drove away.'

There was a pause. Then the Dutchman spoke.

'It was on 5 August, just three days after the invasion. They came bursting into my apartment and held me and another man at gunpoint. There were three women in the apartment at the time as well. They raped all of them, including one who was seven months pregnant. I saw them do it. Four men raped her, in front of her little son, who was four months old – my godson. They were Republican Guards, you could tell them by their red berets.

'One of the officers made the youngest soldier do it – he was hanging back, like he was afraid. He just pushed him forward and made him do it.'

Death became a familiar sight after the Iraqis invaded Kuwait: so familiar, no one did anything much about it. The body of a Kuwaiti who had been shot by the Iraqis lay on one of the bridges in the centre of the city. People just drove over it. The head, hands and legs were all right, but the rest of the body had been flattened by the passing cars, like a road-kill.

Then the two men started reminding each other of people they knew and cases they had heard of.

'There was that woman, was her name Karbazed? Her son was shot in the street in front of her, and they told her not to touch the body. She couldn't help it, she was crying hysterically, and they grabbed her head and rubbed it in the blood.'

'Then there were the al-Awtabis, they were a big family, very famous. They shot the son in front of the father, so he would know his line had ended, then they shot him too.'

'Abdullah al-Darmi was tortured and shot because they found a copy of the resistance newsletter in his flat. Someone had just pushed it under his door – that was how they delivered them. But they shot him.'

'I knew a doctor, Dr Hisham al-Obudan I think his name was. He worked in the As-Sabah Maternity Hospital. They caught him leaving one night with a piece of saline tube in his pocket. They thought he must be going to help some foreigners, or maybe someone in the resistance. Anyway, they shot him in the back of the head in front of the kitchen staff. It turned out he was taking it home for someone in his family who needed a saline drip.'

According to the Red Crescent, an average of between four and five bodies were brought to their centre in Kuwait City every day during the period of the Iraqi occupation. On some days there were as many as ten. Altogether, anything up to thirty bodies were found each day in the city as a whole. Many had been shot through the back of the head at point-blank range.

Looting was the only industry in Kuwait for the six months of the Iraqi occupation. This is a small, random and incomplete selection of what was stolen by the Iraqis in Kuwait City:

28 out of 40 dental units from the main hospital, and 12 more
    dental units from the other hospitals;
7 of the 9 ambulances at the Amiri Hospital;
100 out of 120 ambulances at the Subham depot;
all the hearses and mechanical diggers at the three main
    cemeteries;
all the equipment from the city's three main sports centres;
the entire library and medical records from the Kuwaiti Medical
    School;
the entire library of Kuwait University;

all the equipment and records from the Institute for Scientific
  Research;
all the emergency fire equipment at the civil airport, all the
  navigational equipment, all the unloading gear, all flight and
  maintenance simulators, all machine-shop tools;
every single movable object from the National Bank of Kuwait,
  including safes, desks, chairs, bookshelves, computers, hat
  stands, soap dispensers and towel rails.

The big Matana shopping centre required ten days' continuous looting
before it was emptied of everything. In an interview which Saddam
Hussein recorded for ITN in November 1990, Trevor McDonald asked
him, 'How can you justify the atrocities committed by Iraqi troops in
your name?'

'What is certain,' Saddam answered blandly, 'is that I have not
heard of any such acts. It is possible that . . . the Western media is
trying to fill the minds of people everywhere, every day with lies about
the situation . . . It is also possible that some false reports may come
out of Kuwait, claiming the sort of things you have described.'

The looting and destruction and murder in Kuwait was in fact
done on orders which emanated in general terms from Saddam Hussein
himself. But he had always found that if he said point-blank that
things which were thoroughly documented were untrue, someone
would believe him. They believed him now. The newspapers in Amman
carried articles condemning the Western media for their crude propaganda. Politicians and some journalists in Britain, Germany and France
who were against the war complained about the way the newspapers,
television and radio were trying to push the world into war by
inventing atrocity stories. There is no doubt that those who wanted
war found atrocity stories very useful, but this did not mean there
were no atrocities.

Wherever there is resistance to an occupying force, there are
usually war crimes. By October the armed resistance to the Iraqis was
relatively low; nevertheless around 100 Iraqi soldiers were killed by
the resistance movement over the entire period of occupation, and that
argues a high level of urban guerrilla operation in a small city with
few hiding-places. Resistance took other forms as well. The inhabitants
of Kuwait City would wake up in the morning and find that new
slogans had been painted on the walls:

Long Live Free Kuwait!

Iraqis, You Have No Right Here!

The Kuwaiti People Are Free!

Iraqis, We Will Never Surrender And Never Forgive!

For many Kuwaitis the easiest form of resistance was simply to go on to the rooftops and shout, '*Allah-u Akbar*' – 'God is most great'. A Kuwaiti housewife described the beneficial effects of this to Amnesty International:

> The children were in a perpetual state of fright. Many of them developed a stutter and could not talk normally. Others began suffering from uncontrolled urination. We tried to control their stutter by taking them up to the rooftops with us where we shouted, '*Allah-u Akbar!*' in protest at the Iraqi invasion. At first the children had difficulty in getting the words out, but we urged them to shout at the tops of their voices. After several attempts, some of them regained normal speech.

There were, of course, many acts of cowardice and betrayal; occupation always produces them. But there were also acts of extraordinary self-sacrifice. Many foreigners, who could not leave their homes for fear of being arrested, received food and other help from their Kuwaiti and Palestinian neighbours. The penalty for doing this could be death. According to one British woman,

> There was a Palestinian family in the building and they knew we were around. They came and asked us very early on if they could help us, and they brought us food two or three times a week. Every time they came I would say, 'Are you sure you can carry on doing this?' And they always said, 'We're your neighbours, of course we're going to help you.' Sometimes I thought they might be getting too frightened to go on, but they always did, right up until the time we left. They were wonderful. What can you do to thank people who risk their lives for you, just because they live in the same building? However can you thank them enough?

Perhaps the greatest success of the resistance was the recovery of the body of the Emir's half-brother, Fahd al-Ahmad as-Sabah, who had died on the steps of the Dasman Palace when the Iraqis invaded. It was

kept under guard, but in September a group of resisters slipped into
the morgue where it was being held and took it away for secret burial.
When the word went round, it had a huge effect on Kuwaiti morale.

The morning after the Irishman and the Dutchman had come to
see me, I and my BBC colleagues went with them to the airport. A
pleasant and efficient Indian woman was travelling with them. It took
me a little time to realize that she was one of those whose rape by
Iraqi soldiers they had described to me the previous evening.

There was a great deal of tension as the three of them went through
the complexities of the airport system. One of them was found to have
Kuwaiti dinars on him, and was taken off to a side office. We waited
outside, in full view of the officials through the glass door, until he
was let out. The dinars, of course, were taken off him. But the papers
they had amassed on the crimes and the looting were not discovered.
I watched as the three of them made their way on to the aircraft
which would take them to Amman and safety.

My colleagues and I drove back into the centre of town. I was
beginning to feel at home here. I did not feel safe, exactly, because no
one in a country like Saddam's Iraq should allow themselves to feel
entirely safe. But as a result of the things the two men had told me I
looked at the people I knew in a slightly different light now: the
drivers, the hotel staff, the merchants in the *souq*, the other Iraqi
friends I had made.

They came from the same background as the looters, the executioners, the torturers, the officer who had ordered the youngest recruit
in his unit to take part in the gang-rape of the pleasant, dignified
Indian woman I had just said goodbye to, the soldier who had hacked
off the leg of a passing motorist after a traffic accident, the doctor who
had switched off the oxygen supply to a sick man in hospital because
he happened to be a Kuwaiti.

There is no value in blaming individuals for what groups of their
fellow-countrymen have done: people are people, and have a right to be
treated as they are and for what they do themselves. Nevertheless it can
be instructive to reflect what a society is capable of doing under certain
circumstances. The rape of Kuwait was the work of people operating
under the circumstances which Saddam Hussein had created for them.
At the very least, I reflected, as long as I knew what this society was
capable of doing, I would not suffer any unpleasant surprises.

I also remembered the demonstration by Iraqi children the previous day: 'Iraqi Children Love Their Leader Because He Cares For Childhood.' It was pretty cynical to present the entire crisis as an attack by the outside world on Iraqi children, when the children of Kuwait were reduced to stuttering and incontinence by the ferocity of Iraq's soldiers. The years of Saddam's rule had encouraged some ugly propensities in a nation which seemed on the surface to be so peaceable and easy-going.

I glanced at yet another vast portrait of Saddam, grinning down on his people and holding out his hand in a way that seemed more imperious than inviting. They would never, I reflected, be able to come to terms with what he had done to them, any more than the people of Kuwait would. Like Stalin, like Hitler, like Ceausescu, like Pol Pot, like Idi Amin, he had damaged the lives of his people for generations to come.

Whatever happened now – whether there was a war, whether he died or lived to fight another war and survive that, or whether he was overthrown and died in some miserable shoot-out – he would remain inside them, working away like a cancer, for the rest of their lives, and their children's lives, and their children's children's lives. 'Saddam, We Are Yours Forever,' another placard at the demonstration had said. They certainly would be.

30. THE ABANDONED

Back in Amman, my colleagues and I went out to celebrate the fact that we had completed our tour of duty safely, and had hopes of returning to Baghdad after a short spell at home. We were walking back to our hotel after a good meal and wine that tasted sensational after so many weeks of shortage, when a crowded bus drew up beside us. It was filthy, and covered with the dust of a long trip across the desert. Such buses were coming in all the time from Kuwait and Baghdad, bringing former hostages who had been allowed to leave. If they were Europeans, there was always a gang of photographers and cameramen hanging round to capture the moment when they arrived in the freedom of Jordan. There would be plenty of reporters to ask them questions and hope to elicit stories which would allow them – if they worked for the British tabloids – to use words like 'fiends' and 'evil butchers' about the Iraqis.

There were no journalists or cameramen waiting for this bus. There seemed to be as many people standing up as sitting down inside it, and the driver started pushing and kicking them out onto the pavement. They sat there among their cardboard boxes and bundles tied up in headscarves. The children with them began to cry. Some of the mothers looked no older than sixteen or seventeen themselves, and just as much in need of comfort.

'Where are you from?' I asked one of the older women.

'Please,' she answered, looking nervously up at me, 'we are from Philippines.'

The bus had brought them all the way from Kuwait. The journey had taken more than thirty hours and there had been very few rest-stops. They had only once been given food and water.

They were skinny and feeble, these women, and looked quite incapable of looking after themselves. Some had been locked up by their employers in the houses where they had worked as servants, until the Iraqi soldiers broke in and turned them loose. Many of them had apparently been raped.

Now there was nothing for them to do, nowhere for them to sleep, no food to eat and no water to drink. The reception centre available for people like them was full to overflowing already, so the only place they could sleep was in the front garden. Their embassies had not sent anyone to help them or check their details. Virgin Air-lines had volunteered in a blaze of publicity to fly home the British women and children from Kuwait free. No one had laid on a charter flight for these people. The Reverend Jesse Jackson, who had flown to Baghdad and Kuwait to get the American hostages out (his busi-ness manager had told us when we asked if we could have seats on his plane, 'We aren't into chequebook journalism, but that'll be $100,000!'), wouldn't be coming to rescue them. The British tabloids weren't polishing up their adjectives to describe what they had gone through.

The fifty or sixty Filipinas sat despondently in the warm darkness, quiet now except for the occasional whimpering of a tired child. My colleagues and I hung around awkwardly for a while. The one thing we could do to help them was to fetch our camera from the hotel and film them, in the hope that some foreign government might feel obliged to intervene. As we went off to get the equipment I looked back. They were still watching us, but no one complained that we seemed to be deserting them. Life had taught them that there was no point in complaining, and no one to complain to anyway.

31. THE BUILD-UP

Helicopters rose like pheasants in a field, clattering nervously into the air. In the heat of Saudi Arabia they had no fixity of shape, and swelled or contracted randomly as they moved away across the desert. Their rotors drew the sand up towards them, and it blew across the landing-strip like a net curtain fluttering across a window.

The sand was as omnipresent as air: colourless, creeping effortlessly into the most intimate crevices of your body, working its way between your tongue and the roof of your mouth, between your upper and lower molars, between your waistband and your skin. Anything that could possibly rub became an emery-board of redness and discomfort. Sand studded your soap and infiltrated the controls of your Walkman. It covered you like the lightest and most delicate of sheets as you slept. It was the medium in which you lived and moved and breathed.

The temperature was 118 degrees Fahrenheit in the shade; but there was no shade. A detachment of US Marines marched across the sandy parade-ground, floppy hats shading brown faces and non-regulation sunglasses. To a British eye they looked a little sloppy, a little slow, a little overweight and unfit. But the US Marine Corps had equipment that no other country on earth could match. It had come off the ships in staggering amounts: tons of tents and blankets and tables and chairs and filing cabinets, entire containers filled with ice cream, steaks, prawns. There was a mile of frankfurters, a lake of coffee, a sea of soft drinks. There were trucks called roach-coaches which could stop anywhere and provide a detachment of men with a three-course meal and all the soda they could drink. Armies are like the societies they come from. Here in the Saudi desert the US forces were a consumer society.

A colonel showed the press around his field hospital. It was better than many capital cities could boast: 500 beds, 800 staff, four intensive care units, a beautifully equipped operating theatre, protective suits so the surgeons could carry on working in the event of a chemical, biological or nuclear attack. The air-conditioning hummed quietly, the camp-beds were arranged in perfect lines, the plasma bags were hanging ready. After the stunning heat outside it was so fine and cool and new in here that you almost wanted to be ill.

The war was coming, and coming soon – as long, the soldiers said, as the politicians didn't screw it up. By screwing it up they meant negotiating a peaceful outcome. During the last three months of 1990 everyone found themselves looking northwards time and again; northwards was where the Iraqis were dug in.

This war was the conscious, precise opposite of the cliché: everything the generals did was designed to avoid fighting the last war.

'Whatever else we do,' President Bush had said in August 1990, 'we aren't going to do it the Vietnam way.'

The US military establishment, and particularly the Chairman of the Joint Chiefs of Staff, General Colin L. Powell, believed that the United States had lost the Vietnam War because of the slow build-up of forces over months and years. The very word 'escalation' came into general use in 1966–7 to describe the process by which the American military slowly increased the scope of their activities, and demanded ever greater levels of manpower to carry out the new tasks.

Now the plan would be to make the most accurate assessment possible of the forces which would be required, and put them in place in full. There would be no limited offensives. The US military leadership believed the problem in Vietnam had been that the profusion of small-scale attacks far from the enemy capital had sucked in far too many troops over too long a period.

This time there would be a massive onslaught on the capital itself, to destroy Iraq's decision-making and its communications. 'Smart' weapons like the Tomahawk cruise missile would be used to avoid the heavy civilian casualties which had so revolted public opinion in the Vietnam War. We started to hear the expression 'surgical strike': clean, precise and somehow comforting. This wouldn't be war, it would be surgery – the kind of thing that went on in that beautiful tented hospital. After which the patient would slowly recover.

The memory of Vietnam and of the clumsy, botched attack on Libya in 1986 made people deeply sceptical of the notion of the surgical strike. Pilots who had bombed Hanoi in the 1960s and 70s had found it hard to hit even the biggest targets.

'Surgical strikes,' a naval pilot who had flown many missions in Vietnam told the *New York Times* in September 1990, 'exist only in think-tanks and mental institutions.'

It was a neat encapsulation of what many people felt about the blunderings of the military mind, and it was taken up and quoted widely. But the Tomahawk missile had never been tried out in action, and no one except the military knew its capability. Precision bombing was indeed a serious reality, and the coming war would prove it.

An entirely new era in warfare was about to open. Brutal concepts like carpet-bombing and the deliberate targeting of large numbers of civilians would not be the way the United States would fight in future. Appalling mistakes would still be made, but the sheer scale of killing would be far smaller.

And it was a war which had wide international support. In the waters of the Gulf the United States had the backing of the British, French and Soviet navies, plus ships from Canada, Australia, Spain, Italy, Greece, Turkey, Norway, Denmark, the Netherlands, Belgium and Argentina. Fourteen countries supported the Coalition with troops or aircraft: the US, Britain, France, Canada, Italy, Saudi Arabia, Egypt, Morocco, Turkey, the UAE, Bahrain, Pakistan, Bangladesh and, intriguingly, Syria. Some of the leaders of these countries – President Ozal of Turkey, for instance – were taking a risk in supporting the American line. Opinion polls indicated that 55 per cent of Turkish people favoured Saddam Hussein, not the United States. Public opinion in Egypt was also clearly against, but that mattered less to President Mubarak than the promise by the US and the Gulf states to write off half of Egypt's debts. By the end of the Gulf War the country's annual debt repayments were cut from nearly $6 billion to $1.5 billion.

To have gained the support of President Hafez al-Assad for an attack on an Arab country was an extraordinary diplomatic achievement for the United States. It was fairly cynical on both sides. President

Assad had a human rights record which was only marginally better than Saddam Hussein's own, and he joined the alliance partly because of his personal feud with Saddam and partly because Syria's strategic position in the Middle East was inevitably opposed to Iraq's. He saw it as a short cut to a better relationship with the United States. He also counted on being able to regain full control of Lebanon if UN sanctions prevented the Iraqi-backed Lebanese Christian warlord, General Michel Aoun, from getting any further weapons from Saddam.

The United States had long attacked Syria as a supporter of international terrorism: as it indeed was. Suddenly, the complaints from Washington went silent. The Palestinian splinter-groups which had settled in Damascus and been funded by Syria continued to live there; the Syrian officials who liaised with them and suggested useful targets remained in their posts.

But it suited the US to welcome Assad as an honorary member of a club dedicated to upholding the rule of international law, and Syrian soldiers in their mildly absurd coral-coloured camouflage (the Pink Panthers, as they were immediately nicknamed) took up positions in the desert alongside the British, French and American forces. As a result Assad was accorded a meeting with President Bush.

It really was starting to look as though a new world order might be opening up. If Russia and Syria could side with the United States against a rogue Arab leader, then you could begin to imagine a world in which right-minded countries would join in the business of policing the world against unacceptable behaviour of all kinds, irrespective of ideology and religion. It wouldn't last, of course, but American diplomacy gave sufficient reason for otherwise sane and balanced observers to believe that something was changing in the world.

No one was in any doubt who the leader of the new world order was. There was very little serious consultation between Washington and the countries that were taking part in the enterprise. They were there to give credibility to an American effort, and that was all. American politicians often criticized the Europeans, in particular, for their unwillingness to commit more men, planes and ships; the Democratic leader in the House of Representatives, Dick Gephardt, complained that Britain wasn't doing enough, and the chairman of the Ways and Means Committee, Dan Rostenkpowski, read all the Coalition parties a lesson.

'We're going to have to expect more cooperation from the twenty-two countries that are participating,' he announced.

Soon afterwards Margaret Thatcher, unwilling to see Britain listed as one of the allies which wasn't pulling its weight, announced a sizeable increase in the British contingent.

The general view in the United States was that there was far too much consultation with the Coalition countries. A cartoon in the *Christian Science Monitor* showed an American soldier in the desert reading out his orders:

> In the case of attack the US will confer with French, British, and other Allied force commanders, coordinating with Soviet contacts, then jointly confer with Gulf states, the Syrians, the Egyptians, King Fahd and all 250 of his immediate family, the Emir of Kuwait, Senator Nunn and General Schwarzkopf. You may then fire at will.

In fact there was very little consultation, and even Britain, which supplied the largest fighting contingent after the US (though admittedly a long way after), was often informed of key decisions only once they had been made. The Italian foreign minister, Gianni de Michelis, said acidly in September that the Americans had based themselves on the principle of taxation without representation. The Europeans, he said, were taking a considerable share of the Gulf operation, yet were not listened to when the big decisions were made.

Popular opinion in the US was, as ever, that the Europeans were simply not doing enough. A sizeable minority of opinion, sometimes as high as a third, thought the Europeans were doing nothing at all to help. This was partly because it has become part of the American self-image that the United States does all the work and its allies do little or nothing, and partly because of the US television networks' total absorption in the American build-up. In the months of August, September and October 1990 none of the networks devoted a single report to the British or French forces. In the absence of information, many people assumed that none were taking part.

There was often outright anger at the Germans and Japanese, whose constitutions (heavily influenced by the United States after the end of the Second World War) strictly forbade them to send troops to fight abroad.

'They [the Japanese] have proved once again,' said a Republican senator, John McCain, 'that they have the world's most flexible constitution.'

He was entirely, comprehensively, and perhaps intentionally wrong; the Japanese constitution is rigid in the extreme. But no American politician ever lost votes by telling people that their friends abroad were shirkers.

Many Americans were infuriated that France, which had sold radar and surface-to-air missile systems to Saddam Hussein, refused to supply the Americans with details of these systems' capabilities. There was anxiety in France that its future as an arms manufacturer would be compromised if it released information like this, as well as a definite sense that the United States would use this information to help its own arms manufacturers. But during the Falklands War President Mitterrand had given Britain information about the Exocet missiles it had supplied to Argentina, and felt obliged eventually to give the Americans as much information about the Iraqi systems as they wanted.

Saudi Arabia had originally proposed that King Fahd should be the overall commander of the Gulf forces, with the senior US officer, General H. Norman Schwarzkopf, as one of his deputies. President Bush disagreed strongly. The two sides eventually agreed that there should be separate but parallel commands: the United States and its NATO allies in one, Saudi and Islamic forces in the other.

Norman Schwarzkopf was not what he seemed. Six feet three inches tall, bull-necked, he scarcely looked like a sensitive man, and even less like a good diplomat. There was indeed a volcanic element in his nature, and he wasn't always popular with his staff. But he spoke French and German well, was passionately fond of opera, and almost as enthusiastic about Bob Dylan. In Vietnam, where he had reached the rank of lieutenant-colonel, he had a reputation for looking after the safety of his men, not necessarily a very common quality at that time. After he was appointed commander of the Gulf force he showed a remarkable sensitivity to non-military concerns.

'In a lot of ways I am a pacifist,' he told one interviewer.

He was surprisingly diplomatic in his dealings with the politicians and generals of the other countries involved in Operations Desert Shield and Desert Storm – both the British and French soldiers he dealt with had great respect for him – and his press conferences earned him the respect of a good many journalists, who found him intelligent and relatively honest with them.

This was not something the majority of journalists felt about the military public relations team as a whole. The briefers spewed out huge quantities of neologisms, acronyms and euphemisms. They would speak of HARMs (high-speed anti-radiation missiles), JAATs (joint air attack teams), TADS (target acquisition and designation sights), SLAR (side-looking airborne radar), SLAMs (stand-off land attack missiles) and SLIPARs (short light-pulse alerting receivers).

Many journalists, embarrassingly, took to wearing NBC (nuclear, biological and chemical) suits, just in case. With less justification, some wore military camouflage to match the verbal camouflage they willingly imported into their reporting from the military: MIAs (missing in action), WIAs (wounded in action), KIAs (killed in action). For the KIAs, in place of body-bags there were now HRPs: human remains pouches.

Then there was the famous 'collateral damage', which was coined to refer to the effects of a near miss but came to mean civilian casualties. Some military men, a little franker than the rest, spoke of 'civilian impacting'; it meant the same thing.

Often, the military and the politicians and journalists who supported them used language as another form of camouflage, to obscure reality and make it look prettier than it was. As the preparations for war intensified, it became less and less acceptable to talk about them openly. The public emphasis was entirely on peace, and when on 17 September 1990 the chief of staff of the US Air Force told an interviewer it was America's intention to bomb Baghdad and if possible to kill Saddam Hussein himself, he was relieved of his duties. For the moment, this was still a war which dare not speak its name.

Such opposition as there was in the United States often came from the right rather than the left. Patrick Buchanan, an ultra-conservative newspaper columnist, announced against all the evidence of the opinion polls that the American people were against President Bush's threat to use force against Saddam Hussein. By contrast Todd Gitlin, a former president of Students for a Democratic Society and an important figure in the 1960s protest movement, came out in favour of Bush's decision to work with the United Nations in confronting Saddam Hussein.

'Not only do all generals fight the last war,' he wrote, 'but anti-war people fight the last war too.'

Former members of the Reagan administration, such as Richard Perle and Donald Rumsfeld, who had made himself so useful to Saddam Hussein, now announced that if Saddam were not dealt with firmly now, he would be more troublesome later. Most American politicians and newspapers seemed content to leave it to President Bush to decide the matter for them, though they complained he didn't tell them clearly enough.

'I'd be happy to support the policy,' said Senator Malcolm Wallop perplexedly, 'if I knew what it was.'

In Britain, there were occasional signs of war hysteria. The Home Office ordered a number of arrests, and told the *Daily Mail* that the security service had detained seven Palestinians who were plotting to carry out explosions. The Palestinian writer Abbas Shiblak was picked up just as the war was about to get under way, and found himself in Pentonville prison where he met six other Palestinians; he realized that between them they made up the seven the *Daily Mail* had written about. One was completely apolitical, and had worked for the embassy of a Gulf state, while another had renounced politics in the 1970s. Shiblak later said he was sad to have discovered the other face of a system he had always assumed was just and fair.

'Britain has been our home for the past seventeen years,' he wrote. 'It is a country which gave me an education, shelter, and a sense of freedom . . . [Y]et suddenly I found myself completely helpless and defenceless, held in prison and threatened with the destruction of my future without any reason being given, without any legal defence. It is a terror I do not wish on anyone.'

Under the 1974 Prevention of Terrorism Act there was no require-ment to tell people who were accused of threatening national security the nature of the accusation against them. In this case the law was a direct encouragement to official sloppiness and inadequate police work, while the gullible attitude of some newspapers gave the result an air of legitimacy. Finally, an outcry on behalf of Shiblak and the other two men, all of them entirely innocent, won them their release, and the deportation orders against them were revoked, but in the atmosphere of heightened nervousness it was a close-run thing.

Sometimes the nervousness became outright hysteria. The journalist Peregrine Worsthorne declared in the *Sunday Telegraph* that Islam 'had degenerated into a primitive enemy fit only to be sensibly subjugated'. For him and for many who thought like him, Islam, Saddam Hussein and terrorism had merged into one great incomprehensible whole, irredeemably hostile, which could not be understood or approached on a rational basis, but had to be smashed. As the likelihood of war grew, many people felt they didn't want to know anything more about the nature of the threat, they just wanted it to be 'sensibly subjugated'.

32. PAUSE FOR PEACE

On 27 October 1990 the weather broke in Baghdad. As I looked out from the twelfth floor of the al-Rashid Hotel towards the western part of the city, rainclouds covered the green of the park, the absurd crossed scimitars, the large bulk of the Ba'ath Party headquarters, the vast menacing white block which housed the Mukhabarat close to the racecourse in Mansour. Great warm drops of rain fell and the dusty ground gave out an unfamiliar smell, sweet, pungent and musty. Cars slithered about on the slick roads. Ripe dates, knocked from the palm trees by the rain, made walking dangerous. I watched it all with a certain frisson: Yasser Arafat had told me privately, after meeting Saddam, that the Iraqi forces were on standby for an attack by the Americans soon after the first rains. Lightning flickered on the horizon, and my bedside lamp flickered in sympathy.

Something else was in the wind: a definite feeling, encouraged by my meeting with Arafat, that his proposal for a withdrawal of Iraqi forces from all but the northernmost third of Kuwait had met with Saddam's favour. That day, too, Iraqi embassies around the world had issued a new map which showed only the top third as Iraqi territory.

Yevgeny Primakov, President Gorbachev's special envoy, arrived from Moscow on what seemed to be a last attempt to get a negotiated solution. A solidly built, tough-minded *muzhik*, Primakov was more hostile and suspicious towards the West than his boss. Nevertheless after the first Gulf War he produced a book about his experiences in

Iraq called *The War Which Need Not Have Been*, which showed a clear understanding of Saddam Hussein's true nature. Primakov found him impressive, but detected signs of cruelty and ferocity. He also remarked on the exaggerated notions of honour and national dignity which obsessed Saddam.

The Iraqis were disappointed in Russia, and it was clear that neither Saddam nor Tariq Aziz understood the nature of the changes that had taken place since the fall of the Berlin Wall. Now, sitting in the interview room in Saddam's palace, with its tasteless gilt furniture and its glass-fronted bookcase full of unread books, Primakov had to wait while Saddam read the strongly worded letter he had brought from Gorbachev. The Soviet position was fiercer than it might have been, because Saddam had personally decided not to release the Russians who, like other foreigners, were still being held hostage.

When Saddam had finished reading, he launched into an angry justification for his invasion of Kuwait. There was, he said, a conspiracy between the United States, Britain, Israel, Saudi Arabia and Kuwait to destroy Iraq. Primakov was half-inclined to believe some of it, and indeed it seems clear that the Americans in particular wanted to put the screws on Saddam and that the other countries were prepared to go along with that.

According to his own account, Primakov asked Saddam if he had a Masada complex: that is, if he was considering pulling the entire country down around him. Saddam, Primakov said, nodded.

'But then your actions will to a great extent be determined by the logic of a doomed man,' Primakov said.

Saddam didn't answer, but Primakov felt he agreed. He went on to tell Saddam that there would be war if he didn't pull out of Kuwait.

'If it is a choice between going down on my knees and fighting,' Primakov quoted him as saying, 'then I will fight. But I am a realist. I am prepared to ease the conditions which I made on 12 August.' These linked an Iraqi withdrawal from Kuwait to an Israeli withdrawal from the Occupied Territories. He seemed to be saying that the timing and method of these withdrawals would be matters for negotiation.

Primakov was highly sceptical about the idea; it would reward Saddam's invasion of Kuwait. Anyway, this was all simply a matter of helping Saddam save face; he had not invaded Kuwait in order to solve the conflict between Israel and the Palestinians. On his way back to

Moscow he stopped off in London and told Mrs Thatcher what Saddam had said. She wasn't interested. She merely wanted to 'break the back' of Iraq's military and perhaps industrial potential. Did she, he asked, see any alternative to war?

'No,' she answered, and closed her mouth like a trap.

Yet others were in favour of a deal along the lines Saddam seemed to be suggesting: France, Germany, the Palestinians (whose idea it had originally been). The Saudi defence minister said he saw 'no harm in any Arab country giving its Arab sister land, a site, or a position on the sea'.

Not, however, President Bush. It became more and more clear that he, like Margaret Thatcher, wanted an outcome which would destroy Saddam and his dangerous war machine. On 10 November he announced a doubling of the US ground forces in Saudi Arabia: 1,000 more tanks, 200,000 more men. His defence secretary, Richard Cheney, was clearly in favour of war; his secretary of state, James Baker, was more concerned with forcing Saddam Hussein into a humiliating withdrawal.

On 22 November the war party lost its fiercest member when Margaret Thatcher decided in the face of a surprisingly hostile vote among the Conservatives in Parliament not to stand again for the prime ministership. She had fallen victim to a particularly savage political coup, which had nothing whatever to do with the approaching war with Saddam and everything to do with her confrontational style of government. So the longest-serving British prime minister since 1827, a leader who had restored her country's international position and prestige, left Downing Street in the back of her official car, wiping unfamiliar tears from her eyes.

In Baghdad there was rejoicing; the assumption was that the coalition against Saddam Hussein was falling apart. The Gulf crisis, Naji al-Haddithi said, had buried Mrs Thatcher just as the 1956 Suez crisis had ruined Sir Anthony Eden. A week later there seemed to be some grounds for the Iraqi optimism: James Baker, who was in favour of a negotiated peace, would be sent for face-to-face talks with Saddam Hussein, while Tariq Aziz would be invited to Washington.

'Bush has blinked first,' said a senior Egyptian diplomat. 'He's looking for a way out.' And he added, 'Bush wouldn't have done this if Thatcher was still around.'

But that wasn't the case. In a speech, Bush called the negotiation 'going the extra mile for peace', but it quickly became clear that it was merely a way of making sure that James Baker did not resign in protest that a peaceful outcome had not been sought. Bush telephoned Mrs Thatcher's successor, John Major, saying that there was no thought in his mind of climbing down.

Saddam Hussein, however, interpreted Bush's 'pause for peace' as weakness, and he reacted in his instinctive gangster fashion: weakness on your opponent's part means that you should be even harder than ever. It confirmed everything he believed: that Margaret Thatcher had been the only really tough leader on the Coalition side, that the United States had no stomach for war and could not accept casualties, and that democracies had no fixity of purpose.

'How many losses can an American president take before he falls?' Latif Jassim, the information minister, asked me. 'Five thousand? Ten thousand?'

I tried to explain that an American president does not fall unless he has committed some sort of crime, but Jassim was so buoyed up with his master's mood of triumphalism he didn't listen.

By now Saddam was insisting that he was too busy to meet James Baker until 12 January, which was only three days before the UN deadline for Iraq to withdraw from Kuwait. But as ever, he overplayed his hand. It was clear he was no longer interested in a settlement which would give Iraq a certain amount of Kuwaiti territory and allow its troops to withdraw with honour. Saddam was pushing for victory, not compromise. I talked with several Iraqi ministers and leading civil servants, and went back to the al-Rashid Hotel and put it all together in a piece to camera for that evening's television news:

> There's no mistaking the feeling here that President Saddam Hussein has got the Americans on the run. Washington used to insist it would never talk to him while his troops were still in Kuwait – and yet the two sides are arguing now about the dates for the talking to start. The Iraqis seem convinced that they can go further, and force the Americans to back down on the UN ultimatum to withdraw from Kuwait by 15 January.

At that stage I had only been back in Baghdad for a day after three weeks back in London, but I was certain there would be a war. Saddam would not yield, and the Americans had not blinked. When we had edited our report and it had been satellited to London, I went upstairs to my new room on the eleventh floor, on the opposite side of the al-Rashid. In the fading light I looked out at the view towards the Tigris and the old centre of the city. I had smuggled a telescope past the Iraqi airport security officers, and now I peered through it.

An anti-aircraft post had gone up on the roof of a government ministry close to the hotel. The gunners were lounging around in the evening sunlight, sipping tea, laughing and joking. I tried to think what it would be like when they were firing at planes and missiles, but my imagination wasn't up to it. I snapped the telescope shut, and hid it away.

33. FINAL EFFORTS

On 4 December Saddam held a conference in Baghdad with King Hussein of Jordan, Yasser Arafat of the PLO, and the vice-president of Yemen, Ali Salem al-Bidh. Arafat took the lead in pleading for the release of all the remaining foreign hostages, and the others agreed. Saddam seemed to want to be convinced, and two days later he announced that everyone held against their will could go. Once the war had begun, he came to regard this as a major error, and he characteristically blamed Arafat for persuading him to do it.

Saddam Hussein, like Mussolini, always had to be right, so it stood to reason that any mistake he made was someone else's fault. In fact the real mistake had been to take the hostages in the first place – another of Saddam's sudden decisions, taken without any serious reflection. It had alienated the Soviet Union, whose citizens were refused permission to leave Iraq, and it prevented various countries which might have been sympathetic from supporting him.

He was wrong, however, to think that if Arafat had not persuaded him to let the hostages go, the Coalition countries would have been too intimidated to bomb Iraq's cities, air defences, and key installations because the hostages were held there; as early as September the Allies had decided that if it came to war, the presence of hostages at their major targets wouldn't stop them bombing.

Arafat had urged the release of the hostages because he was, as ever, trying to promote a deal. He could see the damage that taking them in the first place had done to Saddam's cause, and he realized the damage that a war with Iraq would do to the Palestinians' hopes of an agreement with Israel. He had become hugely unpopular with Western governments for establishing himself in Baghdad during the crisis, and he knew he had to come up with some obvious diplomatic success if he were to dig himself out of trouble.

I went to see him at his villa in the Baghdad suburbs. Armed guards moved a set of tyre-spikes aside and we parked in front of his bungalow. It could have been a quiet estate in the outer suburbs of London, except for the Republican Guards in their red berets.

Arafat was his usual ebullient self, and I had always had a soft spot for him. His hands were bandaged and covered with ointment; he explained in an embarrassed way that his doctor had warned him the extraordinary hours he kept, rising in the late afternoon and staying up all night, were damaging his health. If you can't get out into the sunlight, the doctor said, at least invest in a sun-lamp. Get thirty minutes' ultra-violet a week, but on no account stay under more than a few minutes at a time.

Arafat nodded, and forgot the warning. After a week with no sun-lamp he thought he'd better make up for it by taking his thirty minutes in one session. It did real damage to his skin.

Now he took my reluctant hand and held it in both of his. The bandages were grubby, and the ointment on them squelched unpleasantly. I interviewed him at length. His voice went up and down from middle-range to high-pitched, the bandaged hands made their usual extravagant gestures, and he was relentlessly optimistic.

'There will not be any war. You will see. Do you think the Americans would be so foolish as to start a war over so little? There will be no war, I promise you. There will be an agreement. No one will suffer. They [the UN Security Council] will set another deadline, later than the fifteenth of January. Then there will be an arrangement – perhaps with the Europeans, perhaps with the Arabs. Someone.'

It was like asking a carpet-salesman if the trade in carpets would come to an end; Arafat the deal-maker could not envisage a world where a deal could not be reached.

'But if there is a war – just supposing there is, for the sake of argument – will you, will the Palestinians engage in acts of terror?'

He laughed, showing his yellow teeth. It was an awkward question for him, because Saddam Hussein was pushing hard for the Palestinians to launch attacks on British and American targets around the world, and Arafat knew the disasters that would bring.

I had to press him, so that he was obliged to answer.

'I cannot be certain, because it would not be my decision. But I do not think you will see any attacks.'

In fact, behind the scenes Arafat was using every ounce of influence he had to ensure that the various Palestinian groups did nothing which would prevent the Americans and Israelis negotiating with him once the Iraqi crisis was over. There was not a single bombing, not a single hijacking. The government of Iran was using its influence in the same way; Iran, like the PLO, was looking to the future.

Over lunch afterwards, a big, subdued man sat eating noisily at the end of the table. He looked like someone's thuggish bodyguard, but in fact it was Abu Abbas, the man who had carried out the attack on the Italian cruise ship *Achille Lauro*, throwing a disabled Jewish passenger into the sea. In May 1990 Abu Abbas staged a series of amphibious landings on the Israeli coast, all quite pointless.

Arafat had reason to believe at the time that the British were just about to recognize the PLO as the legitimate representatives of the Palestinian people, and the landings destroyed any chance of that. He told me he had said to Abu Abbas that when he used the Arab expression 'I will cut off your hands' to him, meaning he would make sure he was powerless, he meant it literally. Certainly Abu Abbas was a humble, deferential figure now. He said nothing to anyone over lunch and slunk away as fast as he could.

Christmas drew closer. Saddam went on television to give a speech marking Army Day. He looked and sounded tired, and there were no close-ups. His mouth seemed drawn down on the left-hand side, his speech was thick and slightly indistinct. But he was entirely unyielding.

'The Mother of All Battles will soon begin. It will widen into a greater war for the Holy Places and the rights of the Palestinians. The soldiers of Iraq are privileged to be called upon to fight in a war as noble and as holy as the early wars of Muslim history.'

Yet he still didn't believe there would be a war. President Bush said on Christmas morning that he was hoping to bring the troops back from the Gulf without a shot being fired. It looked like further vacillation from the United States.

The Ministry of Information allowed us to go filming at the house of an Assyrian Christian called Jabril, an educated, intelligent former servant who had to drive a taxi in order to keep his family afloat, and who asked us to call him James. The house was old-fashioned, and built round a courtyard, and his wife and daughter laboured away in the freezing cold while he and his sons sat round and ate small pastries like mince pies. A cage full of budgerigars chirruped and preened in the corner. Eventually Chistmas dinner was ready.

'It is the head of a sheep,' James announced proudly, lifting the lid of a very large saucepan.

Something threshed in the pot: I caught a glimpse of teeth. The others in my team ate almost nothing, but with the whole family watching me, nodding and smiling, I felt obliged to finish my plate and took a small cup of scalding coffee in the hope of killing the taste.

On the wall were a series of icons to ward off trouble: the Virgin Mary, St James, several crucifixes, and a large picture of Saddam. That was likely to ward off the worst of the trouble they might experience. I looked round at the pleasant faces of the family: they were happy to have shared their Christmas with guests, and nervous about the possible consequences. James gripped my arm as we left.

'Will everything be safe?'

It was an appeal, as though I could protect them against missiles and secret policemen.

'Absolutely,' I mumbled, though I didn't think it would be true.

There was one last splendid evening. The people of Baghdad, secular and jolly, love New Year's Eve, the best of all festivals. We decided to go to a big restaurant in the centre of town to film. We arrived around 11 p.m. and found everything in full swing.

The noise and heat were stupefying. People were clambering on the tables, taking endless photographs of one another and squirting one another with party foam. Older women made a lot of noise and flirted with everyone, especially us. Girls danced with portly old men, with other girls, and, just occasionally, with their boyfriends. A man wearing a mask like the Face of God ran round the tables trying to catch girls. Waiters sweated and held trays with bottles of dreadfully bad champagne high over their heads and made their perilous way between the tables and across the dance-floor.

Someone stood on a chair and announced that we were from the BBC. People clustered round us, proffering glasses of champagne, handshakes, kisses. A man tipped his glass high above his head and emptied the contents down his throat.

'BBC very good. England very good. Hello,' he called out. 'Hello' is, for some surreal reason, what Iraqis say when they mean goodbye. Then he sank into a chair and took no further part in the proceedings.

Midnight drew closer: the midnight which would bring in an unknown and probably terrible new year. The gaiety grew wilder, the Face of God ran faster and caught more girls, the dance-floor was crammed beyond any possibility of serious movement, musicians sweated over their instruments.

The lights went out. There was laughing and singing and the first candles were lit. I looked round at the gleaming faces, the excited eyes shining in the candle flames, the hands reaching out to one another as people sang softly and smiled at one another. Only fifteen days away, I thought.

An old man, bald and fat, was sitting silently. Across the table from him sat a woman who was probably his wife, though she was young enough to be his daughter. She was plain and rather fat too, but her face was bright with the pleasure of the moment and she bounced a child on her knee, making it clap its pudgy hands in time to the music which was just starting up again. The old man sat in the middle of all the noise and jollity. His eyes were focused on the ceiling, and tears were running unchecked down his fat grey cheeks.

34. DEADLINE

There was some last-minute diplomacy. The Russians and the French tried their hand, but nothing came of it. On 9 January 1991 James Baker, the US secretary of state, met Tariq Aziz in Geneva. Most people thought there would be a deal. I had been told on excellent authority, though, that Saddam was telling his friends and supporters in private that he was not prepared to give way.

'Even if I withdraw our troops from Kuwait City but still keep control of a third of Kuwaiti territory,' he told Yasser Arafat, 'my generals will take this as weakness. Someone will overthrow me.'

This was the possibility which the United States was most anxious about.

'If he'd done that,' said Brent Scowcroft, Bush's national security adviser long after the war, 'our position would have been very difficult. Most of our Coalition would crumble away, and we couldn't have gone on with just the British and one or two others. He [Saddam] would have gotten away with the rewards of his aggression.'

But Saddam Hussein misread the situation, as he so often did. He demanded that the United States should make the first concession, by agreeing to implement the UN resolutions on Israel and the Occupied Territories. Only then would he start to withdraw.

He told Yasser Arafat that he wasn't afraid of the coming onslaught.

'We will only have to face two airstrikes. Then it'll be ended. The consequences will be so terrible that international opinion will force the Americans to stop.'

No one, it is true, had any real idea what an all-out attack by cruise missiles would be like, since they had never been tried out in war. We heard terrible stories about American weapons which would turn our brains to jelly, force all the breath out of our bodies, shake the fillings out of our teeth, crush us to pulp.

On 15 January, the day of the UN deadline, the shops were shuttered and their windows taped against blast. The midwinter sun cast long shadows. Most government officials seemed to have given up altogether. Even the old terror of Saddam and his henchmen was fading: the paralysing fear of an all-out attack by the world's most advanced military powers overrode even that.

Our information ministry minders became preoccupied, their eyes focused on the middle distance, their attention harder to obtain. Poor men: they were a nuisance to us, but they were only in the job because they spoke good English, which argued some kind of interest in a world away from Saddam. One particularly stern and difficult figure even turned out to have a brother in the Arabic service of the BBC, though he never told us; no doubt that was why he himself was obliged to make himself stern and difficult.

Corrupt officials, of whom there were large numbers, became more reckless in their demands for cash. The operators at the central telephone exchange often failed to answer for twenty minutes at a time. In our hotel, the staff were beginning to melt away. Each morning, when I swam in the hotel pool, the heated water was a little cooler and a little less clear. Fungus spread between the tiles. On the hotel lawn sewage seeped to the surface. A nasty smell of decay hung over many places in the city.

In great confidence the British ambassador told the ITN correspondent, who had gone round to see him, that the embassy staff would be pulling out early the following morning. He asked him to pass the information on to me, but the correspondent seemed to forget. Fortunately for us, Sky News got wind of it and told us.

And so at five the next morning, as the cocks crowed and the embassy lights glared out into the darkness, we found the embassy staff loading up their four-wheel-drives. They left two hours later, hooting their goodbyes and their relief at getting out. Silence settled over the embassy. A few ashes whirled in the wind: the remains of the embassy's confidential papers. A tomcat snuffled through the garbage with the practised ease of a secret agent. In the silence of the inner courtyard a First World War field gun stood beside an inscription recording the British capture of Baghdad in 1917. Now, finally, the British had evacuated the city again.

They didn't tell the locally hired staff, however: men and women, but mostly women, some of whom who had worked for the embassy for years. A British woman, who was married to an Iraqi, turned up to collect something for the British Council, where she worked.

'How could they just go off without telling us?'

'Orders from the Foreign Office, dear,' a pleasant, motherly Iraqi lady of a certain age told her.

Everyone felt abandoned. I went around, telling them that the BBC hadn't left and that we would do everything we could to help them, but they must have known, as I did, how little we would be able to do if they got into trouble.

The American ambassador went out noisily. He had visited the al-Rashid the day before, saying his goodbyes to the journalists there with the help of a little electronic gadget that said in a squeaky voice, 'Fuck you! You're an asshole!' He did a good deal of studied phrase-making, in order to make those of us who had decided to stay think again.

'We're leaving because we don't want to be a pound of ground round,' he said; and, 'There's gonna be no more level terrain here, there's only gonna be rolling craters'; and, 'We're gonna pound these guys so far down you're gonna have to pipe in the sunlight.'

The BBC management thought it was going to be too dangerous for us to stay in Baghdad, and put a good deal of pressure on us. As a result, some of my team decided to leave. Only three of us, two reporters and a producer, were willing to remain. The coming war would be hard enough to cover for television; now, without a camera team or a picture editor, I would have serious problems.

But we weren't the only ones. President Bush rang the heads of the different American television networks personally and asked them to ensure that their employees left. CNN behaved professionally and took no notice.

American newspaper editors, faced with the same pressure, became increasingly peremptory.

'If you aren't out by the fifteenth,' one American editor told his correspondent in Baghdad, 'I'll regard it as a personal betrayal.' It seemed like the very antithesis of proper journalism.

Virtually all the American citizens did leave; Marie Colvin of the *Sunday Times*, and Peter Arnett of CNN and his team did not. Theirs would be the real honours in the coming war. Otherwise, the majority of those who remained to face whatever the war would bring were British, and there were the usual nationalities you find at times of war: French, Italians, Australians, New Zealanders and Canadians. The Spanish reporter Alfonso Rojo became known all over the world for his reporting from Baghdad.

Those who left often tried to convince the rest of us that we should join them; the bombing, they said, would be too dangerous.

'Man, I wouldn't be in that shelter when one of those mothers comes out of the sky,' a large reporter confided to me. 'I saw them used in 'Nam. You'll be dead meat, man. The vibration's gonna shake the fillings right outa your teeth.'

He laughed the comfortable, easy laugh of someone who would

only read about it all in the newspapers over breakfast in an expensive hotel somewhere completely different.

I ran my tongue around my fillings, familiar and smooth. How bad would the vibration have to be to shake them? I found myself looking out of the window for minutes at a time, thinking about things at home; or I would walk down the dark, empty corridors of the al-Rashid Hotel, wondering what damage a cruise missile or a B-52 bomber would do to a structure which seemed so solid. Suppose Iraq fired its missiles at Israel, and Israel replied with nuclear weapons?

Several of us started showing physical signs of nervousness. I started to pick at my fingers again; something I thought I had given up. One of my colleagues had a flare-up of eczema.

A variety of things kept us in Baghdad: curiosity, a sense of duty, the knowledge that we would be letting our colleagues down if we left. I remembered, too, what Robert Wiener of CNN had said when I met him on the day we flew to Baghdad: I didn't want to have to spend the rest of my life feeling I had let myself and others down. A Latin tag, a small piece of wreckage from a long-distant classical education, came floating towards me from across the years. It was, I think, from Virgil's *Aeneid*: *fato profugus*, driven on by fate.

The next morning, early mist had blotted out the city. Baghdad had closed down entirely. You could walk down the middle of Rashid Street in the centre of town without having to look over your shoulder for cars. I could only find one shop open. The man behind the counter gripped my hand.

'You are from England? There won't be any bombing, I think?'

'I'm sure you'll be all right,' I said with deliberate ambiguity; this man had wagered his entire life and future on a political judgement, and it seemed cruel to undercut him. I took a cake of soap from the shelf.

'*Inshallah*. You are our friend. Welcome.' He put the soap in a special bag, and tied it with a flourish. 'Hello,' he said in Iraqi through-the-looking-glass fashion, and bowed his goodbyes.

The Iraqi government didn't care much about us – these were the days before the emergence of BBC World – but it badly wanted CNN to stay. Saddam Hussein's strategy was dependent upon showing terrible scenes of destruction and massacre to the world; that way, he believed, the Americans would be forced to stop the bombing and back away. For this reason, although the government had announced the complete evacuation of large parts of the city, nothing of the sort had taken place.

We went to a school in the pleasant suburb of al-Amiriyah. The girls were still arriving, made late by the morning's fog. The minute hand on the classroom clock flicked to 8 a.m. Eight time zones away, at UN headquarters in New York, the deadline for withdrawal from Kuwait had just run out.

The girls sat in rows in their neat navy-blue uniforms, repeating the English words their teacher had written on the blackboard, their dark faces frowning in concentration: I am happy, you are kind, he is sad, they are good.

'They are GOOD.' The teacher's voice was sharp.

'They are GOOOOOOOD,' the girls repeated obediently. Frowns intensified, brown eyes glanced up occasionally to see if we were still looking at them.

In the beautiful wintry afternoon we went to the races. The greatest bombardment in human history was about to begin, but nothing could stop the racing fraternity. Streaks of pink cirrus lay across the sky, and the sun slanted sharply across the 1940s racetrack. The horses were small and spirited and probably drugged, with their ears curled in Indian fashion. There were several thousand racegoers, each apparently convinced there would be no war. Many of them had flat caps on their heads and tweed jackets over their *dishdashas*, as though they had suddenly been transported to some race meeting in rural Ireland and hadn't had time to change. I had been to the races here before; like the teahouses and the life beside the Tigris and the little shops on Rashid Street, it represented the Iraq I had come to love.

The betting was heaviest on Scheherazade at 5 to 1, with Lulu next at 9 to 1. A big greasy bookmaker with a pleasant, crooked smile and a wad of 25-dinar notes took my bet, and asked me what I thought of the situation. I told him. He shook his head, waving the wad for emphasis.

'There will be no war. Nobody wants it.'

Everyone in the small crowd around us agreed. In that atmosphere I almost agreed too. Things were so relaxed, so normal, so pleasant. Only the large white tower of the Mukhabarat headquarters, looking over the racetrack, was a reminder that a less attractive world existed.

I turned to look at the race. The horses were rounding the final bend and heading into the straight. The late afternoon sun shone through the dust their hooves threw up, so they raced towards us in a golden penumbra, heads straining forward, eyes flashing. Everyone in the stands jumped up as though an anthem was being played, waving their racecards and shouting. There was a drumming of hooves, a blur of colour, and Scheherazade duly won. At the Baghdad Horsemanship Ground the favourite always does. The big, greasy bookmaker was counting out notes to people, but he was smiling. Things had gone well for him today.

35. BOMBING

There was a shout of anger from the next room: the phones had been cut. Things would start happening soon now. I remembered Saddam's words: there would be only two strikes on Baghdad, which would be so terrible and destructive that world opinion would force the United States to stop. As our team gathered together, I looked at my watch: 2.20 a.m. on 17 January 1991. It was the moment we had prepared for and worried about for months.

The producer, Eamonn Matthews, called over the young English cameraman who had been abandoned by his organization and had volunteered to work for us. His name was Anthony Wood. The three of us ran downstairs in the darkness and scattered the security men who tried to stop us in the mausoleum-like marble entrance hall of the al-Rashid.

'But where are you going?' a voice wailed behind us.

Outside the night air felt cold and sweet and businesslike. Anthony had had the foresight to hire a driver for the entire night. The trouble was, the man was a thoroughgoing coward and an undoubted spook. But there was no one else.

We hadn't considered where to go: merely getting out of the hotel had been the limit of our planning. Now we all yelled different instructions, and the driver took the turning to the 14 July Bridge over the Tigris.

'No bridges!' I shouted. I knew the bridges would be the first targets to go, and if we were stranded on the other bank of the river and cut off from the hotel we might be lynched by angry crowds.

The driver swerved alarmingly round a bend in the empty road, tyres squealing, and at that precise moment the guns opened up all round us.

The darkness and silence exploded into mind-numbing noise, and the car shook with the reverberation. Red and white tracer shot up into the sky in an almost liquid rush, like water from a hosepipe. We had to scream at each other to be heard over the extraordinary noise. Our driver's face was lit up by the red tracer; I could see it in the mirror. He was badly frightened. Now he pulled the car round in a screaming semi-circle just as the sirens began their belated wailing. Before we could stop him – and I don't think we could have stopped him anyway – he headed straight back to the hotel and in through the gates. We were back in the one place we wanted to be away from.

Inside the lobby we were grabbed by angry hands and forced down a narrow staircase into the shelter beneath. The smell of frightened people in a confined space was beginning to take over. Women and children were sobbing; men too. We were fifty feet below ground, and there were fourteen storeys of hotel above us. I tried to slow everything down, keep calm, establish control over small things and extend it to larger ones.

There was no escaping from the shelter for the time being; guards armed with Kalashnikovs were at the exits. By now there was scarcely room enough to lie down. In the general panic, normal patterns of behaviour were collapsing. A woman wearing only a coat and a bathtowel took them off in full view of everyone, and put on clothes she had brought in a bag; in the flickering light from a few bulbs no one seemed to pay the slightest attention. Outside the ground was quaking as each new missile struck the city. The structure of the hotel swayed and shivered.

Anthony Wood and I found each other in the crowd and agreed to make our way up to our rooms, where we could film what was happening. No matter how much more dangerous it might be there, anything was better than being down in this mass grave. We had to fight our way, literally, past the guards, but they did not shoot.

Upstairs, in the silence of the empty hotel, things were much calmer. A group of my colleagues had gathered in one of the rooms and were filming the falling bombs. A 2,000-pound penetration missile struck a building close by; I saw it and felt it, but contrary to what I had been led to believe my eyeballs did not implode and my fillings did not come out. For the first time I began to think I might even survive this experience.

It was the heaviest bombardment any city on earth had undergone since the destruction of Hiroshima and Nagasaki; yet when the morning came, dull and unremarkable, the extraordinary fact became clear that there was no widespread damage. The precision of the weapons, which had been so much questioned, was proven. Baghdad was being systematically stripped of its essential functions as a city: electricity, broadcasting, water-pumping, lighting, communications were all in the process of disappearing; yet when Anthony Wood and I succeeded in finding a driver and got out into the streets we saw that the missile and bombing strikes had been so accurate that, although entire government ministries and other buildings had been destroyed, the areas round them were almost unaffected. Down one side-street we found a building which was probably a branch office of the Mukhabarat. It had been cored like an apple, burned out, and every floor had fallen down on the one below; yet the glass in the windows of the buildings opposite, scarcely thirty yards away, was intact. Those terrifying rumblings through the earth as the bombs burrowed deep into it, those flashes which turned the entire horizon as bright as day, the fires which erupted and burned for hours – they all seemed so precise that nothing around them had been destroyed.

Now the streets were empty, except for soldiers trying to hitch a lift. Their faces were as strained and vacant as those of the people in the shelter the previous night. Even in the few places where groups had gathered, there seemed to be no talking. A woman dragged her child along by its arm, the child crying and rubbing its eyes. The woman's face was grimy and streaked with sweat, and her clothes were stained with mud. A few old men squatted beside the road with a pile of oranges or a few packs of cigarettes in front of them.

Back at the hotel, we were starting to realize that the cruise missiles were following the line of the main road behind the building as their route into town. The Tomahawk was a curious weapon, eighteen feet in length, and moving at 500 miles per hour: slow enough for an onlooker to be able to register everything about it – its blackness, its lack of markings, its rudimentary, stubby wings, the absence of a fiery trail, its strange lack of menace.

Seeing one was at first like seeing the Loch Ness monster, but slowly, as we became more used to them, I felt they came more to resemble some other large but not necessarily dangerous sea-animal: a walrus, or maybe a dugong. They were extraordinarily dangerous, of course, each one carrying half a ton of high explosive, yet as we watched them fly past (one actually turned left at the traffic lights) they seemed to be well enough directed for us to feel moderately safe.

The pattern for the rest of the air war was now established. Despite the appalling destruction, civilian casualties were low. The real danger came from drinking contaminated water, rather than from being killed by a bomb. A certain half-life returned to the streets: people emerged in the daytime, when the bombing was less intensive, to buy and sell simple foodstuffs. They were slowly starting to realize, as the people of Belgrade and Kabul were also to learn during the next ten years, that an all-out attack by the most powerful weapons systems in the world did not necessarily mean widespread casualties. The ratio of civilian deaths to the tonnage of warheads was less than it had been during the Siege of Paris in 1870. That was the result of a lack of efficacy; now it was because the missiles were so precise.

They did, of course, miss their targets from time to time, or hit buildings which had been wrongly identified as targets by the military planners. Yet although it was the first time this technology had been used in warfare, the number of buildings which were mistakenly destroyed was less than in the NATO attack on Belgrade in 1999 and the American and British bombing of Kabul in 2001. If it had not been for the bombing of the al-Amiriyah bomb shelter, where more than 300 people, mostly women and children, were taking cover, the figures for civilian casualties would have been lower too.

The al-Amiriyah attack took place early on the morning of 13 February. Aerial photographs had shown that the cars of high-level officials were stopping off and delivering people at the entrance to the shelter. There was a specially hardened bomb shelter in the basement of the building, which had been designed and constructed by a Finnish company. To the analysts who examined the photographs, this meant that the building was a significant target. They put it on the list to be bombed.

It was in fact a public shelter. A few weeks later I visited it, and saw the sign still hanging by the entrance: 'Department of Civil Defence. Shelter 35.' In their anxiety to get their families into a place of safety, government officials had been dropping them off at the shelter. Mostly, though, women and children would simply turn up at the door of the shelter, and were rarely turned away. The al-Amiriyah building was not, as the Americans tried to maintain with increasing embarrassment afterwards, a major command and control centre; it was just a big office block constructed during the Iran–Iraq War with an air-raid shelter in the basement.

At around five o'clock in the morning a 2,000-pound penetration bomb cut its way cleanly down through the building and into the ten feet of reinforced concrete and steel of the shelter's roof. The shelter was on two levels. The upper level was a dormitory, and most of the victims were killed here. They died instantly. Those on the lower level died much worse deaths from fire and smoke. The rescuers saw sights of a kind which only the late twentieth century could have devised: bodies fused together so that they formed entire blocks of flesh, a layer of melted human fat an inch deep lying on the surface of the water pumped in by the firemen.

It was a dreadful, disgusting mistake. Yet instead of acknowledging that, the American military tried for almost a week to justify what they had done: the building had been transmitting wireless messages, the signature of radio patterns from it indicated that Saddam Hussein himself might be there. General Thomas Kelly, director of operations for the Joint Chiefs of Staff, went furthest of all: Saddam might, he said, have taken 'a cold-blooded decision . . . to put civilians without our knowledge into a facility and have them bombed'.

The more gullible American and British newspapers accepted all this. It was a British reporter, my colleague and friend Jeremy Bowen, who had gone to the shelter soon after the attack had happened, and the Murdoch press and the traditionally anti-BBC *Daily Mail* launched savage attacks on his professional reputation and honesty.

The *Mail* even suggested that the violently angry people who shouted at Bowen's camera in English – 'You animals, you sons of bitches, is this the way to win back Kuwait?' – had been sent there by Saddam's officials for Bowen to interview. Al-Amariyah was an expensive area where a good many educated people lived; and most educated people in Iraq speak English as a matter of course.

Some American newspapers seemed prepared to swallow anything, rather than accept that a mistake had been made. According to one story, all the military bodies in the shelter had been moved out so the journalists could not see them; according to another, a secret basement, fully equipped to communicate with generals at the front, had been flooded to ensure the journalists on the spot could not find it.

No one explained why, if the al-Amiriyah building had been so important, the Americans had waited until the twenty-eighth day of the war to hit it. By this stage other buildings in Baghdad had been hit twenty or thirty times because of the limited number of targets available. Perhaps the military planners were starting to take risks, and thought there was a good chance of killing some senior Ba'ath Party officials. Instead they slaughtered large numbers of ordinary women and children, in some of the most appalling ways imaginable.

When I went back there, after the war was over, the local feeling was still so great that my driver, a decent man and a good friend, would not let me get out of the vehicle. People would think I was an American and would lynch me, he said. We paused long enough for me to see the sign beside the shelter and the school next door. That confirmed the fear I had had ever since I first heard about the bombing of the shelter.

It was the place we had visited on the morning the UN deadline ran out. I remembered the dark faces, the sidelong glances, and the English lesson:

'I am happy, you are kind, he is sad, they are GOOOOOD.'

Some of those girls would have been in the shelter when the worst death imaginable had visited it.

36. DESERT WAR

It was miserable in the desert at the end of January. The temperature was almost down to zero, and the streaming rain turned the sand to a nasty pale mud. In the vastness of the desert, many of the American soldiers felt a powerful sense of claustrophobia. They sat on their rainproof ponchos and went through the motions, faces reddened and roughened by the sun and the desert wind, waiting nervously or enthusiastically for the moment when the big attack would begin.

But the Iraqis got in first. General Wadoud, who commanded the Iraqi 3rd Corps in Kuwait, was a proactive commander – one of the very few in the Iraqi army – who sent a series of radio messages to Saddam Hussein warning him of the attrition his men were suffering under the Coalition air attacks and demanding to be allowed to counter-attack. Saddam disliked successful generals and stalled, but when he saw an ITN report re-broadcast by CNN, he relented. The ITN team had visited the Saudi town of Khafji, twelve miles south of the Kuwaiti border, and found it empty and unguarded. Saddam suggested that General Wadoud should capture Khafji.

It was little more than a skirmish, but in the tense period before the big Coalition attack it made headlines around the world. It also seemed to show that the Iraqis should be taken seriously. Twelve US Marines were killed in the first twenty-four hours of the operation, and there were casualties among the Saudi troops who were sent to recapture the town. They succeeded eventually, but the Iraqis had caught the allies napping. Saddam Hussein received all the credit, and people across the Arab world came out into the streets when they heard the news of the attack, chanting and waving Saddam's picture. General Wadoud's part in it all was almost ignored.

There was some particularly good newspaper and television reporting of the attack from the so-called 'unilaterals' – journalists who remained outside the official pool system. Often the unilaterals had to get by on their wits: the BBC correspondent Mark Urban, who had served in the Royal Tank Corps, put on his old army beret and found himself being waved forward down the road to Khafji. He and his team reached it just before the Iraqis, and watched the entire battle.

'It was as good a view,' Urban said later, 'as watching the Battle of Inkerman from the Heights.'

The official pool correspondents arrived much later, and an officious NBC reporter called Brad Willis tried to get Urban and the other unilaterals ejected from Khafji on the grounds that they were there without official permission. When everyone finally returned to the main army headquarters at Dhahran after the battle was over, Urban had to endure a lecture from an American reservist called, absurdly, Captain Koko. He was an insurance executive from Kentucky acting as a press liaison officer.

'You are just rogue journalists,' Captain Koko said. 'You're like cockroaches scuttling round a tenement building. It's my job to make life miserable for you.'

Not surprisingly the unilaterals looked down on the official pool system, feeling it did no good to the journalists who belonged to it. The distinction between the journalists and the military units they were reporting on became blurred, especially when the journalists put on military uniform and appeared on camera.

Yet in the end, and despite the best efforts of people like Brad Willis and Captain Koko, the unilaterals had a much better time of it than the pool reporters. They were free to do the more adventurous and more informative reporting, and they usually saw more action. The ground war, when it came, would be over so fast that the entire British and French contingents, and many of the best American units, were largely sidelined. As a result the journalists attached to them saw little of the fighting.

To fight a tank war in the desert is to play Nelson at Trafalgar. The sand is like water, a medium through which the battle progresses. There are no real geographical features to attack or defend; the two sides flow through it to get to each other.

In traditional fashion Schwarzkopf decided to mislead the enemy about his intentions. The US Marine Corps carried out a series of exercises designed to give the impression that part of the Coalition force would storm ashore and capture Kuwait from the sea. This is what Saddam's generals would have preferred, since the coastline was guarded by ten Iraqi divisions. Schwarzkopf also gave the impression that the main attack would come from the south, where the main body of troops had spent the previous four months.

If Saddam had invested $2.35 in a copy of the previous week's *Time* magazine he would have learned that the real thrust of the attack would come from the west, though by that stage it scarcely mattered. In London a thief stole a laptop computer from the car of an unfortunate RAF officer who was carrying the entire Schwarzkopf plan in it. He left his car for a matter of minutes, and the laptop disappeared. The British Ministry of Defence and the Pentagon agreed that it was too much of a coincidence, and that an Iraqi agent must have stolen it; but before General Schwarzkopf had time to alter his plan the computer was handed in at a nearby police station, together with a note.

'I may be a thief,' the note said, 'but I am not a traitor.' No attempt had been made to hand the plans to the Iraqis.

By 23 February a quarter of a million men and thousands of tanks had taken up positions in the Saudi desert west of Kuwait. In any normal conflict it would have been impossible for this many troops to gather undetected, but the Iraqis were blind. They had lost their entire air force, and had no other way of gathering intelligence about the American strategy. Soviet satellites passed over the area at least twice a day, but the Russians did not pass on their information to the Iraqis.

The ground war began just before dawn on Sunday 24 February. Dozens of M270 multiple rocket launchers opened fire with almost paralysing effect, the long, slender rockets shooting up in batches of seven or eight at a time, too fast for the human eye to catch them, the towering columns of smoke they left behind them intertwining in the air.

The gunners grunted and shouted their responses and sweated uncontrollably as the shells in their red cloth jackets were passed from hand to hand and placed in the breeches of the guns. Self-propelled M109 guns on tracks like tanks fired their 95-pound high explosive shells on targets twelve miles away. The British fired more shells and rockets than at any time since the Korean War, forty years before. Interviewed, the artillerymen talked in their usual laconic way about having a job of work to do.

'The lads have been feeling slightly frustrated,' one British officer told a television crew. 'We've been here for a hundred and twenty-five days. It's been a long wait.'

Gaps had been bulldozed in the berms, the large banks of sand which marked the Saudi–Kuwait border. Markers with arrows and brigade symbols were planted in the desert to mark the way through, just like El Alamein. But an older battle haunted the imaginations of some commanders: tanks and fighting vehicles had to queue up at the gaps in the berms much as the troops on the first day of the Somme had had to line up at the gaps in the barbed wire. They would make superb targets for Iraqi gas and chemical weapons.

Shortly before dawn, the American VII and XVIII Corps moved into the undefended Iraqi desert. The XVIII Corps headed north, to block off the Iraqis' escape. The French captured the desert town of as-Salman. The British accompanied the VII Corps, which took the Iraqis in the flank in the approved cavalry manner. They found that the Iraqi tanks were often dug into positions facing in entirely the wrong direction. There were blazing tanks everywhere.

Right from the start it was clear there was no fight in the Iraqis after all. Deserters flooded across, waving the leaflets which had been dropped in their tens of thousands over the Iraqi positions during the previous days. They brought with them stories of food shortages and low morale. Many had no medical supplies and just a little rice and bread each day.

'When we showed him [their first prisoner] the roach-coach,' said a US Marine, referring to one of the mobile catering vans the Americans were using, 'I thought he was gonna lose it altogether. He just kind of stood there lookin' at it and cryin'.'

There was little resistance, just an occasional incoming shell. Yet even now the Coalition commanders were worried: they thought the Iraqis might be husbanding their resources for a big counter-attack.

This was a war fought out between more than half a million soldiers, yet no journalists working within the American or British pool system saw any fighting with their own eyes, or obtained a single image of a dead body. Those who controlled the system seemed mostly concerned with preventing journalists from witnessing what was going on. And there was an intensive effort to make sure that the scale of Iraqi losses was hidden from the world.

When, for instance, the US 1st Mechanized Division attacked the Iraqi front line soon after dawn on 24 February, the barrage from howitzers and rocket-launchers must have killed hundreds of Iraqi soldiers who were sheltering in their trenches. Then the armour broke through, and the real slaughter began.

It was nine years before General Schwarzkopf would say even roughly in public how many soldiers he thought the Iraqi military had lost during the war, but during a television interview in 2000 he finally put the figure at 'tens of thousands'. The killing was a brutal, industrial business, with little or no danger to the American soldiers who carried it out. Bradley fighting vehicles drove right up to the trenches where the Iraqi soldiers lay, and poured devastating quantities of 7.62mm ammunition into them. A single 7.62 bullet can tear a man's arm off; these guns were capable of firing dozens of bullets a minute.

At the same time Abrams battle tanks fitted with huge ploughs and scrapers approached the trenches and shovelled tons of earth over the soldiers who were there: the living, the dying, the dead.

'I came through right after the lead company,' Colonel Anthony Moreno told a journalist afterwards; he commanded the lead brigade of the 1st Mechanized. 'What you saw was a bunch of buried trenches with people's arms and legs sticking out of them. For all I know, we could have killed thousands.'

After them came the ACEs – the Armoured Combat Earthmovers. They smoothed out the ground, pushing the arms and legs and heads out of sight.

And then, thirty-six hours or so afterwards, late on the afternoon of 25 February, the pool journalists were finally allowed to inspect the site. There was, of course, nothing much to be seen except the Iraqi soldiers who had been lucky enough to surrender: no bodies, no barbed wire, not even any trenches. It was too ugly for the public to be told about, and for that reason it had all been thoroughly tidied away.

This wasn't a battle like El Alamein or D-Day. In fact it wasn't a battle at all; merely the slaughter of tens of thousands of Third World soldiers armed only with weapons incapable of penetrating American armour. Almost every Iraqi soldier would have willingly given himself up if he had been given the chance. I have never yet seen a war that was noble and glorious, but this one was as noble and glorious as the morning shift in an abbatoir.

The Coalition's losses were mostly caused by the Americans too. That morning, two British Warrior fighting vehicles, clearly carrying the Coalition recognition markings, were hit by Maverick missiles fired by American A-10 Thunderbolt aircraft. Nine British soldiers died, eleven were injured. There was considerable bitterness about the incident on the British side afterwards, and the British Ministry of Defence, anxious not to encourage anti-Americanism in the British forces or in Britain generally, did its best to cover up the full circumstances of the men's deaths.

After forty hours of relentless advance, the Americans (with relatively little help from their British and French allies, who were sidelined) had effectively destroyed the resistance of the Iraqi army. This was an extremely dangerous moment for Saddam Hussein. Almost as soon as the air war had begun, more than a month earlier, it had been plain that his bluff, on which he had staked everything, had failed: the Coalition airstrikes had been overwhelming, yet they had not caused anything like the huge loss of life he had expected. There had been no worldwide revulsion, no mass demonstrations in the streets of American cities.

He faced utter defeat. Earlier, during the efforts to reach a peaceful conclusion to the crisis, Saddam had refused to compromise because he believed his generals would think he was weak, and perhaps overthrow him. Now the army was no longer a potential threat to him: it was his only defence, his sole protection. With the generals reporting a military collapse all along the line, it would be safer to surrender Kuwait than to see the army destroyed altogether.

And so, on the evening of Monday 25 February, Saddam Hussein effectively threw in the towel. At seven o'clock he contacted the Soviet ambassador in Baghdad and told him he was now prepared to comply with all the UN resolutions on Kuwait. Soon afterwards a statement was broadcast on Baghdad Radio:

> Orders have been issued to our armed forces to withdraw in an organized manner to the positions they held prior to 1 August 1990. This is regarded as practical compliance with Resolution 660. Our armed forces, which have proven their ability to fight

and stand fast, will confront any attempt to harm them while they are carrying out the withdrawal order.

The statement, drafted by Saddam and Tariq Aziz in the underground bunker they occasionally occupied near the al-Rashid Hotel, was a prime example of Saddam's instinct for political manoeuvring even when there was a loaded gun pointing directly at his head. Its wording was an attempt to minimize his personal humiliation while in effect asking the Coalition to stop destroying his forces.

It was accompanied by a breathtaking act of destructive defiance. As early as January he had given his generals their instructions in the event of a collapse in Iraqi communications. If they were forced to withdraw from Kuwait, he told them, they should blow up all the main oil installations.

At the end of January the Iraqi military had already opened the valves on the oil pipeline leading to Kuwait's Sea Island loading terminal, offshore from the Mina al-Ahmadi complex, south of Kuwait City. The millions of barrels which gushed out into the sea caused a slick thirty-five miles by ten miles: it was the biggest oil spillage that had ever occurred.

Now, with the war definitively lost, the Iraqi army set off the explosives planted at all Kuwait's oil installations, setting fire to the gases which were mixed in with the oil. Flames sprang up all along the horizon, turning the sand dunes black and darkening the sun at noon. In Saudi Arabia people had to drive around in the hours of daylight with their headlights full on, and it was impossible for aircraft to take off or land at a large proportion of Saudi airfields. It was an act of terrible, premeditated vengeance, which effectively ended the war.

By Tuesday 26 February, two days into the ground offensive, the Coalition forces had captured 23,500 prisoners; the number of American casualties only equalled the number killed and injured at home in road accidents during the same period. The American First Cavalry Division was engaged on the longest advance US soldiers had ever made to engage an enemy, swinging round to the north of Kuwait, and were starting to close in on the Republican Guard divisions which were their target. Then they heard news that a ceasefire was in the offing. The ground war had run out before their extraordinary advance could bring them into action.

General Norman Schwarzkopf said later that he thought the troops should have gone on for another couple of days, and at the time it was clear he wanted them to take Baghdad; he had to apologize to President Bush for making his thoughts public. But going on to Baghdad was out of the question: if American and allied forces invaded Iraqi soil, the Coalition which had been so skilfully constructed would collapse. Of all the various Arab contingents in the force, only the Kuwaitis would support the Americans if they pressed on. It was too dangerous an adventure, and President Bush was not by instinct an adventurous man. He decided against crossing into Iraq.

Watching the television pictures in Washington, Bush knew the fighting had to stop now. The television crews were just arriving at the scene of utter destruction at the Mutla Ridge on the road to the Iraqi border from Kuwait City, and the scenes were enough to disgust public opinion in the United States and elsewhere with the entire enterprise.

Aircraft from the USAF and the RAF had caught the last column of trucks to leave Kuwait City on the part of the road leading up to the Ridge, and blasted away until every one of them was destroyed.

The drivers were for the most part the last of the looters, delayed by their efforts to find everything they could lay their hands on. Some of them are thought to have been intelligence officers who had based themselves at the Nayef Palace in Kuwait City, the main torture centre during the Iraqi occupation. They were among the last Iraqis out of Kuwait, and they left the instruments of their trade behind them: electricity cable, buckets, bloodstained hunting knives, axes. Men and women had been slowly tortured to death for enjoyment here.

As they left, a number of these and the other remaining Iraqis grabbed people off the streets to act as hostages, perhaps hoping they could ransom them for money later. So of the 400 or so bodies burned to a crisp in the trucks or lying on the sand beside the road at the Mutla Ridge, some will have been those of entirely innocent people.

The Coalition forces insisted that until there was a formal stop to the fighting, the trucks which were heading for the Iraqi border were part of a retreating army. The official line was that the men in them would be safe only if they stopped, abandoned their weapons, and left the vehicles. The retreating Iraqis knew nothing of this, of course. Caught in a long traffic jam on the road, they were easy targets for the pilots who attacked them. By doing so, the Coalition was not contravening the Hague Convention of 1907, which merely forbids attacks on soldiers who have already surrendered. These men had no chance to surrender. But it was an ugly, cruel business, and the pilots who came back exulting in the 'turkey-shoot' often found that their own comrades disapproved of what they had done.

Now the journalists who reached the scene found an eerie silence, with just the wind blowing through the empty, burned-out vehicles and turning over the litter of stolen goods lying on the sand: handbags, plastic toys, clothes, cheap jewellery. These things had brought the deaths of the terrible grinning corpses lying curled up beside the vehicles or still gripping the carbonized steering-wheels. It was the abiding image of a vicious war.

That day a CBS correspondent, Bob McKeown, was the first man into Kuwait City, some way ahead of the allied troops. It was a remarkable achievement. He and his team were 'unilaterals', unshackled by the press liaison officers who managed to hold the pool journalists back. They received an ecstatic welcome from the people of the city as they drove through it. Yet it was a sobering moment for him.

> Beyond the jubilation we felt there is desolation. Buildings have been destroyed, or partially destroyed. There are hulks of auto-mobiles and Iraqi vehicles, and there is a sense of desertedness . . .
> A lot of homes have been appropriated, a lot of the hotels along the seafront have been burned. The streets have been barricaded. There is a Beirut-like sense to parts of downtown Kuwait.

It was a shocking sight, the damaged buildings standing out against the orange and black clouds from the burning oilfields.

The war was over, the Iraqis had been driven out, Kuwait was liberated. The price in lives had not been anywhere near as high as either the Pentagon or the anti-war protestors had thought; but the cost in terms of physical destruction and human misery was incalculable.

In Baghdad that morning the BBC correspondent Jeremy Bowen was awakened early by the sound of gunfire. He went to the window and looked out: the Mukhabarat guards from the al-Rashid were out in the streets firing their guns in the air in celebration. The word was going round that the Americans and British were on their way to Baghdad, and that Saddam Hussein was finished.

It is a serious moment for a tyrant when even the secret policemen are rejoicing in his imminent downfall. But Saddam Hussein wasn't finished after all. One of the most remarkable escapes of modern times was about to be enacted.

37. NO CONTEST

If the air war had been devastating, the ground war had been one of the great anti-climaxes of modern times.

Every journalist, every soldier seemed to repeat the formulation that Iraq was the fourth largest military power in the world. It is always as well to question these bland statements; and in the case of the first Gulf War it amounted almost to a confidence trick. Much of the data the Pentagon used in its public statements and in assembling its computer predictions was completely wrong – absurdly over-estimated for political effect and to encourage the US government, the American people, and international opinion to take the enterprise seriously. Added together, the smaller over-estimates produced one enormous over-estimate: the notion that the Coalition was taking on a serious army. It dignified the efforts that President Bush and his allies were making to dislodge Saddam Hussein from Kuwait.

The Pentagon, estimating that there were 540,000 Iraqi troops in the theatre of war, assembled a force of almost 525,000, of which 350,000 were American. The British contingent was 32,000, and the French 12,000. But the figure for the Iraqi forces was grossly exaggerated. Even when they were at full strength, in early January, there were only 260,000 of them.

Directly the bombing began, the Iraqi troops began deserting at an extraordinary rate. According to General Schwarzkopf, who was refreshingly honest about the entire situation, the desertion rate among the conscripted men in the front line was sometimes more than 30 per cent. The rate among the Republican Guard, where the men were better paid, was lower. But the total forces which the Coalition faced were probably less than 200,000, giving the Americans and their allies a numerical superiority of between 2 and 2.5 to 1, depending on the precise rate of desertion. It was no contest.

The quality of the Iraqi military machine was as inflated as its numerical size. According to a study carried out for the US Army War College,

> Iraq is superb on the defense. Its army is well-equipped and trained to carry out mobile defense operations.

The study failed to point out that the Iraqi army had only been superb when it had sheltered behind the huge defences constructed for it by the Soviet Union. Its equipment was a mixed bag, bought from half a dozen different suppliers in deals which were often heavily influenced by bribes. The army, for instance, had six different types of tank: Soviet T-55s, T-62s and T-72s, Chinese T-59s and T-69s, and British Chieftains. Keeping such a wide range of equipment properly equipped and maintained was extraordinarily difficult. The Iraqi military found it hard to get even basic equipment for its foot-soldiers, and in Kuwait City the troops often had orders to forage for their own food.

It gradually became clear that the men who had volunteered for service in Kuwait had mostly gone there for two reasons: first, because they were certain there would be no war, and second, because they were further away from the informers and surveillance of Iraq proper. Iraqi tank commanders would settle into the positions allocated to them, and would then routinely take out the tank's battery and use it to power hi-fi systems, television sets, microwave ovens and any number of other gadgets looted from Kuwait City. They had no desire to fight a war, and it didn't occur to them that it might eventually be necessary. Even the punishment squads which were based behind the Iraqi lines to shoot deserters had little interest in obeying their orders. Many of them planned to desert themselves.

The daily and nightly air strikes by Coalition planes on Iraqi positions destroyed Iraqi morale to a much greater extent than was realized. By the third week of January, when the air strikes were at their height, you could buy a Kalashnikov at the main Baghdad bus station for twenty dinars: three dollars at black-market rates. A month later, when the ground war was imminent, the price had dropped to eight dinars. Iraqi soldiers were deserting in huge numbers, and selling everything they had in order to get the bus fare home.

Yet the Coalition commanders failed to understand the nature and extent of the Iraqi collapse. They were still conditioned by the Pentagon's computer projections, which had originally forecast allied casualties as high as 40,000, and although these were scaled down to a suggested figure of 5,000 before the attack began, the computers were still estimating that the ground war would last between seven and ten days.

Partly this was because the Coalition needed to exaggerate the danger which was posed by Saddam Hussein (a familiar theme in the second Gulf War, of course) in order to convince public opinion that this was a war worth fighting. But partly it was because of Saddam Hussein himself. His strategy was entirely based on bluff, and the bluff was remarkably successful. When he issued bloodcurdling threats about what his army would do to the invaders, people in the outside world tended to believe him. Not in Iraq, though: his own people had heard it all before, and knew it amounted to nothing.

The process was helped by the curious lack of interest the Western media showed in the reality of Saddam Hussein and the nature of his regime. Their main concern was with the build-up of Coalition forces. Saddam represented our worst fears, and we showed a curious reluctance to give them up by examining the man or his methods. The Western media generally ignored the clear evidence from Baghdad that there was no great support for Saddam there. Many newspapers and television stations were still talking in terms of mass rallies and fanatical crowds of supporters until the very end. That was what the viewers and readers expected, and that was what they got.

Before the ground war began, it was widely believed that Iraq would use chemical weapons. President George Bush said he expected it; the British government agreed.

When the first Iraqi Scud missile hit Tel Aviv, there was an immediate fear that it contained poison gas. A CNN anchorman in Atlanta panicked entertainingly on air.

'We're ordering you not to open that window!' he shouted, when a correspondent in Tel Aviv suggested a simple way of finding out.

The correspondent, ludicrously enough, was wearing a gas mask to broadcast in.

Several British and American newspapers reported that the missile had indeed been armed with a chemical warhead, and not all of them retracted the story the following day. Journalists and servicemen in Saudi Arabia carried gas masks wherever they went. The Israeli High

Court of Justice ruled that it was patent discrimination and a scandal that Jewish settlers in the Occupied Territories were issued with masks when Palestinians were not. In countries as far away as Germany, sales of gas masks were reported.

There was no reported use of any chemical weapon at any stage during the war. The United States attributed this to a warning from President Bush about the severest consequences of any attack, yet it seems that Saddam Hussein never intended to use his unconventional weaponry against Coalition troops. For him, the most important thing was to survive the war, and he knew that if he used chemical, biological or nuclear weapons the allies would hunt him down and kill him.

After the war, one of the best British defence correspondents, Robert Fox, stumbled across one of Gerald Bull's G-5 super-guns, which was supposed to fire huge projectiles enormous distances. It was lying useless in the desert, having never been fired. It was clear too how inferior the Iraqis' conventional weaponry had been. (Except for rifles: the Kalashnikov was largely unaffected by sand – unlike the unnecessarily complex weapons used by the Americans and British.)

The Iraqi T-55 tanks were simply updated versions of the main Soviet battle-tank of the Second World War, and were hopelessly outclassed by the American Abrams and the British Challenger. For the most part the T-55s were used as artillery. Advancing Allied soldiers would come across them in well-prepared, rather comfortable positions, incapable of moving, their guns able to traverse only a few degrees. The war in the air had been serious. The ground offensive was simply a mopping up of illusions.

There was no real will to fight, and no discernible support for Saddam Hussein's gamble in invading Kuwait. The Coalition forces owed a great deal to the Iraqis. The ground war was a walkover, because the Iraqis had taken a conscious, collective decision not to resist. We heard a great deal afterwards about General Schwarzkopf's tactical brilliance and his victorious strategy based on a careful study of the battle of El Alamein. Very little was said about the refusal of ordinary Iraqi officers and their men to fight for Saddam, yet that, rather than the tactics of the Coalition, was what won the war for the allied countries.

38. UPRISING

At the Safwan air base on the border of Kuwait and Iraq, three tents had been fitted together to make one large enough for the ceremony. There was a plain table in the middle, with half a dozen hard chairs set round it and a row of others behind. There was a notepad on the table in front of each place, a bottle of water, and a white coffee cup. Little bowls in the centre of the table held potato crisps and hummus.

Outside, field-guns and even a battery of Patriot missiles had been deployed. At 11.30 a.m. two US Army vehicles approached, escorted by Bradley fighting vehicles bearing large white flags with red crescents on them. A couple of Apache helicopters hovered overhead, keeping to the speed of the convoy. It was Sunday 3 March: the culminating day of the careers of the men who were waiting. For the men who were being brought to the tent it must have been both painful and dangerous.

General Schwarzkopf gave particular proof of his thoughtfulness and sensitivity on this occasion. As the eight senior Iraqi officers arrived and came into the tent, he introduced them to his deputies: the Saudi, British, French, Kuwaiti and other commanders. He had ordered the cameras not to film them as they were searched for weapons, because he did not want them to be humiliated, and he was the first to submit himself to a search in front of them.

The Iraqis were probably concerned less with being humiliated and more with what Saddam Hussein would think when he saw the television pictures of the surrender ceremony. Lt-General Sultan Hashim Ahmad, looking a little like Saddam himself only pleasanter, sat side by side with Lt-General Saleh Abbud Mahmud, their aides behind them. A word spoken out of place, a glance, might lead to their execution. Saddam had at first refused to send his military commanders to the ceremony, but had been persuaded by the Soviet ambassador.

The meeting went on for little more than an hour, and the Iraqis agreed to everything. Saddam wanted it all dealt with as quickly as possible; a little humiliation now would safeguard him later. There were ten points to the final agreement. They included:

the immediate release of all allied prisoners;
the return of all goods stolen from Kuwait during the occupation;
the return of all abducted Kuwaiti citizens;
the clearance of all mines laid in Kuwait;
the clearance of booby traps inside foreign embassies in Kuwait
City;
and no movement of Iraqi aircraft without permission.

But that last stipulation wasn't enough. It was followed by a serious mistake on Schwarzkopf's part – a mistake which would allow Saddam Hussein to pick himself up off the ground and eventually get back to something like his former power.

It was introduced in a craftily diffident way by Lt-General Sultan Hashim Ahmad. Far from offending his master, he eventually rose to become defence minister during the second Iraq War.

We have a point, one point. You might very well know the situation of the roads and bridges and communications. We would like to agree that helicopter flights sometimes are needed to carry some of the officials, government officials, or any member that is needed to be transported from one place to another because the roads and bridges are out.

Why should Schwarzkopf worry about a little thing like that? The Iraqis were utterly defeated; no need to punish them unnecessarily.

Schwarzkopf: I want to make sure that's recorded, that military helicopters can fly over Iraq. Not fighters, not bombers.
Hashim Ahmad: So you mean even helicopters that is armed in the Iraqi skies can fly, but not the fighters?
Schwarzkopf: Yeah, I will instruct our Air Force not to shoot at any helicopters that are flying over the territory of Iraq where we are not located.

These few words sentenced 50,000 Shi'ites to death, and exiled hundreds of thousands of innocent Kurdish civilians. To add to his error of judgement (those probing words 'even helicopters that is armed' should perhaps have alerted him), Schwarzkopf made no mention of tanks and artillery either. Saddam had his means of retribution now.

No one except Saddam and his advisers realized this at the time. There were two conflicting views in Washington: one, that Saddam should be overthrown as quickly as possible, and the other that Iraq, without its strongman to keep it together, would fall into its constituent parts and create chaos in the entire region. Better, this argument went, to weaken the strongman than to throw him out. For the moment, though, George Bush inclined to the view that Saddam should be got rid of. General Schwarzkopf certainly did.

By 1.20 p.m. the agreement was signed, and everyone trooped out. Then something unexpected happened. Schwarzkopf stopped the Iraqi delegation as they were leaving and invited them into his tent. They stayed there for twenty minutes. Schwarzkopf told them in plain terms that it was up to them as military men to get rid of Saddam Hussein. Iraq could never be a normal country while he was in power, Schwarzkopf said. Watching the television broadcast, Saddam saw the Iraqi officers go into Schwarzkopf's tent, and he must have known what was being said to them. It would be some time before he could be certain of their complete loyalty.

The defeat was not as final as the Americans and their allies at first assumed. Twenty-nine Iraqi divisions had been destroyed, but it became clear later that they were mostly from the regular army and were made up of ordinary conscripts. Many of the Republican Guard divisions, much better trained and manned by professional soldiers, had been kept back from the slaughter. They were still intact, and Saddam had ordered his generals to move them back to Iraq before the ground offensive ended. He would need them for the difficult days to come.

The soldiers who were now crossing back into Iraq were a chaotic, completely undisciplined body of men, leaderless and panic-stricken, who had been through terrible experiences. Their only concern was to get to safety. They headed instinctively towards Basra, hungry, frightened and embittered, their loyalties and their sense of values in complete turmoil. Many openly blamed Saddam Hussein, and cursed him for what had happened to them. On the evening of Friday 1 March, the day after President Bush called a halt to the Allied attack, a major uprising broke out.

For the first time, ordinary Iraqi citizens understood what a catastrophic defeat their army had suffered. Soldiers surged through the streets of Basra, jamming the roads with their vehicles and firing their guns in the air. The city was almost entirely Shi'ite, and the old resentments against the rule of the Sunni Muslims gave a sudden focus to the mood of anger and chaos. It was a revolutionary moment.

Crowds of ordinary people, supported by the soldiers with their guns, stormed through the centre of the city, attacking everything connected with Saddam Hussein and his rule. The governor's palace was burned, the Ba'ath Party headquarters was ransacked, the Mukhabarat offices were looted and all files destroyed. The rebellious soldiers set up road-blocks on the approaches to the city, to prevent loyalist troops from retaking it. At this stage the leaders of the uprising were all local people or mutineers.

By the late afternoon of Saturday 2 March new leaders had taken over. Shi'ite fundamentalists loyal to Mohammed Bakr al-Hakim began arriving in considerable numbers from across the border in Iran, helped on their way by the Iranian government. Al-Hakim was an Iraqi, a long-standing opponent of Saddam Hussein, and his organization, the Supreme Council of the Islamic Revolution in Iraq (SCIRI), was based in Tehran.

Now the entire tone of the uprising changed. It was no longer simply a rebellion against Saddam Hussein and his regime; it had became a fundamentalist revolution. An angry crowd attacked the Sheraton Hotel in Basra, smashing the bars and the casino. In the centre of the city a large group of men and women, the women dressed in *chadors*, began proclaiming a Shi'ite Islamic Republic. They had been brought to Basra in buses supplied by the Iranian government.

At this point the soldiers who had escaped from Kuwait were faced with a major decision. Many were themselves Shi'ites, and half-inclined to go along with the fundamentalists. But a good proportion were Sunnis, especially the officers, who in the Iraqi army were often drawn from the area around Mosul in the north of the country. If the revolutionaries had continued to concentrate on the overthrow of Saddam Hussein and the Ba'ath Party, they would almost certainly have kept the support of the soldiers. But the army had been encouraged to think of itself as the cement of the Iraqi nation, and the fundamentalists seemed to offer only sectarianism and the break-up of the country. The officers began to rally their men against the revolutionaries.

The fighting which followed was bitter. I could not get to Basra until four weeks later, but when I finally arrived the evidence was still scattered around everywhere: armoured personnel carriers upturned by the side of the road, helmets and abandoned equipment lying on the ground. Hundreds of ordinary civilians were killed. Basra had fallen to the insurgents for a time, but the army had regained it.

On 1 March the feeling in Washington and London was still that Saddam Hussein should be overthrown. President Bush spoke publicly of the economic hardship Iraq was undergoing.

'The Iraqi people should put him aside,' he said, 'and that would facilitate the solution of all these problems.'

Douglas Hurd, the British foreign secretary, agreed.

'Iraq,' he told the House of Commons, 'cannot expect to be readmitted to the community of nations while it has a delinquent regime.'

The message to the people of Iraq was clear: overthrow Saddam and all will be well. It was the same message General Schwarzkopf had given the generals in his tent at Safwan.

In the south, eight provinces fell under rebel control: Basra itself, Nasiriyah, Amara, Kut, Simawa, Diwaniya, Najaf and Kerbala. Yet what had happened in Basra was replicated in each of the other provinces: at first there was a popular uprising, then the fundamentalists moved in and the more moderate forces turned against them. Old scores were settled, and people accused of being government informers were attacked and lynched. Often, it was said, the government informers would get in first with their accusations in order to protect their own skins. There was no control, no coordination, and little thought given to defending against the inevitable counter-attack by loyalist forces.

On 5 March, only four days after President Bush had encouraged the people of Iraq to come out and overthrow Saddam, the presidential spokesman Marlin Fitzwater made a very different statement.

'We don't,' he said at the daily White House briefing, 'intend to get involved . . . in Iraq's internal affairs.'

In other words, there would be no help for the rebels. General Colin Powell, the chief of staff, whose record twelve years later as secretary of state was weak and unimpressive, argued that it was no concern of the United States to help the rebels, and might cost American lives. For an administration which had taken plenty of risks with American lives already, Powell's argument was the clincher. America would do nothing to help the people it had encouraged to rebel. In an interview I recorded later with President Clinton's head of the CIA, James Woolsey, he described it as one of the worst decisions the United States had taken in the entire course of the twentieth century. There is plenty of competition for that particular title, of course, but it was certainly one of the most ignoble policy changes made by the United States, and it ensured that Saddam Hussein would survive the onslaught against him.

The following day, 6 March, the Republican Guard finally succeeded in capturing the centre of Basra. The damage was worse than anything suffered in Iraq during the war against the Coalition. Hundreds of bodies littered the streets, and the dogs ate them where they lay. The executions began. A favourite method was to make prisoners drink petrol, then set them alight.

Saddam Hussein had made Ali Hassan al-Majid, Chemical Ali, his new minister of the interior. The message was uncompromising and unmistakable: the methods which al-Majid had used against the Kurds in 1988–9 would be used now to restore Saddam's full control. In southern Iraq anyone with a beard or a turban was liable to be rounded up, and many were shot.

Ba'ath Party activists around the country were sent a video showing al-Majid haranguing a helicopter pilot who was being sent on a mission against a group of rebels.

'I don't want you back unless you can tell me you've burned them. If you haven't burned them, don't bother to come back.'

Later in the video al-Majid and Mohammed Hamza al-Zubeidi, who would soon become prime minister for his loyal service to the regime, were shown punching and kicking Shi'ite prisoners.

'Let's execute one and make the others confess,' said al-Zubeidi.

There was some resistance, even at the topmost levels. A leading general who was himself a Shi'ite was summoned by Saddam and ordered to take command of the battle against the rebels. It was typical of Saddam's blood-guilt tactics, to bind people to him. The general had anticipated the order, and prepared his response.

'I would rather die,' he told Saddam to his face.

'Then you will get your wish,' Saddam answered, and gave an order. The general was shot within half an hour.

In Kerbala, the second holiest city of Shi'ite Islam, it took six days of constant shelling by tanks and field artillery to subdue the uprising. As the loyalists gradually regained control they hanged dozens of Party and security officials who had escaped rather than staying to deal with the rebellion.

A few months later, in Washington, I came across an Iraqi general who had gone over to the side of the rebels. Realizing that the Republican Guard would soon be heading their way, he went to an Iraqi arms dump close to the border, which was being guarded by American soldiers. He explained to them that they needed weapons to fight Saddam's loyalists.

'The officer in charge contacted his commander, and the commander contacted Schwarzkopf. Maybe Schwarzkopf contacted Bush, I don't know. But the answer was no. I didn't want the Americans to help us, I just wanted to be able to use our own weapons to defend ourselves. And the Americans wouldn't even let us have those.'

What did he think about it now that he was living in safety in Washington, I asked.

'Every day I remember my men who were killed. I was lucky – I didn't want to get away, but we fought our way out and there was no possibility to return. But I feel very bitter. You can imagine: I live here now, but I will not forget that these people would not even let us defend ourselves.'

Three weeks after the Republican Guard had recaptured it, I visited Kerbala. Nothing serious had been done to clear up the extraordinary destruction. The fighting had been fiercest in the shrines themselves, and the damage to one of them had been so great that we were not allowed to see it. The Sunni soldiers who had recaptured the city had had no compunction about shelling Shi'ite holy places.

Outside the shrine of al-Abbas I talked to the crew of a Chieftain tank. They were all loyal to Saddam, and (like him) they were Sunnis. Saddam's picture smiled out at me from in front of the tank's driving seat, where other soldiers might have put a pin-up. What did they think about Shi'ites now, I asked them.

'They're just dirty animals,' one of them said. He spat on to the ground.

In Najaf, the other great holy city of the Shi'ites, soldiers had parked their motorbikes in the mosque, and the golden dome had been hit many times by artillery fire. We were taken to see the Grand

Ayatollah, Abolqassem al-Khoei. He was ninety-three, and in a pitiable state. He chose his words as carefully as possible, but it was clear he had been forced to broadcast an appeal to people not to support the uprising. When he started to complain about the treatment he was receiving, our minders told us we had another appointment, and it was time to leave.

Much of the centre of Najaf had been destroyed. As it began to get dark, the call to prayer started to float out over the devastation and the ruins of the city.

'There is no God but God, and Mohammed is His Prophet,' chanted the *muezzin*.

I listened for the next phrase, which distinguishes Shi'ite observance from Sunni Islam:

'. . . and Ali is His Deputy.'

It didn't come. Now that the Shi'ites had been defeated, even the basis of their religious worship had been stifled.

By Sunday 3 March there was revolution in northern Iraq too. Bands of Kurdish insurgents rose up to attack the Ba'ath Party organization and the security police in a dozen or more towns and cities. At first, as in the south, everything went the rebels' way: outside Dukan hundreds of soldiers from the 24th division surrendered to them, and some volunteered to fight alongside them; significantly, the 24th division was composed of Iraqi Arabs who were assumed to have little sympathy for the Kurds. Even units of the Jash, the fiercely pro-government Kurdish militia whom ordinary Kurds regarded as quislings, were defecting.

Descendants of the Medes and the Scythians, 25 million or more in number, the Kurds are the largest nation on earth which still lacks the right of self-determination. Curiously, it was only in Saddam Hussein's Iraq that they had achieved even a degree of autonomy. The Kurdish language, which at that time was outlawed in Turkey and hardly encouraged in the other countries where they lived – Syria, Iran and the former Soviet Union – was given official status in Iraq. Yet when the Kurds of Halabjah had shown their desire for practical independence from Saddam, his retaliation had been savage.

There are few more heady experiences than being with people who have liberated themselves from some hated regime by their own efforts. Everyone is a brother. Revolutionary crowds cease to be a collection of cowardly, fallible, untrustworthy individuals and become, for a brief moment, something grander and more generous. Portraits of the dictator are smashed, words are spoken that no one has dared to say in public before, the air of liberty is breathed deeply.

It is utterly intoxicating, and people, once free, find it impossible to imagine they will ever be enslaved again. From Prague in 1968 to Tiananmen Square in 1989, they thought that because what had happened was so right, and because so many good and decent people wanted it, their revolution could never be reversed.

This was the feeling in Kurdistan now. People danced for joy in the streets. They broke into the offices and torture-chambers of the Mukhabarat. They savoured the experience of being able to say what they believed for the first time in their lives.

'You don't know what it's like,' a man in his late forties told a BBC reporter, 'not having to think about what you are saying or who you are saying it to, not having to think about who is watching you or who is following you. It is wonderful, wonderful . . . Saddam is finished. We are free. We have got rid of fear.'

The mountains of Kurdistan were still covered with snow, but the valleys and meadows were green and spring torrents were starting to flow fast down to the chilly lakes. In Zakhu and Kirkuk, in Arbil, in Suleimaniyah, a new era had begun. The yellow flag of Kurdistan was everywhere. Massoud Barzani, a squat, heavily built bear of a man, toured the liberated area and addressed enormous crowds in the towns and villages. Barzani was the second generation of his family to lead the Kurdistan Democratic Party ('Kurdistan' not 'Kurdish', out of deference to the non-Kurdish Christians who played an important part in the movement) and he expressed his delight again and again at being able to come openly to places he could scarcely have approached even in secrecy before.

'One second of this day is worth all the wealth in the world!' he told the singing, cheering, laughing crowds.

Barzani was a realist. He knew that a state which took in all or even most of the Kurdish people was an impossibility. So he wasn't looking for independence, he was looking for autonomy within the Iraqi system. To the British correspondents who followed him around he would say he wanted the Kurdish area to be like Scotland; to the Canadians he said he wanted the Kurds to be like French Canadians.

As the Kurdish crowds gathered round him, reaching out their arms to him, you could see why Arab Iraqis regarded them as being so different. Their hair was lighter, some of the children were blond, and many had green eyes. Arab Iraqis tended to think of them as primitive, and the Kurds felt a certain hostility to them, but it was never intense. Their real hatred was directed at Saddam Hussein.

Kurds who had been exiled from Iraq for decades were coming back, from Turkey and Iran and from much farther afield: Britain, France, the United States. They wanted to be in at the beginning, to construct their new motherland from scratch. Even the people who had escaped from Halabjah when it was attacked by Saddam Hussein's cousin, Chemical Ali, in 1988 were heading back to build it up again. It was very painful to go back to a place where so many of their relatives and neighbours had died, but it was a sign that Kurdistan could live again.

This sense of excitement, of nation-building, lasted precisely three weeks. Then, on 26 March, Chemical Ali came back again. In Kirkuk the helicopter gunships appeared over the horizon without warning. In Zakhu and Suleimaniyah the Republican Guard moved in with heavy artillery. It was carefully judged: Chemical Ali would not be using chemicals this time. Saddam, as ever, was prepared to push everything to the edge, but not over it. If he had used weapons of mass destruction against the Kurds a second time, the allies would have intervened.

As it was, they did nothing. President Bush warned Saddam not to attack the Kurds, but Saddam knew that, with the Coalition moving apart and the troops leaving for home, the Americans would do nothing to him unless they really had to. He made sure they wouldn't have to.

Soon, in the mountains of northern Iraq and the marshlands of the south, the people who believed that Saddam was finished and that they were free found themselves fleeing once again as refugees. The Republican Guard divisions which recaptured Basra, Najaf and Kerbala then moved northwards to Kurdistan, where they joined other Guard divisions. Occasionally they attacked the refugees, but mostly they left them alone: nothing must be done to reawaken American anger.

Hundreds of thousands of Kurds walked over the mountains in the rain and freezing temperatures of early spring. Some went east to Iran, some north to Turkey. There was no food on the way. According to the old saying, the mountains were the Kurds' only friend; now they were their worst enemy. Most felt they had been utterly betrayed by the Americans and British, who had done so much for a million Kuwaitis and so little for 5 million Kurds.

In some places Turkish soldiers opened fire on the refugees. In others they stole the supplies of international aid and made the refugees pay for them. At the Isikveren camp near Uludere, where you could smell the stench of excrement long before you reached the entrance, the Turkish soldiers played a game with the Kurds: if the aid packages dropped by allied planes landed nearer the refugees, they could keep them. And if they landed nearer the soldiers, the soldiers could keep them. At the Sendimli camp, where there were no medical facilities, the Turkish commander refused to allow a group of French doctors and nurses to work there. It took days of negotiation before the Turks would allow the refugees to come down from the inhospitable mountainsides to holding areas on the plains. In some places the Turks fed them only once in three days, and when the aid planes came over the hungry refugees fought each other for food parcels with such ferocity that shots fired in the air did not deter them.

Slowly the appalling conditions suffered by the Kurds began to stir the conscience of the international community. John Major, who had been Britain's prime minister in succession to Mrs Thatcher for less than five months, felt a personal duty to do something about the situation. The only way to relieve the sufferings of the refugees, he decided, was to force Saddam Hussein's men back and allow the Kurds to return to their towns and villages. To the dismay of some of his ministers, he proposed a 'safe haven' for the Kurdish refugees inside Iraqi territory. He understood the political dangers to himself.

'I may end up with egg all over my face,' he told a television interviewer. 'But I will tell you this: I would rather end up with egg all over my face having tried and failed than not having put forward solutions to this problem.'

His biggest problem was to persuade the Americans to take part. The Bush administration was determined to get its troops out of Iraq as fast as possible, and there had been much less media coverage of the Kurdish problem in the United States than in Europe; American journalists were still emphasizing the military victory which had been achieved.

In the end, George Bush gave way and agreed to leave several thousand American troops in northern Iraq, alongside the British, the French, the Dutch and others. The creation of a safe haven for the Kurds turned out to be a considerable success, and led at last to the establishment of Iraqi Kurdistan, run jointly (after a good deal of savage fighting) by the Kurdistan Democratic Party and the Patriotic Union of Kurdistan. It was the first time Kurds had governed themselves in centuries. And they were free of Saddam Hussein at last.

39. WEAPONS

By the start of April 1991 it was clear that Saddam Hussein was going to survive. In front of a big crowd of supporters he stood on a balcony and fired his pistol in the air: that showed he was back in business. Pictures of the incident were displayed everywhere in Iraq, in case anyone had any doubts about it.

But now Saddam was obliged to give way to the United Nations demand that he should cooperate with UNSCOM, the UN Special Commission on Disarmament, which had the task of investigating Iraq's capacity to manufacture and use nuclear, chemical and biological weapons. His cooperation was purely tactical, while he regained his power over Iraq, and he set up teams of specialists to work out ways of hiding Iraq's weapons from the UNSCOM inspectors.

For the most part it was impossible to hide or deny the stockpiles of chemical weapons, together with the factories that had made them and the delivery systems that would use them. They had, after all, been heavily used in Iraq's war against Iran, and against the Kurds. But Iraq's nuclear and biological weapons programmes were different. Iraqi officials were carefully trained to deal with the likely questions and tactics of the inspectors.

Saddam's weapons of mass destruction were to become the most contentious aspect of the entire confrontation between Saddam Hussein and the United States. Did they even exist? Plenty of people who were opposed on principle to the sanctions imposed on Iraq, and who were even more strongly opposed to President George W. Bush's war against Iraq in 2003, questioned openly whether Iraq had ever possessed them.

There is absolutely no doubt that Saddam Hussein tried to develop a nuclear weapon. He summoned his chief nuclear scientist, Dr Hussein al-Shahristani, to a meeting together with other members of the Iraqi Atomic Energy Commission in September 1979 and told them that their research should from now on be directed towards 'strategic fields': that is, the development of weapons. Al-Shahristani took the extraordinarily brave decision of telling Saddam to his face that this was wrong. Iraq, he said, had signed the nuclear non-proliferation treaty and could not therefore become involved in the non-peaceful uses of atomic energy.

The result was predictable. Al-Shahristani was arrested, tortured and gaoled. He says that while he was in prison, paralysed from his treatment, Saddam's half-brother Barzan al-Tikriti came to visit him and told him openly that Saddam wanted him to work on an atomic bomb. Al-Shahristani again refused. He spent more than ten years in solitary confinement, still refusing to take part in Saddam's nuclear weapons programme, and eventually managed to escape during the uprisings that followed the first Gulf War.

His friend and deputy, Dr Jafr Dia Jafr, was less high-minded and agreed to work on the programme. When he tried to get al-Shahristani freed from gaol, Saddam had him arrested too, and by ordering that he should be made to watch while several people were tortured to death in front of him, persuaded Dr Jafr to do the research without al-Shahristani. Immense amounts of money were spent on it, even though the war with Iran was at its height. The Saudis helped to fund the programme, apparently in exchange for a promise that some nuclear devices would be made available to them. The United States knew about all this, but decided to take no action until 1989, when Iraq tried to obtain nuclear detonators, the famous 'capacitors', for its bombs. These were sophisticated objects, and showed that the devices Iraq was building were much more elaborate than had previously been thought. Dr Jafr's team, which in total included 8,000 scientists and technical staff, had managed to find a way of using calutrons, huge magnets, which the Americans had experimented with but had discarded as impracticable years before.

Whether because he delayed deliberately, or because it simply was not possible to go any faster, Dr Jafr did not manage to supply Saddam with an atomic bomb by the time the Gulf War broke out in January 1991. Even if he had, Saddam would never have used it. President Bush had warned him clearly that if he used any type of weapon of mass destruction, the United States would reply with devastating force. Saddam, as he showed in his war against Bush's son, wasn't interested in committing suicide. For him, the purpose of being in power was to make sure he stayed in power.

He wanted a nuclear weapon because that would give him far greater influence than he already had. He would use it to menace Israel, not the United States; since Israel already had nuclear weapons, he would have regarded it as evening the balance.

The Americans knew about Saddam's nuclear plans, of course, but they did not know where the bombs were being developed. They attacked a number of sites, and announced at the end of the war that they had destroyed Iraq's nuclear capacity. But the secret was so well kept that it wasn't until after the war, when the UN inspectors were doing their work, that they discovered where the nuclear weapons facility was based. It was at al-Athir, to the south of Baghdad, a huge complex which the Americans and British had not spotted and had not therefore attacked.

Saddam and his ministers did not expect that the weapons inspectors of UNSCOM would be particularly effective. They were used to the short and rather ineffective inspections carried out by the International Atomic Energy Authority, whose teams had been close to the Iraqi nuclear weapons project several times without realizing it. But UNSCOM was different. The quality of its inspectors was higher, and the leading nations behind the campaign to search out and destroy Iraq's weapons of mass destruction kept up the pressure to ensure that the job was done properly.

When the special committee headed by Tariq Aziz had drawn up a detailed declaration listing the weapons of mass destruction which Iraq still held, Rolf Ekeus, the Swede who was in charge of UNSCOM, could see at once that large amounts of weapons and equipment had been left out. By this time the CIA and Britain's SIS had had plenty of time to interview escapers and defectors from Saddam's weapons programmes, and they were getting a better idea than before of what Iraq actually possessed.

According to one leading British intelligence source, they were embarrassed to find how little of Saddam's arsenal had been destroyed by the Coalition during the war. For a start there was the entire nuclear weapons complex at al-Athir. The main biological warfare plant at al-Hakam, where German and other scientists had laboured away to find ways of weaponizing anthrax and other forms of disease, was also completely intact. Then, in spite of all the efforts by the British and American secret services, the various groups of special forces, and the intense efforts of teams of satellite intelligence analysts, not a single Iraqi mobile Scud missile launcher had been destroyed. All this was a considerable victory for Saddam.

Now, though, the Americans were determined to make sure that these weapons systems were destroyed. The Bush administration played a major part in drafting a Security Council resolution, number 687, which insisted that the sanctions already in place against Iraq should continue until Iraq's weapons of mass destruction had been fully accounted for and destroyed.

This was to have terrible consequences for the Iraqi people; though at the time the Bush administration expected that the business of tracking down Saddam's weapons and getting rid of them would be short: a matter of a few months at most. The phrasing of the resolution was vague and more than a little muddled. Paragraph 21 made the selling of foreign goods to Iraq dependent on 'the policies and practices of the government'; Paragraph 22 stipulated that exports from Iraq would be permitted directly the Security Council agreed that Iraq had met the UN's full requirements for getting rid of its arsenal of weapons of mass destruction. That meant the United States and Britain, the two countries which had made all the running on the weapons issue, would be the judges of Iraqi compliance.

Saddam Hussein thought the weapons inspections would be over quickly too. In 2002 I met and interviewed his former head of military intelligence, General Wafiq al-Samarrai, a man in his early sixties with a certain rather raffish style – he dyes his hair raven-black – and a fierce, mordant wit. He told me why, at the end of 1994, he had escaped from Iraq.

'I saw that my predecessor and his predecessor had both been arrested and executed,' he said, 'and I told myself that when I was in their job I would do things differently.' In his case, doing things differently meant organizing an escape route. He slipped away during a visit he was paying in northern Iraq, walked for ten days, and handed himself over to a group of rebels in Iraqi Kurdistan. After a long debriefing he asked for political asylum in London.

'Saddam doesn't bother me,' he said. 'I feel completely safe here.'

It was true that ever since the first Gulf War Saddam Hussein had stopped sending hit-squads to murder Iraqi defectors. But al-Samarrai told me he kept a mobile phone with him at all times, with the number of a twenty-four-hour Special Branch protection unit ready to dial. Just in case.

Before he left, he attended a meeting chaired by Saddam at which ways of dealing with the weapons inspectors of UNSCOM were discussed.

'This Special Commission will not last long,' Saddam said, according to al-Samarrai. 'A few months at most. We will deceive them, and we will bribe them. We must make sure that the inspectors come from countries which are weak, and which believe the sanctions against us should be lifted. You will see: they will leave, and the matter will be finished.'

But there would have to be concessions. The inspectors would get information about weapons systems and equipment which had been imported, and about Iraq's stocks of chemical weapons. The nuclear and biological weapons programmes, however, would remain deeply secret.

The Iraqis were delighted when they knew that Dr Rolf Ekeus of Sweden was to head UNSCOM. He fitted Saddam's criteria perfectly: Sweden was a 'weak' country, which had not complained publicly when Iraq had used chemical weapons at Halabjah, and public opinion there was openly against the use of sanctions against Iraq. Ekeus, too, disliked the sanctions. But he was a man of considerable principle, who had defied his government and personally attacked Iraq's actions at Halabjah during a session of the Conference on Disarmament at Geneva in 1988. Now he set about constructing a team of inspectors whom he knew he could trust.

Very soon it became obvious to him that the Iraqis were not planning to cooperate in any serious way. In June, after a tip-off from American satellite intelligence analysts, David Kay, one of Ekeus's top men, visited the Abu Gharaib military base, in west Baghdad. The analysts had seen a number of large circular objects, which they thought could be electromagnetic isotope separators, or calutrons, being moved on trailers pulled by tractors.

David Kay was a quiet man with an impressive air of self-confidence: the kind of person who had been through enough experiences to know that he could trust himself to behave well. His team was small and not particularly well funded: he and the others had bought some of their equipment out of their own pockets, often at airport duty-free shops. The British gave them a few cast-off Land Rovers, and they hired a small beaten-up coach.

Visiting the Abu Gharaib site turned out to be an exciting episode, and a dangerous one. Kay and his team, crammed into their vehicles, gave their foreign ministry minders the impression they were heading somewhere else altogether. The commander at Abu Gharaib was furious when they turned up there, but Kay forced him to allow three of his men into the base. They climbed up a water-tower and spotted a convoy carrying the calutrons leaving from the back of the site.

One of Kay's Land Rovers chased after them, and an inspector called Rich Lally photographed the calutrons as the Land Rover overtook the convoy. At that point several Iraqi soldiers fired over the top of the vehicle, and one of the escort vehicles cut the Land Rover off and forced it to stop. Lally refused to hand over the film or the camera. The incident showed that the Iraqis were not prepared to cooperate in any serious way with the basic purpose of UNSCOM's mission and with the demands of the Security Council.

Still, it was an awkward moment for Saddam Hussein and his ministers, since they could not openly reject the UN's demands; nor could they deny any longer that Iraq had been pursuing a nuclear weapons programme. And so in early July they took the strategic decision to destroy some of the more obvious elements of the programme, while hiding some of the key aspects for later development and use. A few weeks later, near Tikrit, Saddam's scientists carried out a controlled explosion in which a good deal of the equipment and technology of the programme was blown up. But it was done in secret; UNSCOM's inspectors were not able to verify what had been destroyed, and there would always be a serious dispute about how much of Iraq's nuclear weapons programme had gone, and how much still remained.

Around this time – the late summer of 1991 – it was possible to detect a fundamental shift in American attitudes towards Iraq. Before the first Gulf War the United States had played down the extent of Saddam Hussein's weapons of mass destruction. The discovery that so much had been going on in secret convinced the Department of Defense, in particular, that it would be safer from now on to assume that Iraq would always have more weapons than it acknowledged. It became a settled habit, which increasingly affected opinion within the DoD over the following ten years until a new President effectively took over the approach as his own.

In September 1991 there was a further confrontation, which this time was broadcast around the world. The CIA had received a tip-off from a defector that large numbers of documents relating to Iraq's nuclear programme were being kept at the Central Records Office in Baghdad. A special team of forty-five inspectors, led by David Kay, was assembled for the task of finding them. Kay tipped off a group of Western television crews to go to the car-park of the Central Records Office and see what happened.

Kay's team raided the office, copying papers and taking photographs, and were eventually chased out into the car-park by armed soldiers. The UNSCOM team jumped on to their bus, carrying as many of the documents as they could. They were besieged for four days, but they had done their planning well. Kay had brought a satellite phone with him, and was able to talk to virtually every major radio and television organization in the world.

Eventually Saddam Hussein surrendered, and the siege ended. The UNSCOM team kept the papers they had seized. These provided the final abundant evidence that in spite of all its assurances and denials Iraq had indeed been constructing a nuclear weapon which could be fitted as a warhead on to a missile. Feebly, a government statement in Baghdad admitted that Iraq had been conducting studies to see whether it was possible to construct a nuclear weapon.

This became something of a pattern. Time and again UNSCOM discovered evidence which forced the Iraqis to confess that they had been continuing work on weapons which they had either denied existed, or claimed to have destroyed or discontinued: biological weapons, a radiological bomb, the VX nerve agent, the programme to construct a long-range missile. In every case they were forced to amend their denials. Each time the Iraqi government was asked for information about weapons systems it could not otherwise account for, it claimed they had been destroyed; and yet it was rarely if ever able to produce clear written evidence of instructions to carry out the work of destruction. All this confirmed British and American officials in their assumption that Saddam had no intention of disarming and would use every tactic and every deception to keep whatever weapons he still had.

Yet there were problems inside UNSCOM. The inspectors were supposed to owe their loyalty to the United Nations, but it was strongly alleged that several inspectors had close links with the CIA or SIS. Ekeus's deputy, Bob Gallucci, was an American diplomat and was in constant contact with the State Department in Washington. The State Department would then put out versions of UNSCOM's work which suited the American line. And when Ekeus reprimanded Gallucci, that too was leaked to the press with a distinctly American spin.

Over the years various defectors – chief among them General Wafiq al-Samarrai, and Saddam's own sons-in-law – gave further remarkable evidence of the scale of Iraq's weapons of mass destruction. Not everything defectors say should be taken at face value, of course; their value is in direct proportion to the amount of information they bring, and its acceptability to their new masters. Nevertheless it was hard to ignore the strong possibility that, as General al-Samarrai maintained, Iraq had succeeded in developing VX, the worst chemical nerve agent, and had found ways of loading it into the warheads of missiles.

As a result of the new information it had been receiving, UNSCOM was able to put more pressure on the Iraqi authorities. Eventually they admitted that the huge al-Hakam facility south-west of Baghdad was indeed dedicated to the production of biological weapons. It was eventually blown up under UNSCOM's supervision.

Nevertheless, well over 100 warheads and bombs, and large quantities of VX gas and other chemicals, remained unaccounted for. It was impossible to trust anything Saddam Hussein or his ministers and officials said about these things; one weapons inspector described to me how painful and unpleasant it was to try to break down Iraqi officials and force them to tell the truth, when their colleagues were listening and ready to inform against them.

'I felt real sorry for some of these people. And then I saw there were some fresh graves in this facility, and new-looking bullet-holes in the walls. It was hard to keep on pressing these guys when you knew what the penalties could be for them.'

40. BETRAYED

Saddam Hussein's family seemed to be one of his great strengths. Without the intense loyalty which he could depend on among the different groups in his tribe and clan, he could never have held his difficult and turbulent country together for so long. His half-brothers, his nephews, his cousins – the whole mafia family which was known to every Iraqi as simply 'the Tikritis' – effectively ran the administration and the secret police. Only the army was relatively free of Tikritis, because it required professionals: men with more in their backgrounds than merely a family tie with Saddam Hussein. Like a medieval monarch, Saddam bound those he felt were worthy of the honour closer to him by allowing them to marry his daughters, while his sons married the daughters of some of his most faithful servants.

And yet it was the family which was the source of Saddam's greatest problem, and in one particular sense, perhaps, led to his eventual downfall. There were several fault-lines within it. The clearest of them separated Uday and Qusay, Saddam's two sons, from his three half-brothers, Sabaawi, Watban and Barzan. They had rival claims on Saddam's attention and favour, and each of them had easy access to him. Slowly, and in ways which are still difficult to work out, the two factions began to fall out. Saddam's children were fiercely loyal to one another, and turned against the half-brothers. Raghad was married to General Hussein Kamel al-Majid, who had started out as a body-guard but had impressed Saddam with his intense loyalty and ability. Her sister Rana was married to Hussein Kamel's younger brother; the

Tikritis preferred this tight intertwining of relationships, because they believed it ensured loyalty.

Official propaganda presented the family as affectionate and united, but there were all sorts of tensions beneath the surface. Saddam Hussein himself was responsible for some of them. After years of apparent faithfulness to his wife and cousin Sajida, who shared a great deal of his stubbornness and determination, he fell genuinely in love with Samirah al-Shahabandar, the wife of the head of the national airline. She, according to newspaper reports in Amman, bore him a son called Ali. Sajida is believed to have appealed to Uday to defend her honour. Uday burst into a party attended by the go-between who had put Samirah and Saddam together, and killed him. It was a savage business, made all the worse because it was carried out in front of a delegation from Egypt which included the widow of former President Sadat.

Saddam reportedly tried to discipline Uday, but he was getting out of control. Soon he turned his violent rage on his father's half-brothers, and on Raghad's husband, Hussein Kamel. Hussein Kamel, in self-protection, seems to have sought the help of Watban and the other half-brothers, but it wasn't enough to save him. Hussein Kamel was a pompous, self-regarding man who had begun to think of himself, rather than Uday or Qusay, as the natural heir to Saddam Hussein by right of his marriage to Raghad. The most serious crisis for Saddam Hussein's leadership since the uprisings of 1991 was about to erupt.

Though loyal to her husband, Raghad managed to remain fiercely defensive of her own family. Like many daughters she was still in complete denial of any problems between her parents. In her interview with al-Arabiyah Television, broadcast on 1 August 2003, she made this clear.

'We, as a family, were a most wonderful and ideal family. The relationships between the brothers and sisters were excellent. Similarly, cohesion among the family members was very strong. The relationship between my father and my mother was also strong. The marriage between my father and my mother was based on love. My father defied his uncles on his mother's side, his uncles on his father's side and her uncles on her father's side to marry her.

'But you know that anybody holding the chief executive office is overburdened. As a matter of fact, the people remotely related to us hurt us. They always interfered and constantly applied pressure on my

father over many issues. Their interference and pressure were such that
they recently caused some unfriendliness. I am particularly talking
about his [Saddam's] three brothers, who overburdened the family in
a manner that I cannot—'

One of the interviewers interrupted: 'You mean Sabaawi, Watban
and Barzan al-Tikriti?'

She nodded. 'Since the 1980s, they had overburdened us and
caused us real trouble. They had been hatching plots against Uday,
Qusay and myself. This was because they felt that I was wielding some
influence with my father. As a matter of fact, he respected my opinion.
Whenever I had a topic I wanted to discuss with him, he came quickly
and listened to me. We agreed on many issues together. My arguments
were convincing to him. This continued until 1995.'

1995 was the year when Raghad, her husband and her sister and
brother-in-law defected to Jordan. It was the single most devastating
humiliation Saddam himself had ever suffered, and it arose from
Uday's ferocious ambition. He had been trying to gather more and
more powers in order – some people within the Iraqi political hierarchy
thought – to be able to force his father aside at some future point. As
part of his campaign he had turned the Iraqi Olympic Committee,
which he headed, into a power-base where his own private army had
its headquarters. By using the links which the Committee provided for
him, he began to control several newspapers and television channels,
and slowly built himself up as a major figure in the Iraqi propaganda
field. By the spring of 1995 he felt strong enough to try to push some
of his relatives aside. It was a time of uncertainty and fear, when
bombs were exploding in Baghdad and the opposition seemed to be
making considerable gains.

In April Uday's newspaper, *Babel*, started publishing a series of
articles which were fiercely critical of his uncle Watban al-Tikriti,
Saddam's half-brother. Watban controlled the interior ministry, and
had always been loyal to Saddam, but now appeared to be weak. His
handling of the growing security crisis was certainly poor. Watban
appealed to Saddam to stop Uday continuing with his campaign, but
Saddam seems to have taken no notice; it's possible he was encouraging Uday to take on more power. Watban was obliged to resign from
the interior ministry.

This wasn't enough for Uday. In a repeat of the violent row over his father's relationship with Samirah al-Shahabandar, he attacked Watban at a party in Baghdad, storming in and killing three security men, who were naturally reluctant to open fire on him first. While the guests screamed and took cover, Uday shot Watban in the leg. Several gypsy singers who had been hired to entertain the guests were also killed. Watban's wound was serious, but he maintained nervously afterwards that Uday's gun had gone off by accident.

Many people hoped that Saddam would now deal strongly with Uday, but he didn't. Uday's ferocious drive to win himself more power continued. The next man in his sights was Ali Hassan al-Majid, Chemical Ali, who was sacked as defence minister in July 1995. Saddam had always relied on him to do his worst and dirtiest jobs, and by sidelining him Uday was making a serious bid for power.

The Majid side of the family had suddenly become seriously vulnerable. The next target would obviously be Hussein Kamel al-Majid, whose father, Kamel al-Majid, was the brother of Saddam's real father. Hussein had married Raghad in 1983, and was now the minister in charge of military industry: not a particularly powerful job, but a hugely profitable one.

Uday started to move in on his area of operation, suddenly taking an interest in military aircraft, which could bring in huge amounts of money through bribes and percentages. In mid-July Kamel met his younger brother Saddam Kamel, who was a colonel in the presidential security service, Amn al-Khass, and told him that the two of them would be Uday's next victims. Saddam Kamel was a quiet man, not very bright, who was inclined to let Hussein Kamel make the decisions. His only real importance was that he was married to Saddam's younger daughter, Rana. They had two children; Hussein Kamel and Raghad had three. The brothers decided to escape from Iraq with their families, and to set themselves up as leaders of a revolution against Saddam. On 7 August 1995, around nine at night, a convoy of cars took the brothers, their wives, their five children and fifteen other relatives and friends to the Jordanian border.

In her interview with al-Arabiyah Television, broadcast in August 2003, Raghad was asked if her husband had told her where they were going.

'I was the wife of a civilized man,' she answered. 'Naturally, I would not go on the road to an unknown destiny without knowing where we were going. I am not an uneducated woman, and no one could persuade me with simple words.

'I knew for certain that we were going to Jordan, and nowhere else . . . Unfortunately, when I left with him, I caused a very big wound to my father, without intending to do so; I certainly did not intend to do so. But I was afraid that if Hussein went alone, if he faced difficult conditions or if he left and took the kids with him, people would say I abandoned him. People would say that I stuck by him only when he had a position in the state and in power and enjoyed a certain status, although I had a status as the daughter of the head of state, praised be God. But people would say that that woman did not stick by her husband. So, I had—'

'You were facing two difficult choices,' the interviewer interrupted.

'Yes, I had my father and my family on the one hand, and my husband on the other. So I left. In fact, my departure was a mistake.'

Hussein Kamel, her husband, had brought several million dollars with him. They drove straight for Amman, and checked in at the al-Amra Hotel. A few hours later Hussein Kamel rang the royal palace and asked King Hussein for political asylum. The King agreed.

Uday and the fugitives' cousin, Ali Hassan al-Majid, turned up in Amman two days later. Oddly, their main concern seemed to be to get Kamel to hand over his bank card to them; perhaps they were afraid he would drain Iraq's treasury. Secondly, Uday hoped to persuade his sisters to return. King Hussein wouldn't let Uday see any of them, but he promised them that he would look after Saddam's daughters as if they were his own. Uday had to return empty-handed.

It looked at first as though Saddam Hussein's regime was collapsing in front of the world's eyes. Hussein Kamel, dressed in a superb grey double-breasted suit, appeared at a press conference in the gardens of one of the royal palaces in Amman and announced that he was working to overthrow the regime in Baghdad. He called on the Iraqi army and security services to join him in overthrowing Saddam.

Soon he was talking to the CIA and Britain's SIS. The CIA meeting went badly; Hussein Kamel was offended that the officers who had been sent to see him weren't more senior, and that they couldn't speak Arabic. Their interpreter, an Egyptian, found it hard to understand Hussein Kamel's Tikriti accent. Neither the CIA nor the SIS team thought that

Hussein Kamel represented a credible threat to Saddam, and they dismissed him out of hand as a possible replacement as Iraqi president.

But Hussein Kamel had his uses. He had been in charge of the campaign to hide Iraq's weapons of mass destruction from the UN inspectors, and Rolf Ekeus, the head of UNSCOM, came to debrief him. The first thing Hussein Kamel did was to reveal that Ekeus's Syrian translator was an agent he himself had sent to infiltrate UNSCOM. Otherwise, Hussein Kamel was only moderately forthcoming; the UNSCOM team felt he was always holding things back. But it was a superb opportunity for them to see what the other side had been doing, and other members of the group Hussein Kamel had brought with him provided excellent intelligence about Saddam's weaponry.

UNSCOM obtained a detailed account from them of Iraq's entire weapons programme; this, after all, was the team which had either bought the weapons, or overseen parts of their construction, and then been in charge of hiding them from the UN inspectors. Ekeus now knew all about the VX nerve agent programme, and had the details of a number of chemical weapons factories which UNSCOM had previously known nothing about. The most spectacular piece of information Hussein Kamel gave Ekeus was that Iraq had been only three months away from testing an atomic bomb when the first Gulf War began in January 1991.

In Baghdad, Saddam Hussein had locked himself up in grief and anger for several days, and refused to eat. He blamed Uday for everything, and stripped him of all his posts. The Olympic Committee building was raided, and a number of prisoners held in the cells there on Uday's orders were released. But Saddam realized that he would also have to do something fast to repair the damage caused by Hussein Kamel's revelations about Iraq's weapons programmes.

Rolf Ekeus and his team received an invitation to return to Baghdad, where it was blandly explained to them that Hussein Kamel himself had been responsible for any failure to disclose information about Iraq's weapons systems. The Iraqis admitted that they had managed to manufacture biological weapons, and had found a way of loading them into nearly 200 bombs and missiles. The UN team were directed to a farm, supposedly belonging to Hussein Kamel, where they found huge amounts of documents and photographs relating to the nuclear weapons programme. They realized, though, that some of the key documents had disappeared.

The big winner from Hussein Kamel's defection was Chemical Ali. He had been driven out of power by Uday. Now, he masterminded Saddam's return to full control by means of a referendum in which the question was, 'Do you agree that Saddam Hussein should be President of Iraq?' When the results were counted (assuming, that is, anyone bothered to count them) it was announced that 99.96 per cent had agreed.

The fugitives in Amman, meanwhile, were in a bad way. No one was taking any notice of them now, and Hussein Kamel and Raghad were having noisy rows in their palace within the royal complex, or else hanging round the next-door palace of the King's eldest daughter, Alia, borrowing videos and drinking endless cups of tea and coffee. Alia decided to leave the country. The Iraqi opposition groups in London and Washington, which had once been so interested in Hussein Kamel, now dropped them. He wasn't used to being ignored, and it upset him. When a Jordanian journalist decided to sue him for threatening to kill him, Hussein Kamel couldn't believe it; especially when the Jordanian government made it clear he would have to face the courts if the case went ahead.

All this while Saddam had been trying to persuade them to come back. In February 1996 this approach began to pay off. Hussein Kamel wrote to Saddam asking about the terms on which he could return. His brother, Saddam Kamel, knew it was foolish, but Hussein Kamel insisted.

'Our return was an even bigger mistake,' Raghad told al-Arabiyah Television nearly eight years later. 'Both steps were a mistake. Or we had the choice of not leaving at all and leaving things as they were.'

'But as regards Uday?' the interviewer asked.

'Please excuse me for not answering this part.'

'It is up to you if you do not want to talk about this. But I wish to ask about the return. Who persuaded Lt-General Hussein to return? Did you play any role in that regard? Did you pressure him? Did you receive any assurances? What happened? Can you tell us that story please?'

'I did not have any role in his decision to return,' Raghad

answered. 'Seven months after we left I had totally adapted to the new condition. I was certain that if we returned – I would be lying if I said that I expected what happened, but I knew that I would certainly be very embarrassed with the family and with my father. I preferred to live in Jordan for good. This was especially the case since I lacked nothing here at that time.

'It was his [Hussein Kamel's] decision. He, may God have mercy on his soul, was known as a hasty man and for making hasty decisions. He decided to go back. Also, it was not possible for me to see him going back while I stayed here. That would have been very difficult. If my husband returned, I should return with him. If he left, I should leave with him. So I returned. I would be lying to you if I do not tell you that that was a tragedy, a great calamity, even for my family.'

But, the interviewer pointed out, her husband had received assurances from Saddam Hussein.

'I did not know about any assurances they might have talked about. He did not tell me all the details. If he had told me all the details I would certainly not have let him go back.'

So the two families packed everything up in the same cars and headed back the way they had come, seven months before. Someone who went with them said afterwards that Hussein Kamel stopped more than once, and walked up and down in deep thought; but each time he insisted they should drive on. Uday met them, scowling, at the border, and took Raghad and Rana and their children, Saddam's grandchildren, under his wing. The brothers had to continue the drive alone. They went first to a family house in Tikrit, but got a hostile reception and headed on to Baghdad, where they stayed in their sister's house.

'Father had pardoned them,' Raghad said. 'A republican decree was issued and I heard it when we entered Baghdad, when we approached the al-Radwaniyah area. But the bad apple in the leadership, namely, Ali Hassan al-Majid, turned the tide in his favour with regard to this issue, certainly not out of love for my father. If I love Saddam, how can I make his two young daughters widows on the same day, when one was twenty-seven years old and the other twenty-four, at an age when women their age have not yet got married? What kind of love is this? But this man is evil. His history is very dark.'

Ali Hassan al-Majid, Saddam Hussein's enforcer, the man who did all the dirtiest jobs of a dirty government, was put in charge of killing the two brothers. However little Raghad wanted to believe it, it must have been Saddam who chose him for the job.

'Yes, he commanded the operation. I later learned from other people that he stood at the meeting [with Saddam] and said: Sir, you pardoned him [Hussein Kamel] as a head of state, but we, as a tribe, will not pardon him. He took the entire tribe with him.'

'What was the President's reply?'

'I do not know. This is what I heard. As far as I knew, none of the tribe approved of what happened. They were all forced to join in but none of them was convinced.'

The two brothers were joined at their sister's house by their father and two more brothers. Soon afterwards, Ali Hassan al-Majid surrounded the house with forty men, and sent enough automatic weapons and ammunition into it to ensure that the brothers would be able to defend themselves properly. The honour of the family was being upheld, Mafia-style.

The battle lasted more than twelve hours. In the end, Hussein Kamel appeared in the doorway and shouted to the attackers that they should kill him and let the others live. In reply they shot him down, and Ali Hassan al-Majid walked over and put a bullet in his head. Everyone inside the house died, including the sister and her children.

After the killing of their husbands, Saddam's daughters disappeared from sight completely for three years.

'We refused to see even our closest relatives. I do not mean brothers and sisters, but I mean the relatives outside the immediate family.

'They tried to visit us several times, certainly not out of love but to gloat over our misery or maybe out of curiosity. They probably wanted to see how these two girls and their children would live, and they then could go to tell the news to the other relatives. However, my mother was very keen not to let any news out of the house.'

'There were reports that you were married or that the President had forced you to get married. Is this true?'

'I did not get married. Here I am, sitting with you. Where is my husband?' She smiled. 'I did not marry at all.'

'So this was only a rumour?'

'It was only a rumour.'

'What about your children?'

'I wish that my children will live very far from politics and that their life will be happier than ours and that they live in freedom, peace of mind and full of happiness, God willing. I also hope that God gives them happier days instead of the difficult days they have lived through, in whichever way they choose.'

41. SANCTIONS

The sanctions which had been imposed by the UN Security Council with almost total agreement immediately after Iraq's invasion of Kuwait had long since become internationally unpopular. Now they had to be forced through by the United States and Britain. The man who won the first Gulf War, President George Bush had failed to win a second term in the presidential election of November 1992. The huge wave of popular support which had swept him along during and after the war began to peter out as the US economy suffered a down-turn which was only partly related to the war. Having promised again and again not to raise taxes – 'Read my lips,' he said, 'no more taxes' – he was obliged to do it after all. The American electorate duly punished him.

Bill Clinton, who followed him, represented a complete change from Bush's mandarin, sometimes almost European style. Yet Clinton was in some ways the most European president the United States has had since John Kennedy: a man from the most remote and backward part of the US, who thoroughly understood the outside world and America's place in it. Having watched Clinton closely, both at home and on his foreign travels, I had some glimpses into the extraordinary range of his mind. Whether speaking to groups of politicians or students or the general public, he had a warmth and a breadth of vision which was deeply attractive. Yet this never seemed to translate into his policies.

'Whenever Bill walks past a TV set,' one of his close associates said, 'he always looks at it to see what the news is. And when he sees it, I always get the impression he isn't thinking, "What should I do about this?"; he's thinking, "What do people think I ought to think about it?"'

For a man of such understanding, he wasted a good half of his second term in office – the period when he could have achieved the most – simply trying to stay ahead of the posse as a result of his inability to control his sexual desires. And for a man of undeniable humanity, who really cared about the ordinary people of the world, he spent a great deal of time attacking them and bombing them: in Serbia, in Kosovo, in Sudan, in Afghanistan. And of course in Iraq. Bill Clinton was a remarkable and in many ways a noble man, yet he had more innocent deaths on his conscience than any American president since Richard Nixon.

In 1992 Saddam Hussein, putting his fears of espionage before the interests of his people, introduced a new series of controls and methods of surveillance over the dozens of international aid agencies which were helping to rebuild Iraq after the destruction of the Gulf War. They were so restrictive that most organizations decided to pull out rather than subject themselves to treatment that was often hostile and sometimes put aid workers' lives in danger.

As a result, it was not until 1998, seven years after the end of the first Gulf War, that UNICEF managed to complete a thoroughgoing examination of the health and nutrition of the children of Iraq. The results were highly disturbing. The destruction of the Gulf War had done such damage to the sanitation and drinking water of the country that diarrhoea was the major cause of death in infants, followed by acute respiratory diseases. Millions of Iraqis had been plunged into acute poverty by the UN's sanctions; as a result, malnutrition was also a serious threat to the lives of children.

Before the invasion of Kuwait in 1990, Iraq had entered the front rank of developing nations. There was some poverty, but Iraq's educational and health standards were distinctly higher than those in Egypt or Syria, and were starting to approach the levels of the Gulf States. All this vanished as a result of the invasion and the war. As early as March 1991 the Finnish politician Martti Ahtisaari, visiting Iraq on a fact-finding mission for the United Nations, was seriously alarmed by the consequences of the war.

'The recent conflict has wrought near-apocalyptic results,' he said, 'Iraq has, for some time to come, been relegated to a pre-industrial age.'

Between 1990 and 2000 the mortality rate among children of five or younger increased by 160 per cent. By contrast, the increase in a country like Rwanda, pitched suddenly into a savage civil war, was 13 per cent. During the same period Syria, Iran, Turkey and Egypt registered improvements in the mortality rate of children under five of 35 per cent, 39 per cent, 42 per cent and 54 per cent respectively.

There was no mass starvation in Iraq, because the government introduced a surprisingly effective and satisfactory system of rationing; dictatorship has occasional advantages, and this was one of them. But there was corruption, and even after the rations were cut in 1994, adult Iraqis had only about half the daily nutrition they required to stay healthy.

In 1998 the United Nations sent an Irish Quaker, Denis Halliday, to monitor the system under which Iraq's oil revenues were used by the UN to buy food and other humanitarian supplies for the Iraqi people. The oil-for-food system was, according to Madeleine Albright, then US secretary of state, 'designed to ease the suffering of civilians throughout Iraq'.

It did nothing of the kind. Halliday was appalled by what he saw as he travelled around the country, and resigned from the UN in protest.

'This policy,' he said angrily, 'causes four thousand to five thousand children to die unnecessarily every month due to the impact of sanctions because of the breakdown of water and sanitation, inadequate diet, and the bad internal health situation.'

There is no doubt that Saddam Hussein used the suffering of his people as a lever to get the sanctions against Iraq lifted. It is true, too, that after the first Gulf War, when Iraq was sinking into abject poverty, Saddam built himself a large array of new palaces, and began the construction of the biggest mosque in the world. The Ba'ath Party, the military and the senior levels of government had no problem importing the things they wanted; Jordan made a fortune out of smuggling goods across to Iraq. But ordinary Iraqis, whose interests were supposed to be protected by the oil-for-food programme, rarely saw much benefit from it.

The problem was not the supply of food; Iraq produced a good deal of its own food, and as we have seen the rationing system worked remarkably well. But the country's ability to ensure a system of clean water and proper sanitation was dependent on importing equipment to repair the sewage, water purification and pumping systems, and on the supply of electricity, which was down to less than a third of its pre-1990 level. The American and British representatives on the committee which oversaw the contracts for supplying equipment to Iraq vetoed these deals again and again, on the grounds that they could be used for producing weapons of mass destruction. Altogether, more than a fifth of the contracts were nullified.

The United States, under the presidencies of George Bush senior and Bill Clinton, regarded sanctions as a useful way of controlling Saddam Hussein. Having defeated him, and having decided not to get rid of him, American policy was to keep him in his place; the chosen method was the use of sanctions.

Officially, these were linked to Saddam's compliance with the Security Council's demands for Iraq to disarm, yet as early as 20 May 1991 President Bush made it clear he wanted to tie the process to Saddam's survival.

'At this juncture,' Bush said, 'my view is we don't want to lift these sanctions as long as Saddam Hussein is in power.'

That remained US policy long after Bush had been defeated in the 1992 presidential election by Bill Clinton. His fierce and rather unlovable ambassador to the United Nations, Madeleine Albright, was a strong personal supporter of continuing with sanctions. On 12 May 1996 she appeared on a CBS *60 Minutes* programme, called 'Punishing Saddam', and was interviewed by Leslie Stahl.

> *Stahl:* We have heard that half a million children have died.
> I mean, that's more children than died at Hiroshima.
> And the price is worth it?
> *Albright:* I think this is a very hard choice, but the price – we
> think the price is worth it . . . It is a moral question, but the
> moral question is even a larger one. Don't we owe to the
> American people and to the American military and to the
> other countries in the region that this man not be a threat?
> *Stahl:* Even with the starvation and the lack—
> *Albright:* I think, Leslie – it is hard for me to say this because
> I am a humane person, but my first responsibility is to make
> sure that United States forces do not have to go and refight
> the Gulf War.

Of course, what happened as a direct result of American policy from 1991 onwards, under Bush senior, Clinton, and Bush junior, was that the United States did eventually refight the Gulf War – and an unknown number of Iraqis, most of them children, also died as the direct result of the sanctions which self-confessedly humane people like Madeleine Albright insisted on imposing. So this policy – 'a price worth paying' – ended in failure anyway. The deaths of so many people were just part of a stop-gap approach which eventually failed. The responsibility for so many deaths lies heavily on Madeline Albright and Bill Clinton.

The first Gulf War was imposed on George Bush senior, in the sense that he wouldn't have fought it if Saddam Hussein had not invaded Kuwait. The second Gulf War, as we shall see, was a matter of deliberate choice for his son, George W. But Bill Clinton, who always wanted everyone to think that his heart was in the right place, killed more Iraqis than either of them by a policy of slow strangulation. And the British governments of John Major and Tony Blair, delegating their moral and strategic judgements to the United States, went along with this policy and indeed helped it along.

It is important, at the same time, to be clear in our own minds that this was not a series of aggressions carried out against an innocent government which happened to get in the way of overwhelming American power. If Saddam Hussein had not been in power in Iraq, an active threat to his neighbours, Iraq would not have been attacked and blockaded in this fashion. Saddam was, without question, the source of the problem, but the methods the United States and Britain used to bring him to heel brought terrible suffering to the ordinary people of Iraq.

The United States, with full British backing, regarded sanctions as the best way to keep Saddam Hussein tied up. They could see it wasn't possible to get rid of him – indeed, they didn't really want to get rid of him – but by keeping his country poor they thought they would prevent him from developing more of the kind of weapons systems he had wanted when he had the money. The method for doing this was UN Security Council resolution 687, and the intention was to impose sanctions on Iraq until it complied with all relevant UN resolutions. But, deliberately or not, the wording of two key sections of resolution 687 turned out to conflict with one another. It was Catch-22.

Paragraph 20 prohibited the sale of goods to Iraq, with the exception of medical supplies and-food. Paragraph 21 specified the conditions on which Iraq could import goods from the outside world again: the Security Council, the resolution says,

> *Decides* to review the provisions of paragraph 20 every sixty days in the light of the policies and practices of the Government of Iraq, including the implementation of all relevant resolutions of the Council, for the purpose of determining whether to reduce or lift the prohibitions referred to therein . . .

Paragraph 22, however, imposed a slightly different set of rules for lifting sanctions on Iraq's exports; particularly, of course, oil. The Council, its says,

> *Decides also* that upon . . . Council agreement that Iraq has completed all actions contemplated in paragraphs 8 to 13, the prohibitions against the import of commodities and products originating in Iraq . . . shall have no further force or effect.

Paragraphs 8 to 13 dealt with the destruction of Iraq's arsenal. In other words, Iraq could start selling its oil again once it had destroyed its weapons of mass destruction to the UN's satisfaction. But it could only start importing goods from abroad again when it had complied with 'all relevant resolutions of the Council'.

The British and the Americans decided this meant that Saddam Hussein would have to comply with Resolution 688, which dealt with his treatment of the Shi'ites and the Kurds, before the sanctions could be lifted. But from 1994 onwards, France and Russia (which both had a great deal to gain once Iraq began trading again) began insisting that paragraph 22 was the one that counted, and that directly Iraq had complied with the demand that it should destroy its weapons of mass destruction, the sanctions should be lifted. Both the French and the Russians maintained that virtually all the weapons had already been destroyed.

There is no doubt that a great deal had indeed gone. UNSCOM reported that although Iraq had been pursuing a secret nuclear programme which might have produced a usable weapon by the end of 1992, its stocks of nuclear material had been destroyed, along with most of its long-range delivery systems. The result was that although

Iraq still had the know-how to produce a nuclear bomb, it lacked the necessary fissile material. Millions of litres of chemical agents and nearly 40,000 chemical warheads were destroyed by UNSCOM, and Iraq claimed to have dealt with 30,000 more weapons and large amounts of chemical agents itself. It also claimed to have destroyed large amounts of weapons-grade biological materials, which it confessed to having produced in the run-up to the first Gulf War. None of these claims was ever verified. Maybe they were all true; the trouble was, Saddam and his officials had a bad record, lying outright about the weapons they possessed.

When the International Atomic Energy Agency reported in 1997 that Iraq's entire nuclear weapons programme had been destroyed, France and Russia renewed their demands that the sanctions on Iraq should be lifted. But the United States and Britain disagreed, and the following year the UNSCOM inspectors ran into the kind of difficulties which seemed to indicate that the Iraqis still had plenty to hide. Iraqi negotiators had managed to get 'presidential' sites excluded from the areas the inspectors could visit; in practice this turned out to mean all sorts of places where they suspected that either weapons or documentation could be stored.

The UN secretary-general, Kofi Annan, skilfully negotiated a compromise which allowed the UNSCOM inspectors to continue their work. But the problems persisted. The inspectors pulled out, then returned, then pulled out again in December 1998. Within a few days, the US and Britain started bombing what they maintained were weapons sites in Iraq. Like earlier bombing attacks, this was done without the agreement of the UN Security Council.

Did Iraq have things to hide? Given its long record of hiding its weapons systems from the international community, the suspicion must be reasonably strong that it did. All the same, the Iraqis themselves insisted that they were protecting their national security from what was in effect an elaborate system of on-site espionage. Iraqi officials claimed that UNSCOM inspectors were working for their own governments first, and the UN second, and that Israel, via the United States, was receiving a full account of everything Iraq possessed. There was a certain amount of truth to some of Iraq's complaints. According to Rolf Ekeus, who continued as UNSCOM's boss until 1997, American inspectors often tried to seek out information which had nothing to do with the work of UNSCOM; for instance, where Saddam Hussein lived and worked, and how he travelled around the country.

The US and Britain argued strongly that Iraq had not cooperated fully with Security Council resolutions about its weapons arsenal and its treatment of the Kurds and Shi'ites, and that the sanctions should remain in force. From time to time the two countries would bomb sites where, they maintained, the Iraqis were storing weapons of mass destruction. Often they would attack aircraft or ground installations which were thought to pose a threat to British or American planes.

The entire strategy was in many ways typical of Bill Clinton's approach to foreign affairs. It wasn't exactly a policy; in fact in some ways it was the opposite of a policy. It simply maintained things at an acceptable level, without straying into outright war and without letting Saddam Hussein off the hook. The British government of Tony Blair went along with it, because to do so filled the gap where an active British foreign policy might otherwise have been.

For President Clinton, this business of aggressive containment had another advantage: it provided him with a useful opportunity to distract public attention in the United States at a time when the investigation into his sexual peccadilloes came uncomfortably close. On 20 August 1998, at a time when the special prosecutor, Kenneth Starr, was examining the President's relationship with Monica Lewinsky with a ferocity that many found obsessive, Clinton ordered the firing of cruise missiles at sites in Sudan and Afghanistan as a result of the bombing of American embassies in East Africa. The sites seemed to be almost randomly chosen, but the American media accepted the notion that this was an effective way of punishing Osama bin Laden for the embassy attacks.

The following December, Clinton ordered the bombing of supposed weapons sites in Iraq: it was called Operation Desert Fox. The purpose, he said in a televised broadcast, was to protect the national interests of the United States and of people around the world. Three days later the House of Representatives took a vote on impeaching him for perjury and the obstruction of justice. Many Americans felt this was all a little too much of a coincidence – and that ordinary Iraqis were paying the price of the President's own personal indiscretions.

Under Clinton, the American approach to Iraq was both weak and deeply destructive to the lives of ordinary Iraqis. Yet it was an adjunct, like so much American foreign policy, to purely domestic affairs. The American media paid little sustained attention to the practical effects of sanctions on Iraq: CNN International was the only American network which covered the story on anything like a regular basis, and its reports were only rarely shown on CNN's domestic service.

The US government's approach had the appearance of toughness towards Saddam Hussein, yet the toughness was all directed at Iraqi society. After Kofi Annan visited Baghdad to settle the problem of arms inspections at the so-called 'presidential' sites in February 1998, Saddam Hussein believed he had made a deal with the UN secretary-general: if there was another round of inspections, sanctions would be lifted. This was not at all the case, but the Clinton administration knew that if there were to be another crisis there was nothing the Americans would be able to do. Clinton was not prepared to stage an all-out attack on Iraq, and anyway he had no form of excuse to do it. Firing missiles at sites which might or might not have been weapons installations now clearly lacked any efficacy. The strongest military power on earth had no means of dealing with a weakened, poverty-stricken dictatorship. And so the administration put quiet pressure on the UNSCOM team to be less confrontational in its searches. Washington, it seemed, no longer wanted anything serious to come out of the inspections, and would be happy now if they just faded away.

Unfortunately for President Clinton, the inspectors didn't see it that way. Scott Ritter, the American who was in charge of the Baghdad team, resigned in protest. As he did so, he claimed publicly that Saddam Hussein would be able to deploy three atomic bombs as soon as he managed to obtain sufficient plutonium or uranium 235. Ritter also made the damaging revelation, that he had had close contacts with the Israeli secret service, Mossad, during the seven years he had spent as an inspector. At a stroke, therefore, he showed up Clinton's weakness and gave weight to Saddam Hussein's accusation that weapons inspection was merely espionage under a different name – and Israeli espionage at that.

In October 1998 the US Congress, dominated by Republicans, responded to what was increasingly seen on the American right as Clinton's feebleness towards Saddam, and passed the Iraqi Liberation Act, a piece of largely meaningless theatre which nevertheless poured

$97 million into the pockets of various Iraqi opposition groups based in Europe and the United States.

Events followed closely one after the other as a result. Saddam Hussein, infuriated by the new act, announced that he was ceasing all cooperation with UNSCOM, and the decision was taken at the United Nations in New York that there was no further point in trying to continue with the inspections. The UNSCOM teams withdrew from Iraq altogether.

As a result of this, and given his problems with Congress over Monica Lewinsky, President Clinton ordered Operation Desert Fox. On 16 December 1998 he announced the start of the operation in a televised address to the nation. It was, like many of his speeches, cleverly written, beautifully delivered, and deceptively empty of real meaning.

> [T]he inspectors are saying that, even if they could stay in Iraq, their work would be a sham. Saddam's deception has defeated their effectiveness. Instead of the inspectors disarming Saddam, Saddam has disarmed the inspectors . . .
>
> Heavy as they are, the costs of action must be weighed against the price of inaction. If Saddam defies the world and we fail to respond, we will face a far greater threat in the future. Saddam will strike again at his neighbours; he will make war on his own people. And mark my words, he will develop weapons of mass destruction. He will deploy them, and he will use them. Because we are acting today, it is less likely that we will face these dangers in the future.

But the action Clinton took turned out to be highly ineffective. Four hundred bombing and missile attacks were launched against sites which the inspectors had wanted to see. Yet of the ninety-seven sites targeted, only nine were completely destroyed. Three days and nights of heavy bombing had little effect on Saddam's arsenal of weapons; of eleven biological and chemical weapons plants marked out for destruction, not one was completely put out of action. The essential weakness of an administration which was only prepared to carry out attacks from the air and dared not put its soldiers in on the ground was plain for all to see.

42. NEW APPROACH

In the early months of 1997, when President Clinton was starting his second term in office, a group of mostly Republican politicians, lawyers and academics banded together under the name 'The Project for the New American Century'. The basic notion behind it was that just as the major part of the twentieth century had been dominated by the United States, so the twenty-first century would also be America's.

The historian Francis Fukuyama was one of them. Seven years earlier he had announced the death of history, on the grounds that liberal democracy had triumphed over Marxism-Leninism; his declaration was of course closely followed by the viciously illiberal conflicts in the former Yugoslavia and the former Soviet Union, the appalling genocide in Rwanda, and the resurgence of fundamentalist Islam. For something that had been pronounced dead, history seemed remarkably noisy and full of life.

Some of the most active supporters of the group had worked for the Reagan administrations of 1980–88: Elliott Abrams, Richard L. Armitage, Richard Perle, Donald Rumsfeld and Paul Wolfowitz.

On 26 January these and other supporters of the Project for the New American Century – a representative sample of reinvigorated American neo-conservatism, impatient for power and now barred from it for another term – sent a letter to the newly re-elected President Clinton warning of a threat 'more serious than any we have known since the end of the Cold War'.

'We urge you . . . to enunciate new strategy,' the letter said, 'that would secure the interests of the US and our friends and allies around the world. That strategy should aim, above all, at the removal of Saddam Hussein's regime from power.'

It maintained that the growing difficulties surrounding the UNSCOM arms inspections would make it much harder in future to monitor Iraq's production of weapons of mass destruction.

Given the magnitude of the threat, the current policy, which depends for its success upon the steadfastness of our coalition

partners and upon the cooperation of Saddam Hussein, is dangerously inadequate. The only acceptable strategy is one that
eliminates the possibility that Iraq will be able to use or threaten
to use weapons of mass destruction. In the near term, this means
a willingness to undertake military action as diplomacy is clearly
failing. In the long term, it means removing Saddam Hussein and
his regime from power. That now needs to become the aim of
American foreign policy.

Instead, the focuses of Bill Clinton's foreign policy in his second term
were the former Yugoslavia, where his and Madeleine Albright's
campaign of bombing Serbia and Kosovo came close to splitting
NATO, and an attempt to cobble together an agreement between Israel
and the Palestinians. The Palestinians thought it demanded so great a
sacrifice from them and so small a one from Israel (though Israeli
public opinion certainly did not agree about that) that agreement was
never a serious proposition. Yet it was a mark of the extraordinary
force of Clinton's personality that at one stage it looked as though he
might after all manage it.

The Americans, preoccupied, left Saddam Hussein alone after the
failure of Operation Desert Fox; though the Iraqi people continued to
pay the heavy price of sanctions. American and British planes regularly
bombed targets in Iraq. Mistakes, inevitably, were made, and civilians
were killed. None of this received much attention in the United States
or Britain, partly because Iraq had made it much harder for Western
journalists to go to Baghdad and report on the situation there. The
bombing, the diarrhoea and the typhoid fever claimed their victims in
secrecy.

For more than a year it seemed a reasonable bet that Clinton's
work would be continued by his vice-president, Al Gore, who was the
Democratic candidate for the presidency. His Republican opponent
was a man whom few of the national political correspondents privately
had much time for. George W. Bush was not stupid, and he knew how
to deal with people and win them over to his side, but he often said
and did things that weren't very clever, and he was scarcely very
impressive in the run-up to the election. He made plenty of mistakes,
which his opponents jeered at; including referring to the inhabitants
of Greece as Grecians, and pronouncing 'nuclear' as 'nucular'. He had

scarcely ever been outside the United States, and had little concept of
the outside world. An American institute which administered intelligence tests estimated his IQ at 92, plus or minus 5 per cent: the lowest
estimate for any president in sixty years.

Al Gore, however, was deemed to be boring, and enough people
had been angered by Bill Clinton's behaviour in office for the Democrats to lose their edge slowly. On the day before the election the
opinion polls showed that Democrats were less pleased with Gore as
their candidate than Republicans were with George W. Bush as theirs.
The result, when it came, gave Al Gore a slight majority: he had half a
million more popular votes. There were all sorts of question-marks
over the way some of these votes had been counted, and a complicated
legal battle began, centred mainly on the result in Florida, where
George W. Bush's brother Jeb was governor; the Florida result was
critical for the number of votes in the antiquated Electoral College
system. Eventually the US Supreme Court voted by five votes to four
that George Walker Bush was the duly elected President. It had been
the most farcical election of modern times.

In Europe and the outside world generally, it was a strange
spectacle. A country which prided itself on its openness and democratic
values was to be governed by the second generation of a political
dynasty whose family machinations had brought him victory. Worse,
George W. Bush seemed like a caricature. Cartoonists in Britain,
France, Italy and a variety of other countries regularly exaggerated his
close-set eyes and the slant of his ears and turned him into an ape with
knuckles that dragged along the ground.

In reality, he acted as the chairman of a powerful and experienced
board, and slowly grew into the job. The members of his administration seemed almost self-selecting: like Dick Cheney, who became
vice-president and was widely seen as the real power behind the
administration, or like Condoleezza Rice, the new national security
adviser, they had worked for his father when he was president; or like
Donald Rumsfeld, who had saved Saddam Hussein from defeat and
destruction in his war with Iran by handing him American intelligence,
they had served during Ronald Reagan's presidency.

During the campaign it had been fashionable to say that there
were no serious differences between George W. Bush and Al Gore:
that they were each as uninspired as the other. But directly Bush

created his administration it became clear that the members of it represented the quiet ditching of his father's middle-of-the-road republicanism, in favour of the harder line of the Reagan years. It was essentially a neo-conservative administration, determined to stamp America's power on the world, impatient with institutions like the United Nations which could not be overtly led by America. Some of its most vocal and influential members were close, not just to Israel – that, after all, is an essential association in the United States, and was as true of the Clinton administration as it was of its successor – but to the Likud Party of Ariel Sharon. Like Likud, the neo-conservatives looked to use their power to destroy their opponents, not merely find ways of doing a deal with them, and like Likud, they believed that Saddam Hussein was a serious danger who had to be eliminated.

In foreign policy, the key figure was supposedly Colin Powell, the secretary of state. But Powell, who was something of a liberal (in the European, not the American sense) and was certainly not a figure of the fundamentalist right, quickly showed that he did not have the strength to create the kind of foreign policy he wanted. He became a figurehead. For the first eight months of the new administration, anyway, there was very little interest in foreign affairs at all. Foreign commentators spoke of a return to the twenties and thirties, when America had turned inward and took no serious interest in the events going on in the outside world.

Then came 11 September 2001, and it became fashionable to say that the world changed. It didn't, of course; not, at any rate, for the vast majority of its population. But for the small percentage who were American, it changed radically. The old sense of being protected against terrorism vanished: now the US itself had suffered from the worst and most devastating act of terrorism ever.

Donald Rumsfeld was among those who had signed the letter from the Project for the New American Century, urging Bill Clinton to overthrow Saddam Hussein. On 11 September Rumsfeld was at his desk at the Pentagon when one of the three planes hijacked by Osama bin Laden's suicide bombers crashed into the building. He was hurried away to the National Military Command Center, and at 2.40 p.m. that day his officials jotted down his thoughts. Their notes, which were later broadcast on a CBS News special, show that even at this early stage his thoughts were turning to the possibility of a revenge attack on Iraq.

> Best info fast. Judge whether good enough hit S.H. at same time. Not only U[sama] B[in] L[aden]. Go massive. Sweep it all up. Things related and not.

It is clear from this that Rumsfeld's first thoughts were not so much whether Saddam Hussein might have been behind the attacks, as whether there was sufficient excuse to strike at him.

There never was any evidence to link Saddam Hussein with the 11 September attacks, and nothing serious to link him with al-Qaeda either. To some extent Saddam represented everything that Osama bin Laden was dedicated to overthrowing: Arab statism, the influence of the old Soviet Union and Marxism-Leninism, secularism, the liberation and education of women, even the freedom to buy and sell alcohol.

In the days immediately before the first Gulf War, Saddam had been photographed and filmed a good deal in mosques, praying, though some of these images seem to have been of his leading double. He had also placed the great acclamation of Islam, *Allah-u Akbar*, God is most great, on the national flag of Iraq. But this was mere policy, designed to represent the war against Saddam as somehow a war in which all Muslims should take part. Before the crisis over Kuwait, Ba'athist Iraq had treated Islam as an irritating form of competition, which had to be strictly controlled. One of Saddam's most loyal henchmen, Vice-President Taha Yasin Ramadan, was questioned by Islamic fundamentalists about Iraq's attitude towards the faith when he visited Jordan in the 1980s.

'Muslims are free to practise their faith,' he said. But he added irritably, 'If they try to harm the Ba'athist regime or ridicule its slogans, the regime will break their necks.'

Osama bin Laden knew exactly how secular Saddam's Iraq was. He did not regard it as an ally; on the contrary, the extreme Islamists who thought like him invariably regarded Iraq, like the governments of Saudi Arabia, Jordan, Syria and Egypt, as potential or actual enemies. There was no meeting of minds whatever between bin Laden and Saddam, therefore, except on their mutual hatred of the United States. When the Northern Alliance captured Kabul and drove out the Taliban and their al-Qaeda allies, there were indications that men from many Islamic and Middle Eastern nations had come to Afghanistan as volunteers to fight for al-Qaeda; but there seem to have been no Iraqis among them.

Neither the CIA (which showed no sign of contracting the neo-conservative obsession about Saddam) nor Britain's SIS had any compelling information to link Iraq either with the attack on the Twin Towers, or with al-Qaeda in general. There might, a senior SIS man told me, have been some faint contact at one stage, but Iraq and al-Qaeda were chalk and cheese, and could never have worked together. He confirmed that the CIA, with which SIS works for the most part closely and amicably, believed exactly the same thing.

This wasn't the way Rumsfeld and his deputy, Paul Wolfowitz, saw it. Whether they genuinely believed there were close links between Saddam and al-Qaeda, or whether they merely saw a useful opportunity to get rid of a regime which was a standing reproach to American power and a danger to its neighbours, especially Israel, is difficult to say. Some senior State Department officials seemed to think the latter. Senior figures in the British Foreign Office certainly did.

On Saturday 15 September President Bush summoned his chief advisers to a meeting at Camp David. Paul Wolfowitz was there, and Bush asked him for his opinion. Although Osama bin Laden and his al-Qaeda organization operated from Afghanistan, Wolfowitz said, he felt it was a difficult country to fight a war in. In the account of the meeting given by the journalist Bob Woodward, Wolfowitz's opinion was that Iraq was 'a brittle, oppressive regime that might break easily'. Then he used a word which was to surface again more than once: attacking Iraq was 'do-able'. The foreign minister of Saudi Arabia, Prince Saud al-Faisal, later said that he had despairingly asked Dick Cheney a year later why the United States was so determined to attack Iraq.

'Because it's do-able,' Cheney said.

In other words, Iraq *looked* as though it was a difficult nut to crack, yet it wasn't. It was an opponent the United States could take on without having to worry that its military and political prowess might be damaged. An attack on Syria or Iran, for example, would be a very different matter, but Iraq, almost without an air force, damaged by years of sanctions, ill-equipped militarily, deeply divided internally and with a population that would clearly be grateful to be rid of Saddam Hussein, was an easy target. It was pre-eminently do-able.

Colin Powell seemed unconvinced that Iraq had played a part in the 11 September attacks. The division between him and other members of the Bush administration was becoming clear even at this stage. Powell had always shown considerable caution; at the time of the Shi'ite and Kurdish uprisings in Iraq in 1991 this had led directly to the deaths of tens of thousands of Iraqis. Now his caution led him to oppose the idea that retribution over the attacks on New York and Washington should be extended for reasons of policy.

Wolfowitz and Rumsfeld were very aware that America's close ally, Israel, saw Iraq as the chief threat to its existence, because they thought it was the only Arab state capable of mounting a nuclear attack on it. The 11 September attacks effectively gave the United States the freedom to retaliate as it chose. Wolfowitz and Rumsfeld wanted to use this major opportunity to help Israel as well as to demonstrate American power in a relatively easy way. Powell was determined to limit any attack to getting rid of Taliban rule in Afghanistan, the one country which was demonstrably linked to group responsible for the bombings.

The policy lines were becoming more clearly drawn. The Pentagon was in favour of getting rid of Saddam Hussein, the State Department wanted to keep control over him through sanctions. Before 11 September the issue was still academic. Nevertheless Richard Clarke, a counter-intelligence adviser to Presidents Reagan, Bush, Clinton and George W. Bush before resigning, later maintained that after 11 September George W. Bush asked him to see if Iraq had been involved, in a way that showed he wanted a positive answer. And when Clarke insisted that Afghanistan should be the focus of American attention, Donald Rumsfeld said abruptly that there weren't enough targets there.

By 17 September, a formal plan was drawn up and sent to the Oval Office. Two and a half pages long, it contained the basic strategy by which the United States would eradicate the Taliban in Afghanistan by supporting their enemies, the Northern Alliance, and by bombing both Kabul and Taliban targets generally. The Northern Alliance would do the fighting on the ground. But, at the end, the document instructed the Pentagon to carry out a detailed study of an attack on Iraq which would overthrow Saddam Hussein and his regime. No serious evidence was produced to demonstrate that Saddam had indeed been implicated in the 11 September attacks, beyond a vague and inconsequential report from Czech intelligence about a meeting between a known Iraqi agent and al-Qaeda associates, but the top figures in the Department of Defense were convinced of it, or said they were. George W. Bush agreed with them, even though the CIA and the State Department insisted that the attacks had no connection with Saddam whatsoever.

The operation in October and November 2001 to dislodge the Taliban and destroy al-Qaeda's network in Afghanistan was for the most part smooth and effective. The US air force hit several hospitals and clinics by mistake, and the offices of the Arabic-language television news broadcaster al-Jazeera were deliberately targeted, but for the most part opinion in the United States and around the world was supportive. Despite the doubts about the messianic language which Bush had taken to using, there was a certain sense that America, having been terribly injured, was justified in striking at those who had helped the 11 September attacks to happen.

Those of us who explored al-Qaeda's reception centres and offices in Kabul after the fall of the Taliban failed to find any documents which linked the organization with Iraq in any way. There seemed to be no Iraqi volunteers, no Iraqi money, no Iraqi planning. As I rooted through a heap of documents and passports at one spectacularly untidy al-Qaeda office with my Afghan translator, I remarked on it to him.

'This'll put an end to the idea that Saddam was paying bin Laden,' I said.

At the time, it was uncertain whether Iraq was still on President Bush's hit-list. Even on 28 January 2002, when he referred in his State of the Nation speech to 'an axis of evil, arming to threaten the peace of the world', and revealed that this axis consisted of Iran, Iraq and North Korea – an unlikely threesome – it was by no means certain that he planned to attack any of them; although he added, 'We will not wait on events while dangers gather.'

Tony Blair, sitting in the audience, must have discounted two of the three 'axis' countries as likely targets: Iran and North Korea. But he himself had been worried about Iraq's arsenal ever since he saw the intelligence reports on first coming into office in 1997 and, as he listened to Bush's speech, he may well have found himself in agreement.

Eighteen days later, according to Russian intelligence documents which the *Sunday Telegraph* found in Baghdad soon after Saddam's fall, Blair told the Italian prime minister, Silvio Berlusconi, that the Americans had decided some 'negative things' about Iraq. In April, Bush went public in a briefing he and Blair gave after their meeting in Crawford, Texas.

'I made up my mind that Saddam needs to go,' he said. 'That's all I'm willing to share with you.'

Yet it still wasn't clear whether all this was merely rhetoric. On 1 June 2002 he told an audience at West Point that the United States could and should launch pre-emptive military attacks if its interests or its security were threatened. By that stage he had probably taken the decision privately to launch a major operation to overthrow Saddam Hussein, but it was not until July that the word started to filter down to senior people within his administration that it was really going to happen. It was no longer merely do-able; it was going to be done.

43. RESOLUTION

To his closest colleagues, Tony Blair had all the qualities a visionary leader should possess – except one. He was passionate, highly articulate, quick-witted, a charmer who possessed the human touch. As a young man he spoke to a friend about his longing to achieve something for his country. Tony Blair was a conviction politician, a man who wanted to do things, to change the country for the better, not just a Harold Wilson figure for whom power itself was the aim of politics. But he had one major failing: he wanted to be liked.

This brought all sorts of secondary problems with it. It ensured that he was overly dependent on his close allies: people like Peter Mandelson, Anji Hunter, Alistair Campbell. It made him extremely sensitive to what the newspapers said about him. It lured him into a dangerously dependent relationship with the newspapers of Rupert Murdoch's News International. And it meant that while he dominated British political life, especially in the absence of any imposing figure on the opposition benches, he was inclined to defer to one or two foreign leaders: specifically, Bill Clinton and George W. Bush.

Blair, though an instinctive European, subscribed wholeheartedly to the basic tenet of British foreign policy, which was that Britain's position in the world depended mainly on keeping close to the United States. As a result, when he came to power in 1997, he set out immediately to make himself Bill Clinton's closest ally. It wasn't altogether difficult. Clinton was something of an anglophile, yet he had not been at all close to Blair's predecessor John Major. (Major had ham-fistedly tried to help George Bush senior's chances in the 1992 presidential election by agreeing to a search of British police and security records for anything Clinton did during his time as a Rhodes scholar at Oxford which might be used against him by the Republican Party.)

There were other affinities. In some ways Clinton, and even more his wife Hillary, felt naturally at home with the politics of the Labour Party, while Blair was a natural Democrat: of the left, but not socialist. Clinton had been president for nearly five years by the time Tony Blair became prime minister; he was firmly settled in the job, and had won a second term, while Blair was still a tyro. It wasn't surprising that Clinton should be the dominant partner in the relationship, since he had everything – experience, character and the weight of the world's only hyperpower – behind him.

Everything, then, from Britain's strategic interests to his own character, inclined Blair to go along with what Clinton wanted. When Clinton's personal and political problems urged him on to attack Slobodan Milosevic's Serbia in support of the ethnic Albanians of Kosovo, Tony Blair was there to back him to the hilt and to send in the Royal Air Force and British ground troops as the second largest contingent in the war. Yet it was all done very much on America's terms. The British were allowed into the decision-making process only on condition that they made no decisions of their own. It paid off, to the extent that President Clinton supported a number of British initiatives and policies in other areas, not least towards Hong Kong and Northern Ireland. But it was achieved at the expense of supporting whatever Clinton did.

Margaret Thatcher, as prime minister, had been just as close to the United States, but the effect had been very different. She had much the same ideas as her opposite number, Ronald Reagan, but always had a very clear sense of Britain's separate needs and separate policies. When Reagan staged his invasion of the tiny Commonwealth island of Grenada, in the British West Indies, Thatcher pointedly refused to have anything whatever to do with it, even though Reagan's administration claimed that the Marxist government of Grenada was a threat to American lives.

And when, during the complex strategic weapons negotiations between Reagan and the Soviet leader Mikhail Gorbachev, Reagan agreed to throw British and French nuclear missiles into the pot, Mrs Thatcher was furious, and told Reagan so in as many words. It helped, of course, that Reagan was no intellectual giant and that his mental powers were visibly waning, yet by the time George Bush senior succeeded to the presidency Mrs Thatcher was the dominant character in the Western alliance.

When Clinton left office after the 2000 election, it looked for a moment as though the link between Washington and London had been severed. Tony Blair's close friend had gone, and the new president was a man who had no perceptible knowledge of, or interest in, Britain. The phone from the Oval Office to Downing Street didn't ring. It took a considerable effort on Tony Blair's part to build a good relationship with George W. Bush, and the achievement was entirely Blair's.

But it was based on a realization that the British could perform some necessary functions which the United States could not do for itself. Britain from now on was to play Sancho Panza to America's Don Quixote, puffing slowly and reluctantly behind in the various assaults on windmills, deeply unconvinced about the point of it all, but unable to head off home and leave the master to carry on alone. For the Bush administration, Britain's only function, it seemed, was to say yes to the United States; a single no or even a maybe would have cut the thread altogether.

For Tony Blair, that would have had serious repercussions at home. The Conservatives, demoralized and divided, would immediately have discovered a function for themselves as the saviours of the Atlantic alliance. British opinion would have been disturbed by a wholesale switch from Washington to Europe. Large sections of the British press, and particularly the papers owned by Rupert Murdoch, would have turned on Blair and savaged him. The prospects for a third term in office might well have weakened.

Hard though it was for many people in Britain to understand why their government had to follow the United States so closely, Tony Blair had no real alternative. Any Labour prime minister who had followed a European lead rather than an American one would have been vulnerable to attack from the Conservatives and the majority of the press at the next election. It would have been the end of Tony Blair's efforts to turn Labour into the natural party of government in Britain.

One of his more attractive characteristics was a complete inability to do things by halves. If he decided on a particular line of action, he had to follow it with enthusiasm and passion. He possessed the lawyer's ability to persuade himself of the merits of a case, and the true believer's desire to throw himself into it heart and soul. Blair was an instinctive crusader. He could not go into a war against a man like Saddam Hussein in a lukewarm fashion; he had to adopt it as a cause.

Not that this was necessarily difficult. Saddam Hussein was indeed a thoroughly unpleasant character, and Iraq and the world in general would be a better place without him. An habitual crusader for left-wing causes, the British journalist and author Christopher Hitchens, found after examining the evidence that as much as he disliked George W. Bush, he disliked Saddam Hussein far more. As a result he threw his campaigning efforts into supporting regime change. Some on the left agreed, but not many.

Both Blair and Hitchens felt a fundamental support and loyalty for the United States. For a great many people in Europe, their opposition to an attack on Iraq grew out of a distaste for the way George W. Bush was using American power in the world, and there was more than a little generalized anti-Americanism in their attitude. In January 2003 the British playwright Harold Pinter, an outspoken critic of Clinton's bombing campaign against Serbia in 1999 and Bush's war to overthrow the Taliban in Afghanistan in 2001, published a savage attack on the notion that the United States had the moral right to impose its views on other countries.

God Bless America

Here they go again,
The Yanks in their armoured parade

Chanting their ballads of joy
As they gallop across the big world
Praising America's God.

The gutters are clogged with the dead
The ones who couldn't join in
The others refusing to sing
The ones who are losing their voice
The ones who've forgotten the tune.

The riders have whips which cut
Your head rolls onto the sand
Your head is a pool in the dirt
Your head is a stain in the dust
Your eyes have gone out and your nose
Sniffs only the pong of the dead
And all the dead air is alive
With the smell of America's God.

The Poet Laureate, Andrew Motion, wrote a briefer, more complicated poem which looked at the motives behind George W. Bush's decision to attack Iraq.

Causa Belli

They read good books, and quote,
         but never learn
A language other than the scream
         of rocket-burn
Our straighter talk is drowned
         but ironclad;
elections, money, empire, oil and Dad.

As a hostile critique of George W. Bush's determination to seek the overthrow of Saddam Hussein, the poem's assessment of his motives is not only succinct, but reasonably accurate and inclusive: winning the 2004 presidential election, helping American business, demonstrating American power in the world, protecting American oil supplies, and completing his father's unfinished business.

Oil, in particular, played a more important part in this crisis than it had in the 1990–91 confrontation with Iraq. The United States had a record balance of payments deficit in 2002 of US$484 billion –

almost 5 per cent of its total gross domestic product – and a large proportion of that was due to imports of oil. Ensuring that Iraq was controlled by a government favourable to the United States would protect American oil supplies; it would also ensure that the dollar, rather than the euro, continued to be the world's main reserve currency, and the currency in which oil was priced. If the United States were forced to pay for its oil imports in euros rather than dollars, an already enormous balance of payments deficit might become catastrophic for the American economy.

But there were clearly several more complex motives as well. These included giving Israel a helping hand by taking out its most dangerous opponent, and showing Americans how strong they really were, at a time when their sense of security had been savagely undermined by the events of 11 September 2001. And although no serious evidence was ever produced to show a link between Osama bin Laden and Saddam Hussein, then or afterwards, this didn't necessarily matter: George W. Bush maintained that they were essentially the same.

'You can't distinguish between al-Qaeda and Saddam when you talk about the war on terror,' he said in an address to the nation in September 2002.

It was literally true; large numbers of Americans couldn't distinguish between them. According to one opinion poll, 20.6 per cent of people thought Saddam Hussein and Osama bin Laden were the same person.

Later, in response to a reporter who asked about the link, Bush said bizarrely, 'That's an interesting question. I'm trying to think of something humorous to say but I can't when I think about al-Qaeda and Saddam Hussein.'

It wasn't clear why he would want to be humorous about the subject in the first place; perhaps it was a throwback to his days as governor of Texas and as a presidential candidate, when he would often horse around with the journalists who followed him. They liked him as a person, but found it hard to work up any serious respect for him.

On this occasion he blundered on with nothing to guide him except his memory of the policy which other people had outlined for him, improvising in a way Ronald Reagan had once done. His assertions that al-Qaeda was linked with Iraq were backed by nothing serious in the way of facts.

'The danger is, is that they work in concert. The danger is, is that al-Qaeda becomes an extension of Saddam's madness and his hatred and his capacity to extend weapons of mass destruction around the world.'

Donald Rumsfeld was characteristically fiercer. When he was asked at a hearing of the Armed Services Committee what was so different now, that the United States should be compelled to take action against Iraq, he answered: 'What's different? What's different is three thousand people were killed.'

In other words, Iraq would be made to pay for the attacks of 11 September, whether or not there was proof of its involvement. Did any such proof exist? Condoleezza Rice, the national security adviser, a pleasant but not particularly forceful woman whom I once interviewed for my programme *Simpson's World* and was not impressed by, claimed vaguely that it did.

'There are clearly contacts between al-Qaeda and Iraq that can be documented.'

The trouble was, there weren't. Donald Rumsfeld was more honest about the embarrassing lack of evidence when a journalist asked him for proof of these links.

'This happens to be a piece of intelligence that either we don't have or we don't want to talk about,' he snapped.

This kind of response might be acceptable in the United States, where the mass of the population is usually prepared to take the government's word about matters of foreign affairs, but it wouldn't wash across the Atlantic. Few items on the list of American motives in any way matched the national interests of Britain. It didn't matter to the government of Tony Blair that Bush was re-elected, or American firms prospered from another war, or American oil supplies remained cheaper than bottled water. It did matter, though, that the United States should remain powerful, and it mattered even more that Britain should be close to the innermost circles of power in Washington at a critical moment in American history.

That meant supporting the Pentagon's line. At first, George W. Bush received strong contrary advice from the various older Republicans. Several leading figures from his father's administration, like Brent Scowcroft and James Baker, were against; so was George Bush senior. But the pro-Israel group at the Department of Defense and their allies in the Project for the New American Century were determined that Iraq should be next. So when George W. Bush made it clear he agreed, the British government had to agree too, or risk being entirely sidelined.

The British ambassador in Washington was Sir Christopher Meyer, a clever, witty and perceptive figure whom I had come to know when he was the head of the news department – in effect the chief spokesman – at the Foreign Office during the 1980s. Unlike many other diplomats, he knew the benefits that could be derived from cultivating journalists, both at home and in Washington, and he turned the British embassy into an unrivalled listening-post, tuned to picking up the faintest signals which might indicate a change of policy inside the administration. In April 2002, when Tony Blair was preparing to travel to Texas for a crucial meeting with George W. Bush, Meyer explained to him at length how the Pentagon had persuaded Bush that Saddam's Iraq should be the next target.

Blair knew he had no real alternative but to go along with the basic decision to overthrow Saddam. But he gambled everything on his ability to persuade Bush that his father's policy of keeping the United Nations on side was the best one to follow now. When he went to Camp David he argued that there should be a new round of UN weapons inspections in Iraq; assuming that the inspectors discovered that Saddam Hussein was still up to his old tricks, as British and American intelligence indicated he was, it should be relatively easy to get the necessary UN resolutions to support an attack on Saddam Hussein. This way he could make his own party accept the notion of regime change, and persuade British public opinion in general that it was necessary and worthwhile.

Blair had the tacit support of Colin Powell, the secretary of state, and of Bush's own father. At the time it seemed like a winning combination, and when Blair went to see the President at Camp David in early September 2002 he and Christopher Meyer thought they had succeeded in squaring the circle. Even Dick Cheney, the vice-president, an outspoken critic of the United Nations and its presumption in telling the United States what to do, agreed that there were advantages to winning the UN's support. The entire British team were delighted with their success as they left for home.

Four days later, on 12 September, in the spirit of the agreement he had reached with Tony Blair, Bush made a speech in which he said he wanted to introduce a resolution enabling a new round of weapons inspections to take place, backed by the threat of military action. That, at any rate, was the intention. In fact Bush spoke of 'new resolutions'. It was suggested afterwards that his teleprompter system had dropped out, and that he had been forced to improvise the key part of the speech, though plenty of people preferred the explanation that he had simply made one of his mistakes.

Mistake or not, the notion of having more than one resolution was quickly picked up. It provided Dominique de Villepin, France's foreign minister, with the opportunity to engage in some divisive tactics. He had no problem with a resolution to send the inspectors back in, but France would support a second resolution authorizing the use of force only if Iraq deliberately refused to cooperate with the work of the inspectors.

It took almost two months for Resolution 1441 to be agreed. In that time the fury of the hawks in Washington had plenty of time to vent itself.

'Explain to me why the heck all these people from African dictatorships and bankrupt third-world regimes should have any right to decide what the United States of America is going to do?' demanded a red-faced Republican senator on a television opinion show.

There was as much debate between the different factions in Washington as there was between the other UN members: Powell, the State Department and some of the remnants of George Bush senior's administration were in favour of taking the UN along with them, while Rumsfeld, Wolfowitz and the Pentagon maintained that the United States should not be bound by anything the inspectors or the UN Security Council decided, and wanted the US to have an entirely free hand in deciding what action to take against Iraq. Dick Cheney seemed to be slowly shifting back towards Rumsfeld's line; George W. Bush himself was still influenced by his father and his father's advisers, but also (to the dismay of the British) seemed to be slowly shifting.

The passing of Resolution 1441 was not, as it turned out, an end in itself, just a stage along the way in the continuing debate. The French argued that the UN weapons inspectors would have to finish their work before any final decision could be taken on what the resolution called 'all necessary measures', UN-speak for military action. The resolution had failed to set a timetable for the inspection process, so it looked as though there would be a return to the old pattern established after the first Gulf War: a game of hide-and-seek in which the inspectors had to fight to find out anything about what remained of Iraq's weapons of mass destruction and their documentation, with no clear sanction of force behind it to persuade Saddam Hussein that he should comply fully.

This suited Saddam Hussein very well, of course. It also suited the government of France. Jacques Chirac had been re-elected in May 2002 with a huge majority over the National Front leader Jean-Marie Le Pen. That freed him from the need to work with the Socialists, and he was in a position to follow the policies he wanted. A more closely contested set of elections, in September 2002, brought Gerhard Schroeder back as Chancellor in Germany. He had won only by tapping in to the general hostility among the German electorate towards George W. Bush and his aggressive policy towards Iraq. In the normal way Schroeder would probably have given Washington his reluctant and passive support, but he and his advisers saw the anti-war ticket as the only sure way of keeping the Social Democratic vote together, and fracturing support for the Christian Democrats.

Having been elected in this way, it was impossible for Schroeder to go back on his commitment to oppose a war against Iraq, and although, if left to themselves, neither Germany nor France would probably have come out openly against the United States and Britain, they felt they had the strength to do it as a partnership. In Versailles, at the celebration of the fortieth anniversary of their alliance, they agreed formally to resist any attempt by the United States to attack Iraq either unilaterally or with British support. The fact that Germany had just taken its seat by rotation on the UN Security Council gave added diplomatic strength to their stand.

Yet even now Chirac had probably not decided finally that as one of the five permanent members of the Council (alongside Britain, the United States, Russia and China) France would veto a resolution authorizing force. Over the previous decade it had grown harder for the French, and the British too, to justify their permanent membership of the Council when bigger and richer countries such as Germany and Japan only had rotating membership.

In the early 1990s, as a result of the ending of the Cold War, the Americans had toyed with the idea of proposing an end to Britain's and France's permanent membership, as a sop to both Germany and Japan; the British, in particular, had often found in their dealings with Washington that loyalty was a one-way street, and it was only by using the most intense diplomacy that the government of John Major had succeeded in dissuading Clinton. But as a result both France and Britain had become even more reluctant than before to draw attention to their special status by using their vetoes.

Right up until the third week of January, leading members of Jacques Chirac's party felt morally certain that at the last minute he would veer away from vetoing a resolution authorizing force against Iraq. On 21 January, however, Dominique de Villepin made France's position clear when he was asked at the United Nations if it would indeed use its veto.

'Believe me, we will go all the way to the end as a matter of principle.'

It was an open challenge to American power and influence. With his characteristic aggressiveness and lack of diplomatic skills Donald Rumsfeld, a man used to laying down the law without any fear of contradiction, made things worse by characterizing America's enthusiastic new allies in Eastern Europe, especially Poland, which at this stage in their development would have agreed to anything America wanted, as 'the new Europe', while France, Germany and Belgium were 'old Europe'. 'Old Europe', in American parlance, meant the Europe which appeased and eventually capitulated to Hitler. Maybe there was also a faint accusation of anti-Semitism about it, too.

Typically Rumsfeld, not at all an anglophile, managed to leave Britain out of the comparison altogether. In any administration less confident of its power and influence, the whole episode would have been deeply embarrassing. It was a measure of the Bush administration's immense self-confidence that only a few figures in the State Department even winced at Rumsfeld's crudity.

But the Americans weren't the only ones to worsen the atmosphere with their aggressive approach. When de Villepin, the French foreign minister, announced that France would use its veto as a matter of principle, he also made a declaration which offended the Bush administration from top to bottom.

'Today,' he said grandly, 'nothing justifies considering military action.'

It confirmed many Americans in the slightly fuzzy belief that France was somehow their main underlying cultural and political enemy in the world. But together, France, Germany and Russia had made it impossible for the British and Americans to get a second resolution through the Security Council, authorizing the use of force. As a result, London and Washington had to make do with the vaguer wording of the first resolution, 1441, which could be interpreted as meaning that if Iraq did not comply with the UN's demands, force could be used. But it was hardly satisfactory.

Nor was the short-lived visit paid by the new group of UN arms inspectors to Iraq, under the leadership of the thoughtful and remarkably tough Hans Blix. The Bush administration decided, on the basis of very little information, that because he was Swedish Blix would be a pushover for the Iraqis. This certainly wasn't the case, but Blix himself would have preferred to carry out a thoroughgoing search of weapons sites all over Iraq, lasting months. The Americans, on the other hand, wanted a quick end to the inspections so that the war could begin before the summer heat became too strong.

44. ANOTHER VIEW

George Bush senior, and his closest political ally James Baker, never spoke publicly about their views of Bush junior's handling of the coalition against Saddam Hussein. Yet Baker, whose long-term political career was effectively ended when he told the Likud government of Yitzak Shamir in Israel that since the United States was footing the bill it should get the kind of policies it wanted, cannot have been enthusiastic about the way Likud's friends and supporters in Washington were making the running in this crisis.

Nor can Bush senior, who managed the seemingly impossible trick of persuading the Syrians to join his military coalition and the Iranians to give it their tacit support and approval, have thought particularly highly of the way his son managed to alienate even traditionally close American allies such as France, Germany, Egypt and Saudi Arabia. In the twelve years since the first Gulf War, the world had changed greatly. George W. Bush and Donald Rumsfeld, encouraged by groups like the Project for the New American Century, saw no great need for delicate diplomacy. You were either with America or you didn't count; France and Germany no longer counted.

But other figures from George Bush senior's administration, including his national security adviser Brent Scowcroft, were openly dismayed by this approach.

'As we've seen in the debate about Iraq,' Scowcroft said in March 2003, 'it's already given us an image of arrogance and unilateralism, and we're paying a very high price for that image. If we get to the point where everyone secretly hopes that the United States gets a black eye because we're so obnoxious, then we'll be totally hamstrung in the war on terror. We'll be like Gulliver with the Lilliputians.'

45. FACE TO FACE

In December 2002 I had some hopes of getting an interview with Saddam Hussein, despite my past problems with Iraqi officialdom. If I could get some respected Arab leader to intervene with him personally and ask him to allow me to interview him, then I might stand a chance. One such leader agreed, and the response from Baghdad was remarkably favourable. All that was required, I was told, was the endorsement of the one British politician whom Saddam trusted: George Galloway, the maverick Labour MP. George was very pleasant, and said he'd got several of my books on the shelves of his Westminster office as he spoke, but he explained the troubles he'd had with the BBC, and said he felt he couldn't help. It also appeared that I had competition in my efforts to get an interview with Saddam. Tony Benn, the veteran Labour peace activist, wanted to do the same thing.

Interviewing Saddam, as I have indicated before in this book, is a difficult business. He dominates the occasion; you are merely there to prompt him very occasionally with questions. You are certainly not expected to interrupt him. Nor, if you want to go home in safety, do you point out to him the inconsistencies in his argument. I had worked out ways round this, based on my experience of doing a live television interview with the Serbian warlord Arkan. ('We can do this two ways,' I told him, 'I can ask you hard questions or soft ones; which is it to be?' Arkan opted, of course, for the hard ones – and that made my job a lot easier.)

Tony Benn was everything Saddam wanted in an interviewer, so he, not I, was given the opportunity; if I'd been Saddam I'd have made the same decision. When the two men met and sat down at the inevitable heavy, grossly carved table, Tony Benn was given a slightly smaller chair, and sat forward eagerly in it, smiling and clasping his hands between his knees. Because of the angle of the camera, you could see his hands clearly; it looked as though he was praying. Saddam Hussein, by contrast, sat straight and alert in his grander chair, not allowing the slightest smile to ease the sternness of his demeanour. Alistair Campbell couldn't have organized it better. It looked as though Benn was the supplicant, begging Saddam for peace.

And indeed in a way he was. In one of his soft, unchallenging questions, Benn begged him to 'say something helpful and positive' which the peace movements around the world would be able to use. Saddam wasn't interested. On the contrary, he went into a long account of Iraq's determination to shed its blood in defence of the Motherland; not quite the helpful note Tony Benn was hoping for, presumably. It was the first television interview Saddam had given since 1991, and it wasn't a great success.

Nevertheless he encouraged the growing feeling in many Western countries that Iraq might not, after all, have the kind of weapons which the British and Americans insisted were an imminent danger.

Iraq has no interest in war. No Iraqi official or ordinary citizen has expressed a wish to go to war. The question should be directed at the other side. Are they looking for a pretext so they could justify war against Iraq? If the purpose was to make sure that Iraq is free of nuclear, chemical and biological weapons, then they can do that. These weapons do not come in small pills that you can hide in your pocket. These are weapons of mass destruction, and it is easy to work out if Iraq has them or not. We have said many times before, and we say it again today: Iraq is free of such weapons.

This, at least, was clever and effective. It wasn't necessarily true, of course; biological weapons might not be as small as a pill in your pocket, but enough anthrax to wipe out Kuwait City could be buried under a garage forecourt and no one would know.

Tony Benn was less impressive. It is not a pleasant sight when a free man seems to abase himself before a tyrant, even for the sake of peace, and it would have been a little better if he had shown that he at least understood why some people who had no love for George W. Bush or for America's new imperial role felt it was necessary that Saddam should be overthrown. The trouble was, Tony Benn and some (though by no means all) of the people who thought like him regarded any criticism of Saddam's abominable record in power as being part of the propaganda effort which was propelling Britain and America to war; as though any threat from Washington instantly cleanses a dictator of his sins. Things are rarely so clear-cut that one side is entirely noble and right and the other entirely bestial and wrong. We have to make our decisions about these things by weighing up the available evidence and deciding for ourselves – not by buying a pre-selected package, as though political judgements are like peaches at a supermarket.

46. PROTEST

The peace demonstration in the centre of London on 15 February 2003 was the largest gathering of people in British history, and one of the largest at any time anywhere in the world. Maybe there weren't quite as many as the figure of 2 million which the organizers claimed; but in a country which, by and large, has never been very enthusiastic about demonstrations, this meant something very significant.

Before the war, British public opinion was strongly opposed to the idea of invading Iraq. It swung round when the war began, as opinion usually does in times of national crisis, but afterwards it swung back again. Some very unlikely people were against the idea of the war. When I gave a talk in a tiny village in North Yorkshire, which had never had anything but a Conservative MP in its entire political history, a crowd of 200 – almost the entire population – was clearly wholly opposed to war. When I chaired a panel discussion in London soon afterwards, all the generals and military men present felt the same. It is a remarkable feeling to listen to a soldier famous for his toughness and his fighting record explaining how stupid it is to go to war on an unreasonable pretext.

On the day when the crowds marched through London, there were other vast gatherings in cities right across the world: a million and a quarter in Barcelona, a million in Rome, three-quarters of a million in Madrid, half a million in New York City, 400,000 in Paris, a quarter of a million in San Francisco and in Sydney, 150,000 in Montreal, and so on.

Again and again at speeches in all these places, and in others, the same points were made: there was no established link between Iraq and the attacks of 11 September; the Bush administration had failed to produce any evidence that Iraq posed a threat to the United States, Britain, or the outside world; there was absolutely no certainty that Saddam Hussein possessed weapons of mass destruction any longer.

Instead, the nature of the Bush administration was placed in question: why was it prosecuting another war? What were its long-term motives? How was oil involved in all of this? Did the fact that George W. Bush, Dick Cheney and Donald Rumsfeld all had close links with oil companies affect their approach?

The actions of 10 million people worldwide received relatively little attention on American television news. The networks tended to ignore them as weirdos and malcontents. The American media were getting ready for war, not for a discussion about the merits of peace.

Some of these same demonstrators had marched against the war in Afghanistan. The Taliban had demonstrably supported the people who planned the attacks of 11 September 2001, and had given them an honoured place of refuge. As a result of Taliban rule, Afghanistan had become a political black hole where any kind of violence and lunacy could shelter, and the Taliban had instituted the fiercest and most fundamentalist Islamic regime on the face of the earth. It wasn't the brutal beating of women and the destruction of girls' schools in Afghanistan that brought the crowds out on to the streets in protest; it was the prospect that the United States might be planning the overthrow of one of the world's most brutal systems.

In other words, what made the difference was the American involvement. Some people felt more strongly about that than they did about the regimes the Americans were attacking. There was a confusion about aims and purposes, but it all came down to the basic question of American interventionism: did the United States have the moral right to attack other countries merely because it was powerful enough to be able to?

47. DOSSIER

As early as March 2002, when it was becoming clear that the neo-conservative hawks in the Bush administration would press for an extension of the war against terror to include Saddam Hussein, Downing Street quietly assembled an intelligence fact-pack on Iraq's weapons of mass destruction. It had a very limited circulation, but it was felt to be impressive. By late summer, as public opinion still resolutely refused to swing the government's way, the difficult decision was taken to make the dossier public.

It was clear that MI6 was unhappy about the idea. Making intelligence public, even when it has been carefully doctored to ensure that its sources have left no fingerprints on it, is something that goes seriously against the grain for an intelligence service, especially MI6 (which is more properly known as the Secret Intelligence Service, or SIS). After the disasters of the 1950s, when the 'Cambridge' group of Soviet agents was discovered to be disturbingly close to the heart of British intelligence and Kim Philby was for a time regarded as a possible future head of SIS, the organization had had to rebuild itself painfully from within.

In order to do that, it had gone back to basics – and the most basic value of all was secrecy. It was remarkably successful, and by the time the Cold War ended SIS was a highly effective and much-respected organization. The CIA, by contrast, was riven with dissension, and turned out to have two important Russian agents working at key levels inside it.

Now SIS was being asked by the government to help in the essentially political task of persuading the British people about the risks from Saddam Hussein's Iraq, by breaching the principle which had saved the organization during its worst times. It was a difficult issue for Sir Richard Dearlove, the head of SIS. He had spent his entire career in the organization since leaving Cambridge in 1966, and making his hard-won intelligence public in this way must have seemed a disturbing innovation.

At the same time, SIS had done a good job in building and retaining New Labour's respect for its work; the secret services had often been mistrusted by Labour governments over the years. Government support is important for SIS, which is a relatively small organization compared with American or Soviet intelligence, but is well funded. Secret intelligence does not come cheap, and it is important for SIS to keep in with the government. Dearlove quickly established a good relationship with Tony Blair, and that proved to be a great advantage for SIS.

When the government told Dearlove it wanted to make public the dossier of March 2002 on Iraq's weapons of mass destruction, therefore, he felt on balance that he had to agree. It was a decision which would have long-lasting effects on the reputation of both the government and SIS, and would affect his own career as well.

When I first opened the dossier on the day it was published, 24 September 2002, I had the impression that the force and logic of its fifty pages of detailed information were unanswerable. Tony Blair, writing the preface to the document, had thrown all his presentational skills and his formidable enthusiasm into making it the centrepiece of a highly convincing case.

'I am in no doubt that the threat is serious and current,' he wrote, 'that [Saddam Hussein] has made progress on WMD, and that he has to be stopped . . . Some of these weapons are deployable within 45 minutes of an order to use them.'

Iraq was, the dossier said categorically, developing nuclear weapons with uranium from Niger, in Africa, which had no application for Iraq's civil nuclear programme. It had also developed missiles which could strike at Israel and other targets in the Middle East; the impression left on the reader's mind from all these different items of information was that Iraq was working hard to obtain nuclear missiles, perhaps for use against Israel, which might be fired within forty-five minutes. All in all, the effect of the dossier was that Iraq represented, in the over-used American phrase, a clear and present danger.

In reality, not very much of this impressive collection of information was true. The director-general of the International Atomic Energy Agency denied that Iraq was close to manufacturing a nuclear weapon, and maintained that Iraq hadn't tried to buy uranium in Niger. When Western journalists visited what the dossier called 'facilities of concern' in Iraq, they could see nothing out of the ordinary there.

Saddam Hussein was certainly a past-master at hiding his weapons of mass destruction, and there had never been any doubt in the past that he had done his best to acquire them. It was also true that he had hired some top soldiers and scientists from the former Soviet Union and the former Yugoslavia to work on the deployment and concealment of his weaponry; the Yugoslavs, in particular, had shown a remarkable ability to hide installations, tanks and guns during the NATO bombing campaign against Serbia in 1999.

But did Iraq now possess the kind of weapons the dossier claimed he had? Or could we for once believe Saddam Hussein when he promised that he had destroyed all his weapons of mass destruction? The problem was, the government had included some distinctly questionable elements. Some of the dossier had been lifted without permission from the doctoral thesis of a student of Iraqi origin in the United States. The impression given was that this information came from intelligence sources, when it was in fact added in by a researcher working in Downing Street.

A second dossier presented to the public some months later also contained assertions about Saddam's weaponry which were never proven to be correct.

In the United States George W. Bush had the advantage that, despite the evidence of frequent deceit and untruths over the years, Americans tend to trust their presidents to tell them the truth about what is happening in the world. The CIA, which worked closely with SIS and usually had a high opinion of its information, assured him that the information in the British dossier was reliable, and his speechwriters adapted the section about Iraq's efforts to obtain uranium from Niger into his State of the Union speech. Months later, when the war was over, this turned out to be the issue which Bush's critics turned to in their determination to discredit his entire approach to Iraq's weapons of mass destruction, and in defending the line the Bush administration duly passed the discredit back to its source, British intelligence. It was a thoroughgoing disaster, from which no one emerged unscathed.

In January 2003, before all these things were properly clear, a friend of mine who was a senior figure in the world of intelligence invited me to lunch. It was a pleasant and surprisingly frank occasion. He explained that the government was exerting heavy pressure on the intelligence professionals. He and his colleagues were having to squeeze their agents in the field for the information which the British government needed badly; I had the impression that this pressure might be putting many of them at serious risk.

My friend's great fear was that these people, some of whom sounded as though they might be scientists in Saddam's various weapons programmes, could soon be corralled together by the Iraqi authorities into special living areas where they would no longer be able to communicate with their British handlers. If Saddam's security men did that, then the flow of information would stop altogether. My friend mused for a while, and told me how difficult it was to provide the agents with the new forms of radio equipment they needed to make contact.

I nodded sympathetically, hoping I wouldn't have to explain that even if I made it to Baghdad, which was looking increasingly unlikely, there was nothing I could or would do to help in this way. I don't believe that journalists should be part-time spies; it doesn't do any favours to either side.

To my relief, that wasn't what my friend meant at all, and I knew from the past that he shared my dislike of journalists who crossed the line. Instead, he was worried about the problems of providing the kind of information which the British government was demanding more and more urgently. The pressure was on him and the rest of the intelligence community to give the politicians the necessary ammunition to persuade public opinion of the threat from Saddam Hussein.

Was there a threat? Yes, my friend thought there probably was. Did Iraq still have weapons of mass destruction? Yes, he thought that was certainly possible, though it was going to be difficult to find them.

'Bear in mind,' he said, 'that since the weapons inspectors left in '98 Saddam has had almost four years to hide the stuff or get rid of it. That's a long time.'

I told him about a story I had recently published in my *Sunday Telegraph* column about how President Hosni Mubarak of Egypt had rung Saddam Hussein and told him that he must get rid of what Mubarak called his 'naughty' weapons. The story came from an unimpeachable Middle Eastern source, but it was impossible to verify and I said so in the article. I also said there was no way of verifying the corollary to it – that Mubarak had offered to use Egyptian lorries and ships to spirit the weapons away to Syria, Libya and Egypt itself. But although I had hedged the whole story round with every kind of warning that I couldn't vouch for its authenticity, the Egyptian government came back during the days which followed with such a blast of anger and denial that I thought for the first time that it might be entirely true. Now I hinted at all this to my friend in intelligence, over a rather good glass of claret; he, I noticed, always drank at least one glass fewer than I did.

'H'm,' he said. 'Very interesting.'

Perhaps he meant it, perhaps he didn't. You don't get to the senior levels of intelligence by gushing about how grateful you are to be told something you didn't already know. Nor do you give more information in return.

Maybe the purpose of the lunch from his point of view was to tell me I shouldn't expect that the weapons of mass destruction would be at all easy to find. Intelligence people, like politicians, like to feed these things into the minds of journalists, so the journalists can then pass them on to their viewers, listeners and readers. As long as you know what is going on, you can make sure you are not merely being used, but it is a murky form of communication at the best of times, and it is why I prefer the straight reportage of events to the quiet briefing, the off-the-record lunch, and the deep backgrounder. Out in the real world the rules are clearer.

There was one final piece of information which I stored away for possible use. Over lunch my friend told me that the head of MI6 had received an apology from Downing Street (which I took to mean Tony Blair's communications chief, Alistair Campbell) over the so-called 'dodgy dossier' the one which had contained part of a doctoral thesis from an American-Iraqi student about the nature of Saddam Hussein's rule in Iraq.

In the summer of 2003, at the height of the battle between the government and the BBC over the allegations that information the government made public about Saddam's weapons of mass destruction had been 'sexed up', I passed the news of the apology on to the *Sunday Telegraph*'s editor, Dominic Lawson. Dominic too had heard something of this, and the article duly ran in the paper. I was mildly taken aback that a few words spoken during a lunch six months before might have been front-page news, but that is the nature of this kind of nod-and-a-wink journalism. Downing Street immediately questioned the report, but apparently on a quibble: it probably wasn't a letter of apology, but rather a phone-call of apology. To the unwary, though, it will have seemed that the apology itself was fictional. Such are the ways of spin-doctors.

But who knows? Maybe my friend, who is a past-master at the politics of Whitehall, wanted to plant a bomb with a slow fuse on me, knowing that at some stage it would explode in the faces of the people who had caused his service such difficulties. Or maybe, as journalists so often do, I read much too much into a quick, unguarded aside. But successful and able spies probably don't make unguarded asides about anything; not even the weather or the time of day.

Fundamentally, the problem lay in mixing up intelligence with public relations. The British government, knowing the respect that people tend to accord the intelligence agencies (even if they don't even know their proper names), was using the Secret Intelligence Service and the Security Service (what we still tend to call MI6 and MI5) as witnesses in the government's defence. The Foreign Office, the Home Office, even the police are used to this sort of treatment.

But the essence of the intelligence services is that they keep in the background, providing a discreet flow of information to the politicians to help them make up their own minds on complex issues of policy. The Blair government wanted the intelligence services to do more than that. It wanted them to help in the business of persuading the public that it was right to support the American line in Iraq. The intelligence services, in other words, were being politicized in a way they themselves found unnerving and distasteful.

They saw their product, the intelligence they worked so hard and took so many risks to obtain, being printed in official publications and spread round the media and to the general public. One of the chief rules in my friend's world is never to show people what you know, because they will be able to work out from that what you don't know. Making intelligence assessments public was dangerous in every way. In the short and medium run, MI6 gained greatly by being Tony Blair's favourite arm of government. It received the money it needed, and it was accorded the respect which some other arms of government found themselves lacking. But it did the service no good at all; and at all levels inside MI6 there seems to have been a good deal of unhappiness about the 'outing' of intelligence.

Immediately after the end of the Cold War, Sir Colin McColl's identity as the head of MI6 – 'C', as he was known; the initial went with the job, as did the use of green ink for his signature and jottings – became publicly acknowledged. At that stage MI6 was still finding its way in the new public world it was expected to inhabit. It moved from its anonymous, cramped and rather insecure headquarters at Century House in Lambeth to a grandiose and thoroughly recognizable building on the river at Vauxhall Cross. It formalized the appointment of a senior figure to deal with the press. And, with perceptible nervousness, it invited senior journalists like me to come to lunch and meet its top people.

I went along on several occasions, determined if I could to persuade Sir Colin, and later his successors, to appear on camera and talk to me about the reality of life in the dark regions of espionage. Sir Colin, whom I took to greatly, was very polite and promised to consider the idea. He was an outwardly bluff character who affected to hide his remarkable quickness of intellect, but for all his apparent willingness to think about my offer he plainly never intended to take it up.

He explained that his service had secret agents all over the world, who depended on MI6's remarkable reputation for discretion and integrity to keep their identities hidden. If he went on television and talked about his work, he said, these agents and many others who might think about joining MI6 would see it, and they would immediately ask themselves what other secrets might MI6 consider revealing. A secret organization has to remain entirely secret, he said.

Sir Colin would certainly have argued the same way over the government's desire to make its intelligence on Saddam's weapons of mass destruction public, and no doubt Sir Richard Dearlove, the latest incarnation of the title 'C' at the time of the build-up against Iraq, would have done the same. A secret organization whose work isn't entirely secret is like a hermit crab out of its shell. As a government servant Sir Richard was obliged to go along with what his political masters wanted, but he must have wished they hadn't demanded it of him.

When it was announced that he would be leaving his post in 2004, at the end of a five-year stint, it was generally taken as a sign that he was sick of what the government had done to his service, even though Downing Street immediately pointed out that his two predecessors had also given up after five years. Maybe the chances were less that Sir Richard was retiring in disgust, and more that he realized it would be very hard to continue heading a service which had been so unwillingly opened up to public scrutiny.

But journalists, historians and politicians always think there must be some linking cause, some deeper explanation, which underlies every action that is taken, even though the evidence from our own daily lives shows us this is rarely true. Maybe Sir Richard Dearlove had just come to the end of his five years, and knew it was time to move on.

48. CONSCIENCE

Tony Blair was one of the most remarkable British leaders of modern times. The changes he brought about in Britain's political and constitutional life, and in the alignment of the Labour Party, were necessary and lasting. He was a man of vision, decency, and genuine compassion.

He kept his government in power with the most sophisticated system of press and public relations Europe had ever seen. At its best, it simply meant that the government spoke with one voice and was properly aware of the need for coherent and intelligent coordination. At its worst, and it was often at its worst, it introduced a degree of media manipulation previously unknown in British public life. Alistair Campbell, Downing Street's then head of communications, was a former political editor of the *Daily Mirror* who knew how the press worked and had a considerable (and often justified) contempt for the way many journalists simply wrote what government spokesmen told them. But instead of trying to improve the quality of the reporting, he and his assistants played on the weaknesses of the press and used them for the government's own ends.

During the twelve weeks from March to May 1999, when I was reporting for the BBC from Belgrade on the NATO bombing of Slobodan Milosevic's Serbia, I came in for a good deal of trouble from the British government's press machine, which seemed to want to bludgeon everyone into accepting the view from Downing Street, and to undermine anyone who provided a different version of things.

In my case, directly I started reporting the kind of things from Belgrade that the British government found inconvenient, Campbell (a man for whom, in spite of everything, I still have a genuine respect and even affection) whispered in the ears of lobby correspondents that I had been duped by Milosevic's propaganda. The people I had been interviewing were, Campbell said, just Milosevic plants – only I was too naïve to realize it. A rather less talented woman at the Ministry of Defence press office said worse things, off the record. Tony Blair himself attacked my reporting at Prime Minister's Question Time in the Commons; and two thoroughly unreconstructed Labour MPs, to whom I shall always be grateful, called out in protest.

My fiercest critics at this time, though, were two senior government ministers: Robin Cook, the foreign secretary, and Clare Short, the international development secretary. Neither had much influence inside Tony Blair's government, but it suited them to try to enhance what they had by acting as cheerleaders for the bombing of Serbia.

Clare Short, impelled perhaps by the reputation she had of being 'the conscience of the Labour Party', attacked my reporting from the moral angle; she managed, indeed, to hint not only that I was a sympathizer with Slobodan Milosevic, but that since he was, in her book, the next thing to a Nazi, and I had willingly stayed in this latter-day Berlin in order to broadcast lies to the British people, I must therefore be a bit of a Nazi myself.

In the Serbian crisis Tony Blair did what he later did over Afghanistan and Iraq: he willingly accepted the leadership of the United States and made himself America's lieutenant. It was easier then, because Bill Clinton was genuinely a friend of his and they shared the same general outlook. Yet during the bombing of Serbia, as later in Afghanistan and Iraq, civilians were killed, hospitals were hit, children and old people and pregnant women suffered just as much as soldiers did. Politicians seem not to mind doing these things if they have to, on the principle of the omelette and the breaking of eggs, but they don't like it if journalists are on hand to tell the world when the eggs are being broken.

In fact, I had no sympathies whatever for Milosevic, any more than I did for the Taliban in Afghanistan or Saddam Hussein in Iraq. But I did have a great deal of sympathy for the ordinary people of all three countries, and if you bomb a nation, as opposed to an army, then the taxpayers back home who pay for the war have a right to know where the bombs are landing, and what results they have when they explode. If the bombs are killing civilians, especially civilians they are not intended to kill, then the people back home have a right to know that as well. And if it is inconvenient for the government in power when this comes out, too bad. Maybe it'll mean that the bombs and missiles will be aimed with a little more care next time.

Clare Short seemed to think it was fine to bomb civilians whose governments she didn't like. But while she and the people who thought like her identified Slobodan Milosevic as a second Hitler when he was nothing more than a nasty little nationalist, they seemed prepared to ignore Saddam Hussein's crimes. To me, it seemed like humbug. You either think it matters if ordinary, innocent people are killed, or you think it doesn't matter as long as the cause is right. But can a cause honestly be justified if it is imposed on classrooms and maternity hospitals and mental homes and ordinary, small, poverty-stricken houses with cluster-bombs and high explosives and the cleverest methods of killing people that the munitions manufacturers of the United States and Britain can devise?

Clare Short, the conscience of the Labour Party, thought it could. She had held on tightly to office during the bombing of Serbia by proclaiming the moral value of a war fought to protect the lives of ethnic Albanians. (In fact, Slobodan Milosevic's thugs murdered more ethnic Albanians after the NATO bombing began than they had murdered beforehand; for them it was a matter of simple revenge.) She was quieter during the war against Afghanistan, though that also produced its inevitable quota of clinics bombed and civilian convoys shot up. She clearly believed that she was doing a good job as development secretary, and this should not be jeopardized. So she made it clear to the press that while she wasn't happy, she had decided to stay.

Tony Blair was grateful. Clare Short stood for something in the Labour Party: she had the air of an old-style Labour figure, and adhered to some Old Labour principles. The smaller aid agencies, which she either bullied or ignored, were more inclined to think of her as an old-fashioned statist; she decided that the big agencies were the ones to support, while cutting back heavily on the small niche agencies which did a great deal of good but lacked the turnover.

If she left the government, Blair would have problems. Clare Short was useful to him politically: she did her job well, she provided the government with a fig-leaf with which to cover its pro-American policies at a time when the United States was increasingly unpopular on the left, and she went along quietly enough in Cabinet with what was being done.

Robin Cook was less of a threat. He had been a significant figure in the party for more than a quarter of a century, but his time in office as foreign secretary had curiously diminished his importance. Now he was a markedly shrunken figure, having been pushed aside to take the Leadership of the House. It would be serious if he left, but not dangerous for the government. Now he made it clear that if war with Iraq began without a second UN resolution, he would resign.

Clare Short had to be dealt with much more carefully. On 9 March 2003 she told the BBC she thought Tony Blair had been 'reckless' in allowing Britain to move towards war – a serious accusation to make against the leader of her own government – and laid it out as plainly as words could make it:

'If there isn't UN authority for military action [against Iraq], or if there is not UN authority for the reconstruction of the country, I will not uphold a breach of international law or this undermining of the UN; and I will resign from the government.'

Tony Blair pulled out all the stops at his disposal to persuade her to stay. He reminded her that the war in Kosovo, which she had supported so enthusiastically, had not had the backing of a UN vote, and while UN authority could not be obtained for military action against Iraq, because the French, Russians and Chinese wouldn't agree, he would do his utmost to get the UN involved in reconstructing Iraq after the war. She would, of course, play an important role in the business of reconstruction.

It seems pretty transparent stuff, and it would never have convinced anyone who was clear in their mind about the rights and wrongs of bombing people for purely political reasons. But the fact was, Clare Short wanted to stay. She liked being in office, and she liked getting things done. Tony Blair played on her vanity and her sense of duty equally, and she decided that, after all, she was needed and must remain. The conscience of the party was going to swallow her qualms; but for the time being she kept her decision secret.

Robin Cook behaved according to his principles. He was careful not to give Tony Blair's real enemies within the Labour Party – the irreducible hard left who longed to see Blair overthrown – any unnecessary ammunition. He discussed the manner and timing of his resignation carefully with Alistair Campbell, and did not turn up for another meeting of the Cabinet afterwards. On the evening of 17 March he made a fierce attack on Blair's support for war without a UN resolution, but he did not widen it into an attack on Blair himself, or on his premiership. It was a skilful performance, and one which won him more respect in the House of Commons than he had had for a long time.

A rebel motion in the Commons for debate the next day declared that the case for war was not yet proven. It was a critical moment for Blair and his government. He wouldn't lose the vote, because the Conservatives would support him, but if there were a major rebellion among Labour MPs Blair would be weakened almost fatally. Two junior ministers, Lord Hunt and John Denham, announced that morning they were resigning. By contrast, Clare Short's friends let it be known she would stay.

Tony Blair's speech in the debate was probably the best he had ever given. His words were imbued with the drama and passion of the moment, and he knew he was fighting for his political life. The issue was wider than the future of Iraq and the future of Saddam Hussein: it was the development of the UN, the relationship between Europe and the United States, and the way the US engaged with the rest of the world. The implication was that Britain was in a position to make sure the US did it the right way.

'To retreat now, I believe,' he summed up, 'would put at hazard

Nall that we hold dearest, turn the United Nations back into a talking-shop, stifle the first steps of progress in the Middle East, leave the Iraqi people to the mercy of events on which we would have relinquished all power to influence for the better.'

Labour MPs – though by no means all of them – cheered him as he sat down. Some who did not cheer nevertheless planned to vote for him because they didn't want to help destroy the most successful Labour government since 1945. Blair had made it clear during the course of his speech that he would resign if the motion was defeated, and that brought him some more unwilling votes.

He knew, though, that would never happen; his majority was far too large for him to be defeated. Even so, a big revolt by Labour MPs would begin to undermine him, so that his eventual fall would be dated to the day of the debate.

To counter this, the spin-doctors had put it round that a rebellion by 170 MPs would constitute a serious defeat; they knew the real figure would be nowhere near as big. In the end, though, it was still the largest rebellion in British parliamentary history: 139 Labour MPs voted against their party, and sixteen Conservatives voted against theirs (the Tory leadership supported the motion). They were joined by fifty-three Liberal Democrats, and eleven others. Even so, the House of Commons voted just under two to one to attack Iraq. It was the first time Parliament, rather than the government of the day, had decided whether or not the country should go to war. So it turned into an important constitutional precedent: if and when Britain fights another war, ordinary MPs rather than the government will have the final say.

49. EMBEDDING

We had known for months that journalists would have unrivalled access to cover this war. It wasn't going to be at all like the 1991 campaign. At the BBC, at CNN, at Sky, at al-Jazeera and al-Arabiya, at every national television and radio organization and every news-paper which could afford the considerable outlay, arrangements were made to send reporters and camera teams to cover it. Teams were dispatched to Doha, Kuwait City, northern Iraq and Baghdad itself. Reporters and cameramen were assigned to work alongside the American and British troops who would be carrying out the invasion of Iraq. And by October 2002 we started hearing a new word: 'embedding'.

The idea began with a senior army officer working in the Pentagon, who passed it on with a certain hesitation to his colleagues. There had been a recent flurry of Hollywood films and television series about the Normandy campaign of 1944, and a book about the war bearing the name of the main NBC anchor, Tom Brokaw, had achieved phenomenal sales. Suppose journalists were trained to accompany forward units of the Coalition forces in the forthcoming war, sharing their privations, their dangers, and ultimately their victory?

It required some thinking about, of course. But the expectation in the Pentagon, the basic article of faith, was that this would be a campaign of liberation rather than a hard-fought war; having journalists along would demonstrate to the people back home how fast and how complete America's victory would be. This was not going to be like Vietnam, where cameramen and reporters could hitch rides on helicopters to visit beleaguered and frightened American soldiers stuck in their isolated foxholes, and reveal the extent of their suffering on the evening news. This campaign was to be a blitzkrieg inspired by Donald Rumsfeld himself: a ferocious and unstoppable onslaught against an enemy who, as the Pentagon well knew, was largely incapable of defending itself.

There was a little nervousness: suppose something went wrong, and the cameras were on hand to see it? But the mere suggestion that things could go wrong was heretical. As long as the journalists were properly equipped and properly trained, and could keep up with the soldiers, and wouldn't complain or pass on secret details, then the US forces would accept them. And what the US forces accepted, the British would have to accept as well.

It is usually the generals who dislike having journalists around, because they know how easily things can go wrong and how quickly blame is assigned back at headquarters. The junior officers, NCOs and private soldiers welcome them, because that gives meaning and glamour to the daily grind of campaigning, and their families back home

19. Our team in Arbil, northern Iraq. From left: Commander Nariman of the Kurdish forces; Dragan Petrovic, our Serbian cameraman; Oggy Boytchev, the field producer in charge of the operation; Craig Summers, security adviser; Fred Scott, cameraman; Tom Giles, producer; J.S.

Four colleagues and friends

20. *Above.* Terry Lloyd of ITN, killed March 2003.

21. *Left.* Gaby Rado, Channel 4 News, died March 2003.

22. *Above, right.* Kamaran Abdurrazaq Mohammed, our translator, killed 6 April 2003.

23. *Right.* Kaveh Golestan, the BBC's Tehran cameraman, killed March 2003.

24. The US Air Force bombs the Iraqi front line.

25. With Tom Giles and the Israeli correspondent Ron Ben-Yishai.

26. Waji Barzani (far right), brother of the KDP President and charismatic head of the Kurdish special forces. Two days after this picture was taken he was critically injured in an American 'friendly fire' incident. Kamaran, our translator, who died in the incident, is on the far left.

27. The incident itself. The column of smoke on the right marks the place where the missile landed, a couple of minutes earlier. The smoke on the left comes from the first of the vehicles to blow up.

28. I record a piece to camera. The blood on my face comes from two small shrapnel wounds.

29. American special forces soldiers carry the body of a dead Kurdish soldier.

30. An American medic examines Fred Scott's scalp wound.

31. Abdullah Zaheeruddin, our Afghan photographer, takes a picture of himself in an ambulance soon after the incident. The makeshift bandage on his neck covers a shrapnel wound.

32. Mohammed Saeed al-Sahhaf, Saddam's information minister.
He claimed after the war that Saddam told him to let me go to Baghdad
in order to have me killed, and that he blocked it.

33. This unsourced picture allegedly shows ousted Iraqi leader Saddam Hussein
being dragged out of hiding on 13 December 2003. He was found by US troops
in an underground hole at a farm in the village of ad-Dawr, near his
hometown of Tikrit in northern Iraq. *(Caption: Getty Images)*

can catch occasional glimpses of them on television, or read their names in the newspapers.

So it was in this war, but the generals' anxieties were cancelled out by the Pentagon's enthusiasm for the idea, and the generals had to pretend they liked it. The business of training and equipping the 'embeds' – an entire idiolect had to be developed to describe them – began.

In August 2003, more than three months after President Bush had declared the war over, I had to represent the BBC at a conference in Chicago at which top American military people discussed the phenomenon of 'embedding' with a number of leading journalists. It was a strange business: several of the military people had dealt in one way or another with the disaster which had overtaken my BBC team and me in northern Iraq. Not wanting to offend unnecessarily, I decided not to tell my audience that I had christened the piece of shrapnel in my hip as big as a nine-millimetre bullet, 'George W. Bush'.

But I did tell them what I thought about the careless and often dangerous way the American forces had fought the war. I made few friends in doing so, except among the journalists. Some of the finest reporters involved in covering the war were present, and two of them – John Donvan and John McQuetty, both of ABC News – were forthright in their criticism of the way the Pentagon, the television networks and the politicians had approached the war.

By contrast, the well-coiffured and beautifully dressed Lou Dobbs of CNN described how he had dropped General Wesley Clark, the former NATO commander, from his show 'because he kept intruding politics into his comments' – Clark was a trenchant critic of the war – and summed up his own approach to reporting it by giving the impression that for him the American fighting man could do no wrong; which begs the question how effectively Lou Dobbs would have reported, say, the My Lai massacre in Vietnam.

Both the journalists and the military, broadly speaking, felt the embedding experiment had worked remarkably well. There were one or two complaints from the military about smallish lapses of security in the journalists' reporting, and one or two from the journalists about unnecessary obstacles placed in their way by the military, but for the most part everyone seemed pleased by the experience.

John Donvan, however, raised a particular anxiety about it. Listening to a long account of the way the American television networks had organized the mechanics of it all, he intervened to say that he felt the networks were so enthusiastic about the prospect of covering the war in this excitingly close-up fashion that it coloured their entire attitude to the war itself. They *wanted* it to take place, because they knew how effective the reporting of it would be, and how large the audiences would be. And that meant, he said, that they largely ignored the anti-war protests in the United States and around the world as freakish and irrelevant. The absence of proper reporting of an extraordinary international phenomenon troubled a few (though not many) mainstream American commentators at the time, and perhaps John Donvan was right in his assessment of the basic reasons.

In future, it seems reasonable to assume, the United States will continue the embedding experiment in every war it feels certain of winning easily, which means every war in which it takes the initiative. The British experience, too, was positive. The British army learned as long ago as the early 1970s in Northern Ireland that the best spokesmen for its forces are the sergeants, corporals and privates who talk from their experience and their emotions rather than from a script prepared at army headquarters.

The big point of contention comes over what other areas of the battlefield need reporting. In the second Gulf War the BBC and most of the British media decided that they must also have independent reporters working outside the embedded teams, operating between the armies. Thanks to the carelessness and poor training of the American forces, this proved to be extremely dangerous, and in any future war involving the United States, news organizations will be much more cautious about sending their teams out into no man's land; yet it is their duty to do it, and the teams will simply have to be much more careful and more aware of the dangers.

Finally, the BBC, CNN and many other companies decided they had to be represented in Baghdad. This was unpopular with the British and American governments; they knew that bombs and missiles would go astray from time to time and cause serious civilian casualties, which they would prefer people not to see. But the nature of twenty-four-hour news on dozens of channels around the world is now such that it is impossible to keep these things hidden; and even if none of the big national television organizations had kept teams in Baghdad, the pictures shot by the international agencies would still have appeared on the world's television screens.

This was a conflict in which, for once, the generals did not use the tactics of the previous war; yet they and the politicians failed to understand how the nature of television news had changed. In 1991, thanks to the foresight and flair of the anarchic Ted Turner, CNN was the only global television news organization in existence, and its reporting from Baghdad changed the nature of the first Gulf War. In the second Gulf War the BBC had taken over as the leading news broadcaster, but there were plenty of others in Baghdad, including four twenty-four-hour Arabic language services. CNN was eventually thrown out for its American-flavoured reporting, but the skill and innate balance of the BBC's two main correspondents in Baghdad, Rageh Omaar (himself a Muslim) and Paul Wood, just managed to ensure that the BBC hung on there. In 1991, when I reported the war from Baghdad, there were no more than twenty-five or thirty other reporters from all over the world. This time there were 1,500. The lesson had been learned: nowadays we have a duty to report wars from as many sides as possible.

50. THE NORTH

Personally, much as I appreciated the remarkable possibilities which 'embedded' correspondents would have for reporting from the front line, I could not myself think of joining their number. Maybe I was wrong; if I had, I would not have led my friend and translator Kamaran Abdurrazak Mohammed to his death, nor suffered mild but lasting injuries myself. But you are what you are, and if I had to make the decision again I would do exactly the same thing.

I wanted to go to Baghdad, of course, but as the war came closer and Baghdad seemed as closed to me as ever, I plumped for Kurdish northern Iraq. It had many advantages. It was, technically, still a part of Iraq, and it was possible to get close to Iraqi soldiers there. It seemed pretty likely, before the war started, that the Turkish government would allow American troops to move through Turkey and create a northern front, in which case we stood as good a chance as anyone else of getting to Baghdad first. Finally, northern Iraq was difficult to get to; its neighbours, Syria, Iran and Turkey, were all reluctant to allow too many foreigners across the border, and I would not have to battle through several thousand journalists as I would if I went to Kuwait. But it was a gamble. I realized that I could easily be sidelined.

In Afghanistan in 2001 I had been able to select my own team, and thanks to some luck and some good judgement the BBC was able to cover the true front line in the war and then make it to Kabul before everyone else. This time the luck, and maybe the good judgement too, was less in evidence. I was hoping to hire the famous combat cameraman Peter Jouvenal, who was based in Kabul, but our window of opportunity for getting into northern Iraq was extraordinarily narrow, and at the moment when Peter would have had to start the long and complicated journey to get to Turkey he lay ill in his room at the hotel he had opened in Kabul. (It was Osama bin Laden's old house, as it happens; we had visited it together on the day after Kabul fell, and agreed that it would make a superb place for journalists, politicians and aid workers to stay. Who could resist the attraction of a place in which bin Laden had secretly visited his family?) Now Peter was uncontactable; his servants at Château al-Qaeda said he was too ill to speak to, and by the time he had recovered sufficiently to leave his bed the moment had passed.

Turkey was our only possible route to northern Iraq, because the BBC had managed to offend both the Syrian and Iranian governments at once. Our producer, Oggy Boytchev, managed to get us on the only facility trip which the Turks offered journalists during this entire time, and in the last week of February 2003 our team gathered in Istanbul and flew south to the border, where the Turks shuttled us across by bus. We were supposed to come back a couple of weeks later, but both we and the Turkish authorities knew it wasn't going to happen.

There were six of us: Oggy, a quick-witted, charming, ambitious Bulgarian who had escaped to Britain during the Communist 1980s and joined the BBC's Bulgarian service before moving on to television news; Tom Giles, thoughtful, straight-dealing and courageous, one of the BBC's leading film-makers, who had been in charge of some of my most enjoyable and testing expeditions and was now making a programme for *Panorama* about our war; Fred Scott, a clever and sociable Californian cameraman, who had won various awards in his time and would win more as a result of this trip; Dragan Petrovic, a particular friend of mine from my days in Belgrade, tall and tough and as reliable in his understanding of the situation as in his rock-steady loyalty; Craig Summers, another tough character who had served in the British army and was now attached to us as a security adviser; and myself.

Our task was to report on the fighting in northern Iraq, and then get to Baghdad as quickly as possible. It sounded easy enough, but when we sat round a table at a dirty hotel in the ancient Kurdish city of Arbil and examined a map with some care, all of us were left with a serious feeling of foreboding; or, as Fred Scott put it, our backbones turned to jelly. Reporting the war in the northern sector was fine: whether or not the American army was able to open up a second front here, we would have plenty of news to report. The two main Kurdish political groups, the Kurdistan People's Party (KDP) and the Patriotic Union of Kurdistan (PUK) were both favourably disposed towards the BBC, we had a good set of colleagues working alongside us from the BBC bureau in Tehran – Jim Muir, a good friend of mine, his radio producer Stuart Hughes, and his Iranian cameraman Kaveh Golestan, whom I had known and liked for years – and the situation here was as fluid and open as the front line in Afghanistan had been, eighteen months earlier.

The other journalists in the area were blessedly few in number, and often highly convivial: among them, the glamorous, mercurial Charlie Glass of ABC News in New York, and the most renowned and gentle of war photographers, Don McCullin, now in his mid-sixties but as kind and friendly towards the young journalists who only knew him by name and reputation as he had been when I first met him in 1970 at the long-since destroyed City Hotel in Derry. I felt thoroughly at home in Arbil, and in the evenings we played poker – especially the weird varieties which Fred taught us, like Butcher's Boy and the use of the Death Card and the principle of Frontier Justice – drank whisky, smoked cigars, and talked obsessively about the past and the future.

That much was fine. The problem was, how would we get to Baghdad? There seemed to be two almost inevitable dangers: the Iraqis and the Americans. There were three major cities on our route to Baghdad – Kirkuk, Mosul and Tikrit – and getting from one to the

next as they fell seemed likely to be remarkably hazardous. The
retreating, surrendering Iraqis would be angry and resentful, and
would find an unarmed, heavily equipped television crew easy pickings.
By contrast, I knew the Americans would do what they always do:
shoot first and discover afterwards whom they have killed. The most
dangerous moment would be driving up to any American checkpoint,
since they would impose their own elaborate rules of approach without
necessarily telling anyone else what they were. And no recognition
symbols, no 'TV' signs marked out on the windows and sides of our
vehicles with camera tape, would make the slightest difference. If you
are a scared, indifferently trained, heavily armed nineteen-year-old
from Mobile or San Bernadino, any vehicle which drives up to your
position is a likely threat. And if your officers have told you that the
preservation of your own life comes before any other consideration,
then you are quite likely to shoot someone, just in case.

One night, early on during our time in Arbil, there was another
hotel guest sitting in the dining room. He was about five feet eight, in
his late fifties, lacked a finger on his left hand, and looked tough and
reliable and probably amusing. Just from looking at him, I could tell
he was an Israeli, but what on earth was an Israeli doing in northern
Iraq? It was one of the most dangerous places on earth for him. I asked
if he wanted to join our card game, simply to get in conversation. He
smiled, but shook his head. Card games weren't for him.

'My name is Ron ben-Yishai,' he said, in the kind of accent I
hadn't heard since I last interviewed Ehud Barak. And he added, 'I am
from——' and named a country so ludicrously unlikely that I couldn't
help laughing.

He knew I knew he was an Israeli. Long afterwards he said it had
given him a shock to realize I had twigged immediately, so wedded are
we to our comforting fictions about ourselves. He did indeed have a
passport from the country he had named, but to me that made it all
the more likely that anyone who guessed the truth about his real
citizenship would also assume he was working for Mossad.

I knew he was what he said he was: a television reporter. My hotel
room looked out on to the rooftop where he did his live broadcasts to
Israel. Early every morning he would set up a camera on a tripod, then
walk round, stand in front of it and start talking down some line he

had fixed up to his television station; I was transfixed. Unlike me, he had no back-up whatever, no colleagues, not much equipment, not a lot of cash. Ron was a loner.

My heart went out to a man who had the sheer *cojones* to run every risk imaginable to get good front-line access to this war. The fact that he was on his own, and perhaps that he was my age too, made me determined to help him. Journalists – real journalists, that is, not the characters who peddle their national myths for a living – have a fellow-feeling that overrides every national distinction. Being a journalist is a kind of nationality in itself, and real journalists can talk to each other on a level where national differences play no part.

There are scientists who want to ban Israeli scientists from publishing their research in British or French journals; there used to be bans on South African musicians, black as well as white, simply because they came from a country with a nasty regime. There are audiences in Europe who slow-handclap British businessmen because their government has taken a particular line over Iraq. Pretty stupid, you might think, and it is hard to have much respect for such exercises in mind-closing.

The morning after we had spoken, I saw Ron again. He knew, he said, that I realized where he came from. Could he ask me something? I nodded. If he got into trouble of some kind, would we help him? There was no doubt whatever in my mind; this was a duty. Anything we had, anything we could do, was his. If he wanted, when he wanted, he could be a part of the BBC team, and we would not allow anything to happen to him if we could help it. He held my hand tightly, and I grinned at him. He was a one-off, an extraordincary man. I admired him as a colleague.

For the rest of our time in Iraq, Ron operated in parallel with us, and I was grateful again and again for his wisdom, and for his courage in getting pictures and information which we needed. On balance, I think, we received more help from Ron than he received from us.

He told me how he had managed to get to Iraq. A group of smugglers had brought him in across the border from Turkey in a truck filled with bags of flour. They had constructed a wooden frame around him on the floor of the truck, under a ton or more of bags, and he sat hunched up there for hours, not knowing whether the props which protected him might splinter and break with the jolting of the truck, and leave him to be crushed to death under the weight of the flour.

For the next few weeks, Ron ben-Yishai's mordant humour kept us amused. When, finally, Saddam fell and the big advance came, Ron was in Kirkuk and Mosul before we were; and he allowed us to use the pictures he had shot of the fighting and violence. Showing a little solidarity with a lone journalist on a distinctly dodgy passport was one of the few good things I did during this war.

51. FIRST STRIKE

Tony Blair's assiduous loyalty to President George W. Bush was not reciprocated by Washington when the war began. Blair and his government presented Britain as America's steadfast partner, shoulder to shoulder in the attack on Saddam; for the Bush administration, British support was useful, on the whole, but could be taken more or less for granted. The British were hanging around somewhere in the rear, and would be told when they were wanted.

And so, when President Bush decided to launch the first missiles against Iraq two days before the agreed date, it was not the British whom the Americans told first; it was Israel. There were good reasons for that. Saddam's first response might well be to retaliate against Israel, and there was a very real danger that Israel would then stage an outright attack of its own against Iraq: something which would have been politically disastrous for the Coalition.

Still, exactly as happened in 1991, when the first Gulf War started without any consultation with the British, Tony Blair found out only after the attack had begun. All the Downing Street briefings about Britain's essential part in the planning of the war were shown to be wishful thinking. It was the kind of humiliation that is routinely handed out by a government which feels it has no particular reason to worry if it treads on other people's toes. As for the Australians, who were also taking part, their presence was scarcely even mentioned by the Americans.

Shortly after ten o'clock in the evening on Wednesday 19 March Washington time, three on Thursday morning London time and six on Thursday morning Baghdad time, Bush went on television to announce that the long-awaited war had begun.

> My fellow citizens, at this hour American and Coalition forces are in the early stages of military operations to disarm Iraq, to free its people, and to defend the world from grave danger. On my orders, Coalition forces have been striking selected targets of military importance to undermine Saddam Hussein's ability to wage war.

He stressed that the United States and its allies had no ambition in Iraq except to remove the threat which Saddam posed and to restore control of the country to its own people. His short address ended:

> We will defend our freedom. We will bring freedom to others and we will prevail. May God bless our country and all who defend her.

It sounded as though he was only talking to Americans, and so he was. 'On my orders' meant that there was only one boss of this operation, and the British, whatever they liked to think, had no commanding role in it.

It wasn't only the politicians in Britain who were annoyed; the spies were angry as well. In the run-up to the war the CIA and SIS had worked together closely and effectively, sharing agents and the means of communication with them. But the reason the war had started two days earlier than the British had been told to expect was because the CIA had information about Saddam Hussein's whereabouts which SIS had grounds for believing was false.

The CIA received information which had supposedly come from someone who was thought to be a close aide to Saddam: this said that Saddam was attending an emergency meeting with his two sons, Uday and Qusay, and other senior figures of his administration at al-Dawra Farm, an estate on the southern outskirts of Baghdad which had belonged to Hussein Kamel al-Majid. Now it belonged to his widow, Saddam's daughter Raghad.

More than four months later she told her interviewers at al-Arabiyah what had happened. It did not say much for the quality of the CIA's information.

'At six o'clock in the morning the first missile hit my farm at al-Dawra, when I was with my children. I had two houses at the farm, which were completely destroyed. Praise be to God, we had left the house a few hours before. It is said that the heart of a mother can tell. My mother came to us before dawn. She pleaded with me and my sister to leave the place. She said: Daughter, I feel your end will be here if you stay.

'I actually wanted to stay. They believed I was stubborn. I wanted to stay until the first missile fell on Baghdad and then I would move to the place they had arranged for me. God saved us from this ordeal. My sister left the farm a little while before I left. It was a few moments before the missile could have hit my children, my house or me. We stayed in a very simple military shelter we had built inside the farm. With God's help, the shelter protected us from that fate. We stayed about two and a half hours under the bombing. Ten missiles fell everywhere in my farm. Even the smallest buildings were destroyed, including a farmer's room.'

'So it was not a meeting of the Iraqi leadership?'

'No, not at all. The farm belonged to Hussein [Kamel].'

'Where was former President Saddam Hussein at the time?'

'I certainly did not know where he was. A person of his standing, under those difficult conditions, would not tell his family where he was.'

The information President Bush and his closest advisers were getting from the CIA presented them with a considerable temptation. None of them had any qualms about killing Saddam; on the contrary, they believed that if he died the war would be greatly shortened and lives would be saved. They probably weren't told that Britain's SIS did not believe the CIA's report; even if they had been, they would have taken no notice.

There were other problems about taking this action. A missile attack on al-Dawra would signal that the war had started. The Americans believed that directly this happened Saddam Hussein would order the blowing up of Iraq's oil-wells and the launching of missiles against Israel and the Coalition bases in Kuwait. Even so, Bush and his advisers thought it would be worth the risk. The word was given; ships of the US Navy fired a total of forty-two cruise missiles at al-Dawra, and several F-117A Stealth aircraft dropped 2,000-pound bombs on the site, each capable of burrowing its way deep underground and piercing through many metres of specially reinforced concrete.

It was all entirely wasted. Not only was Saddam not at al-Dawra Farm, he wasn't at any of his other bunkers around the country. According to a credible Iraqi military source, in these early stages of the campaign Saddam was driving around incognito in a small truck which he drove with a single bodyguard. He made no calls from a mobile phone; his instructions were delivered to his lieutenants by hand by trusted messengers.

While the White House and the Pentagon were still discussing the possibility that they had successfully 'decapitated' the Iraqi regime, Saddam Hussein was already working on a speech to show he was still alive. He wrote it himself by hand in a large notebook, and then drove to a small but effective studio which had been set up for his use, probably outside Baghdad. There was nothing on the set except an Iraqi flag and a blue curtain behind him. He recorded his speech, perhaps in a couple of takes, then headed off again. After a suitable interval the technicians drove the recording to Iraqi television so it could be broadcast.

It was obvious that various things were different from his usual television appearances. In his previous speech, a couple of days earlier, he had had the attentions of a trained make-up artist. Now he looked older and more strained, and his moustache seemed greyer; no make-up, therefore. He also wore unfashionably large reading spectacles, peering down at the words he had written in his notebook and turning over the pages in a way he had never had to do before. No teleprompt either, then. Make-up artists and teleprompt operators may ensure a better performance, but for Saddam security was what counted, and security was best served by ensuring that as few people as possible knew where he was.

There were some desultory attempts by Donald Rumsfeld at the Pentagon and by the spokesmen in Doha and Kuwait to suggest that we had seen one of Saddam Hussein's doubles, and that the man himself had been killed. It was foolishness. What distinguished the doubles from the original was that they never spoke in public. A few syllables of that harsh voice with its peasant accent were invariably enough to show that Saddam Hussein himself was speaking.

The performance was a curious one, full not just of the usual bombastic stuff about the eternal courage of Iraq and the struggle of the Palestinian people but containing one or two idiosyncratic touches which he had never put into any of his previous speeches. In particular, at one point he broke into verse which he had apparently written himself. It was empty, mawkish stuff, almost impossible to translate, which tried to imitate classical Arabic poetry but contained several careless lapses into modern idiom which purists found irritating. Only Saddam, who cared for no one's opinion and whom no one ever dared to correct, would have made such a speech.

But it had its effect. The entire direction of the war had been changed on the turn of a card by President Bush, and the gamble had failed. The great attack, built around the concept of 'shock and awe', had lapsed immediately into bathos. There was little shock, and no awe whatsoever. The plan had been to destroy Iraq's ability to exist as a functioning society, and to force out Saddam's regime through brute strength. The Americans had shown in Baghdad twelve years before, and in Belgrade and Kabul more recently, that it was possible to do this if sufficient force were brought to bear, and the strategy didn't have to kill civilians in large numbers if the target intelligence was good enough.

This time, having changed the plan at the very outset, the American missiles had no very devastating effect on Iraq's ability to function. For most of the war, for instance, Iraqi television was up and running, and there was sufficient electricity for most people who were able to receive its programmes to watch Saddam Hussein at least once a day. That was of great value to his supporters, since it gave ordinary Iraqis the sense that even now Saddam was still a major force to be reckoned with.

All the old conspiracy theories about the Americans wanting to keep Saddam in power surfaced in Iraq again, with the result, of course, that even those who genuinely regarded the British and American forces as their liberators were wary of coming out to greet them. If the Americans wanted to keep Saddam as a puppet ruler, people reasoned, then this could simply be a ruse to bring his enemies out into the open where he could recognize them and destroy them.

For all the intense planning that had gone into it, therefore, the war as it was actually fought was an improvised, hurried business. Yet it didn't make much difference. Far worse tactics would have produced the same result, because the odds were so hugely stacked in favour of the Americans and their British and Australian allies. The United States lavished $400 billion on its armed forces – almost half the entire world's spending on defence. Saddam Hussein had only been able to afford about $1 billion.

The Americans had the best-provided army the world had ever seen; the British forces, though far smaller and absurdly badly equipped – Silverman's, the main military outfitters in London, ran out of army boots and a range of other equipment because the soldiers often had to buy their own gear there – were the best trained army anywhere. Side by side with the American forces, British sergeants found they routinely undertook responsibilities which were not allowed to American captains.

This was never likely, therefore, to be much of a contest. In the first Gulf War, as we have seen, there had been much talk about the sheer size of the Iraqi army; in the second, there was great anxiety about the possibility that Saddam Hussein would use chemical or biological weapons, or maybe even nuclear ones. Notions like these gave a brooding sense of uncertainty to the preparations for war, and no one who was involved in the fighting or reporting of either Gulf War was entirely free of anxiety about what was to come.

And yet nothing did come. It was a pushover, with no serious hitches. Often, as in the first Iraq war, the main danger was the Americans themselves, who seemed to find it hard to distinguish between their friends and their enemies.

The wars the United States fought at the end of the twentieth century and the start of the twenty-first were very much the same as the small colonial wars the British fought in the period from 1870 to 1899: set-piece conflicts against native armies which were largely untrained and hopelessly outgunned. Nineteenth-century intellectuals such as Hilaire Belloc found the combination of rampant chauvinism and racial and technological superiority disgusting:

> Whatever happens, we have got
> The Maxim gun, and they have not

he wrote mockingly. He would have recognized the same instincts at work in American public opinion in 2003. The Iraqis had no planes or ground-to-air missiles to speak of, so the Coalition forces had total command of the air. Their forces matched the Iraqis in terms of numbers, and every piece of equipment they had, from assault rifles to tanks, was better designed, better maintained, and more effective. The years of sanctions, the persistent air attacks, the controls on the import of weapons, had reduced Iraq's armed forces to the level of scarecrows. They were useful for only one thing: terrorizing the civilians of Iraq. For Saddam Hussein, that was their most important function.

52. THE KURDS AT WAR

In Arbil, we had an interesting job to do, and the danger was strictly limited. Occasionally, as when the CNN correspondent Brent Sadler was trying to record a piece to camera on a bridge in full sight of the Iraqi troops opposite, there was the possibility of attracting an incoming mortar round; once, a shell passed uncomfortably close over the heads of Julian Mannion of ITN and his crew and narrowly missed the house we used for our forward reporting position.

Our war could not have been more different from that of the embedded journalists travelling with the American and British forces in the south. In many ways it was more intriguing and difficult, but there was no denying that those of us in northern Iraq felt that we were completely in the wrong place. (The BBC News 24 presenter Peter Sissons, who used to present the flagship 10 O'Clock News on BBC 1, pointed this out to me on air; it wasn't particularly kind of him, but I couldn't deny it.) It was only afterwards, when I compared notes with 'embedded' friends of mine, that I realized this was a war in which all but about three or four correspondents felt that everyone else was having a more interesting time than they were.

Nevertheless, we had our moments. One of the best things we did was to hire the services of an Afghan stills photographer called Abdullah Zaheeruddin, a delightful and idiosyncratic companion with the knack of making friends with absolutely everyone. The Kurds loved him, because he habitually wore a black and white Kurdish scarf round his neck, spoke a variety of Persian which they could just understand, and managed to persuade them that Afghans and Kurds were closely related. During the years of Communist rule in Afghanistan Abdullah had been reduced to driving a taxi in order to survive, but he had the good fortune to pick up John Burns of the *New York Times* as a fare, and John immediately spotted his remarkable qualities and hired him for the rest of his visit.

When they parted, John gave him a tip of 100 US dollars – an unthinkably large amount of money in Kabul at the time. Resisting all temptation, Abdullah went straight off and spent the money on a course of English lessons, and when his sketchy English won him more jobs with visiting foreign journalists he ploughed that money, too, into further lessons. I still found it quite hard sometimes to work out what he was saying, but his enthusiasm and good humour gave him a universality which appealed to all of us. He took to poker so well that it was occasionally hard to think he had never played before ('I'm have two ladies and three As,' he once said, artlessly holding up a pair of queens and three aces. It was one of the best full houses of our entire trip, and he scooped the large pool containing dozens of matchsticks, trouser-buttons and dinar notes).

His main contribution to our war coverage was the relationship he built up with the local KDP commander, a big bear of a man called Nariman, who controlled the entire front line in the Arbil sector. This faced both the Iraqi strongholds of Kirkuk and Mosul and straddled the road that led directly to Baghdad, 180 kilometres away to the south. Thanks to Abdullah, whom he loved as a brother, Nariman was superbly accommodating and allowed us to film everywhere we wanted. If he had been able to do it, he would have smuggled Tom Giles and me across the front line into Mosul, but neither he nor a couple of thoroughly dubious local characters whom Craig Summers contacted were able in the end to pull it off. Nevertheless we had the best access to the fighting of any of the journalists working in our area.

Our team grew. In the manner of television crews we hired four-by-four vehicles and drivers and translators and people to read the newspapers, and got special access at a nearby internet café. Everyone knew us: our reports for BBC World seemed to be watched by the entire town. One day, as I walked into the lobby of our hotel, the

Arbil Tower, a tall, bulky man in his early twenties stood up and greeted me. He had a pleasant face, and a thin 1940s moustache. Altogether, I felt, he looked less like a Kurd than a Mexican bandleader, heavily handsome and well dressed, surprisingly quick for his size, and distinctly courtly in manner.

'My name is Kamaran, sir,' he said, with the faintest of bows. 'I have seen you on television, and I would like to work for you.'

Normally I would have asked him to speak to Oggy Boytchev, who was in charge of hiring (and of firing, which he positively seemed to enjoy sometimes). But there was an engaging, slightly artless quality about this Kamaran which I liked. In this matter of hiring translators it is more important to get someone you can trust to tell you the truth and to stick with you in difficult situations than to get someone with perfect English or the right qualifications. Personally, I prefer to hire students, because they usually have an idealism about them which tends to override the calculation and official-speak of older people.

'That's fine by me,' I said, 'but you know that our job is often quite dangerous. We spend a lot of time down at the front line.'

I could feel the gaze of the useless characters behind the reception desk, and the curious glances of the supernumeraries who hung out in the lobby watching al-Jazeera and the BBC on the vast screen against the wall. Any activity attracted their attention, but the hiring of local staff was the most interesting activity of all. I steered Kamaran towards the lifts: there was a broadcast to be done, and I didn't want to hang around. It usually took ages for the sole working lift to appear: the staff liked to use it to go up a single floor, in preference to walking.

Kamaran was still thinking about what I had just said.

'I like adventures,' he said simply. And then he added, in words that went straight to my heart, 'And I would like to be your friend.'

He put his hand out. I shook it, in a gesture which I suppose sealed his fate. He had about another month to live.

Kamaran was a good translator: the best we had. He was also brave. It was distasteful and rather indecent to have to explain to him that we didn't have enough flak-jackets to provide him with one, and even at the time I decided I would never embark on an enterprise like this again without the proper equipment for everyone in the team. Why should I have the most expensive body-armour money could buy, while Kamaran had none at all? Why should my life be regarded as more valuable than his? But he accepted the absence of a flak-jacket as one of the conditions of working with us, and he said he didn't mind.

He was good at explaining the intricacies of Kurdish politics to me, though he knew less about Saddam's Iraq: he had been only thirteen when the Kurds were given their partial independence at the initiative of John Major in 1991. Would he come all the way to Baghdad with us? God willing, he said; that would indeed be a serious adventure.

By the third week in March the Kurdish forces were pressing forward continually, and the Iraqi troops were falling back little by little, abandoning villages and trench-lines and sometimes entire stretches of arid country to them. Once we thought we had found the story of the war so far. At a small village which the Iraqi troops had just evacuated, the Kurds discovered a training school in the use of chemical and biological weapons.

On the door was a piece of card with the name of the officer in charge, and his designation: Chemical Warfare Officer. There was a heap of documents on the floor, and a number of placards pinned to the walls of the classroom. Most of them showed the use and management of poison gas: how the weapons were fired, how soldiers should protect themselves from the effects. I rang the newsdesk; they were excited about the possibility.

Tom Giles and I knew we had to be 100 per cent certain about all this; 99 per cent would not be enough. Unfortunately Kamaran wasn't with us that day. Our stand-in translator was a plausible enough character, but his English was always a little hard to follow and neither Tom nor I felt entirely confident about him. Time was pressing. We took the documents back to our front-line house, which looked across the river at the Iraqi positions, and went through the documents carefully with him, one by one.

The poor man floundered.

'Does it say precisely who is using these weapons?'

The translator went off into a misty, hard-to-follow explanation.

'But what was the officer trying to teach the men? How to use the weapons or how to protect themselves if the Americans used poison gas?'

More impenetrable English.

'I don't think we've got a story,' I said. 'Or at least, I don't think we can be certain we've got one.'

'And we've got to be certain,' Tom agreed.

We both knew how delighted the British and American governments would be if we ran a story that said we had found signs that
Iraqi front-line troops were preparing to use chemical weapons. An
American television team had already done precisely that, but hadn't
produced the final proof. We summoned the poor perplexed translator
back, and gave him another grilling. At one point it all seemed to turn
on whether a verb was in the active or passive form; at another,
whether a word could be translated 'is' or 'could be'. His English
collapsed entirely under the strain, and he went off into Arabic.

'It's not there,' said Tom.

I think I had guessed it all along. At that stage I still believed that
the Iraqis had tactical weapons of mass destruction which they might
possibly use at some stage, but if they had been available to relatively
low-level combat troops like this, then surely someone would have
used them before now.

An hour after I had had to ring the newsdesk to tell them we
wouldn't have a report for that night's news, the translator walked
triumphantly into the room with a couple of documents under his arm.

'They not using them, just teaching,' he announced.

At least we knew we'd done the right thing. But I was very sorry
we'd left Kamaran behind that day; he would never have taken so long
to tell us we didn't have a story.

53. GETTING IT WRONG

It's always difficult to admit you have made a mistake; especially
publicly. There are always detractors and, alas, colleagues who will
seek to use your confessions against you. But if you are in the truth
business, or at any rate set out to be a purveyor of accuracy, it is
unavoidable from time to time. You have to grit your teeth, find the
right words, and hit the 'send' button; and it's surprising, afterwards,
how much better you feel.

I never supported or opposed the idea of a second Iraqi war in
my *Sunday Telegraph* column, of course, but I did make it clear that

I expected that most Iraqis would come out in full support of the invaders, not because they liked the Americans and British, but because they hated Saddam Hussein.

Maybe, if the Coalition had made it abundantly clear from the start that they were determined to overthrow Saddam once and for all, the Iraqi people would have shown more enthusiasm towards them. But they allowed Saddam's television service to remain on the air, and that persuaded most Iraqis that they would play the same game they had played in 1991, and allow him back into power again.

When the invasion started, and the Iraqis were obviously hesitant about coming forward to greet the invaders, it slowly became clear that there was a much greater level of opposition to the Coalition forces this time than there had been in 1991. I had got it wrong. I assumed the Iraqi military would simply surrender in enormous numbers, and I quoted King Abdullah of Jordan as saying that the Coalition's chief problems would be deciding which among the dozens of generals driving out to meet them with white flags they would be able to trust.

I wrote an article for the *Sunday Telegraph* which admitted that I had been wrong. It caused a minor fuss, and I must have been interviewed for about twenty programmes inside and outside the BBC. Some of the interviewers sounded as though they could scarcely contain their delight, although I felt that was the kind of thing I had to endure for being wrong in the first place. But I felt better afterwards, all the same.

In February 2003, a month before the invasion began, I sat in a studio at Central Hall, Westminster, together with sixty or so other people, taking part in a *Panorama* discussion about the coming war in Iraq. I knew it was pointless my being there: if you divided the length of airtime available for the programme by the number of guests who had been invited to speak, it was plain that only a quarter of us could hope to see our words broadcast. And as a BBC employee (family, therefore) my contribution was even less likely to be used than those of more exotic guests: ministers, ambassadors, luminaries of different kinds.

On a huge screen overhanging the studio appeared the dark, louring features of Richard Perle, the closest figure the programme's organizers could get to the Pentagon. In fact Perle had recently been obliged to resign his position over a conflict-of-interest issue, but he certainly spoke for Donald Rumsfeld and Paul Wolfowitz, and was himself one of the leading influences behind the new imperialist thrust of the Bush administration.

What, he was asked, did he expect would happen when American troops invaded Iraq and fought their way through to Baghdad? People would come pouring out to greet them as liberators, he replied.

There was a snort of contempt from the handsome, grey-haired figure beside me: Tariq Ali, no longer the sixties firebrand but a trenchant critic of American influence in the world. Beside him an answering snort came from Bianca Jagger, whom I had rather less time for, having once observed a grandstanding visit she made to her native Nicaragua at a time of hunger and great deprivation, and seen the amount of clothes she had brought with her.

'Never!' she said.

I muttered something about socialite politicos to my other neighbour. What did either of them know about the likely reaction of Iraqis who had been enslaved by Saddam Hussein's brutal system for so long? It seemed to me, perhaps wrongly, that these two had bought into the notion which seemed always to float unspokenly in the air when opponents of American action were gathered together: that Saddam was exactly what he claimed to be, a popular leader beloved of his entire people. Much the same people had said much the same thing about the Taliban, who were so loathed by most Afghans. Once upon a time they had said much the same thing about Nicolae Ceausescu and Todor Zhivkov and the rest of the gang who ran Eastern Europe for the Russians; and about the Soviet system itself, which crashed unwanted in a matter of days.

I found myself in the middle of all this. My six months in Baghdad in 1990–91 had convinced me that every single Iraqi except those whose fortunes were most closely tied to Saddam's longed to get rid of him. Nobody – the civil servants, the soldiers, the secret policemen, the politicians, the generals, the shopkeepers, the housewives – wanted Saddam Hussein to rule them any more. His regime meant bloodshed and poverty and national isolation. 'The one who confronts' had lived up to his name far too well. The Iraqis overwhelmingly wanted a quieter and better life, and I felt they deserved it.

At the same time, I found the rhetoric and the ideas of the ultra-right in America deeply distasteful, and the thought that a new imperial force was trying to establish itself in the world seemed as wrong as it was absurd. I was, therefore, what Americans would call 'conflicted'. I could understand the attitude of the radical British (but increasingly American) journalist Christopher Hitchens, who felt Saddam's crimes were so disgusting that he was even prepared to support George W. Bush in overthrowing him, but I could also understand the opinions of the writer and film-maker Michael Moore, a man I took to for his wit and his humanity the moment I met him, who shouted an attack on Bush and the war above the howls of outrage (and the applause) at the 2003 Oscars ceremony.

> We like non-fiction and we live in fictitious times. We live in a time where we have fictitious election results that elect a fictitious president. We live in a time where we have a man sending us to war for fictitious reasons.

I did, however, expect that people would come out and greet the British and American troops with gratitude as liberators. But I had not been allowed back to Iraq during those twelve years, and I failed to understand all the many changes that had come over the country since then. In particular, I got three things wrong.

For a start, I completely underestimated the extent to which the United States had become identified as Saddam Hussein's ally. It was, after all, George Bush senior's terrible miscalculation to have urged the Shi'ites and Kurds to rise up against Saddam, then allowed Colin Powell to talk him out of doing anything to help them. By betraying the uprisings and allowing Saddam to remain in power and wreak his vengeance on them, the United States had made itself as much the enemy of large sections of the Iraqi people as Saddam himself was.

The second mistake I made was to forget what an impact twelve years of American- and British-sponsored sanctions had had on the people of Iraq. The poor starved, and their children died in unprecedented numbers; the well-to-do watched their savings and their assets evaporate as they too sank into abject poverty. Pretty stupid, you might think, to believe the Americans and British could destroy a country and then expect the victims to come out and cheer them in the streets.

Third, I forgot the effect it was likely to have on the people of a country to invade them, bomb their cities and kill their soldiers while maintaining they were only there as liberators. If the Americans had succeeded in killing Saddam on that first morning, 20 March, at al-Dawra Farm, then most Iraqis would have greeted them with gratitude. But it didn't happen. The Americans didn't even manage to kill him or capture him for months after the end of the war. Everything was done ham-fistedly and without proper thought, and none of us should have been surprised that what the Coalition thought was a simple, surgical process was in fact clumsy, unskilful and much resented.

54. ADVANCING

It didn't turn out as the military had predicted. Certainly the Iraqi troops surrendered in large numbers, as we had all expected. But that did not mean the end of resistance. On the contrary, Saddam Hussein's careful planning ensured that there were hundreds of specially trained troops from the so-called Saddam Brigade hidden in the towns and villages along the invasion route of the Americans and British, and they staged a courageous guerrilla campaign which held the invaders at bay for an embarrassing length of time.

Nothing like this had occurred during the first Gulf War, and it was clear that in spite of all the empty, boastful rhetoric that issued from Saddam and his ministers about the dauntless will of the Iraqi people, they had a very clear idea of what was likely to happen this time. They planned for it accordingly.

By contrast, it seems that the American military leadership were expecting a re-run of the first Gulf War, and were surprised by the extent of the resistance. The pattern of the war's opening stages was set at Umm Qasr, a little port just across the Kuwaiti border. An American military spokesman announced within hours that US forces had captured Umm Qasr; instead, snipers hidden in private houses and old, abandoned warehouses waited until the American marines who had spearheaded the attack were past, then opened fire on them.

Over the next six days, fewer than fifty guerrillas endured everything the Americans could throw at them. The invaders' firepower was overwhelming, yet the Iraqis still held out. It created a legend of resistance which even those who welcomed the eventual overthrow of Saddam Hussein would take pride in. The guerrillas did not, of course, fight in uniform; they seemed like any other civilians until they opened up with automatic weapons or threw hand grenades. This led to another, equally disturbing feature of the fighting: the lack of discrimination on the part of the American forces. As had happened thirty years before in Vietnam, any civilian the Americans spotted was in danger of being killed as an enemy.

The battle for Umm Qasr was not to be the pattern for the rest of the war. The Iraqi guerrillas who fought there were specially chosen for the task, and knew they had to sell their lives dearly. At Safwan, not far away, there was no real resistance. Yet it was obvious that the inhabitants were scared of welcoming the invaders; they remembered the terrible penalty people had paid in 1991 for coming out to greet the Coalition forces. In towns and villages throughout southern Iraq, the Americans found to their surprise that people didn't believe they were there to overthrow Saddam Hussein; they had drawn all the wrong conclusions from the events of twelve years before.

Saddam's strategy seemed to be based on the certainty that the Americans and British would win, but he wanted the victory to be as slow and embarrassing as possible for them. After that his main imperative would be to remain at large, and hope that the guerrilla war his followers were fighting would eventually bring so many American casualties that Washington would be forced to withdraw from Iraq altogether.

The Coalition's strategy was, in its way, simpler. The attack would be composed of three main thrusts: the first would head along the eastern bank of the Euphrates; the second would move along the western bank to Kerbala and on to Baghdad, and the third would make its way north between the Tigris and Euphrates via Kut al-Amara, the scene of one of the British army's worst defeats in the First World War. The Americans and British would capture Basra, Iraq's second city, and the British would occupy it, pacifying southern Iraq while the Americans headed on northwards. The Coalition forces would, where possible, avoid the bigger centres of population and leave it till later to subdue them. There would be no painfully slow progress, capturing one town and moving on to the next. Getting to Baghdad was the prize.

The expectation on the Coalition side had been that the Shi'ite population of southern Iraq would mostly greet the Americans and British as liberators. This turned out to be wrong. It wasn't merely the result of being betrayed in 1991; those Shi'ites who were most opposed to Saddam were also most likely to be anti-Western, thanks to the radicalizing influence of Iran. The Shi'ites had also suffered disproportionately from sanctions.

But there was never the slightest doubt that the Americans would win. In the open desert and countryside their advance was fast and often unopposed; and where it was opposed the intensity of US firepower ensured there would only be one possible outcome. The problems always came in the towns. One of the toughest battles came in the area of Nasiriyah, south-east of Baghdad, where the roads to the north cross the Euphrates. The US casualties were relatively heavy here, and inevitably Iraqi civilians as well as guerrillas died in sizeable numbers. These things meant the Americans were not greatly loved; something they found hard to understand. They knew they were there as liberators. How come the Iraqis didn't realize it?

The fundamental mistake about the way the Coalition forces were likely to be received affected the British as well. A military spokesman forecast that the Americans would be in Baghdad in a matter of days – a serious underestimate. It also presumably gave rise to the British claim that an uprising against Saddam's forces had begun in Basra. On the basis of what happened in the first Gulf War that seemed entirely feasible, but it wasn't true, and caused a good deal of embarrassment for the British. They described Shi'ite casualties as 'horrific'. Then a correspondent for the Arabic-language television news channel al-Jazeera inside Basra reported that no uprising of any kind had taken place. It all seemed like official propaganda of the worst kind, and a serious misunderstanding of the effect that television reporting was to have on the conduct of the war.

At the end of the first week the American advance was bogged down in the worst sandstorm for ten years. The sand worked its way into everything: the gearboxes of 'desertized' engines, the most carefully protected parts of a gun's mechanism, the most intimate parts of the body. From experience I knew how it felt in your eyes and on everything you touched, rubbing and grinding and clogging everything, and turning the entire world a strange reddish colour.

In other ways too it was becoming clear that what Donald Rumsfeld had called 'the best-planned campaign in the history of warfare' was not going as it should. Logistically, the military effort was superb; not even in the first Gulf War had medical aid, food and water been so easily available to the troops. Yet no one at the Pentagon seems to have reflected on the fact that in the age of the television war, old-fashioned delays in looking after the needs of civilians would not look particularly impressive.

At Safwan, Zubayr and other towns the Americans dropped supplies from the air, but found that this led only to terrible fights on the ground, which the fittest and most able invariably won while the television news cameras captured the results. At Umm Qasr, close enough to the Kuwaiti border to be able to see the explosions from there with the naked eye, it was three long days before the British were able to bring in supplies on a sufficient scale to satisfy the needs of the population. There too the locals fought each other for food and water. It was ugly, and reflected badly on the entire military effort.

There was a distinct feeling of unease in London, where a leading official called it 'a Week One wobble'; in Washington, where the realization that American troops were being treated more as enemies than liberators was starting to sink in; and on the ground among the Coalition forces.

'The enemy we're fighting is different from the one we'd wargamed against,' said the commander of the US Fifth Corps, Lt-General William Wallace, and although he was much criticized by guests on Rupert Murdoch's super-patriotic Fox News for saying so, it was plainly true.

In 2003, as in 1991, the people of Baghdad quickly came to realize that the weapons which were being used against their city were usually precise, and at first they decided they had nothing very much to fear from them. The missiles and bombs tended to fall at particular times, and the notion of 'shock and awe' had been forgotten to such an extent that the old Iraqi suspicion that the Coalition wanted Saddam to survive was once again beginning to surface. Many of the sites which were being bombed again and again were places ordinary Iraqis would not be able to approach anyway: Saddam's palaces, and the premises of the military, the security services and the Ba'ath Party.

This appearance of accuracy encouraged many American correspondents to repeat the kind of thing the Pentagon told them, without troubling to examine the reality. One correspondent, Jim Miklasz-ewski, was certain about it.

> More than a thousand bombs and missiles were dropped on Baghdad [in the first two evenings of the war], three times the entire number from the entire Gulf War. And this time, they're all precision-guided, deadly accurate, designed to kill only the targets, not innocent civilians.

It was guilt-free warfare. These precision-guided missiles were able to detect the secrets of the heart, seeking out only the guilty while allowing the innocent to rest easy.

Unfortunately, it wasn't like that. On the seventh day of the war, with the dust from the desert sandstorm hanging blood-red in the air, there was a savage reminder that there was no such thing as deadly accuracy. By error or misjudgement an American aircraft dropped two bombs on a busy market in the working-class suburb of Shaab, in northern Baghdad. The Iraqi government, whose casualty figures were often surprisingly accurate, announced that thirty-six people had been killed and more than 200 injured. Given that the explosions blew up a petrol tanker as well as a dozen or more vehicles, this is not impossible.

At US Central Command in Doha, where the set on which the American, British and Australian spokespeople appeared had been planned by a team of Hollywood designers, the hapless Brigadier Vincent Brooks, who always seemed liable to get things wrong, tried to suggest that the Coalition was not responsible.

'We think it is entirely possible that this may have been an Iraqi missile,' he said.

It seldom pays to underestimate people's intelligence, and in this case it didn't work at all. There was never any serious question that the bombs were dropped by Coalition planes, and although the American press and television gamely carried Brigadier Brooks's attempted disclaimer, it was treated as absurd everywhere else in the world.

Two days later, still with no proper admission of liability from the Americans, there was an even worse disaster: up to sixty civilians were killed by a huge explosion at Shawala in southern Baghdad.

If there ever had been a possibility that a quick, successful invasion, welcomed by the mass of the Iraqi people, would silence the critics of the war around the world, this was the moment when it finally evaporated. The war was an ugly business, often carelessly and brutally fought, and it would not win over anyone who had originally had doubts about it. The British government had tried hard to present it in terms of a moral crusade, but it was now clearly all about power: the American ability to blast through any obstacle and conquer.

It had become reminiscent of the Boer War, in which Britain's military superiority had suddenly been placed in question and it had to win, whatever tactics might be necessary. Wars are never easy, pleasant things, but this one had become particularly brutal, very fast: bigger payloads of explosive were being used closer to civilian centres, cluster bombs were being used by both the Americans and the British (though, as during the NATO attack on Serbia, the British were able to deny on a technicality that they were using them). Cluster bombs are some of the most vicious weapons of modern warfare, deliberately designed to kill people in large numbers. When used in towns and cities (for instance Nis in Serbia, and Nasiriyah, Najaf and Kerbala in Iraq), there may well be a case for inquiring whether their use constitutes a war crime.

By 31 March the American Marines' Fifth Regiment were only an hour's drive away from Baghdad. The Republican Guards, about whom so much had been written, had scarcely been seen. Somehow, though, this did not calm the anxieties of the Coalition troops; maybe the Iraqis were simply trying to draw them into the streets of Baghdad, where they would fight a ferocious urban guerrilla war – or maybe they would even unleash the weapons we had all been told so much about. This entire middle part of the war was a time of growing uneasiness, which the military spin-doctors tried to assuage with a calming fantasy: the rescue of Private Jessica Lynch from an Iraqi hospital. Private Lynch was a nineteen-year-old from Virginia who had suffered serious injuries and had behaved – so the spin-doctors maintained – with remarkable heroism. She was young and frail and rather pretty, and the entire rescue, which was a model of good planning and minimal force, was filmed in the eerie green light of a night-sight.

Unfortunately, to borrow Michael Moore's savage expression, her own exploits were fictitious. But the American press loved the story, and magazines and newspapers across the country predictably reproduced the headline 'Saving Private Lynch', a reference to the fictional treatment of a real rescue in a real war. This was a real rescue too, but it certainly wasn't D-Day and the requisite elements of danger and heroism were distinctly on the light side.

The story as presented by the official US spokesmen centred on the ambush on 23 March by Iraqi guerrillas of a detachment from the US 507th Maintenance Company, largely made up of cooks and mechanics. It was a serious setback by Coalition standards: eleven Americans were killed and six, including Private Jessica Lynch, were captured. Maybe the extent of the disaster, which was on a scale the Iraqis experienced every day but which produced the worst casualties of the war at that stage for the Americans, encouraged the Pentagon's press department to put a favourable spin on the story and deflect anxieties back home.

The more gullible newspapers and television and radio outlets reported it in these terms – including a ninety-minute fight to the death where Private Lynch had defended her comrades by blasting away at an overwhelming number of Iraqi soldiers until she finally collapsed from bullet and stab wounds. She was carried to a hospital where, the stories hinted, she had been badly treated. Not long afterwards a group of American special forces soldiers surrounded the hospital in Nasiriyah and, after a fierce battle, rescued Jessica Lynch and the other American patients.

In July 2003, a US army investigation into the circumstances surrounding the incident indicated that most of the 'Saving Private Lynch' story had been invented. The report showed there had been little heroism involved, and it seems that the Iraqi soldiers who attacked the convoy had been few in number. It is possible to detect a certain military disdain coming through the text of the report for the way the entire business was handled.

It all had been a serious mistake, though the report concluded that each member of the unit had performed honourably and done his or her duty. The original problem had arisen when the column of eighteen vehicles and thirty-three soldiers was trying to find a road, code-named Route Jackson, around the town of Nasiriyah. Somehow the commander of the column, Captain Troy King, managed to lose contact with the 600 other Coalition vehicles he was travelling with and took a road which led directly into the centre of the town. At that stage Nasiriyah was still controlled by forces loyal to Saddam Hussein. Captain King and his party had been on the road for nearly seventy hours and they were very tired.

When Captain King realized his mistake he tried to turn back, and at that point his vehicles came under what the report called 'sporadic small arms fire'. Disasters followed each other in quick succession: some of the group's radio batteries were dead, one vehicle ran out of fuel, the main 50-calibre machine-gun and several other weapons jammed. They fought until they couldn't resist any more. Only eight vehicles containing sixteen soldiers managed to escape. As for Private Lynch, the report said she sustained her numerous injuries when her vehicle was hit by a rocket-propelled grenade and crashed into one of the other vehicles. The four other passengers in the vehicle were killed.

So she had no stab wounds, and she wasn't shot. Nor did she fight for her own or anyone else's life. As for the suggestion that she might have been mistreated by the staff at the Iraqi hospital, the report did not dignify that by investigating it. Nor did it say anything about the technicolored accounts of her last stand which the army spin doctors passed on to the American press.

Private Lynch's experiences were unquestionably pretty horrific, and no doubt she behaved with considerable courage. Tactfully, she always insisted that she couldn't remember what happened when she was injured: her memory, she said, went blank. None of the absurd hype that surrounded the case came from her; it was all the invention of the US Army spinners, and a credulous press desperate for some genuine heroics in a war which seemed disturbingly short of gallantry. Genuine heroics are hard to get in a war this one-sided, so they had been invented to order. Fortunately the US Army inquiry was properly conducted and honest.

As for the rescue from the hospital, that too seems to have been largely fictional. A BBC team which visited it later found that the Iraqi army had fled from the place the day before the rescue happened. There had been a great deal of shooting, but none of it was directed at the rescue party. All the evidence was that they sprayed bullets everywhere to deter anyone from firing at them, and it worked. The sound-track sounded extraordinary on the television pictures, but the viewer had no way of knowing that the guns were all being fired by the Americans.

It would be interesting to know what the US special forces who carried out the rescue at the hospital thought about the whole thing. Both in northern Iraq and two years earlier in Afghanistan I had come across a number of these men and found them impressive. They were well trained and, unlike so many of the US marines and ordinary soldiers who took part in the second Gulf War, fully aware of the nature of the fighting they were involved with. In Afghanistan their comments on the behaviour of the rest of the US army were blisteringly contemptuous; they sympathized with the Afghan and Pakistani victims, and I sometimes had the feeling they thought more highly of their al-Qaeda enemies than they did of their fellow-soldiers.

What really happened in the case of Private Jessica Lynch, therefore, was that she was injured in the kind of accident that happens in wartime, taken to hospital by the Iraqis, cared for quite well, then 'rescued' by troops who in reality faced no threat to themselves. The real victims in this particular firefight were the international press, who believed everything the American military authorities told them, without troubling to check the facts or put in the necessary caveats.

But then sections of the American media were acting as irregular forces for the Bush administration anyway. A couple of commentators on Fox News agreed that the Coalition should target Iraqi journalists.

> *John Gibson:* Should we take Iraqi TV off the air? Should we put one down the stove-pipe there?
> *Bill O'Reilly:* Why haven't they taken out the Iraqi television towers yet?

On 26 March, the seventh day of the war, a joint US/UK bombing mission did indeed take out the Iraqi television station, maintaining that it was 'part of a command and control centre', and that the station was housed in 'a key telecommunications vault' for satellite communications. The television station was in a residential area, and several civilians were killed. The Iraqi authorities had been expecting an attack, so Iraqi TV was broadcasting again very quickly. The International Press Institute declared that the attack was a violation of the Geneva Convention and of the Universal Declaration of Human Rights; Amnesty International questioned whether it might constitute a war crime; Human Rights Watch and Reporters Sans Frontières both condemned it outright.

John Gibson of Fox News, by contrast, claimed the credit for this attack.

'Fox's criticism about allowing Saddam Hussein to talk to his citizens and lie to them has had an effect,' he said.

For me, it was an unpleasant reminder of the attack on Serbian television during the NATO bombing campaign of 1999. The government of Slobodan Milosevic seemed to regard the attack as a propaganda bonus, and had warned the management to stay away from the building at night-time, when the bombs tended to fall. The only people who were in the building, and who died when it was attacked, were ordinary employees: the make-up lady who used to get me ready for live broadcasts, for instance, and the studio cameramen who operated the equipment. Then, too, the American military (backed by the British) maintained that there were special operational reasons for attacking the television station; then, too, it was broadcasting again within hours.

It was certainly true that by allowing Iraqi television to continue broadcasting, the Coalition gave Iraqis the impression that Saddam Hussein was still in firm control, and perhaps even that that was how the Americans wanted it. But there were plenty of ways to disrupt the broadcasts, as they had found in Belgrade. There was no need to destroy the building and the people working inside it, especially since it only knocked Iraqi TV off the air for a short while. Both attacks were ineffectual.

Fox News's motto was 'Real Journalism, Fair and Balanced'. Constantly repeated, this had an Orwellian flavour to it.

'The only word with any truth in it is "and",' the American columnist Tom Shales remarked.

Fox's star reporter from the Afghanistan campaign, Geraldo Rivera, had a less successful time in the second Gulf War; failing to get into northern Iraq, he was eventually embedded with American forces in the south, but was thrown out for revealing the position of the forces he was with, and their intention to stage an attack in the near future. Others managed to maintain the standard of reporting, all the same. Bill O'Reilly, who was so keen on 'taking out' Iraqi TV, rejected the caution of the retired generals whom he interviewed on his programme, and declared that the United States should just go in and 'splatter' the Iraqis.

The Fox formula of fierce opinion violently expressed was bettered by MSNBC, which broadcast a radio programme aptly called 'Savage Nation', in which a man called Michael Savage raved into the microphone.

'We are the good ones, and they, the Arabs, are the evil ones. They must be snuffed out from the planet, and not in a court of law.'

A media consulting firm, Frank Megid Associates, reinforced the sense that there was only one opinion which counted when it warned its clients that carrying reports on protests against the war might well frighten off advertisers. In its rare coverage of the peace demonstrations Fox News contributors spoke of 'the usual protestors', and on one occasion of 'the great unwashed'.

The advance on Baghdad continued. As they drew closer, the American soldiers found it bewilderingly difficult to work out what the people they encountered thought of them. Were they hostile? Or did they truly welcome them but were scared to show it? Most Iraqis experienced a mixture of emotions: Saddam was a monster whom they would be far better off without, but they often saw the Americans as a dangerously trigger-happy army of invasion.

Nevertheless, as in the holy city of Najaf, which had suffered badly under Saddam Hussein in the Shi'ite uprising which followed the first Gulf War, the Americans were sometimes greeted as liberators. Grand Ayatollah Sistani even told his Shi'ite supporters to allow the Americans through unhindered. Sometimes people stood by the sides of the road, cheering and waving as the Americans passed; sometimes they leant out of their cars and shouted their good wishes. But did they mean it? The Americans were never able to tell.

In Baghdad the defence minister, General Sultan Hashim Ahmed (whom we last saw in 1991, in General Schwarzkopf's tent), told a press conference on 27 March that Iraq expected the Americans to surround the city within five or ten days, which turned out to be a fairly accurate estimate. But this, he said, would only be the beginning.

'In the end, the invaders will have to enter it [the city]. Baghdad is the capital of civilization. We inherited it from our forefathers, and history will see how we defend it.'

These predictions were distinctly unnerving. The Americans had so far swept through largely undefended territory, covering an average of seventy-five miles a day. Donald Rumsfeld's strategy of a fast, relatively small, heavily armed force cleaving through almost non-existent opposition had so far been mostly successful. But was it possible they were just heading into a trap?

55. CASUALTIES

This was the thirty-fourth war I had covered, and in some ways it was the worst. During the course of it, I lost four friends: Terry Lloyd of ITN, Gaby Rado of Channel 4 News, Kaveh Golestan, the BBC cameraman in Tehran, and my own translator, Kamaran Abdurrazak Mohammed.

Terry, like the rest of us, knew the serious dangers of being out in front, between the Americans and the Iraqis. Yet it was his choice to operate as he did, and he will have weighed up the chances carefully. He and his team of four crossed the border from Kuwait – not necessarily an easy thing to do – and headed north.

On the third day of the war, 22 March, the vehicle he was travelling in together with his French cameraman, Fred Nerac, his Lebanese translator, Hussein Othman, and another French cameraman, Daniel Demoustier, was making its way through the village of Iman Anas, south of Basra. They passed a group of American marines and headed on into no man's land. A short distance further on they came face to face with some Iraqi tanks and other vehicles. They turned round as fast as they could and hurtled back towards the Americans with at least one Iraqi vehicle following them.

Although they had clear television and Coalition markings on their vehicle, and had been seen only a few minutes before by the US marines they were driving towards, the Americans opened fire on them. Somehow, Daniel Demoustier threw himself out of the vehicle and was uninjured. Terry, however, was killed at once. As for what happened to Nerac and Othman, nothing more could be discovered about them. ITN later sent out a team of investigators to search for them, but their bodies were never discovered. It seems inconceivable that they could have survived.

Terry was a highly experienced reporter who had covered wars in

Cambodia, Bosnia and Kosovo, and he and I were in Halabjah together in 1988 when we saw the after-effects of Saddam Hussein's use of chemical weapons. He was a pleasant, friendly, easy-going man who was never caught up in boring professional rivalry with colleagues like me. At the same time, he was one of the best television reporters in Britain. It seems terrible that a man with such talent and such a love for life can have been silenced by a panicky teenager with a gun who could not recognize the most simple and obvious of signs.

Kaveh's death was equally unnecessary. It happened on Wednesday 2 April: the fourteenth day of the war. Kaveh was with Jim Muir, the BBC's Tehran correspondent, Stuart Hughes, a BBC radio producer, and a Kurdish translator. They drove towards a forward position at Kifri, in north-eastern Iraq, which was manned by the Patriotic Union of Kurdistan. They tried to park their car in the shelter of a concrete building which stood virtually on the front line. A PUK officer waved them away, and told them to go and park on a stretch of grass beside the road. Jim Muir, who was driving, asked if there was any danger the ground might be mined, but the PUK man assured him there wasn't.

Jim parked where the man suggested, and Stuart opened the car door and put one foot out on to the grass. It detonated a mine, which blew a piece of Stuart's foot off. Kaveh was on the side of the car away from the mine, but he thought their vehicle had come under mortar fire, jumped out and ran round to shelter in the lee of the vehicle. He trod on one mine, which blew his leg off, and fell forward on to another, which killed him instantly. The others threw down metal camera boxes to check there were no more mines. Then their translator, Rebeen, crawled over them and recovered Kaveh's body.

Stuart Hughes was given good medical care, but eventually his leg had to be amputated. It fell to Jim Muir to drive back for two hours or more with the remains of Kaveh, who had become a close friend of his, on the back seat of the car.

56. REACHING BAGHDAD

Saddam Hussein, his commanders and his military advisers, who included Russians and Serbs, had always planned that the real line of resistance to the Coalition forces would lie around Baghdad. The idea was that the Americans would be encouraged to race through the empty countryside, finding relatively little opposition, and when their supply lines were stretched to the utmost they would meet the real strength of Iraq's defence. There was no great secret about the strategy; Tariq Aziz, the deputy prime minister, had made it plain some weeks earlier.

'People say to me, you are not the Vietnamese; you have no jungles and swamps to hide in. I reply, let our cities be our swamps, and our buildings be our jungles.'

As a strategy, it required only one thing from the Iraqi defenders: a willingness to fight for Saddam. He himself was certain the willingness was there, and his ministers and generals naturally reinforced his self-assurance, since anyone who told him differently would receive a bullet in the back of the neck before nightfall. He put some of his most trusted officers in charge of the project, and fully expected that his regular soldiers and the ordinary inhabitants of the city would fulfil his expectations.

The Coalition forces also assumed that this would happen. The British commander in Iraq, Air Marshal Brian Burridge, one of the brightest and best of the leading military figures on the Coalition side, was quite clear in his own mind about it.

'The enemy is going for a Stalingrad siege,' he said. 'He wants to entice us into urban warfare.'

There was no real way of avoiding it. The war couldn't be won without capturing Baghdad, and the Americans had decided to use as much force as would be required in order to make certain that they wouldn't be dragged into a long-lasting urban campaign.

But something had happened during the rapid American advance on the city. After the long period when Iraqis seemed uncertain whether Saddam might not, once again, survive the onslaught and return to power, opinion seemed to swing round. People began to believe that this time he really would be overthrown. The Special Republican Guard, who were expected to ensure that the American troops came nowhere near the outskirts of the city, vanished from sight.

As a result, the advancing American troops started to find, as they drew nearer to Baghdad, the kind of welcome they had been told to expect from the start. Groups of people, sometimes few in number but sometimes in the hundreds, gathered by the roadside waving and cheering and occasionally throwing flowers. At the same time, the officers whom Saddam had put in charge of leading the guerrilla war inside the city also decided that the result was a foregone conclusion, and that there was no point in obeying their orders. This was critical to the way the endgame played out.

Finally, the US 3rd Infantry demonstrated the unstoppable ferocity of the American advance by capturing Saddam International Airport, on the western edge of the capital. Even though there was little resistance, it was a major achievement for the Coalition, and the reports of one of the most successful of the embedded journalists, Bob Schmidt of ABC, captured the excitement of the moment and established the real value of the embedding system to the military once and for all.

Mohammed Saheed al-Sahhaf, the Iraqi information minister, remained loyal to his master to the very end. His press conferences had a hypnotic quality which captured the attention of people around the world, largely because of his denials of the patent reality around him. It was soon after the capture of the airport that the newspapers in Britain began calling him Comical Ali; the reference was, of course, to Ali Hassan al-Majid, Chemical Ali.

Now, after the airport fell, al-Sahhaf denied that Coalition troops were even within 100 miles of Baghdad, and people unused to deliberate lying began to wonder whether the Americans had indeed captured the airport or not. Bob Schmidt's reports, as he tracked the American soldiers through what was recognizably the main terminal building and then on to the VIP section, showed incontestably that they had. The crunch of their boots on the broken glass which lay all over the marble floor provided the requisite sound effects.

It had taken the Americans sixteen days to reach the outskirts of the capital: a remarkably short space of time in any campaign, even against a critically weakened enemy like Iraq. Donald Rumsfeld's *blitzkrieg* tactics, carried out with remarkably small numbers of troops, had succeeded triumphantly. Now the city was under attack from every side except the north. That, therefore, was the way the refugees took, piling their vehicles high with boxes and suitcases and driving out to escape the bloodbath they still thought would come. The poor, and some of the rich, decided to stay: the poor because they couldn't afford to leave, the rich because they were reluctant to abandon their houses to the looters.

Now it was clear the end was in sight. Young men of military age, delighted at being free of the burden of fighting, waved at the advancing Americans from the sides of the roads, turning to set about the inevitable portraits of Saddam Hussein, smashing them or firing their guns at his face, shouting and laughing with the sudden bravado of the moment. Some of the iconoclasts might well have marched proudly in front of Saddam in the past. But once the cracks started showing and his weakness was made evident, the mob turned as mobs do. Fear and the need to conform had made them his worshippers, and directly the fear and the need evaporated they became his enemies.

The American mistake had been to assume that this meant everyone was potentially pro-American. The soldiers who were now starting to arrive on the outskirts of Baghdad were shocked to find that many people in the city wanted them as little as they wanted Saddam Hussein.

Some, indeed, were determined to do what Saddam had demanded of them. There were suicide bombings, which killed Americans and Iraqis indiscriminately. Videos of the kind we have seen so often from Lebanon and Palestine started to appear on the Arabic twenty-four-hour news channels, showing men and sometimes women dressed as martyrs, holding copies of the Holy Koran and announcing their determination to kill as many of God's enemies as possible.

On 4 April Iraqi television, which remarkably enough was still on the air, broke into a programme about Saddam Hussein and the glories of Iraq to show unedited pictures of the man himself, walking round the streets in Adhamiya, an outer suburb of Baghdad, with his younger son Qusay and a few bodyguards. He was dressed in army uniform, and looked relaxed and jolly, even though he had been on the run for sixteen days, spending each night in a different place and sometimes moving twice or more during the night.

But the people who were in the street at the time came flocking round, some cheering and waving rifles in the air; you could see clearly from the video how nervous this made some of his bodyguards. Some people in the crowd came forward and kissed him on the hands, and even on the cheeks. It was a very clever piece of public relations, and a classic example of Saddam's ability to capture the limelight. But although it gave heart to his loyalists and supporters everywhere, and added to the Saddam legend, it couldn't do anything to alter the basic fact that the Americans were on the outskirts of Baghdad.

On the morning of the following day, Saturday 5 April, an extraordinary mistake by the Americans turned into a major portent of the coming victory. A support column from the 3rd Infantry Division, coming up from the south, was supposed to drive around the city to the west, heading for the airport to re-supply the troops there. The soldiers on board were not combat troops; they were mechanics, cooks, medics: very much the same kind of people who had been in Private Jessica Lynch's convoy when it was ambushed. And, in a disturbing repeat of that episode, the column took the wrong turning and headed straight for the centre of Baghdad.

If there had been any concerted opposition in the city, they would never have made it. But the idea that Saddam Hussein's forces would draw the Americans into the city and destroy them was shown to be nothing more than an Iraqi PR fantasy. When the line of dots, each representing an American vehicle, appeared on the wall-mounted plasma screens of the Blue Force Tracker system at Joint Operations Centre in Doha, there was an audible intake of breath from the American controllers. But their nerve held. The order was given to the column to head on to Qadisya, on the left bank of the Tigris, then turn sharp west and head for the airport. It was absolutely the right thing to do: by stopping and turning round, Jessica Lynch's commander had shown that he was nervous and lost; the 3rd Infantry support column looked as though it knew exactly where it was going. It reached the airport in safety.

The Americans could now stage what they called 'an armed reconnaissance': a fast drive right into the centre by a force of twenty-five Abrams tanks and twelve Bradley fighting vehicles. They headed into the outer suburb of al-Dawra, where Saddam's daughter Raghad had her farm, retracing the route the supply column had taken, and firing as they went. They too looped around, then returned to the airport.

It was one of the best moments of the entire war for 'embedded' journalism. A team from Fox News, the stridently pro-war channel owned by Rupert Murdoch, travelled with the column and broadcast some extraordinary scenes live from the operation, including what looked like an attack by a suicide bomber in a car. No one knows how many civilians were killed during this foray, though American officials in Doha said the number could have been as high as 2,000. It had been an extremely bold and clever tactic, worked out on the spur of the moment; but it was disturbing to see how little attention was paid to the lives and safety of the ordinary people whom the Americans were supposed to be liberating. When they fired their missiles or dropped their 'smart' bombs on carefully pre-planned targets, they claimed to be careful to avoid unnecessary civilian casualties. The soldiers in the armoured column do not seem to have been under any such instructions; they blasted away with their heavy machine-guns at anything which might possibly constitute a threat.

According to Saddam Hussein's daughter Raghad, interviewed later by al-Arabiyah Television, the city was betrayed by Saddam's own closest supporters when it fell to the Americans on 9 April.

'It was a big shock. How can you explain it? The explanation is very clear. Regrettably, the people in whom he placed his full trust and whom he considered his right-hand men were the main sources of treason.

'History will judge them before it judges us. Even if I do not like you, I should not betray you at all. Treason is not one of the Arabs' traits. This was treason and this was really painful. Besides, they betrayed their country before they betrayed Saddam Hussein and his family. We are Iraqis, just like they are. We would go, others would come and there were others before us. But it remains my country. When I am faced with a situation in which I have to defend it as a man, I should not surrender easily.'

Raghad obviously believed that Saddam had a master-plan for the defence of Baghdad, which would mean drawing the Americans into the city then trapping them; and that leading figures in the regime had run away before the plan could be put into action. Perhaps she was trying to put the blame on Ali Hassan al-Majid, Chemical Ali, who was responsible for killing her husband. Other leading Iraqis, such as Tariq Aziz, also clearly expected that a last stand would be made inside Baghdad. Perhaps those who were supposed to be in charge of the resistance really did simply melt away, though there was plenty of resistance afterwards, and it was only a matter of weeks before the number of American soldiers who died in combat was overtaken by the number who had died in the attacks of urban guerrillas.

After the war Uday Hussein's personal bodyguard told a British newspaper that Saddam Hussein and his two sons had stayed in Baghdad for at least a week after its fall, taking refuge in houses in Adhamiya, where Saddam went for his walkabout. The guard said that in the last days of the war Saddam guessed that there was a traitor in his immediate entourage, because a number of his safe houses had been bombed. An army captain came under suspicion, and Saddam asked him to set up a meeting in a house behind a restaurant in the Mansour district. Saddam and his sons arrived there, the report said, then left very quickly. Ten minutes later the house was bombed. The captain was shot immediately afterwards.

According to the newspaper, Saddam and his sons went to Friday prayers at the main mosque in Adhamiya on 11 April, two days after the fall of Baghdad. An old woman went up to him and asked what he had done to them. Saddam clapped his hand to his head.

'What can I do?' he said. 'I trusted the commanders but they were traitors, and they betrayed Iraq.'

Perhaps it was just an invention, and Saddam left Baghdad on 9 April, as most people believed. But it all helped to create the legend.

57. DISASTER

In the north, too, the Iraqis were crumbling. For more than two weeks we had been moving forward with the Kurdish forces from one front line to another, as the Iraqis had pulled back. It was exciting and sometimes dangerous, but it was nothing like as spectacular as the action to the south of us: apart from anything else, our war was fought with light weapons and the occasional mortar round, while the Americans and British were using the most up-to-date armaments.

I had long given up any hope that I might play a major role in reporting the war. Al-Sahhaf, Comical Ali, had, I thought made sure of that. What I didn't realize then was that the war was so widespread that none of my colleagues, inside the BBC or outside it, felt they had a clear view of it, and all of them seem at some stage to have felt completely sidelined. No doubt this has always been true of large-scale wars; my problem was, perhaps, that I had been reporting smaller ones for the past twelve years, and was used to being able to see almost all the action from one place, like a nineteenth-century war correspondent basing himself on a hill overlooking the battlefield.

On the evening of Saturday 5 April, the day the Americans first accidentally, then deliberately, carved their way through Baghdad, my team and I found ourselves in the small village of Shemamer, on the front north-west of Kirkuk. The Iraqi front line was less than a kilometre away, and the fifty Kurdish Pesh Merga troops in the village had the support of eight American special forces soldiers, who were both impressive and very pleasant. They kept themselves to themselves, and we were careful not to film them, but we had access to all sorts of things they might want, especially satellite phones, and we had hopes of being able to talk to them quietly that evening. The next day was clearly going to be an important one, and we needed to keep close to them. We were hamstrung by not knowing what the broader American strategy might be: were they planning to capture Kirkuk and Mosul before Baghdad fell, or to allow it to collapse once Saddam had vanished? Maybe, if we got friendly with the special forces people, they might give us some indication.

One of the Americans was sitting on the flat roof of a building in the middle of Shemamer with a powerful pair of binoculars, watching the village of Haweira, ten kilometres away in Iraqi territory. A couple of American planes were circling it, and we heard some explosions and saw a column of black smoke going up. The American on the roof called down something to his colleagues. (Later they told us that a column of five Iraqi vehicles had set out from Haweira in order to attack us at Shemamer, but had been destroyed by the Americans from the air.)

We had obtained some good material and I wanted to send it to London in a better fashion than our jerky, awkward videophone would allow. Our hotel was only forty minutes' drive away in Arbil, and the big satellite dish we had been using was still set up on the roof; I could go back there, while Tom Giles, Fred Scott, Dragan Petrovic and Craig Summers could all try to charm the Americans in their different ways. It also occurred to me that I could sleep in a bed and have a bath and a shave before I came back the next morning for what was obviously going to be an important day. At fifty-eight, I liked whatever comforts I could get.

The next morning, Sunday 6 April, was the day Kaveh Golestan was to be buried in Tehran. I got up early and was back at the village before seven, to find everyone starting to stir. It had been a long night: the American soldiers had liked the whisky they had brought, and they had all sat singing songs and talking about the campaign until the early hours. The Americans had been remarkably friendly and, as I had expected, everyone in our team had brought something to the relationship: Tom because he had worked alongside American special forces before, and had spent time, like them, in Afghanistan; Fred because he was Californian and knew the right songs and the right variants of poker; Craig because he had been a soldier and spoke the soldiers' language; Dragan because he can charm anyone on earth.

We had another secret weapon too. We had made contact with Dumeetha Lewthra, a freelance reporter who had previously worked for the BBC and was with me in Afghanistan in 2001. She was always good at finding out what was going on, and seemed to be entirely fearless. For some reason the BBC, instead of promoting her, had allowed her to go off and become a freelance. Fortunately, she was happy to work alongside us and tell us what she found out.

Now everyone looked and sounded rough. They had slept anywhere they could find, and had only just woken up. But they were pleased with the relationship they had struck up with the soldiers, who had been generous and friendly. Special forces soldiers are rarely too worried about discipline, and unlike regular troops they often feel a sense of kinship with journalists, who can go where they want and make their own decisions. They had been scathing about the training levels and attitudes of the main body of American troops; partly, perhaps, this was the superiority which an elite group feels towards the rank and file, but it also arose from a genuine professional disapproval.

While the others cleaned up, I strolled around the village, which until the day before had been occupied by the Iraqis. Kamaran came with me, translating the different signs and notices and pointing out the big portrait of Saddam Hussein which no one had yet touched: there wasn't even a bullet-mark on the face.

Was the work all right? I asked him. He had been talking to the other translators, he said, and they had told him to ask for more money. I left that side of things entirely to Oggy Boytchev, but I promised to see if we could afford some more. I knew there were one or two other problems: the lack of a flak-jacket, for instance. But did he want to continue?

We stopped and faced each other as the sun came up over the distant hillside and I felt its warmth. Kamaran's pleasant, open face with its Mexican moustache was immobile for a moment, as he thought about it.

'Yes, I want to continue, Mr John. I like the work, and I like you and the others. But I have many costs, and I have to pay for my mother and my sisters.'

'Do they know the work you are doing?'

'No, they think I stay in the hotel and translate the newspapers. It is easier that way.'

'So – no other problems?'

'No, Mr John. I told you: I like adventures.'

I smiled at him; he was usually so well turned-out, but he looked rumpled and dirty. He grinned back at me, the sun lighting his face.

There was shouting down the road, and the sound of vehicles starting up. In the usual haphazard fashion, another advance was just beginning. The Iraqis had pulled back during the night from their front line just opposite us. We jumped in our cars: Dragan with Fred and me and our driver; Tom, Abdullah, Kamaran in the other, with Craig driving. We scarcely had time to look at the abandoned front line as we passed it and headed on to the village of Haweira behind. On the way we passed the column of burned-out Iraqi vehicles which had set out to attack us the previous afternoon and had been comprehensively destroyed by American aircraft.

In Haweira itself the locals had already trashed the Ba'ath Party headquarters. Someone was raising the Kurdish flag in place of the Iraqi one, and others were going round shooting up pictures of Saddam and replacing them with photos of Kurdish heroes. I walked up and down the main street dictating copy to London into my phone and answering the questions of the presenters in various BBC radio and television studios. They didn't sound very interested.

We headed on to a village where we had spent time before: Pir Daoud. Commander Nariman, whom Abdullah, our Afghan photographer, had spent so much time cultivating had a base here, but when we arrived he was busy trying to work out what to do with all the Iraqi prisoners who had been sent there. We couldn't film them properly, and there seemed little point in staying, especially when we heard that the nearby town of Dibarjan had been captured by the Kurds. Dibarjan lay between Mosul and Kirkuk, and seemed a good jumping-off place for the Kurds to attack either city from.

We had watched and filmed the road leading to Dibarjan many times in the past. It made an evocative sight, running off in the heat haze into the heart of enemy territory, and I had often wondered if we would ever travel down it. Now we could. We headed out, with Dragan in Craig's car this time and Kamaran with Fred and me.

It was eerie. The road was entirely empty, and we had no clear knowledge of what might lie ahead – just someone's assertion that Dibarjan had fallen. There were occasional loud explosions coming from somewhere, but it was hard to know where. Our car was in the lead, and Fred and I were becoming less and less certain about carrying on. The driver, sensing our feelings, slowed down; at that moment there was a roar of engines behind us in the distance, and a cloud of dust. Instinctively, our driver pulled over to the side of the road.

There must have been sixteen of them: big Land Cruisers, new and still quite shiny. The first couple bore big KDP flags, and after the Kurdish part of the convoy had passed there were several American vehicles with big Stars and Stripes carrying special forces soldiers.

'It's Waji,' said Kamaran.

Waji Barzani was an impressive character: the younger brother of the KDP president, and the leader of the Pesh Merga's special forces. We had interviewed him a couple of days before. This was a very high-level group indeed, and it would be excellent for us to stick with them. Our driver slotted in behind them on the road. The dust welled up all round us. At one point we stopped. The Iraqis had dug mines into the road, and we had to make a wide detour over a muddy hillside to get past them. A couple of American planes were circling overhead, I noticed.

Ahead of us lay a ridge, and the Kurdish and American vehicles were stopping there.

'Flak-jacket time,' I said.

At times like these, the speed with which you do things can change everything. If we had taken more time to catch up, or if we had stayed a little longer in our cars, we would have burned to death as so many of the other people around us would shortly do. They, and Kamaran, had only a few minutes of life left.

The convoy had stopped at a crossroads on the top of the hill, and Waji Barzani and his men were standing there looking down into the valley beyond, in the direction of Dibarjan. Someone was pointing towards a couple of Iraqi tanks about a mile away in the valley below us, and I realized then that the thin column of black smoke which was still hanging in the air a few hundred yards behind us had come from a shell fired by one of the tanks. The American special forces vehicles were drawn up alongside each other close by, each flying a gigantic Stars and Stripes. A little way ahead of us, down the road, several American armoured personnel carriers had also stopped. They too carried vast flags.

The rest of the vehicles in the convoy, a dozen or so of them, all displayed big panels of orange material on their roofs, clearly visible from the air. Our vehicles had them too. In other words, if you were a pilot flying reasonably low you could not have glanced at the scene on the ground and mistaken us for an enemy. I heard the sound of a radio crackling; one of the Americans was calling in an airstrike against the tanks. By chance, there was a wrecked Iraqi tank lying right beside the crossroads; it must have been attacked and destroyed earlier in the day. It's not impossible that the presence of this tank, when an attack was being requested on another tank nearby, caused the disaster that followed.

The two US Navy F-14s were flying very low; about 1,000 feet.

Fred Scott wanted to film them as we were standing near the group around Waji Barzani, and called out to Tom Giles that he needed his tripod to film the planes.

'OK – tripod,' I heard Tom shout back. He and Craig headed off back to our vehicles.

I was aware of Fred standing quite close to me, and Kamaran about six feet away. Dragan was also there somewhere: he said something too, which I couldn't hear. The noise of the planes overhead was too loud.

Just as Tom was getting the tripod out of the vehicle, his phone rang. It was his birthday, and his mother was calling to wish him many happy returns. He thanked her, then held the phone up in the air so she could hear the noise the planes were making.

'Listen, Mum, that's the sound of freedom,' he said, to tease her; she was strongly against the war.

As she listened, there was a huge whistling roar at the other end of the phone, followed by a terrible explosion. For an instant she must have thought Tom was dead, but then she heard his voice swearing. He had forgotten she was there, and was blundering around in the smoke that was rising from the centre of the crossroads, still holding the phone. Car alarms were starting to go off, and all round there were the screams and groans of injured and dying men.

Twenty yards away, on the other side of the parked cars, Fred and I both saw the bomb as it landed. I found it hard afterwards to credit my senses, but when I checked what I had seen with Fred I realized it was true. There was an immense downward force, hitting the ground at an acute angle, and I had the impression of something white and red. Late in 2003, Tom Giles and I were given a reluctant briefing by the Pentagon about the attack. We were told it had been a 1000-lb bomb which had been dropped on us. The angle of its detonation was so acute that anyone standing outside the vector of its blast, as we were, had a chance of surviving. Most of my team and I were between ten and twelve yards away.

Fourteen pieces of shrapnel hit me altogether, and I was knocked to the ground. Most were pretty small, like the ones that hit me in the face and head, but two the size of bullets were big enough to have killed me. One lodged in my left hip, the other stuck in the plastic plate of my flak-jacket right over the spine. I was wearing a pair of those trousers that unzip to turn into shorts; the left leg section was entirely blasted off its zip by the explosion, leaving my leg naked and bleeding.

I lost consciousness for an instant, then felt myself being pulled up. Dragan, instead of running for shelter, had come back to help me, thinking that the plane might drop a second bomb on us. People have won medals for less bravery than he showed. He ran across the grass, pulling me along by the wrist, so fast that I fell over again.

'Fucking leave me alone,' I shouted at him; it was scarcely gracious.

He and I stumbled across the grass, and it was only later that I remembered what had happened to Kaveh Golestan and realized we had already come across a line of mines across the road half a mile back. Fortunately no one had laid any mines here.

The roar of the explosion was still in my ears, but I slowly realized it was worse than that: my left eardrum seemed to have gone.

Ahead of us, Fred was kneeling behind a small hillock, his glasses and face entirely covered with thick, viscous blood. It was a shocking sight.

'Is my eye OK?' he kept asking.

Dragan told him it was fine, though neither of us thought it could be.

'We've got to film this,' I shouted above the racket of the car alarms. There were smaller explosions too, which I couldn't quite understand.

The two planes were still circling overhead.

'Call your bloody friends off,' I shouted at the Americans on the ground; but they had already done so. The pilots must have been circling to get some estimate of the damage they'd done.

Fred switched his camera on, and peered at the lens to check that it hadn't been shattered. A large drop of blood landed on it, and he had to wipe it off with a bloody finger a second or so later. The blood on the lens summed up the entire appalling business.

In circumstances like these, it is often easier to do what you know best. Fred and Dragan behaved with great calmness and courage, and I found myself trying to work out what we needed to make this into a proper television news report; so often when sudden violence happens you find yourself forgetting to do the essential things.

Fred and I peered over the lip of our defensive position. Almost all the Land Cruisers were on fire now, and the explosions were much fiercer and louder.

'They're cookin' off,' Fred shouted.

He was right: the vehicles were packed with ammunition and rocket-propelled grenades, and as the fire got to them they exploded in every direction. As he filmed, a grenade flew just inches over our heads.

'Christ!'

I went off to find the others, but apart from Dragan I couldn't see anyone else. There was terrible screaming from close by, and a man staggered past me with his arms full of his intestines, gleaming and salmon-pink in the sunlight. He looked around for a place to sit down and collapsed there. The next time I looked he was dead. Nearby a man was burning to death, the flames curling round him, his arms held rigidly in front of him as he knelt on the ground. There was nothing I could do to save him. The stench made me gag, and I stumbled away.

I stared at the inferno where the cars were burning and exploding, and tried to tell myself that Tom and the others were there somewhere; but I couldn't see where they were. I stopped myself thinking what might have happened to them.

'We should do a piece to camera,' I said when the bullets and rockets seemed to have died down a little.

We stood out gingerly in the open, with the cars blazing away, but at that moment Craig came staggering through the smoke.

'Kamaran? Where's Kamaran?' He pronounced it as though it was spelt 'Cameron'.

'Is Tom OK?' I bellowed, and then Tom appeared through the smoke behind him.

I dialled the BBC in London and got through to Traffic: one of the great broadcasting institutions, it's the department which takes in all foreign reports and distributes them to the right programmes. There was quite a wait, and I felt extremely vulnerable as I stood out in the open with the occasional bullet and grenade still firing off. I'm going to die here, I thought, because someone can't take a decision quickly enough.

'Put me on the fucking air,' I shouted, then immediately felt bad about it. Whoever was to blame for keeping me hanging around like this, it certainly wasn't the Traffic manager. 'Sorry,' I mumbled.

Soon a calm studio presenter was asking me sensible, thoughtful questions, and I realized I was much too worked up and would have to quieten down a little.

'Well, it's been a bit of a disaster,' I replied, before realizing it was important not to downplay what was happening too much.

'It was an American plane that dropped the bomb right beside us. I saw it land about ten yards, twelve yards away, I think. This is just a scene from hell here. All the vehicles are on fire.'

I turned and looked at the man who was burning to death, and at another who was lying on the ground, the flames still licking around him.

'There are bodies lying around, there are bits of bodies on the ground. This is a really bad own goal by the Americans.'

While I was talking, an American soldier came up to me. In my confused state, I got the idea that he was going to try to stop me reporting the news of an American disaster.

'Shut up, I'm broadcasting,' I shouted at him.

He took it well, and explained he just wanted to help because he could see I was bleeding from the head. I let him look at me while I carried on talking to the programme in London.

'Just a couple of bits of shrapnel,' he said, and went off to help someone else.

They had found Kamaran by now. The blast must have flung his considerable weight on to a bank of earth five yards or more from where he and I had stood near each other. One foot seemed to have been mostly blown off, and they were trying to put a tourniquet round his thigh and give him an intravenous injection. Tom was kneeling beside him.

Death isn't a neat, convenient thing, and we sometimes behave as badly in dying as we do in living. Kamaran, horribly shocked by what had happened and traumatized by his massive injuries, fought off his helpers with all his weight and strength, while the blood that might have saved his life pumped out of him even faster. Sometimes he called out Tom's name, recognizing his face among all the others bending over him.

'It's Tom here. You'll be all right. Everything's fine.'

But he could see that Kamaran wouldn't last much longer.

I badly wanted to stay, because it was all my fault that Kamaran was there; I had led him into this, and I couldn't bear to walk away from him. But the American medics were round him, and Tom was with him. I knew I had to do a piece to camera while the full force of this terrible business was still around us.

Fred had cleaned the right lens of his glasses now and could see what he was filming, though his face was still covered with congealed blood and more leaked out of the wound high up on his forehead. I recorded a longish piece to camera, trying not to rail against the Americans for doing this to us. After all, it was Americans who had tried to help Kamaran; they had suffered too – I didn't yet know if any of them had been killed – and the look on the face of the special forces officer who had actually called in the airstrike was terrible to see. I spoke to him briefly, and he answered me like a man who was sleepwalking.

Whether he had mistakenly given the plane our own coordinates instead of the coordinates of the Iraqi tank, or whether it was the pilot and navigator of the F-14 who mixed them up, or whether they had looked down and seen only the wrecked Iraqi tank by the roadside and fired at that before registering the presence of so many vehicles with Coalition markings, was impossible to say. There was no proper, systematic investigation into the incident, and no information about it was made public.

There was still one member of the team whom we hadn't found: Abdullah. When the missile landed he had been wandering around, separate from the rest of us, taking photographs. We searched for him everywhere. The fires had mostly burned out by now, and it was safe enough to get close to the vehicles; but examining one burned corpse after another to look for any faint sign that one of them might have been Abdullah was an unpleasant task. I thought at one point I'd found his body, charred and lying under an upturned jeep, but just as I was about to call the others someone shouted that Abdullah had been taken away in another vehicle and was getting medical care. He had taken a chunk of shrapnel in the neck, and another piece in the leg, but neither of them had done him any serious injury.

While I was searching for Abdullah, Tom and Dragan were helping to pick up Kamaran and get him on to a small flatbed truck which had driven up. Knowing the state of the road it would have to take, I could see he would never stand the slightest chance of getting to Arbil alive.

Dragan and one of the Kurds hoisted his heavy body on to the back of the vehicle. He was still alive, but only just. Tom and I were given a lift in another vehicle which had arrived, but we had gone only half a mile when we saw an ambulance in the road. Somehow, in an extraordinarily short space of time, Oggy Boytchev had managed to summon it up in Arbil and had made it all the way to the road where the disaster had happened.

'Kamaran was pronounced dead when he got here,' Oggy said.

Although I had seen him lying on the ground and had looked at his injuries, I felt angry and somehow cheated. All the rest of us had survived with only the most superficial wounds. Tom thought he wasn't hurt at all, until we were driving along in the ambulance and noticed that there was a hole in his shoe. An inch-long piece of shrapnel had entered his toe, but had done no serious harm. Fred's cut was a flesh wound, though his left eardrum was perforated – the second time this had happened to him. Dragan had a perforated eardrum too, and had been hit by a piece of shrapnel which had severed some of the nerves in his leg. Craig was peppered with a few pieces of shrapnel, but they were only specks. Of the five of us, I suppose my injuries were the worst: my left eardrum was completely blown away, and the shrapnel in my hip will probably remain slightly painful for the rest of my life.

But that was it. Our drivers were slightly hurt, though not badly. Our bags and equipment had been rescued unharmed from our third vehicle: Craig, with great presence of mind, had pulled them out while it was burning – he even rescued my Tilley hat out of the car, with a shrapnel hole in it the size of a fifty-pence piece. With eighteen people killed around us and forty-five wounded, we had had one of the most extraordinary escapes any of us had ever heard of.

Yet Kamaran had escaped nothing. It was as though we had used up all the team's luck ourselves, and hadn't left any for him. It had nothing to do with the lack of a flak-jacket; he could have worn the best and most expensive body armour in the world, and still have died from the chunk of shrapnel which hit him in the leg and ruptured the artery. I looked at his pale arm and pale face as the flatbed truck carried him joltingly, cruelly, down the unmade track, and thought with unbearable force of that moment in the hotel lobby.

'I like adventures. And I would like to be your friend.'

That afternoon, after we had been to the American special forces hospital and been treated for our minor injuries, I went with Tom and Oggy to see Kamaran's mother. Neither Tom nor I had yet had a chance to change our clothes; my trouser-leg was still ripped off at the knee, while Tom's jeans and shoes were still soaked in Kamaran's blood where he had held him and cradled him as he lay dying.

The courtyard of the house was full of family and friends. Many of them were weeping. Kamaran's mother, who was probably only fifty but looked like an old woman, was too exhausted from grief to weep any more. I had thought she might rail at me and accuse me of killing him, as I accused myself. Instead, as I sat and held her hand, she could only ask me why it had happened.

'He told me he never went to the front line; why was he there?'

And, 'The Americans know everything. How could they not know they were attacking you?'

These were questions I couldn't answer. I just held her hand and looked at her worn, uninteresting face and felt an unbearable degree of guilt. Why should the life of an Englishman of fifty-eight – older than she was – be more valuable than that of her young, lively, adventure-loving son of twenty-five? I read the question in her face; and even if I only imagined it, she had a perfect right to ask it. I was the one with no answers. I was the one who had led him to his death.

I made all the promises I was empowered to about compensation, and in due course the BBC acted responsibly and generously towards the family. They now have enough to own their own house and look after the old lady – for so she seems to me – and her unmarried daughters.

There was a lot to do that night: reports to edit, live two-way questions to answer. Fred's pictures, when we saw them, were worthy of the highest awards. A moment of absurdity intervened as I stood in my hotel room sponging the blood off my face and clothes: someone rang on behalf of Mohammed Saeed al-Sahhaf, Comical Ali, to say that I could have a visa to Baghdad if I wanted one.

That night I slept heavily and without dreaming, but in the morning I turned the television on to see what was happening in the war and found that BBC World was still running our report. I watched the pictures of Dragan helping to lift the heavy, inert, unnaturally pale body on to the back of the truck, and found the tears running unstoppably down my face. Staring at the television screen I could only say, over and over again, 'I'm so sorry. I'm so very, very sorry.'

58. BBC BAGHDAD

For the international television audience there was one real star of the show, as far as the reporting of the war was concerned. True, there was some excellent front-line work: the quality of people like Ben Brown, Gavin Hewitt, Clive Myrie and David Willis of the BBC, Jeremy Thompson and David Chater of Sky, Mark Austin of ITN, and from American television news Ted Koppel of ABC *Nightline* and Walter Rodgers of CNN, both men of my own age or older, shone through. Greg Kelly of Fox News did very well too, and seemed a real journalist compared with the irreflective presenters in their studios back in the United States.

Television exerts a glamorizing quality, which it often sheds on just one person in a complex situation like this. In the 1991 Gulf War it was Arthur Kent of NBC News; in 2003 it was Rageh Omaar, the BBC's Johannesburg correspondent, who combined grace and intelligence in a way the viewers found compelling.

People in television news tend to be fiercely competitive; it is, indeed, one of the fiercest areas on earth to work in. Yet no one, as far as I could see, begrudged Rageh the fame he received. In an industry where the loudest voice often attracts the most attention, his voice is noticeably quiet and thoughtful; but he has an ability to get himself into the most difficult of places and stay there by sheer force of character. Through the fact of his Muslim faith he managed to persuade the Taliban to allow him into Kabul not long before the city fell in 2001; as a result, the BBC was the only Western news organization represented there.

In the mid-1990s he was based in Jordan; and whereas most correspondents there had previously concentrated on the events in Israel and Palestine, Rageh turned his attention eastward to Iraq: much more difficult and problematic. Somehow, he charmed some of the unpleasant and corrupt characters in the Ministry of Information, whose job it was to let a few Western correspondents in while keeping most of them out.

A good proportion of those who went there tried to please their hosts by reporting only those things the Iraqis wanted them to show; interestingly, the Iraqi officials usually saw through this at once. Rageh, by contrast, provided a flow of good, honest reporting, while managing to stay in Baghdad for long periods of time by the judicious use of a word here or an image there which kept Saddam's officials happy. Merely to call him 'President Saddam Hussein' instead of simply 'Saddam' was sometimes enough to calm the anger of the Iraqi authorities, while avoiding a word like 'regime' and referring to 'government' instead kept them happy without any sacrifice of objectivity. Rageh Omaar found that a natural politeness worked wonders in Baghdad, and it helped him every time he wanted another visa to go there.

Inevitably, his reporting during the war itself attracted the ire of the British government. In that respect, if no other, Alistair Campbell, the head of information in Downing Street, was rather similar to the Iraqi government: if you didn't report what he liked, you were regarded as an enemy, and all sorts of stories would be passed around about the low quality of your reporting. In Rageh's case suggestions floated out from Downing Street and Whitehall that he was much too sympathetic to the Iraqi side; very much, indeed, what Campbell and his juniors had said about my reporting from Belgrade during the NATO bombing campaign of 1999. Fortunately, as it showed then, the BBC is a good deal more robust about defending its correspondents from government attack than it was in the distant past, and Rageh continued to broadcast from Baghdad.

This was important to the BBC. In 1991 CNN showed that in order to succeed in international television news you have to have a foot in every camp. The CNN team, headed by Peter Arnett and Robert Wiener, stayed on in Baghdad when almost everyone else, myself included, was thrown out. During the 1990s the BBC slowly caught up with CNN in terms of reputation, and then somewhere between 1999 and 2002 overtook it.

CNN International (that is, the non-domestic arm of the organization) is impressively run and has some good talent, but during the second Gulf War it wasn't entirely able to ring-fence its international broadcasts from its domestic ones, and inside the United States itself some of CNN's broadcasting was embarrassingly nationalistic. Anchors like Lou Dobbs wanted to demonstrate their patriotism to a domestic audience, without realizing what it sounded like when it was broadcast around the world to non-American viewers. The basic art of international broadcasting is to realize that your audience doesn't understand what you mean by words like 'our' and 'we'.

In Baghdad Saddam Hussein and his officials were so irritated by the American flags on screen and the unthinking insults of the studio guests that they eventually threw out the unfortunate CNN team, whose broadcasting had in fact been careful and unbiased. It was a serious blow to CNN International, which had done a good job under difficult conditions, and it may well indicate that no broadcasting organization so closely tied to American interests and values can succeed for long at a time when the United States is widely unpopular.

Rageh Omaar himself came near to being thrown out, together with his colleagues. It was a danger which always hung over them. Caroline Hawley, the BBC's Amman correspondent and a fluent Arabic speaker, was ordered to leave the country after being asked a thoughtless question from a London studio presenter about her official minders; the minders took offence. For the rest of the war Paul Wood, a clear-minded and highly articulate correspondent with experience of difficult and touchy regimes in the Balkans, made his way through the Baghdad minefield with equal skill.

Andrew Gilligan, whose reporting after the war became a major source of controversy, worked mainly for the *Today* programme from Baghdad. The man in overall charge of the operation was Paul Danahar, whom I had worked with in Pakistan before the 2001 invasion of Afghanistan: tough, idiosyncratic and not inclined to beat about the bush, he was told from the BBC foreign desk in London that the government was accusing them of being too favourable to the Iraqis.

'Favourable to them?' he shouted down the open line for the Iraqis to hear. 'We hate the bastards!'

They had the services of three excellent cameramen, who were to remain calm and impassive under the most considerable danger: Duncan Stone, a tall, laid-back and witty Englishman, Andrew Kilrain, tough and stocky, an Australian who had worked in just about every unpleasant place on the face of the earth, and Malek Kenaan, who had gained his experience in the dangerous conflict on the West Bank.

Being in Baghdad was central, therefore, to the BBC's reporting of the war. There were plenty of other journalists there, but the only ones who really mattered as far as Saddam Hussein and his ministers were concerned were CNN and the BBC. If the others occasionally said or wrote things that the regime might not like, it scarcely mattered; the chances were that no one would ever find out. But Saddam himself watched CNN and the BBC. If he took offence at what was said, there would be trouble, and even if he hadn't been watching when something awkward was broadcast, his officials had to assume he might come to hear about it.

For Rageh Omaar and his colleagues, the man who mattered most in their lives was Mohammed Saeed al-Sahhaf, the information minister. His command of English gave him the job in the first place and ensured that he eventually became an oddly attractive, iconic figure whom Western audiences found almost endearing.

But only once it was clear that nothing he said was likely to be true. At first he sounded as menacing as any of the other gangster-like figures around Saddam; Rageh Omaar, writing about him later, spoke of 'his own parallel version of reality where the British and American forces were concerned'.

'I am sure that they are stupid, and they will never succeed . . .' al-Sahhaf said. 'At the same time, this is a good testimony, a good proof that they are killers, they are criminals and they believe in assassination.'

Just as, back in January 1991, Saddam had expected two enormous onslaughts by American bombs and missiles, so now he and his ministers thought there would be more than 3,000 missile attacks in the first forty-eight hours of the war. That, perhaps, is what he would have done himself. So Rageh found there was a palpable sense of relief among Iraqi officials when the so-called 'shock and awe' tactics were at first neither shocking nor awful.

'We can absorb all military threats,' al-Sahhaf crowed. 'This is no problem for us.'

That night, however, the BBC team watched from their office on the thirteenth floor of the Palestine Hotel as an immense bombardment lasting an hour and a half destroyed many of the structures of Ba'athist power, and the palaces and buildings associated with Saddam Hussein himself.

'At times,' Rageh wrote, 'it was hard to find the language to convey the other-worldly nature of this onslaught: its sheer violence, the thunderous noise which reverberated through every street and avenue of the city, and the terrifying sight of plumes of debris being hurled at least 100 metres into the air. And all of this was taking place only a few hundred metres from where we were.'

The Palestine's windows would shudder and buckle inwards, and the entire structure would sway with the blast.

The Iraqis had no serious defences. Their anti-aircraft guns couldn't hit the American planes, and rarely seemed able to knock down any of the missiles which the Americans and British fired at them. Their only tactic was to light fires around the city, their black fumes sticking in everyone's throat, in a feeble attempt to confuse the bombers. Since every target was checked by satellite and fixed by the most precise calculations, the entire effort was pointless, but perhaps it gave the people of Baghdad a sense that something, however small, was being done to protect them.

As in 1991, the Iraqi government's assessment of civilian casualties was surprisingly accurate. They could easily have exaggerated the figures; no one would have known any better, and the inflated numbers would have been used by the anti-war movements throughout the world as truth. Instead, their figures were in the hundreds rather than thousands. The Iraqis were accurate in other ways too; when they claimed that cluster bombs had been used, it generally seemed to have been true.

Counter-intuitively, it was the strategic situation which the Iraqis invariably lied about: al-Sahhaf denied that the Americans and British were advancing, when it was plain from the reports of the embedded correspondents that this was unquestionable fact. Perhaps he hoped until the end that the attackers would be turned back at the gates of Baghdad. In spite of all the lies he had told, he never seriously exaggerated the civilian death toll. If he had claimed it was a hundred or a thousand times greater, his lies might have had some effect. As it was, they didn't. Perhaps it was simply that no one in the information ministry thought about doing it. Left to their own devices the officials at the interior ministry, whose main concern was to make sure there was no wild panic, simply issued figures which were broadly accurate.

From the point of view of propaganda and spin, therefore, the Iraqis' failed badly. The Iraqi government, used to issuing the most absurd lies and expecting them to be meekly passed on by the country's press and television, had no real idea how information could be manipulated in more sophisticated societies. It showed how at sea Saddam's officials were directly they moved outside the narrow area of information-control which they themselves maintained inside Iraq, a country where no one could check anything, and tried to influence the thinking of the real world.

At seven in the morning of 7 April, Paul Danahar rang Rageh's room at the Palestine Hotel.

'Take a look outside your window at the other side of the river,' he said.

Two American Bradley fighting vehicles were stationed outside the presidential palace. Troops from the 3rd Infantry Division were attacking the compound, firing as they went. Rageh could see the Iraqi soldiers running away. Many of them had torn off their uniforms and were dressed only in their underpants. Saddam Hussein was finished, and his power-structure had collapsed. Soon his huge, clumsy statue in Paradise Square would be pulled down by an armoured personnel carrier. That was the moment which appeared on the front pages of all the newspapers and most of the books about the war. But the real image which showed Saddam's fall was the sight of dozens of skinny young men wearing nothing but their underwear, giving up any attempt to resist the implacable force which had overthrown him.

59. TARGETS

The twenty-four-hour Arabic language station al-Jazeera, 'The Pearl', achieved one of the great successes of the war. Al-Jazeera, like its rivals al-Arabiya and Lebanon Broadcasting Company, has altered the entire polity of the Middle East. It isn't possible any longer for Arab governments to insist that the only truth that can be heard and seen is their truth.

Al-Jazeera may share most if not all the feelings and prejudices of its viewers; so does, say, Fox News in America. But unlike Fox News, it does allow a certain amount of airtime to people whose views it doesn't approve of. An Arabic-speaking spokesman for the Israeli government makes frequent appearances on al-Jazeera; Tony Blair justified his support for the American war against Iraq at length on one of its interview programmes; American supporters of George W. Bush made their case against Saddam again and again on al-Jazeera. Fox News would never have offered the same scope to supporters of Iraq.

Al-Jazeera's entire tone and approach, certainly, showed that its editors and correspondents knew they were broadcasting to people who believed the American and British invasion of Iraq was an unjustified aggression, and its language often reflected that. The BBC, for instance, would not have wanted to broadcast in such one-sided terms. But neither would it have wanted to use the kind of tone and language which Fox News habitually employed; on the whole I think al-Jazeera was the less biased of the two.

The American and British governments both professed themselves horrified when al-Jazeera broadcast pictures it had obtained from Iraqi television of dead and captured American soldiers, and Donald Rumsfeld seemed to think that broadcasting footage of American prisoners being asked where they came from contravened the Hague Convention. There was no truth in this; the prisoners were not being humiliated or ill-treated in any way, and the prisoners' families themselves agreed to allow the pictures to be broadcast.

As for the dead bodies, neither British nor American television stations would have wanted to show the pictures, because both countries share a cultural dislike of graphic, close-up images of death and injury. But discreet pictures of dead Iraqi soldiers had certainly appeared on American television, and we had seen Iraqi prisoners being herded around, humiliated and screamed at by British and American soldiers; neither Donald Rumsfeld nor Tony Blair had felt called upon to come out and complain about that.

There was a good deal of humbug in both countries about al-Jazeera, but it seemed to arise from an anxiety that anything other than the British and American version of events was getting round. Al-Jazeera had one or two embedded correspondents, but they found they were so marginalized and isolated with the Coalition forces that it was very hard for them to operate.

Yet while the British and American military regarded al-Jazeera as little more than a propaganda agency for Saddam Hussein, the Iraqis accused them of doing the Americans' work for them. After the Ministry of Information headquarters in Baghdad was bombed, Mohammed Saeed al-Sahhaf stormed round with a gun in his hand to see the correspondent who had broadcast pictures of the wreckage. He called him an American spy, and screamed that he would cut off his arms at the shoulders and throw them over the border. As for the rest of al-Jazeera's correspondents in Iraq, al-Sahhaf threatened that their broadcasting would be strictly controlled from now on.

The al-Jazeera management in Qatar made precisely the right response. If its correspondents couldn't operate properly in Iraq, it said, then they would withdraw from the country altogether. Two days later the Ministry of Information quietly withdrew all its threats, and al-Jazeera stayed in Iraq. Even so, in a completely unrelated incident, two of its correspondents were later expelled from Baghdad because the Iraqi government objected to the kind of thing they were reporting.

It is certainly true that whereas American reporting concentrated almost exclusively on what the American forces were doing, al-Jazeera directed much of its attention to reporting the effects of the Coalition attacks on the civilians of Iraq. Neither the British nor the American government seemed to have suggested that al-Jazeera broadcast phoney pictures of Iraqi casualties and deaths; they simply found it inconvenient that the pictures were being seen around the world.

There's nothing particularly wrong with governments trying to push their view of events into the public consciousness; they do it everywhere, all the time. But there is everything wrong if journalists in a free society echo this view without ensuring that it is true. Al-Jazeera, which is a remarkably free organization, broadcasting throughout the Middle East to people who will otherwise only get their own government's view, acted as a reality-check on the British and American version of events. Its motto, which appears everywhere in its offices, right down to the coffee-mugs, is 'Where there is one opinion, there is another one.' This is a minimalist, un-pompous, rather world-weary creed, which is mercifully free of grander appeals to Truth and Idealism. Al-Jazeera might not have been perfect, certainly, but it provided a remarkably balanced service. And it was a damned sight more honest than some of the American channels.

One of the best people al-Jazeera employed was Tariq Ayoub, a quiet, pleasant Jordanian of thirty-five. He was invariably polite, and not inclined to force his opinions about the war either on the people around or on the viewers who watched his reports. He often showed a hint of nervousness on camera as the missiles and bombs landed, but as a viewer I liked that. I didn't want to see some macho man defying the worst the Americans could throw at him. Ayoub seemed to me to share the vulnerability of the people of Baghdad whom he reported on.

At around 7 a.m. on Monday 7 April, just as Rageh Omaar looked out of his window and saw the Americans storming the presidential palace, two rockets were fired at the building, some way from the Palestine Hotel, where al-Jazeera had its office. Tariq Ayoub was crouched down on camera at the time, plainly terrified, reporting on the explosions around him. One of the rockets killed him as we watched. It was horrible, disgusting.

Was the attack deliberate? Perhaps not, given the amount of high explosive that was being fired off everywhere that morning. Nevertheless it was disturbing that al-Jazeera's offices had been hit twice in two consecutive wars – in Kabul in 2001 and now in Baghdad – and that on each occasion the Americans had complained that al-Jazeera was supporting the enemy. (In Afghanistan it persisted in showing video messages from Osama bin Laden. If the BBC had received them first we too would have rushed them on to the air and made great play with what we had obtained; would the United States have regarded us as an enemy too?)

During the NATO bombing of Belgrade in 1999, Serbian state television had been treated as an enemy target and bombed. All the senior editorial figures had been warned to keep away that night, but a number of people much lower down the scale had to work as usual and were killed. That attack, certainly, was intentional, just as the Kabul one was. There are those who believe it was a war crime, which should be punished as such.

Whether Tariq Ayoub was killed deliberately or in error, it was a shocking business. Soon afterwards, as the American tanks moved closer to the Palestine Hotel, a spotter on one of them thought he saw an anti-tank weapon on the roof of the building, where a sizeable group of journalists were watching their approach. It was of course a television camera. The tank fired, and killed a Reuters cameraman of Ukrainian origin, Taras Protsyuk. José Couso, a cameraman working for the Spanish channel Tele Cinco, was wounded and died soon afterwards. The American military command issued a statement which was essentially wrong:

'Commanders on the ground reported that Coalition forces received significant enemy fire from the Palestine Hotel, and consistent with the inherent right of self-defence Coalition forces returned fire.'

There was, of course, no fire from the Palestine Hotel, significant or otherwise. The attack was the work of a jittery officer who knew that the only law he needed to obey was the law of self-preservation. Neither he nor anyone else was called to account for the deaths of the two cameramen or the injuries to three other members of the Reuters team at the Palestine.

Some weeks later, at the conference I attended on the outskirts of Chicago, I met the American colonel who had been in overall command of the tank that day. He was a sharp, intelligent man, still young, who will no doubt make it to the top levels of the American military. I criticized him and his colleagues for their carelessness and lack of proper concern for civilian lives; he replied that he had received a great deal of hate-mail for what had happened, but insisted that his men had obeyed their instructions to the letter. He was particularly annoyed with me for suggesting that there had been no proper investigation of what had happened; he insisted that a careful examination of the entire incident had taken place.

The examination did not include the evidence of David Chater, the Sky News correspondent in Baghdad. A former officer in the British army, he was himself badly injured in the former Yugoslavia but continues to report from some of the most dangerous situations. He was watching the scene below from a balcony of the Palestine Hotel.

'I never heard a single shot coming from any of the area around here, certainly not from the hotel,' he reported on camera immediately afterwards. 'I noticed one of the tanks had its barrel pointed up at the building. We went inside and there was an almighty crash. That tank shell, if it was indeed an American tank shell, was aimed directly at this hotel and directly at journalists. This wasn't an accident, it seems to be a very accurate shot.'

No one, of course, was held accountable for the deaths, the injuries, the destruction. The colonel's men, understandably nervous and perhaps over-excitable, perpetually thought their lives were at risk, and in the US forces, that seems to be more important than ensuring the safety of the civilians around them.

The war against Saddam Hussein in 2003 saw a greater loss of life among journalists than in any comparable period of time: sixteen deaths in less than four weeks. Only in the Iran–Iraq War of 1980–88 and the Vietnam War were journalists killed on such a scale during the past fifty years. This war, against Saddam Hussein, was so one-sided and so brief that it is hard to understand how it was possible for so many reporters and their colleagues to die.

This is the full list:

Tariq Ayoub of al-Jazeera television, **Taras Protsyuk**, and **José Couso**, killed in Baghdad.

Julio Anguita Parrado – correspondent for the Spanish newspaper *El Mundo*, and **Christian Liebig**, correspondent for the German magazine *Focus*, killed when an Iraqi shell hit an American base outside Baghdad.

Kamaran Abdurrazak Mohammed – a Kurdish translator working for the BBC in northern Iraq, killed by an American missile in a so-called 'friendly fire' incident.

Michael Kelly – a correspondent for *Atlantic Monthly* and the *Washington Post*, killed when his military vehicle overturned.

Kaveh Golestan – an Iranian cameraman for the BBC, killed by a landmine in northern Iraq.

Gaby Rado – a correspondent for Britain's Channel 4 News, died in an accident.

Paul Moran – a cameraman for ABC Australia, killed by a suicide bomber in northern Iraq.

Terry Lloyd – a correspondent for Britain's ITN, killed, probably by American forces, in southern Iraq.

Fred Nerac – a French cameraman for ITN, and **Hussein Othman**, their translator, are both still missing, presumed dead, after the same incident.

Veronica Cabrera and **Mario Podesta** from Argentina's America TV, killed in a road accident.

David Bloom – a correspondent for NBC TV in America, died from deep-vein thrombosis after travelling for two days in an American military vehicle.

Sixteen people. Sixteen good, conscientious colleagues, who knew the risks they were running but were more concerned with reporting on the war than with their own safety. Nothing can mitigate the loss their families and friends feel, but we have a duty, it seems to me, to keep their memories alive. And perhaps, too, we have a duty to examine why they died.

Some, like Veronica Cabrera and Mario Podesta, were killed as a result of car crashes. These things are a constant danger for those who work in difficult places, and indeed even now, after a terrible twelve years of losses and injuries, more people from BBC News have died as the result of traffic accidents than from bombs and bullets. The mines which killed Kaveh Golestan and injured BBC producer Stuart Hughes are a constant danger in countries like Iraq and Afghanistan; in a way, we are lucky that more journalists weren't killed like this. Gaby Rado and David Bloom died in the kind of accidents that can happen anywhere; it doesn't make our sense of loss any easier, but there aren't many lessons to be learned from what happened to them.

So five deaths out of sixteen are depressingly explicable. That leaves eleven people who died from some kind of military action. One was Paul Moran, the Australian photojournalist who died when a suicide bomber blew him up: another terrible loss, but again something that was impossible to guard against.

Of the remaining ten, three were killed by the Iraqis. Michael Kelly died because his Humvee crashed after it had come under Iraqi fire. Julio Anguita Parrado and Christian Liebig were killed when an Iraqi shell hit the American base where they were staying.

That leaves seven: Taras Protsyuk, José Couso, Tariq Ayoub, Kamaran Abdurrazak Mohammed, Terry Lloyd, and Fred Nerac and

Hussein Othman, presumed dead though their bodies haven't been recovered. All of them were killed by American fire.

Seven out of ten of the journalists who died as a direct result of military action, therefore, were killed by American bombs, bullets and missiles. As far as the reporting of this war goes, the American forces were more than twice as dangerous to journalists as the Iraqis. As far as I know, there have been no public apologies for the deaths which have taken place, and any official investigations have yet to be concluded and their results brought to light.

This is not a political issue, nor an attempt to criticize either the fact that the war was fought at all, or the way it was fought. But I do think it's incumbent on us to try to find out why the Americans killed so many journalists, if only to persuade the Bush administration and American public opinion that something went very wrong this time, and that in the next war – if there is one, that is – the military should be a great deal more careful. The people who died, like the rest of us, were only doing their job, and that job is the kind of thing a country which regards itself as fighting a war for democracy should respect.

The British forces with the Coalition were not perfect. A cameraman from al-Jazeera TV, Akil Abdul-Amir, came under fire from British artillery while they were filming the shelling of food warehouses west of Basra. The vehicle he was in, which was unmarked, was hit. This is, however, the only incident I have come across where British forces attacked journalists.

Why did these things happen? I believe that it was the decision to embed reporters and camera crews with the American and British forces which was at the root of everything that followed. Around 600 people were embedded altogether, and in many ways the decision helped to give first-class television, radio and newspaper coverage of the war.

On the few occasions when the Iraqi military put up a fight, television's habit of leading its viewers to assume that the small-scale action we are watching on our screen is only part of something larger gave the impression that the momentary hold-ups were something really serious; hence the feeling at the end of the first week that things weren't going the Coalition's way. But no army which is completely without air cover and whose morale and weaponry are as poor as each other is likely to hold up a super-power for long, and from the second week onwards the war was fought with the kind of success which the American company Fox News told its viewers was being achieved all along. In that way at least Fox News was right.

In the unlikely event that the United States were to take on a country with a serious army and air force – Iran, for instance – I doubt if journalists and cameramen would be embedded then; instead, I imagine the Pentagon would try to imitate the British Ministry of Defence during the Falklands War, and do its best to keep any pictures back for as long as possible. But against Iraq, the embedded correspondents and cameramen were welcomed by soldiers and officials whose normal instinct would be to keep journalists as far away as possible.

Yet there is a price to be paid for this kind of closeness. That, after all, is why it was offered to us. The price was that it became quite difficult for all but the hardest-nosed reporters to be absolutely honest about the soldiers who fed them, transported them, gave them the power they needed for their equipment, and (when necessary) saved their lives from the enemy. That mere word, 'enemy', shows how a mind-set was created, and the word was used by plenty of reporters who didn't work for Fox News. If you are with one side in a war, your fortunes and those of the soldiers you are with are pretty tightly intertwined; deep down, you are praying that they won't fail. 'All I wanted,' wrote the London *Times* reporter Chris Ayres with engaging sincerity after the war was over, 'was for the Americans to win quickly; for my own safety, rather than any political reasons.'

And, of course, it's harder to write stories about hold-ups, lack of success, deficient morale, looting, war crimes. Chris Ayres did write about these things.

'When I reached the headquarters of the 1st Marine Division in central Iraq, a senior public affairs officer called me "a piss-poor journalist" because I had written a story saying that the supply lines were being attacked by the Iraqis and that we hadn't moved from our positions in several days.'

Chris Ayres goes on to quote him.

' "I'm glad you're leaving, because otherwise I would be kicking your ass out of here," he said. A Marine behind him, overhearing the conversation, grabbed my camping-chair and pulled it away. "You can sit in the fucking dirt," he said. "I ought to be fucking shooting you." '

It's only fair to say that Chris Ayres's experience wasn't by any means typical of the way that journalists were treated by the Americans. But this was the reason why many of us who were free to choose where we went preferred not to be embedded. We didn't want to be beholden to the very people whose actions we were obliged to report on impartially. Nor did we think that it was right that the only reporting on this war should come from the embedded correspondents or else from those based in Baghdad.

Reporting independently turned out to be every bit as dangerous as we feared it might; not so much because of the Iraqis, though plenty of journalists found themselves being held up and threatened by them, but because of the Americans. It was clear that the only journalists who the American soldiers and pilots were aware of, were those who were embedded. Anyone who was out there in the open was a potential target.

American soldiers tend to obey orders unthinkingly and without using their personal discrimination. They shoot rather than investigate, if they have the faintest sense that their own safety might be endangered. You do not feel safe around American soldiers when they are out in the open and liable to come under fire.

Nor, as I discovered, were we safe when American aircraft were overhead. Many of their crews were ordered to take Dexedrine or other speed-like drugs to keep them awake during their long patrols, and that was bound to have an effect on their behaviour and judgement. In the war against the Taliban in Afghanistan in 2001, some bomber and fighter pilots are reported to have taken Modafinil, which is far stronger than Dexedrine and can keep you going for forty hours without sleep.

The Defense Advanced Research Projects Agency, DARPA, has been instructed by the Pentagon to find ways of keeping soldiers awake and alert for a week or more, and they may be succeeding. In the next war, we may even see such drugs used. But soldiers aren't, or at least shouldn't be, automata: their judgement is the most important weapon they have.

The trouble is they don't use it, even at present. Who seriously thought someone was genuinely sniping at them from the Palestine Hotel in Baghdad – the incident in which a tank fired and killed Taras Protsyuk and José Couso? Who really thought a car which had 'TV' on it in big letters, and which had driven past them a few minutes before carrying Terry Lloyd and his ITN team, had suddenly turned into an Iraqi hit-squad?

I genuinely don't think American soldiers were trying to teach the media a lesson. I believe it was blind panic, inadequate street training, and complete ignorance.

When journalists are killed by mistake, this should be the subject of rigorous investigation and the punishment of those concerned; not because journalists are so wonderful, not because they are special in any way, but because their activities have a direct bearing on some of our most important liberties and the general health of our society. A failure to investigate and, where necessary, punish those who kill journalists is a failure to uphold the liberties which Western governments are pledged to maintain. This, after all, is the ultimate censorship – censorship of the kind approved by Saddam Hussein, who had Farzad Bazoft of the *Observer* executed in 1990 for investigating Iraq's weapons of mass destruction. The United States was so concerned with winning a small war against a weakened opponent that it betrayed some of its deepest-held convictions.

60. MOVING ON

We all dealt with the disaster that had befallen us in our own ways. Dragan Petrovic shut himself up in his room, which worried me. Fred Scott did the same, but he was watching movies. Abdullah the Afghan photographer lay in bed, telling a little group of respectful, sympathetic cleaning-ladies the story of his injuries. One brushed away a tear as I came into the room.

The rest of us talked it all over obsessively, and found that better than any course of treatment with a trauma therapist. I got further consolation from reading Fielding's *Tom Jones*, with a glass of single malt and a cigar beside me. *Sub specie aeternitatis*, I started the process of putting it all into perspective. I didn't dream about it, and the nasty things I'd seen didn't fill my head; not, at any rate, after I'd talked about them to the others.

On Wednesday 9 April, the day Baghdad fell, we went back for an examination at the American special forces hospital in Arbil. In my case the news was bad: the entire eardrum had been blasted away, leaving the inner ear exposed.

'Hey, that's interesting,' said the doctor, an engaging man who usually worked in the emergency unit of a big inner-city hospital in the US; he felt a lot safer here in Iraq, he said. 'I can see right through into your head. Never done that before. Not with someone alive, anyhow.'

He made me lie down on a gurney, and probed the wound in my hip to see if he could find the piece of shrapnel. The probe went down an inch and a half, but he couldn't reach it.

'Nowadays they don't take these things out anyway,' he told me. 'Causes too much nerve damage. It'll just grow to be a part of you, that's all.'

He was right. When I got back to England the specialists all agreed to let it stay where it was. It's still there: a chunk of aluminium the size and general shape of a bullet, which could have done things to me, but instead lodged in a part of the body where it could do no damage apart from causing a certain low but continuous level of pain. If only, I thought, the remarkable chance that guided the shrapnel into the one part of my body where it would do no harm had protected Kamaran against it too.

At lunchtime we sat in the dining-room of our hotel and talked about what we should do next. Through a contact of ours, I had discovered the American plan for dealing with Kirkuk and Mosul: the two towns, still held by Saddam's forces, which we had been waiting for weeks to enter. The big attack on them would come within four and five days respectively, and I was anxious to be there when it did. This was, after all, why we had come here.

I outlined the plan to the others as I understood it. We would go to Kirkuk first, then head westwards across country to Mosul, getting there hopefully in time for it to fall. Then we would turn south and go as fast as we could to Tikrit, Saddam's stronghold, where everyone expected the final battle of the war would take place. From there we would go to Baghdad, do a spot of reporting, then head back to England, home and beauty. I sat back and grinned at them. I was rather pleased with myself.

There was a silence, and I understood suddenly that not everybody saw things in quite the way I did. After what had happened to us,

Fred, who had done such a superb job when the missile fell on us, wanted to go home. He had already suffered a perforated eardrum some years before; now the same eardrum had been damaged again, and he was worried that if he was involved in any more front-line action he might lose his hearing altogether: a terrible loss for a cameraman. He wanted treatment as quickly as possible, though a specialist I spoke to in London told me over the phone that all of us with damaged eardrums would have to wait for weeks before it was possible to know whether they would heal of their own accord, or whether we would need operations.

Craig Summers, the security officer who was responsible for our safety, had escaped any real injury, though he'd been peppered with small pieces of shrapnel. He sat there now, looking at the marks on his arms and trying to dig the little bits out with his fingernail. He had problems back at base: one of the small-time jacks-in-office who make everyone's lives so hard in a big organization like the BBC had been insisting he should go home.

I myself was keen that Dragan Petrovic should leave, because he was worried that the piece of shrapnel which had lodged in his leg might mean he could lose his foot. And since he hadn't yet seen his daughter Andrea, who was now almost two months old, it seemed essential to get him across the border to Turkey, and then on to Belgrade. Abdullah, the photographer, needed to get back as well.

That left three of us: Oggy Boytchev, who had to stay with the satellite dish we were using, and its Anglo-Italian crew, even though he had been ill and needed an operation, Tom Giles, and me. Tom had a pronounced limp from the piece of shrapnel which had sliced into his little toe (there really can't have been much room inside it, considering the shrapnel didn't touch the bone) and the cut seemed to be turning mildly septic. He had to wear a slipper on his foot with a plastic bag over it to protect against the constant rain. I was limping too, and was as deaf as a post. When the two of us walked down the street we looked like a couple of vagrants trying to find a doorway to kip in.

I'd known Tom for a long time. Although there is a twenty-three-year gap in our ages, we come from backgrounds which aren't all that different: middle-class, broken homes, even the same school. While we were in Iraq he confessed he had written me a letter when he was still at St Paul's, asking how he could get into television journalism. I answered his letter, apparently; thank God for that, given the amount of time we have spent together on the road and the scope we have had for arguments.

Tom and I have worked alongside each other in some dreadful places, and usually managed to find the experience amusing. Tom has progressed rapidly in the BBC, but each new promotion seems to offer some opportunity for us to work together from time to time: in Afghanistan, and now in Iraq. I am a terrible trial to him. I have sudden bouts of irritability with people Tom has patiently been cultivating, and offend them horribly; I announce at the last moment that something has come up to prevent my leaving for an important filming trip on time; I insist that he must stretch his budgets beyond breaking-point so I can fly business class; I disagree so strongly with him about the direction of a story that it makes his life intolerable; but though he is no shrinking violet, and can be aggressive and demanding himself, we always come to some mutually acceptable agreement.

So now we were sitting in the dining-room of the Arbil Tower Hotel, with a glass of over-sweetened tea in front of us and the marks of yet another chicken and rice dish on the dirty tablecloth, and I was listening to reasons why everyone else wanted to leave. I hadn't yet spoken to Tom. He was sitting on my right. It was time to ask him.

I had a sudden and unreasonable flashback to January 1991, when most of the team decided to leave Baghdad on the night before the missiles began to land, and only three of us stayed. Suppose, I thought to myself, Tom refuses to stay? It wasn't the prospect of covering the last chapter of the war alone that worried me; I used to be a radio reporter, and radio reporters always work alone. It was just that I'd feel such a sense of betrayal. I'd have to rethink my entire judgement of character if he turned me down.

Tom had been as badly injured as any of the others, and had been lucky not to lose his foot, like poor Stuart the radio producer in northern Iraq. Perhaps I should also ask myself how I manage to get into these situations, where my colleagues feel they have to leave me? Is it me or is it them? And if it's me, should I do something about it?

I messed around for a moment with my empty glass, and arranged the knife and fork with some care. At last I couldn't put it off any longer. I turned to face him.

'So, are you going or staying?'

I was much more brusque than I meant to be, and simply succeeded in annoying him.

'Of course I'm staying. What do you think?'

Relief flooded through me. Apart from anything else, he knew what was needed for the documentary. He could also use a camera.

'So we'll do it on our own?'

'We've got Hiwa.'

That was a relief too. Hiwa Osman worked for BBC Monitoring in England, but his father was a famous figure among the Kurds and Hiwa's contacts and his nose for a story were unrivalled. The three of us might be a bit short on the technical side, but we would be able to turn in some excellent work. But the thought that Tom, at least, hadn't turned me down made everything seem good again.

'You must remember,' said Ron ben-Yishai, the Israeli, when I told him, 'you and I are reporters. We have a lot to gain from staying. Tom – he is the same, and he comes from the same background. He's a gentleman.'

The words had an antique sound, but I knew what he meant.

We said goodbye to everyone and headed off eastwards to Suleimaniyah, where we were told the assault on Kirkuk would come from. It was, in a way, exhilarating to be on our own. The problems would be far greater, but so was the challenge; and at last, after the weeks of feeling that we were in the wrong place, the focus of the war had shifted to northern Iraq and we were on hand to report it.

61. THE CITIES FALL

Suleimaniyah was a large, relatively attractive town which had greatly prospered during the years of Iraqi Kurdistan's freedom from Saddam. It was the stronghold of the PUK, where Hiwa's contacts were particularly good. He took us straight round to the house of the PUK prime minister, Dr Varham Salih. He wasn't there, but a group of thirty armed and uniformed men were hanging around in the street outside. A year before to the day, a group of Islamic extremists linked to Iran had attacked the house and tried to kill him; five of his bodyguards had died, and ever since then the PUK had taken no chances. We sat and drank endless cups of tea and waited.

There was a sudden flurry. Dr Salih strode into the room and gripped my hand. He was a studious-looking but energetic man who had been educated at Liverpool University and had been partly responsible for designing the M20 motorway in Britain. He gave us dinner, and in his decisive way announced that from now on we would have five members of the PUK President's personal bodyguard to travel with us and protect us. To be honest, I wasn't keen. Armed men, in my experience, get you into more trouble than they can protect you from. I have never yet found a confrontation I couldn't talk myself out of, though I freely admit this could change quite quickly.

Now there was no alternative: I could see it in Dr Salih's determined eyes. He knew it would be dangerous for Tom, Hiwa and me to go to Kirkuk and Mosul, and five highly trained bodyguards were, for him, the answer. He bade us an affectionate farewell, and we went out to start our evening's broadcasting. Suleimaniyah Television had set up a camera position outside the main hotel, and I broadcast all evening as the town went wild in its celebrations of the fall of Baghdad. The streets were packed with hooting cars and cheering crowds. People held up pictures of George W. Bush and Tony Blair, and flew the Stars and Stripes, the Union Jack and the PUK flag. This was the kind of thing Bush and Blair had been expecting would happen throughout Iraq; if they watched our pictures that night they must have felt that here at least their actions had been justified.

We were going to spend that night in the Suleimaniyah Palace Hotel, which was far better than the place we had stayed in Arbil, with its flies and cockroaches. Our suite was the one the BBC had occupied for weeks past. It was from here that Jim Muir, Stuart Hughes and Kaveh Golestan had left on the morning of the day they hit the minefield: a sobering thought to send us to sleep before the next morning's attack on Kirkuk.

We had found a cameraman: rather a good one, in fact. Dana was pot-bellied and shaven-headed, and he had only the little digital camera we gave him, but his instincts seemed right and he was a pleasant, easy-going companion. Our driver was an old Pesh Merga fighter, gnarled and small and humorous, who reminded me slightly of a rather jolly gnome. He was inclined, as he drove along, to break into a sudden snort of amusement and beat the steering-wheel with his fist. Maybe he was remembering old campaigns; he had fought the Iraqi army just about everywhere in northern Iraq. We went in front in our four-wheel drive, and the bodyguards stayed behind us in their black vehicle.

In the distance we could hear the sound of bombing. I passed the time as we drew closer by jotting down some notes:

> Tozhkermatoo (can it really be called that?) has fallen. We decide to go there, on main Kirkuk–Baghdad road. We have no idea what lies beyond, and we have two enemies – retreating Iraqis and nervous Americans (remember Terry Lloyd). But, Hiwa says, 'the boys' – i.e. our guards – 'are up for it'. I suppose we are too.
>
> Road up ridge from Chamchamal still mined on either side. We come to (PUK) roadblock, and turn off left along a small side-road. Feeling very vulnerable.
>
> Glorious blue sky, open green meadows. With the cottonwool in my damaged ear, I've retreated into a world of silence. Have to sit at an angle in front seat, because of drain inserted into wound. Quite painful.
>
> 'This place has no man's land written all over it,' says Tom. 'They always have this delightful quality.'
>
> A whole Iraqi division is, we're told by a PUK officer we meet, nearby and fighting ferociously. He points: I can see a column of black smoke going up about three miles away. The B-52s are clearly visible, high in the sky like silver crosses.
>
> Hiwa takes a call on his satphone.
>
> 'Our forces are in Kirkuk,' he says, grinning.
>
> It turns out that the PUK have pulled a fast one. Instead of waiting for the Americans, as they agreed, they infiltrated the city during the night. Now there's fighting. We have to get there fast. I ring Malcolm [Downing, the BBC's foreign editor] and tell him we're going there the quickest way. We turn round in the minefield where we stopped – no mines on road, fortunately – and head back. Two huge fires from oil wells dominate the skyline: the Iraqis have blown them up.
>
> On the road as we go into Kirkuk there are abandoned olive-green uniform jackets and trousers everywhere: Saddam's men have done a runner. Oil trenches, just as in Baghdad: broad, black, soaking into ground. A picture of Saddam, shot up.

I jotted down a report to send for radio:

Cue: Kirkuk has fallen. JS.

The centre of the city reeks of smoke from government buildings
and the symbols of Saddam Hussein's control. A column of dark
smoke is going up from one of the nearest oil wells to the city, and
there's another one farther off. Oil, too, lies in trenches round the
city, apparently dug to deter attackers. But they didn't deter the
Kurdish special forces, who slipped in during the night and created
the rebellion which overthrew the Ba'ath Party's control . . .

The overthrow of Saddam's reign in Kirkuk came with extraordinary speed. Unlike the other towns and cities in Iraq, this
place simply imploded . . .

The Kurds have gone much farther and faster than the Americans wanted, and for now this city is in the hands of Kurdish
irregular troops. They're everywhere, firing their guns in the air
and hooting their horns as they drive triumphantly through the
streets they themselves have liberated.

In the park in the centre of the town Saddam's statue lay at an angle
where it had been pushed down in the approved revolutionary fashion,
its head almost touching the ground, resting on its broken arm. It was
Saddam dressed as an Arab sheikh – the Kurds here had always hated
that – and people were taking off their shoes and bashing its head with
the soles, or climbing up on to the plinth and chanting, 'Thank you,
USA.' Kurds and Shi'ites were both there together – something that
was important for the peace of this town, which was originally almost
entirely Kurdish until Saddam planted thousands of Sunni Arabs and
Shi'ites here as well.

As it turned out, though, the ethnic problem here was less serious
than the law and order problem. Something seemed to snap inside the
heads of Iraqis directly they knew that Saddam was finished. I watched,
appalled, as we went to a nearby hospital to see if we could get some
painkillers, and found the entire building being ransacked by a crowd
of laughing, shouting, jostling people. They were dragging anything
and everything out of the place: bits of computers, beds, hospital
records, emergency equipment. Maybe they thought these things had a
value and could be resold. Maybe they just wanted to get their hands
on something they believed Saddam had taken from them. It was a

terrible wound to inflict on themselves, but in the absence of any form of control they were as likely to sack a hospital as they were to loot a department store or a bank.

'This is independence?' a man screamed as he saw our camera. 'This is not independence. Some are shooting, some are stealing. This is not independence!'

With splendid timing, Oggy Boytchev joined us with the crew of the satellite dish, but their efforts were vitiated by the fact that the editing machines had gone home with Fred Scott. We were unable to put a proper report together, therefore: a shame, since I seemed at that stage to be the only television reporter in the town. Back in the hotel, I was recording tracks for agency pictures of the things we had seen and filmed for ourselves but were unable to edit, when I got up to speak to someone outside in the corridor and somehow found myself on the floor. I stayed there for a few minutes, until Oggy came and very solicitously helped me up and got me to lie down on the bed. A doctor came round and gave me an intravenous painkiller and some intravenous antibiotics, and I had a brief nap before doing some more broadcasting. After that I slept long and well for hours.

> *Friday 11 April.* We go to Chemical Ali's house. [Ali Hassan al-Majid, Saddam's enforcer, had crushed the Kurds in the past, notably at Halabjah, and used this house as his base whenever he was here. He had been there only a short time before.] Cheap, smelly, dirty and entirely characterless. I don't necessarily believe the stories about his drunkenness and the belly dancers which the head watchman enthusiastically retails: maybe true, but I've heard so much of this kind of thing. It's the lack of taste which is so characteristic of him. These people were just low-life bandits. No education, no culture, no taste, no right to govern except the gun. The looters have been here too, but there's enough left to see how Chemical Ali lived: the plastic fittings, the imitation gold taps, the lavatory that must have been blocked months ago and never seen to.

The next day, 12 April, we headed on to Mosul. After all the weeks we had watched it from a distance, filming the bright flashes in the sky as American bombs and missiles struck it, we finally approached it in the morning. Now the people in the city had overthrown Saddam's regime and were starting to confront each other: Kurds against Sunni Arabs against Shi'ites.

> A cloud of acrid smoke is hanging over the city, and along the road every shop is closed for fear of rioting, and burned-out cars litter the side-streets. The uprising here has gone very badly wrong . . .
>
> We reach Camera Hill: combination of shaken journalists who've come out of Mosul, and nervous ones who haven't gone in. Oggy joins us with dish. Tom and I don't see how we can decently stay here on city outskirts, and decide to drive in. Our driver is particularly good, but Hiwa even better. He fixes up with Farhan Sharifani, head of Kurdish Sharifani tribe, to meet us and escort us in. Terrible scenes of destruction on way, but Kurdish area more peaceful and some shops even open. Our bodyguards have put UN plates on cars – suitably, from UN water and sewage authority.
>
> Sharifani's house is surrounded by armed men, dozens of them, and all sorts of weird characters have gathered there. We meet a general from Saddam's security service, plus Arab leaders and two of Izzat Ibrahim's bodyguards. He seems to have escaped to Syria.

He had indeed. Izzat Ibrahim was effectively Saddam's deputy, a strange-looking man, skeletal and with a brilliant mop of red hair. We established that the day before we arrived he had driven through Mosul, stopped at the Central Bank, ordered the unfortunate manager at gunpoint to give him all the gold and dollar reserves in the vaults, loaded it all into a fleet of Mercedes, and driven off in the direction of the Syrian border.

> Sharifani, together with senior Arab leaders, made the rising happen. But they expected the Americans to come in, and they didn't: hence the looting and violence.
>
> There are all sorts of goings-on now. Hiwa explains quietly to me that Saddam's minister of defence is trying to negotiate his surrender with Sharifani. Apparently the minister is sitting some-where in the desert with a satphone.
>
> We interview the security general. He's loathsome – the real equivalent of some surrendered Nazi. Yes, the regime was terrible, and no one was safe from informers and execution. Yet he,

apparently alone, had clean hands. He could assure me of that. Terrible things were done to him and his family, but he just did his job (as a secret policeman, of course) and tried to help people.

Afterwards Tom does an imitation of me interviewing the general: it sounds like John Humphrys speaking to a government minister. 'How can you possibly sit there and say that?'

The bodyguards are worried with all these renegades around, and want to sleep in my room. I refuse; they compromise, and sleep in the corridor.

More trouble in the night – a lot of shooting, though some say it's because they've heard Tikrit has fallen. [In the morning] Tom is limping around and eating an old piece of bread and meat from last night's dinner. 'Faced with a choice between starvation and food-poisoning,' he says, but fails to complete the sentence.

2 US planes fly right over us, presumably attacking vehicles on the road from Tikrit. Strange how uneasy it makes me. I check with Tom: he feels the same. Neither of us has any great fear of guns, but bombs are suddenly a real terror. Especially US ones.

We drive through centre of Mosul. Very eerie, like the world after nuclear attack. Little gangs of would-be rioters hang round but do nothing, because PUK guards are everywhere. Our bodyguards not happy about us here. Money, stolen from banks and ripped up into thousands of little pieces because entirely worthless, whirls in wind and flutters along gutter like coloured butterflies.

The next day we drove on to Tikrit. The sky was red and angry; as red and angry as the small wounds on my arms and legs and head where the American shrapnel had hit me. The hot wind whirled and fretted the dust of the vast, open, waterless, dun-coloured plain as we drove through.

'Mount Hamrin,' Hiwa murmured. He pointed through the windscreen at a long ridge stretching across the horizon ahead of us. It was the borderline between Kurdish Iraq and Arab Iraq. Beside the road were the scrapings in the sand and the sandbagged positions and the smashed guns where Saddam Hussein's army had been until that morning. They had deserted eight hours before.

We were late: worryingly so. It was 6.45 now, and the sun was sloping down fast to our right. This was not good country to be caught in at night.

'TIKRIT 70 km', announced a signpost beside the road.

'*Yalla, yalla,*' I said to the gnomelike driver, quite unnecessarily, since he didn't want to spend the night here in the open, with bandits and angry, defeated soldiers on the loose, any more than I did. Twenty yards behind us was the vehicle containing our bodyguards: five tough, well-trained characters in uniform who had been given to us (slightly against our better judgement) by the president of the PUK movement in Kurdistan. He had told them that if we were killed, they shouldn't come back. They took their duties very seriously, and you couldn't get out and relieve yourself by the roadside without having a man with an AK-47 standing guard on you.

And now we were heading towards the place where, it seemed reasonable to assume, the last battle would take place. I remembered Tikrit from 1991: Saddam Hussein had put 200 or more tanks round the place, in case the Coalition forces invaded Iraq and captured Baghdad. It was to have been the city where the culminating battle was fought; maybe now, twelve years later, the same would happen.

Thirty miles or so from Tikrit, there was a new anxiety. Vehicle after vehicle with 'Press' or 'TV' marked on it came away from Tikrit at speed. As they flashed past us our driver, a tough little character who had been a Pesh Merga, or Kurdish fighter, years before, would lift his hands off the steering-wheel, palms upwards, in a sign that meant, 'What's going on?' The answer never seemed clear. 'Everything's fine,' a Spanish reporter called out, stopping briefly. 'Go back!' shouted another, scarcely slackening his speed. It was impossible to know what to do. So we carried on.

62. TIKRIT: OUR ARRIVAL

As the sun set, we reached the bridge over the Tigris which is the main entrance to Tikrit from the north. The Americans had been here for most of the day, and had entered the city without any of the fighting I, for one, had expected.

But there was no last stand. The American marines had driven into the city with scarcely a shot fired at them. It was the final big action of the war. Yet the atmosphere was tense enough, even here at the bridge. On the bluff above us was one of Saddam Hussein's palaces – his favourite anywhere in Iraq, so it was said – which the marines had taken over as their headquarters. It was a natural target for attack, and as we were passing this way the following day the marines discovered what they thought was a car-bomb. Everyone was very jittery.

The ordinary soldiers were polite, all the same, and when I said we were from the BBC it produced a gratifying response.

'Just 'bout every one of us listens to BBC here,' said a short, pudgy black marine, giving us a gap-toothed grin. ''S the one way we get to find out what's happenin' in this war.'

I explained what we were doing, and why we were being followed by a car containing five men in Iraqi military uniform. An officer walked across. He, too, listened to the BBC.

'No problems about them, sir, but we can't let your guards take weapons into the town. They'll have to leave them with us.'

I knew this would be difficult for the bodyguards, because they were sworn to defend Tom and me to the death. But Hiwa got out and explained the situation to them tactfully, and they handed over their AK-47s.

''Preciate your cooperation, sir,' said the marine officer. 'You guys have been real nice.'

So had these marines. Our vehicles rumbled across the bridge into Tikrit, with the shadows lengthening fast.

It was a different town from the one I had passed through in 1991. Then it had seemed just another untidy, backward little place; now, real money had been spent on it. Several of the buildings were faced with marble, and were five storeys high. A statue of Saddam on horseback – rather a good likeness, I thought – stood at the junction where the road from the bridge met the main street which ran through the town. I stared up at the imperious features, the proud, straight back: it was hard enough for me to imagine that after all this time Saddam was gone. For the locals it must have been virtually impossible.

'Stop right there.' Another group of US marines stood across the road. There was much more tension in the voice that called out to us. I explained everything all over again, showing them my little piece of

BBC plastic with the photograph accidentally reversed on it, and an expiry date which had passed some months before. It didn't even occur to me to worry that someone might notice that; no one ever did.

The marines here didn't say anything about listening to the BBC. They were frightened and jumpy, and inclined to shout, and no one seemed to listen when I explained about the five men in the vehicle immediately behind us. I started to shout too, giving contrary instructions to the driver. I wanted him to pull forward and park by the side of the road so that we could get out and do some filming, and I was so concerned with that, and the fact that someone had set up a live television camera on the pavement and was filming our arrival, that I paid no attention to what was happening to the other vehicle.

Then I looked in the rear-view mirror. A marine was pulling one of the bodyguards out by the arm. Another was dragging the chief bodyguard along the street.

'They're armed!' someone else was shouting, and another marine was screaming, 'These are Eye-raqi Republican Guards!'

Quietly, but tensely, Hiwa said, 'They kept their side-arms.'

Of course they would have; they would rather have walked through Tikrit naked than followed us unarmed. I jumped out, my blood boiling. The rather dapper bodyguard with a small, well-cut moustache was lying in the road with a marine's boot on the back of his neck. I could see his face; it was contorted and dark red with rage. There would be serious violence here soon. I hobbled over, waving my stick in fury.

'Get your fucking foot off him. These are BBC people. They all are. Leave them alone at once.'

An officer, pleasant and rather impressive under other circumstances, was standing ineffectually nearby, watching all this. Now he stepped forward. But the strange thing was that the marines obeyed me; perhaps it was the yelling. The officer started to apologize. He, too, listened to the BBC.

At that point another marine came running across the road, his rifle swinging dangerously around. As the bodyguards, whose uniforms did indeed look rather like those of the Iraqi Republican Guard, picked themselves up and stared resentfully at the men who had humiliated them, the marine screamed, 'Sniper!' and pointed his rifle at a nearby rooftop.

I looked up. In the gathering darkness an elderly man was shuffling around trying to fold up a blanket which had been left out to air in the afternoon sun.

'If you fire that rifle,' I shouted, 'I shall be a witness at your trial for murder.' It took me a second or two to get the words out, but he lowered his weapon. I must have sounded like Peter Sellers as the RAF officer in *Dr Strangelove* trying to get Colonel Bat Guano to lend him the money to call the Pentagon and stop an all-out nuclear attack on Russia; we had watched the video back in Arbil, two weeks earlier.

The marine officer was full of remorse. I could certainly understand the earlier mistake: our bodyguards might very well have been members of Saddam's Republican Guard. But I couldn't understand their lack of self-control – their near-hysteria, indeed. Nor could I understand why, as the only troops holding the main street of Saddam's home town, they weren't equipped with an Arabic translator. But they paid a price for their excitability: the entire incident had been broadcast live on al-Jazeera Television, and the broadcast had been picked up, also live, by CNN International. It had been seen in every Arab country, and in many parts of the wider world.

For a moment or two I felt some remorse of my own; what kind of figure must I have cut, lurching around like a comic actor from an early sixties movie, threatening US marines with my walking-stick? But the moment passed, while the marine captain's apologies continued. Two of his men, he said pointedly, would be round later on to apologize to the bodyguards in person. After Hiwa told them that, the redness began to leave their eyes. These were men whose pride was more important to them than their lives, but to have American marines apologizing to them would make up for a great deal.

63. TIKRIT: SADDAM'S LEGACY

There was no question who this city belonged to. Even now that he was gone, Saddam's picture decorated every lamppost, every shop window, every wide place in the road. Whatever they might be doing everywhere else in Iraq, no one toppled his statue or shot the eyes out of his portraits here. In Tikrit, Saddam remained a living presence. He was exhorting them, rewarding them, threatening them as though the American invasion had never happened and he was still in charge of their lives.

The next day I recorded an edition of my programme *Simpson's World* in the centre of Tikrit. It is part of the programme's style to present the place which we are filming exactly as it is for those twenty-five minutes, so when there was a sudden downpour of rain we carried on filming, and I interviewed a group of eight or nine people from the town who were taking shelter, as we were, outside a row of shops.

The range of opinions was extraordinary; so was the fact that anyone was prepared to speak to me at all, given that only thirty-six hours earlier they would have risked death if they had criticized Saddam Hussein in public to a Western journalist.

There are different kinds and grades of dictator. Some merely command the bodies of their subjects: Pinochet in Chile, Mugabe in Zimbabwe, Leonid Brezhnev in the Soviet Union. They are savage enough to anyone who steps out of line, but are usually satisfied with outward compliance. Others, like Mao Zedong or Nicolae Ceausescu, burrow their way into people's minds, turning them into the policemen of themselves, hypnotizing them with the fear of being disloyal and the desire to become acceptable in the Leader's eyes.

Saddam Hussein was the latter type: an inner voice inside every-one's head, a permanent, twenty-four-hour-a-day terror. There was nowhere you could be safe from him, no moment when you could relax. Your wife, your husband, your children might all betray you for thought-crime against the Leader. Some people did, of course, defy him; Iraqis are a fierce people and not easily cowed. But if they were discovered they usually paid a terrible price for it. The fear which each arrest, each torture session, each execution engendered radiated out through society, eating into everyone's minds, so that you had to be very brave or very stupid indeed to do anything that might attract official mistrust and anger.

Saddam Hussein's duller opponents routinely called him another Hitler, another Stalin, but because these were merely easy insults does not mean they were untrue. On his smaller scale – and the scale wasn't always *that* small; how many other Third World dictators have sparked off a war which killed a million people? – Saddam was to his people and his enemies what Hitler and Stalin were to theirs. But he was a man who made foolish, elementary strategic mistakes and then had to get out of the trouble he had made for himself by the cleverest of tactics.

Like Stalin, whom he hero-worshipped as a young man, Saddam was a dull companion whose only real fascination lay in the terrible power he could wield. He was no conversationalist, no wit, no intellectual, and he appeared to have no insight into himself and his own motives. He collected nothing of interest, and built nothing of interest; in other words, he devoted the enormous resources of the Iraqi state, which he treated as his own, to little more than the celebration of his own power and the fostering of terror.

Still, he had a fine eye for the siting of his various palaces. During the 1990s he built a huge palace complex in Tikrit overlooking the river Tigris, where he, his wife and his mistress lived in a state of mutual recrimination and sometimes open hostility. Like so much of the building work Saddam ordered, it was poorly done; he was ripped off time and again by the contractors, many of them Westerners. The limestone facing comes away like a badly applied veneer, revealing the carelessly laid cinder blocks underneath. Damp rises up from the foundations, iron-laden water dribbles down the façades, leaving its characteristic stain. Soon, the doors cease to fit properly and the curtains come off their poles.

We met up with another BBC team, who had come up from Baghdad: Fergal Keane and Glen Middleton, particular friends of mine, and Caroline Hawley, the BBC correspondent who had been thrown out of Baghdad on a trumped-up charge some weeks before. With them as a safety adviser was a tough, impressive former SAS man, Ian Watt. Since the war in Bosnia, television organizations have increasingly hired people like him to work with their teams in difficult places. They are not, of course, armed, but they know how to look after themselves and the people they are working with, and their knowledge of military affairs can be extremely useful.

That night I had one of the weirdest meals of my life. With nothing more to light us than a three-quarter moon, we sat at a rickety table outside a teahouse on the pavement of the main street of Tikrit, eating tough kebabs wrapped in bread with the general consistency of coarse cardboard, and drinking strong tea. From time to time, over to the south-west, we could hear the low booming of explosions as American planes bombed some more unfortunates into submission. A passing patrol of US marines warned us that we had less than an hour to be out in the street, but anyway there was broadcasting to be done, and the kebabs were not worth lingering over. I still tasted the fat on my palate an hour afterwards.

An American officer came up as we were about to leave. He had, he told us urgently, received intelligence that Jordanian and Syrian *fedayeen* had taken refuge in a mosque only sixty metres away from us. He was obviously trying to be helpful, but I could somehow tell it wasn't true; that kind of story never is. There wasn't anything we could do about it anyway.

We spent that night in and around the police station, with the mosquitoes infiltrating everywhere. I slept in our vehicle, with a mosquito net wrapped ineffectively around me; I must have looked like Miss Havisham.

64. TIKRIT: THE PALACE

The next day, as we stumbled around the compound or shaved in the reflection of windows or car mirrors, groaning with the discomforts of the night and scratching our bites, the desire came over us more and more strongly to move somewhere a little less uncomfortable: and Saddam's palace came forcibly to mind. Once the idea had been broached, it grew powerfully within us and could not be set aside. The combination of palatial comfort and the opportunity to boast that we had been Saddam's guests was an unbeatable one. Whatever it takes, I said to Oggy Boytchev; whatever it takes.

It turned out to take a good deal. The US marines were based there, and their mood was not made easier by the discovery of a car-bomb on the bridge beside the palace. Oggy negotiated for what seemed like hours to get us in: the marines didn't want us, and the group of journalists who were hoping to get in was growing. One team was there already, a television crew from Fox News which had persuaded the US military (which liked Fox's noisy, irreflective, triumphalist style, and couldn't understand why everyone couldn't be like that) to allow them in to report on the marines and their doings. From the area where the Fox team had set up their equipment I heard the loud and unmusical voice of an otherwise moderately attractive young blonde from, possibly, Austria, raised above the surrounding noise: 'This is *my* embed, and I'm not sharing it with anyone.' Non-Americans who work for the American news networks are sometimes very hard to take.

Finally we were allowed to drive through the gates to the huge palace grounds – the gatehouse was bigger than my flat in London – and up the winding hill towards the complex of marble buildings above us. I spotted Oggy standing by the side of the road trying to placate the sizeable lieutenant-colonel who seemed to be in charge here. Things, clearly, had got to the colonel.

'There's marine blood been spilled up here,' he was shouting.

This seemed to mean that the hill-top was too sacred for the sacrilegious sweepings of the world's press to be allowed to profane; though when I spoke to a more rational marine later he told me that the only marine blood which had been spilled, as far as he knew, was that of a sergeant whose knife had slipped as he was trying to open a bag containing an MRE – 'Meal Ready to Eat'.

There seemed to be two types of American marine, officers and men. One was the colonel's type, with protruding eyes, expanded chest, and a patriotic sentiment waiting to explode at any moment; another officer lectured us about doing our work in a way which wasn't brazen, and managed to get the American Bill of Rights into his homily to us, together with a warning that if we didn't like it here we should pack our shit and get out.

The other type of officer was far more relaxed, even in the difficult circumstances of newly liberated Tikrit, and it seemed to me that several of the more sensible types thought these little displays of infarctive excitability were absurd and embarrassing. You must never generalize where Americans are concerned. For every popping-eyed extremist you will find someone who is calm and sane and unexcitable, and usually very funny.

The palace compound somehow lent itself to extremism, though. There were eight or nine palaces spread over the hillside, set in gardens which were beginning to show the first obvious signs of neglect.

Saddam hadn't been around for some time, clearly. From a distance they were rather impressive, especially Saddam's own: a huge, rambling affair with extra wings and floors erupting out of the central block like a vast, overcooked soufflé. It had the best view over the Tigris, naturally, and its decoration was more elaborate than any of the others: curlicues and pinnacles and arches exploded out of it, as though Gaudí had returned to earth and been hired to design a prison.

Personally, I would have been reluctant to stay there. Some years before, I had met some of the contractors who had been involved in the job, and they were neither paid properly nor allowed to leave when their tasks were finished; there was some dispute, inevitably, about money and workmanship. As a result, they told me, they had taken their revenge by linking the sewage system in some way with the air-conditioning; Saddam's main palace may not have been the haven he had planned for himself.

There were smaller palaces dotted around the complex on the top of the hill. One of them belonged to Saddam's first wife, Sajida, who was the mother of his children. There were guest palaces where Saddam's sons Uday and Qusay occasionally stayed with their entourages. Another was where Saddam's mistress, Samirah al-Shahabandar, used to stay when Sajida was not on hand. It was this relationship which led to the worst of the feuds within Saddam's dysfunctional family, and had a major effect on the development of the wider Iraqi crisis.

As darkness fell, it started to rain heavily. Could we, Oggy asked, take refuge in one of the empty palaces for the night? The US marine colonel exploded again. These palaces belonged to the Iraqi people, and he had ordered his men not to set foot inside them; and if US marines couldn't sleep there, no one else sure as hell could. What was more, his men would patrol the little lanes which connected the palaces all night long to ensure that we didn't creep inside to get out of the rain. If US marines had to sleep in the rain, then . . . But we had got the message.

Our former SAS adviser, Ian Watt, slipped into one of the outlying palaces to reconnoitre. There were, he found, mattresses on the beds there, and he lugged them out between patrols. I sat in the shelter of one of the grand doorways with Fergal Keane and Caroline Hawley, eating spicy meatballs from some military MRE packs. Television

journalism is a highly competitive business, and it is not always easy
for correspondents like ourselves to coexist while covering a story.
Fergal, however, made the relationship between us work with gener-
osity and grace, suggesting that Glen Middleton, his cameraman,
should work for Tom and me whenever we needed him, and then – an
act of almost unheard-of altruism – letting me take alternate puffs of
the only cigar he had left.

The marines who were ordered to patrol the palaces in the rain
were men of a rather more human stamp than their commanding
officer. They would stop and talk to us, partly for company and partly
to get a little shelter, and we would ask them insinuatingly if they had
had a chance to talk to their wives or girlfriends recently. None of
them had been able to speak to the people back home since they had
arrived in Iraq. In exchange for a call on one of our mobile satellite
phones, they agreed to all sorts of minor services, the best of which
was to turn a blind eye to the mattresses from the palace which no one
was to enter.

I wandered round the outside of the palace, examining it in the
light of my head-torch. The design of all these places was remarkably
eclectic, and this one was partly oriental and partly Greek. It reminded
me somehow of the Christian Science church I used to go to when I
was a child: square, marble, simple, the precise opposite of the Gothic
styles of the established church. Someone had smashed the glass of a
window at the back, and I slipped inside, my feet crunching on the
glass slivers lying on the marble floor. It was very eerie; the huge pieces
of furniture cast shadows twelve feet high on the walls, and the wind
whipped the curtains out through the windows and lashed them like
frenzied ghosts. I peered at the paintings on the walls: they were the
kind of cheap, talentless stuff you see in any exhibition of amateur art
in the Arab world, except that here the painters had hit it rich and
very lucky with their scenes of alpine hillsides and fat, unrealistic
cattle.

The toilets stank; so did the area round them. Saddam's family
might be hugely wealthy and powerful, but they and their entourage
seemed to be largely un-house-trained. The carpets, as far as I could
see by the light of my torch, were badly stained and poorly fitted.
But this in a way was an indication of the kind of people they were.

Saddam did not feel at home with luxury. His childhood had been of the poorest, and the most formative part of his life had been spent as a fugitive. Sleeping rough was natural to him, and to some extent, it seemed, his family had followed his example.

These absurdly grand and expensive surroundings meant nothing as far as they were concerned – they were just the outward and visible signs of the huge power which the President of Iraq and his family wielded. Saddam's sons might have known nothing except marble palaces and expensive cars, but he himself showed no interest in these things whatsoever. He was a revolutionary, a man of the resistance, a figure of the underground. He was never so happy as when outside force obliged him to leave his marble palaces and head out into the open with just a driver for company.

I found my way back to the broken window and eased my way out again. It would be hard to sleep in the palace; the stench from the toilets would keep me awake. Instead, I lugged my mattress round in the rain to the grand doorway at the back, which matched the one where I had sat and talked with Fergal at the front of the building, and unrolled it in the slender patch of shelter where the rain wouldn't get to me.

I could hear the tread of the marines and their occasional whispers, and the mysterious night-noises which came from the gardens close by me: scratchings and the shaking of branches and the movement of birds and small animals. But for the most part, as the rain grew lighter and the moon appeared occasionally through the clouds, I lay and thought of the extraordinary and ferocious character who had grown up outside Tikrit and clawed his way to supreme power through alliances with other people from this place, and had eventually built this palace here, preferring it to all his others. Modern Iraq had been constructed in his image and likeness, a terrifying society where your worst enemies could well be your children, who might report any sign of thought-crime to the authorities, and where every word and every movement had to be carefully controlled for fear of arrest, torture, possible execution.

But was it the nation which had created Saddam, or Saddam who created the nation? And what part had the British and Americans, who had established the country in the first place, rescued him when he was close to disaster, and finally overthrown him, played in the process? I was still turning these things over in my mind, with half an ear on the disturbing noises of the night, when I fell asleep.

65. LOOTING

It was already obvious in Baghdad that Donald Rumsfeld's strategy, which had won the war quickly, was not going to win the peace. There were too few American troops in the streets to maintain order, and those few were understandably nervous and inclined to be trigger-happy. People in Baghdad had been prepared to welcome the arrival of the Coalition's forces not just because they meant the end of Saddam Hussein, but because they expected that it also meant the end of poverty and deprivation. Instead, even the things which had been readily available under the old regime were now in short supply: drinking water, proper sanitation, electricity, oil, petrol.

Worst of all was the looting. The American soldiers seemed to have orders to protect themselves, but not to trouble about the breakdown of law and order which was happening in front of their eyes. The looting began, as it had done in Kirkuk, Mosul, Tikrit and the other towns we had passed through, with the Ba'ath Party and Mukhabarat offices. From there the mobs moved to any government buildings they came across. Then, by extension, they went for everything else that had been run by the government: hospitals, schools, museums.

It was pay-back time. People who felt they had been deprived of everything under Saddam Hussein now grabbed anything they could lay their hands on, regardless of the consequences to anyone else. This was the world of Thomas Hobbes, with a vengeance: a powerful ruler had been deposed, and the 'war of every man against every man' had commenced. You could see people struggling over broken items of office furniture, trying to grab them from the rest of the looters. Carpeting was ripped up, light fixtures wrenched out, even the insulation pulled out from the ceilings.

Occasionally, when the American soldiers got nervous, they would fire a shot or two in the air, and the crowds would shrink back and take a few minutes to gather again. Soon, when they realized the firing was only being done for effect, they would take no notice beyond flinching at the sudden noise. They had no objection to being filmed by the television cameramen who were now everywhere. There was no point in their hiding their faces, because there was no authority to be frightened of.

'Can you understand what it is like for us?' one old man asked a reporter. 'Yesterday we had Saddam, and we could be arrested for anything we did. Today we have America, and we can do anything, and nobody stops us.'

He didn't regard this as freedom; he saw it as a new and worse type of tyranny.

The Americans were baffled. They had assumed they would be regarded as liberators, and instead they were simply onlookers, irrelevant to the real concerns of life as it had suddenly become in Baghdad. They were neither loved nor hated, liked nor disliked; they were just another factor which had to be taken into account in the Hobbesian business of trying to stay alive. If you didn't understand the commands they screamed at you in their own language, you could die.

'Well, *everyone* understands the word "stop",' an American soldier explained to a television cameraman who asked him how he could control a crowd without speaking a single word of Arabic. As it happens, 'stop' is not one of the English words which Iraqis have adopted. In the weeks that followed the American capture of Baghdad, more than twenty people were shot and killed because they couldn't understand it.

Within three days of the city's fall, a crowd attacked the National Museum and began looting the storage rooms. In the first Gulf War many of the greatest treasures had been moved to secure storage areas, but in 2003 there simply wasn't the manpower or the available space to move everything. Because the collection survived the first war intact, there was less urgency the second time around. No one seems to have anticipated the possibility that the museum would be attacked by mobs of looters.

It was clear that many of the men who converged on the museum had a clear idea what to look for. Forty-seven important pieces vanished from the main exhibition halls, of which seven were first-class masterpieces of international importance. In the storage rooms, 13,000 objects vanished: inscriptions, figures, pottery, terracottas, decorated or inscribed bricks. Many of these pieces surfaced in the *souks* in the days and weeks after the fall of the city, and prices gradually rose. Some of the foreign journalists who were in Baghdad at the time bought stolen items, and the authorities at the Jordanian border belatedly realized they had to try to stop the outflow. As my colleagues and I left Iraq, a Jordanian customs officer searched our suitcases and equipment boxes thoroughly. A Japanese reporter who came through at the same time as us was found to have a brick with a cuneiform inscription hidden in his luggage, and was arrested.

Approximately 1,500 pieces were later brought back to the museum, often by people who said they had taken them for safe-keeping; unfortunately, many of these objects turned out to be replicas or fakes. According to one American academic, most of the 10,000 or so archaeological sites across Iraq were looted in one way or another, though Babylon and Ur were protected by their security staff. It was altogether a depressing end to the Coalition campaign, and yet some-how a symbolic one: as Saddam Hussein fled his capital, the country had turned on itself and destroyed some of the things that most characterized it.

The Bush administration couldn't be blamed for the strange and violent mood of self-harm that suddenly possessed Iraq, but it was guilty of a serious lack of forethought. Perhaps, to be frank, President Bush, Donald Rumsfeld and the others had no very great interest in what would follow the collapse of Saddam's regime: according to the *laissez-faire* model, that was the Iraqis' own business. America's was simply to liberate them. In the weeks that followed, several of the more thoughtful American administrators were highly critical of the absence of any serious planning to follow the regime change which was so important a feature of discussion in Washington before the war.

Later, at a press conference I went to in London, Condoleezza Rice, the President's national security adviser, admitted that the admin-istration had found Iraq's condition to be far worse than it had expected, and she blamed this on Saddam's thirty years of brutality. She made no reference to twelve years of the grinding sanctions the

United States, with British help, had insisted on imposing on Iraq; such is the way politicians can airbrush away the inconvenient facts of history. No one in the audience, which was filled with senior diplomats and politicians, reminded her of this.

Tim Carney, a former US ambassador who spent two months at the Iraqi Ministry of Industry and Minerals in an attempt to revive its work, complained that the White House had not thought through its post-war plans; there was, he said, a lack of resources and priority given to reconstruction. The team which was supposed to be in charge of the task was led by military men under a retired general, Jay Garner. This, Mr Carney said, was 'a grievous flaw', because the military either didn't understand the need to rebuild Iraq, or didn't think it was important enough.

'The coalition has been announcing trivial amounts of money in the tens and twenties of millions of US dollars' worth of projects,' he said. 'It's time to get serious about resources, to announce a package of several billion US dollars, and to address some of the urgent needs of infrastructure and updating of antiquated plants in the many state-owned enterprises.'

But it wasn't done; or at least not in time. The feeling grew that the Bush administration had been concerned purely with the business of toppling Saddam Hussein; after its spectacular victory, it seemed to have no great interest in the wrecked and demoralized society it had chosen to take control of.

66. BACK TO BAGHDAD

We said an affectionate goodbye to our Kurdish bodyguards, who were going back to Suleimaniyah, and an equally affectionate one to the BBC team in Tikrit, and headed off to Baghdad. We drove past Saddam Hussein's home village, al-Awja, a dull earth-coloured place, and on to the site of Balad. Back in 1987 someone from here fired a shot at Saddam's motorcade as he drove through, and the village was completely erased: the buildings destroyed, the land ploughed over. To try to shoot Saddam was so unthinkable, no one would ever think again of the place where it happened.

We had been making good time until we reached an American road-block: there were, they said, *fedayeen* further down the road. Three days ago, this road had been open. Now a new war was starting, a war of sniping and occasional guerrilla attacks. The only answer the American forces had was a heavy one. Cobra helicopter gunships flew low over us, and I noticed that Tom looked as uncomfortable as I felt; suppose they mistook us for Iraqis again? They hovered in the air, firing their rockets, and in the distance an Iraqi arms dump went up like Guy Fawkes Night.

Sitting in the sunshine, waiting to be allowed to continue our journey, I realized how bone-tired I was. This was my fifty-third day on the road – almost eight weeks in which I had not had a single day off. For the last six nights I'd been sleeping rough, and hadn't even changed my clothes. I smelled rank in my own nostrils. My shrapnel ached, my left ear sang constantly like a seashell. I didn't care much about anything now, except just to get to Baghdad, because Baghdad was a major step on the way to going home.

We decided to cut across country, and headed for the Kirkuk–Baghdad road. We had to cross the Tigris, and waited interminably for a fierce knot of traffic to untie itself on the Bailey bridge which some sweating British subaltern must have thrown across the river eighty years before. We found ourselves sitting next to a bunch of fierce-looking, unshaven, heavily armed characters in green uniforms; maybe they belonged to the new police force, but it was hard to be certain at this stage in Iraq's collapse. Without our bodyguards we felt remarkably vulnerable.

Suddenly, two US helicopters came flying along the line of the river at no more than fifty feet: I could even see the cables leading from the pilots' helmets, and watched them turn their heads to look at us. For an instant it seemed certain to me that they were going to blast us, but the heads turned forward again and they carried on along the river. It wasn't simply that I was frightened of being killed. Rather it was that having got this far, and getting so close to surviving, I was terrified I wouldn't make it home.

We negotiated our way through a difficult and potentially hostile village, half Sunni and half Shi'ite, and found ourselves on the high road. There was the old, familiar sense of unreality: Saddam had clearly hired the people who did the signage for British motorways to do the job here as well. BAGHDAD: after all these years it was strange to see the name on the road-signs again. We put on our flak-jackets; from now on, anything could happen.

We headed into the city centre, along streets that had left a faint trace in my memory. American soldiers in the desert I had come to accept fully; to see Americans patrolling the streets of Baghdad felt unnatural. There were burned-out tanks all the way down the side of the road here. I noticed one which, by some extraordinary trick of blast, which can do the oddest things, had had its gun-turret thrown up in the air and turned round, so that the barrel of the gun was stuck in the ragged open hole where the turret had previously fitted.

I started to orient myself as we got closer to the Palestine Hotel and the Sheraton opposite. Saddam's statue, overthrown several days before, still pointed inexorably downwards at the ground, his head close to it as though he was inspecting the concrete very intently. We parked, and an American soldier searched me. While this happened an old man tried to drive through the bewildering chicane the Americans had set up. Someone screamed at him to stop, and fortunately he heard the note of panicky aggression in the voice and obeyed. All the rifles that had been aimed at him were lowered again.

I had to fight the emotions inside me as I walked up the ramp of the Palestine after all this time and went in through the glass doors. It was, somehow, the reverse of nostalgia: a kind of revulsion, or at least of recoil from all the shaven-headed US soldiers and the clean, eager journalists who had just arrived after a long wait in the hotels of Amman, and whose clothes would never be as dirty as mine. It was as though these people had all intruded into some particular area I had reserved for my own use. I felt wholly out of place – a relic from some earlier period in human history, isolated by my deafness and my limp from the unrecognizable new world which was slowly taking shape here.

There was no power in the hotel, and therefore no lights and no lifts and no food. You had to walk up all the stairs, pushing and being pushed in the darkness, smelling the stench of a large building without sanitation. For most of these people, the new arrivals, it was a form of contact with the war – 'It was *still* hell when I got there.' For me, six days without having washed or taken my clothes off, it was just a disappointment, and more isolating than ever.

I was led like a blind man up the darkest of stairs, tap-tapping with my stick, and came out on the part of the hotel roof where the television satellite dishes had been set up. It was all so foreign: this had been a city where information was rationed, was handed out in small, dangerous parcels, was utterly controlled. Now information was being sprayed out across the world with no concern for its dangers or its effects, and with no danger of comeback. It wasn't the Baghdad I had known, in any sense.

And at that moment I saw one single figure from the old Baghdad: Hassan, one of our drivers from the war of 1991, large and shapeless and now distinctly elderly, one of only two local drivers who had stayed with us when things became really difficult. I can't say I had ever particularly liked him; he had been inclined to fawn and be over-generous, bringing us gifts of melons or dates in order to safeguard a job which was his anyway. Now, though, he represented something entirely different: evidence that an older, more difficult Baghdad than this sudden new open, westernized Baghdad had really existed, and that I had had a small part in it.

Hassan was proof of my separate identity. We kissed each other, and I found tears springing to my eyes. Poor old Hassan: he had come down in the world, and had shown up at the BBC with pictures of me and of Jeremy Bowen and of one or two others from 1991, to bolster his claim to have worked for us and his appeal to work for the BBC again. In the haste and flurry of getting going, no one had been interested in an old man with a set of fading photos, and he hadn't even had a hearing.

'You are safe,' he said, and pointed to heaven; it wasn't clear whether it was because this was where the missile or my protection had come from. '*Hamdil'ullah*.'

I promised to do everything I could to get him a driving job, though he didn't return at the appointed time the next morning, and may have found another employer. Poor old Hassan: I was grateful to him for being there, and for reaffirming my independent existence. I was a person again, not just a revenant.

Soon there was someone else: a man I found it hard to identify, an elderly, unshaven man in grubby clothes with a broken front tooth.

'Mr John – I am Sa'ad. You remember Sa'ad? We had good times together in 1991.'

I did now remember Sa'ad. He had been the most dapper and pleasant of our government minders, always well turned-out in dark double-breasted suits and clean shirts, no more helpful than the others because that would have been too dangerous for him, but as decent a man as Saddam Hussein's system would permit. Now he was like the country itself: decayed, sad, troubled. He was working as an occasional fill-in guide for the BBC and delighted to be getting the small amount of money he was paid.

'My wife, I am sorry to have to tell you this, is very ill. It is like sleeping in the bed with death.'

Mr Sa'ad smiled his broken smile, as apologetic for raising such an unhappy thought as he had once been to tell me that it was impossible to film such and such a scene or use such and such a phrase.

I found myself being greeted with wonderful warmth by the BBC people, and chatted with friends and colleagues, the new inhabitants of the journalistic city, while visitors from the new state the Americans were trying to establish came in to be interviewed by the different television stations which had established their temporary studios here on the hotel roof.

A tall, fat Arab in a perfect *dishdasha*, a long white robe, and a *k'fir* or headdress, was propelled through the crowd by a group of sweating, shaven-headed American soldiers; someone said he was going to be the new mayor of Baghdad. Good luck to him, I thought – a more thankless task, performed at the point of American bayonets, it would be hard to imagine. Lots of disturbingly attractive young women shouted at each other in American accents: the US networks were here in force, and for them television was life.

Fortunately there were older people here too, people of my own age and experience, people who knew that television wasn't the only life there is: Dick Blystone of CNN, a renowned writer of attractive, interesting scripts; Mike Boettscher of CNN, whom I knew from Central America in the 1980s, thoughtful and concerned about the wrecking of entire countries; Peter Arnett, who had had his problems with his old employer, CNN, and with his newer one, NBC, who had at first supported him after he had given an ill-considered interview to Baghdad television during this most recent war of liberation, then sacked him when the pressure built up.

As I spoke to old friends and colleagues, I found the invisible curtain between myself and the world around me dissolve. I was no longer observing this new existence without being seen myself, like Scrooge with the ghost of Christmas past. I had, I discovered, become a kind of monument. People came up shyly and shook my hand, or gave me their business cards, and I instinctively patted my pockets, as though after fifty-three days I might still find a card of my own tucked away somewhere. Photographers and cameramen got shots of me, until I found myself slipping round corners and behind large objects to avoid them. From one half-life to another: now I scarcely seemed to exist outside a television set myself.

67. PAYBACK

'You will see,' said an Arab friend of mine who knew Saddam Hussein and the family. It was the same intermediary who had passed on Mohammed Saeed al-Sahhaf's message to me about owing him a favour. 'The two sons were born with a silver spoon in their mouths. They can't live anywhere except a palace, with people bringing them food and girls. They'll be caught. But the old man [Saddam] is different. He doesn't want to have anything to do with them, because he knows he'll be caught as well if he does.'

And so it came to pass. Saddam's two sons, Uday and Qusay, met up after the Americans captured Baghdad, or maybe, in spite of their mutual dislike, they had stayed together all along. At first they tried to organize the resistance, but that became impossible, and anyway it wasn't necessary: the resistance instinctively broke down into small, self-motivating cells which didn't require overall control. At some stage the brothers decided to head for the north. Perhaps, like Uday's father-in-law, Izzat Ibrahim, they thought they should seek refuge across the Syrian border, but by the time they reached the area it was clearly unsafe to cross. So they went to Mosul instead, and took refuge at a house on the northern outskirts belonging to a local tribal leader, Nawaf al-Zaydan Mohammed. The house was not far from the one where Tom, Hiwa and I had stayed, some weeks before, though it was grander and more isolated.

It was also full of people. Tribal leaders in Iraq are expected to play host to large numbers of guests, putting them up and feeding them. In the house of Farhan Sharifani, the head of the Sharifani tribe, there must have been fifty people during the daytime and at least twenty staying there at night. Most would be trustworthy enough, but given that Uday and Qusay each had a price of 15 million dollars on their heads it is not entirely surprising that they were betrayed. They were foolish to have sought shelter there; but as my friend said, they were used to houses and food and company. They couldn't operate on their own.

Perhaps it was Nawaf al-Zaydan Mohammed and his son Shalan who betrayed them, though that would go against every conceivable tenet of tribal duty and hospitality; perhaps it was someone who had visited the house. There were reports afterwards that al-Zaydan's brother had been arrested by the Mukhabarat for falsely claiming to be a member of Saddam Hussein's tribe; this, it was said, had weakened al-Zaydan's loyalty to Saddam and his sons. Whoever it was who betrayed Uday and Qusay approached the American military on the evening of Monday 21 July (the Americans confirmed later it was a 'walk-in') and told them that Uday and Qusay were there. All through the night the American forces planned the operation.

At around nine-thirty on the morning of Tuesday 22 July, a sizeable force of ground troops and armoured vehicles closed off the area around the house and took up their positions. It was an easy target to attack, not at all like Sharifani's house, which was in a small side-street. In choosing their place of refuge the brothers scarcely seem to have considered the possibility of defending themselves. The attack began half an hour later. A group of soldiers ran up to the front door, and an officer with a megaphone demanded that everyone inside the house should come out with their hands up.

Local people said afterwards that Nawaf al-Zaydan Mohammed and Shalan, his son, came out with their hands on their heads and were taken away, though the official American account of the operation made no mention of them whatever. Other neighbours later told reporters they had seen the two men sitting drinking water and eating fruit with American soldiers while the battle to take their home began. One even said he had seen al-Zaydan embracing one of the American soldiers.

Ten minutes later the attack team entered the house, and the two brothers and their bodyguards opened fire on them from behind a barricade set up on the first floor, wounding three soldiers who were making their way up the stairs and another who was outside the building. The troops withdrew quickly, and a more heavily armed group was brought in. The brothers continued to fire out at them from the house. At 10.45 the big weaponry came into play: grenade-launchers, rockets and heavy calibre machine-guns.

Soon further reinforcements turned up: by now there was a virtual army pouring fire into the house. At 11.45 Delta helicopters joined in. The siege ended soon afterwards. Qusay, his fourteen-year-old son Mustafa and a third man, who may have been a bodyguard, were killed by a TOW missile which was fired at the house; Uday, who was injured, shot himself rather than be captured.

There followed a sequence of events which reflected little credit on the American military in Iraq. Secretary of Defense Donald Rumsfeld, who had expressed such outrage during the war at al-Jazeera Television's decision to show pictures of the unidentifiable bodies of dead American soldiers, permitted the publication of photographs showing the bodies of the dead brothers. When many Iraqis doubted that the brothers were really dead, the US military shaved the corpses' heads and used rudimentary embalming techniques to demonstrate that the identification was right.

Twelve days after the shoot-out, the bodies of Uday, Qusay and Mustafa, wrapped in Iraqi flags, were buried near Tikrit in the cemetery of al-Awja, the village where Saddam Hussein had been born. It was a brief, unceremonious affair, and the American soldiers who surrounded the cemetery would allow only 150 mourners to enter.

'We took them to the cemetery's mosque. We prayed and we buried them in the family grave,' said Thawrah Abed Bakr, the director of the Red Crescent Society in the Tikrit area. 'Everything was finished by twelve-thirty. I had been told to do it secretly by the family and the tribe.'

The three graves were also draped with Iraqi flags, and throughout the day small groups of loyalists came to pray beside them. A few hours later there was an explosion in Tikrit, and three American soldiers were injured. In Iraq as a whole, however, most people seemed delighted at the thought that Uday was finally dead. He was a vicious character, thoroughly out of control, who had murdered, raped and tortured an unknown number of people. Qusay was quieter, cleverer and more in control of himself, but deeply unloved. It was not the fact of their deaths which was troubling, so much as the manner of their treatment afterwards. In that, as in so many other ways, the Americans seemed to many intelligent and thoughtful Iraqis to have behaved less like liberators and more like conquerors.

68. DOUBTS

The first Gulf War was a necessity, imposed on President George Bush senior by the unthinking adventurism of Saddam Hussein. No matter that it was a war fought about oil; no American President could have ignored a challenge to the international order of this kind, which would have damaged the economic interests of the entire developed world. The campaign was fought intelligently and quickly, with relatively little bloodshed. Bush senior's great and unforgivable mistake was to listen to the advice of Colin Powell and let slip the opportunity of allowing the Iraqi people to get rid of Saddam themselves once the war was over.

After 11 September 2002 the campaign to rid Afghanistan of the Taliban and their unwanted guests, al-Qaeda, was exemplary: swift, intelligent and largely bloodless. After a ferocious attack like the ones on the Twin Towers and the Pentagon, there was scarcely a nation on earth which questioned the right of the United States to strike back at the man who had planned the attack, and at the near-lunatic and much-hated government which had given him shelter and encouragement. Even Saddam Hussein expressed a certain sympathy for the United States after 11 September; not something the Americans chose to recall afterwards.

The war to overthrow Saddam Hussein was of a completely different order from the other two. There was no outrage, no attack, no *casus belli*, to make it inevitable, and if there was ever any real evidence that Saddam Hussein suddenly constituted a new threat to the United States or its friends, it was never convincingly produced. Leading figures in the Clinton administration had exhaustively examined the question of Saddam's weapons of mass destruction and the danger they posed, and had come to the conclusion that no military action needed to be taken.

What changed was that a new set of people were in government, with a new and crusading approach to American power. Several of them had identified Saddam Hussein before the 2000 election as an enemy of the United States and of its ally Israel, and had already decided that something should be done about him. It would be a sign to the entire world of American power in the new century; and if anyone thought, after 11 September, that America was in any way weakened, then attacking and overthrowing Saddam Hussein would show that this was not the case. Those who killed Americans through acts of terror would be hunted down and killed wherever they were; that was the settled policy of the Likud Party in Israel, and Likud's friends in the Pentagon and the White House wanted to adopt it as America's policy too.

So – did Saddam Hussein genuinely represent a threat to the United States, or was he simply a useful target which would allow the United States to demonstrate the range and extent of its military power? Anthony Zinni, a former Marine Corps general and special representative in the Middle East for Presidents Clinton and George W. Bush, was an experienced and thoughtful man. A reporter put this question to General Zinni early in the crisis. Yes, he answered, Iraq did indeed constitute a threat to the United States, but he would put it at around number seven on the list, and he didn't think there was any good reason to take any action against anyone beyond number five.

Saddam Hussein was certainly a potential danger to his neighbours, but neither an imminent nor a very serious one. His main concern was simply to continue in power, and if he had been closely monitored and carefully controlled he would not have troubled the outside world again. In the opinion of the CIA and the British SIS he had no perceptible links with al-Qaeda or Osama bin Laden or the Taliban in

Afghanistan. In other words, many of the things the Bush administration and the Blair government said about the threat from Iraq before the war were exaggerated or even untrue.

On 7 August 2002 Vice-President Dick Cheney said, 'It's the judgement of many of us that in the not-too-distant-future, he [Saddam Hussein] will acquire nuclear weapons.'

Less than a month later, speaking to journalists at Camp David with Tony Blair beside him, President Bush had shortened that forecast and made it much more precise: Saddam, he said, was 'six months away' from developing a nuclear weapon.

In January 2003, in his State of the Union message, the President spoke of evidence from British intelligence that 'yellow cake' uranium was being smuggled into Iraq from Africa.

On 5 February 2003, the American secretary of state, Colin Powell, told the United Nations that Iraq was importing high-strength aluminium tubes as part of a uranium enrichment programme.

Tony Blair followed the same trajectory.

24 September 2002: '[Saddam's] weapons of mass destruction programme is active, detailed and growing. The policy of containment is not working. The weapons of mass destruction programme is not shut down. It is up and running . . .

'The intelligence picture [the intelligence services] paint is one accumulated over the past four years. It is extensive, detailed and authoritative.

'It concludes that Iraq has chemical and biological weapons, that Saddam has continued to produce them, that he has existing and active military plans for the use of chemical and biological weapons, which could be activated within forty-five minutes, including against his own Shia population; and that he is actively trying to acquire nuclear weapons capability . . .'

This claim about the forty-five minutes acted as a lightning conductor for the entire, complicated dispute. On the face of it, the precise length of time in which weapons like these could be activated was a relatively small detail, especially if the fundamental question was whether Iraq actually had the weapons at all. Yet it often happens in a highly complicated dispute that everything narrows down to a single detail, if only because our minds find it difficult to take in the vast range of other evidence. The human brain has a need to simplify.

The forty-five-minute claim was first openly challenged in an interview on the BBC Radio 4 *Today* programme, soon after six o'clock in the morning. The programme's defence correspondent, Andrew Gilligan, revealed that he had been talking to a leading source who had told him that the government had 'sexed up' the intelligence in the dossier it had placed before the public, and that in particular Downing Street had insisted on inserting the detail about the forty-five minutes against the wishes of the intelligence community.

This claim immediately roused the Downing Street director of communications, Alistair Campbell, to a fury. He demanded an apology from the BBC. The BBC defended itself strongly, and the row became worse and worse. Campbell kept demanding an apology from the BBC; the BBC, knowing that if it apologized it would be seen around the world as the British government's poodle, refused. Intense pressure within the government machine flushed out the source of Gilligan's information: Dr David Kelly, a leading Ministry of Defence weapons expert who knew what he was talking about but was not himself involved in intelligence work. As a result of the intense pressure, both within the Whitehall system and from the media, Dr Kelly apparently committed suicide. In the horror of the moment, the government set up the Hutton inquiry to investigate the circumstances leading to Dr Kelly's death.

As more and more senior figures in intelligence, defence and broadcasting appeared before the tribunal, it seemed impossible that the government, the intelligence services or the BBC itself would escape unscathed. Alistair Campbell announced he was leaving Downing Street – for family reasons. Tony Blair's standing in the opinion polls dropped alarmingly. The BBC examined the dangers involved in allowing less experienced reporters (Andrew Gilligan was a recent recruit from newspaper journalism, and relatively new to the BBC's ways of operating) to speak off the cuff in live interviews. The Murdoch press attacked the BBC with a ferocity which surprised even writers on *The Times* and the *Sunday Times*: their proprietor could see the financial advantages to himself of the BBC's apparent weakness.

In all of this, the original issues were in danger of becoming almost forgotten. On 15 September 2003, a year after the forty-five-minute claim had first been put forward in the government's dossier, Sir

Richard Dearlove, head of SIS, gave evidence to the Hutton inquiry via an audio link in terms of remarkable and fascinating opacity.

'It could be argued that [the claim] was given undue prominence, given the misinterpretation that was placed on the forty-five-minute intelligence. With the benefit of hindsight you could say that is a valid criticism.

'But I am confident that the intelligence was accurate, and that the use made of it was entirely consistent with the original report.

'It did come from an established and reliable source, equating a senior Iraqi military officer who was certainly in a position to know this information.'

The intelligence dossier in which the forty-five-minute claim had appeared related to chemical and biological weapons, he said, and the intelligence assessment staff had supposed that these were weapons which could be used on the battlefield. But when the dossier was made public, people who read it thought it referred to long-range weapons.

The problem, of course, was that the British government, like the Bush administration, was anxious to mobilize public opinion behind an attack on Iraq, and was keen to seize on anything which would have that effect. No wonder the intelligence professionals were nervous about making their information public in a dossier; no wonder the senior SIS figure I spoke to over lunch had told me about the pressure they were under to produce more and better intelligence from inside Iraq.

In the determination to convince public opinion, corners were cut; and although the BBC's report was vulnerable in at least two aspects, the basic fact was that the British government did intervene to make the public believe the position was more alarming than it turned out to be.

At the time of writing, April 2004, no evidence whatever has been discovered of any of the weapons of mass destruction which Saddam Hussein was supposed to have been able to deploy; and if not him, then his two sons – though that was another claim which Downing Street sought to exaggerate. Hans Blix, the former UN chief weapons inspector, declared soon after the war that he thought Iraq had destroyed most of its weapons of mass destruction ten years before, but had kept up the pretence that it still had them in order to deter the

United States from attacking it. That may well turn out to be the case. Yet the work of Hans Blix and his team of UN inspectors revealed a wide range of weapons which were known to have existed and were nevertheless unaccounted for: about 31,600 chemical munitions, 550 mustard gas bombs, and 4,000 tons of chemical precursors.

As late as February 1998 UNSCOM discovered that shells taken from Iraq in 1996 contained 97 per cent pure mustard gas, indicating that it was freshly produced. Although a number of defectors and other witnesses agreed that Iraq had produced VX nerve agent, no stockpiles of it were ever found. Merely because the British and American governments exaggerated the threat does not mean no weapons existed, though in the summer of 2003 the CIA admitted that most of the evidence about Iraq's weapons on which it had based its assessments was a good five years out of date.

It is an irony that the US government exaggerated the threat more than the British government did, yet at first George W. Bush encountered nothing like the storm of criticism suffered by Tony Blair as a result. Bush had benefited greatly at home from his handling of the savage attacks of 11 September 2001. Americans wanted somebody to hit back at, and this feeling was not entirely assuaged after the collapse of the Taliban in Afghanistan. They felt a need to see American troops on the ground defeating an enemy, and Iraq provided the opportunity. It was, as we saw earlier, 'do-able': that is, it looked hard to the uninitiated, but was perfectly easy in reality. There is always a tendency in the minds of the American public to accept what the President of the day tells them, especially about the world outside America, which is a country where less than 19 per cent of the population even owns a passport.

In Britain, there was always a deep unease about George W. Bush. The best cartoonists of the day represented him as a kind of Neanderthal, and sometimes as an ape. His links with the oil industry, his hostility to international measures to deal with global warming, the ferocious and often questionable legislation which was introduced after 11 September – all these things made it hard for Europeans in general and British people in particular to accept him as a leader. By hitching his own political fortunes to George W. Bush's policy cavalcade, Tony Blair was taking a very serious risk indeed; and the risk did not pay off.

He argued his case with a passion that was entirely his own, but essentially his argument was that Britain should do what America did. Before the election of 2000 which brought George W. Bush to power, President Clinton was strongly against intervening in Iraq; Tony Blair was therefore against it too. When the Bush administration was in favour of it, Tony Blair was too, and because he was the person he was, he was as passionate about the new cause he had espoused as he had been about the old one. His foreign secretary, Jack Straw, is said to have argued privately that the failure to get a second UN resolution meant that Britain should restrict itself to offering full political and moral support to the United States, but shouldn't get involved militarily. That would have offered a possible way out of the problem, but Tony Blair overruled him. For him, it was all or nothing.

Although few British people seemed to realize it, what they objected to was not so much the personality and abilities of George W. Bush, but the nature of the fiercely conservative government he headed. 'We can do it because we are America,' Bush said about a task unrelated to the Iraq crisis, and that sense of being the world's dominant – others would say domineering – power was something that Europeans in general found repellent. Many smaller elements played a part in the general dislike: the appearance, manner and attitude of Donald Rumsfeld, for instance. But the essence of America's unpopularity lay in its complete lack of interest in what any other country thought, and its determination to do what it perceived was best for America.

'They are drunk with power,' Nelson Mandela told a television interviewer, and his words struck a chord with many people, right across the world.

One of Bush's speechwriters, in London to plug a book about the President, berated the British for their lack of sympathy with what America had become.

'We are what you used to be,' he said, and indeed there was a real and unashamed sense among Bush's supporters in Washington that America had become the greatest power in history, and had the right to use its strength as it saw fit. Suddenly 'imperial' wasn't a word to avoid any longer, as it had once been. There were very real similarities between the United States at the turn of the twenty-first century and Britain at the turn of the twentieth; not least that both countries were being overtaken economically by their rivals, yet still had the immense political power which their economic supremacy had once given them. From 1999 to 2003 America has been fighting its wars at the rate the British empire fought them in the last quarter of the nineteenth century; and there is the same disparity of power.

America's advantage in the war was overwhelming. It took on a defeatist, poorly equipped army which was completely lacking in air cover, and smashed it utterly in what was effectively a small colonial campaign against a devastated enemy. It was, no doubt, well and efficiently fought, but military historians are unlikely to rank it alongside the Battle of the Bulge or D-Day as a great and honourable American victory.

One hugely unequal American war now overlays the next in the public memory, recording over it like videotape. Who still remembers the American-led onslaught on Serbia and Kosovo in 1999? That was overtaken by the attack on the Taliban in Afghanistan in 2001, and now, in turn, we have had the second Gulf War of 2003, which has largely obliterated the memory of both of them. The generals may understand that there are problems, but the public merely sees the succession of victories, and doesn't pause to consider what might happen to the enemy on the receiving end of the bayonets and the Gatling guns.

Objectives have been achieved, targets hit with meticulous accuracy, yet thousands of ordinary people have been killed and injured in these wars, and there have been grotesque mistakes such as the bombing of hospitals and civilian convoys: incidents which the military authorities responsible have usually apologized for and moved on, and which the peace movements throughout the world regard as evidence that wars of this kind are both immoral in purpose and fundamentally flawed in execution.

Saddam Hussein's Iraq, then, was the test-bed for a new America, which was determined to act up to its full presumed power. The fact that he was genuinely the nastiest dictator on earth became less important than the fact that the Bush administration had chosen him to demonstrate America's strength; not so much to the outside world, which featured very little in Washington's thinking, but to Americans themselves. They had been thoroughly scared and unsettled by the attacks of 11 September 2001. The war against Saddam in 2003 was President Bush's way of assuring them that everything was still all right.

69. RETROSPECTIVE

The invasion of Iraq in 2003 was carried out for a variety of stated reasons, and one or two unstated ones, which were probably more important. It was done, we were told, in order to overthrow a particularly unpleasant tyrant, to protect the world from his dangerous weapons, to undercut the threat from international terrorism, to make the Middle East more democratic. It was also done, though no one put it into such words, to give Americans the sense that they had struck back at the dark forces which had reached out and attacked the heart of the American system on 11 September 2001. In addition, there must have been several people at the top of the Bush administration who thought that destroying Saddam Hussein would help to safeguard the position of Israel. As for the president himself, he may well have felt, privately, that going one step further than his father had gone would ensure his re-election in 2004.

It didn't quite work out as expected.

The Middle East did not become more democratic as a result, nor was Israel's position made any safer; and the world in general, as the appalling bomb attacks in Madrid and elsewhere in 2004 demonstrated, was just as vulnerable to international terrorism as before; indeed, the invasion of Iraq recruited thousands of new volunteers for the cause around the world. The war revealed something else as well: America's ability to fight and win a set-piece war against a feeble enemy was never in question, but its capacity to police a complex and little-understood country for a long period of time was much more doubtful.

As events in Northern Ireland and the Basque country have shown, people who want to commit acts of terrorism cannot easily be stopped; but they will not achieve their political purpose if governments employ patience, good police work, and a determination to look objectively at the situation and redress whatever wrongs exist. That way, the terrorists become isolated in their communities, and eventually their cause fades into inactivity.

The British and Spanish governments did all these things, and thereby won the support of neighbouring countries where there had previously been a certain sympathy for the ultimate goals of the terrorists. The terrorism of a few ETA and IRA diehards still erupts in a small way from time to time, but it is clear that the basic purpose of both organizations has been fatally undermined. The British and Spanish governments had to reform themselves and their habits, and work hard to get rid of the very real causes for terrorism. It was a slow process, and there were no short cuts: certainly not attacking other countries, murdering the terrorist leaders, or bombing their supporters. Such tactics please the voters for a while, but they are the best and quickest way to ensure failure and further bloodshed in the longer run.

The United States, under George W. Bush, chose to ignore the examples of Northern Ireland and the Basques, and to follow Israel's practice instead. As a result, terrorism was treated as a national enemy instead of a serious crime. In the towns and cities of Iraq, the US army consciously adopted the tactics used by the Israeli army in the West Bank. At the same time the Bush administration did nothing serious to bring about a peace agreement between Israel and the Palestinians: the one area of political change which might have undermined support for fundamentalist terrorism. History is likely to be hard on George W. Bush and his administration.

The period during which these things happened saw a remarkable upturn in the national fortunes of Britain. For decades the British had become used to thinking of themselves as being in decline; but by the end of the 1990s it started to become clear that they were in fact doing rather well. The British economy overtook that of France to become the fourth largest in the world, and there were forecasts that by 2012 it would be larger than Germany's. British influence had always been greater than most people in Britain realized; now, it seemed, the British had a new relationship with the United States which gave them greater strength and a louder voice in the world than ever.

Yet instead of being regarded as America's strong and loyal supporter, Tony Blair was represented around the world as George W. Bush's lapdog, prepared to do any tricks for a good word from his master. But although this was the general public perception, it was not, in fact, the way Bush treated him at all. On two separate occasions, anxious about the political fallout in Britain of Blair's support for the invasion of Iraq, Bush suggested that he might prefer not to send British soldiers to Iraq. On both occasions Blair insisted firmly that he would.

None of this did Tony Blair any good at all. The moral authority which he had exercised when he came to power in 1997 had inevitably lessened considerably, but the war against Saddam drew off the remainder of it. His assurance that Iraq had weapons of mass destruction which would eventually come to light did serious damage to his standing. But his close association with an American president who stood for so many things which a majority of British people found distasteful harmed Tony Blair even more.

Bush's almost unquestioning support for the government and policies of Arial Sharon in Israel, his espousal of capital punishment and other conservative issues in the United States, and his fundamentalist form of Christianity made George W. Bush seem a very foreign figure to most British people. The cartoonists' vision of Bush as a stupid, hairy ape with close-set eyes came to dominate the public perception in Britain, and no one who chose to be identified closely with Bush was likely to receive much public respect as a result. No matter how long he might continue in the job, Tony Blair's authority as prime minister was seriously damaged by the beginning of 2004.

For better and for worse, the tone of his government was set by his communications director, Alistair Campbell. It was Campbell who brought a new degree of sophistication to the concept of 'spin' in British politics, paying a degree of attention to appearances which was entirely foreign to the Labour Party. Many civil servants believed his approach blurred the previously clear-cut distinction between public service and political action, and disapproved of his influence accordingly.

The powerful divisions which the war created within the country and the Labour Party made Campbell even noisier, angrier and more interventionist than before. The end of the fighting in Iraq in May 2003 did nothing to calm the atmosphere; in fact, the debate about weapons of mass destruction and the rights and wrongs of attacking Saddam Hussein continued more forcefully than ever. Alistair Campbell had had an exhausting few months, and his temper, always fierce, grew worse.

The main target for his anger was the BBC, which, annoyingly, insisted on being even-handed on this issue, as on every other matter of controversy. Campbell would sometimes ring the director of news, Richard Sambrook, several times a day to complain about something he had heard or watched. His calls were not quiet and calm. On the contrary, he would shout his threats down the phone line with abandon.

He was aware how effective this kind of aggression had been in the past, when the BBC had been more timid. But Sambrook, though a peaceable man himself, knew that he was in charge of the largest and best-respected television news organization in the world, and was not prepared to be bullied. His senior staff backed him strongly, even fiercely, and perhaps this was counter-productive. With hindsight, the tone should have been more careful, more balanced, more self-searching. But we only realized that later.

For some years previously the *Today* programme on Radio 4 had been edited by Rod Liddle, a highly talented man who could be appallingly rude to his staff. He was much more of an independent operator than many other BBC programme editors, and wrote a column for the *Guardian*. He had resigned after a storm of protest about an attack he made on the supporters of the Countryside Alliance, in which he said the sight of them reminded you why you voted Labour at the last election: not the most balanced of lines to take. Not long before the invasion of Iraq the BBC gave him the choice of continuing to edit *Today* or continuing to write his column. He chose the column.

Characteristically, Liddell was often impatient of the BBC news correspondents who were assigned to his programme, because he felt they did not provide the cutting-edge journalism he demanded and he began appointing some correspondents of his own choosing. One of them seemed a stoutish, rather obsessive man who had previously worked for the *Sunday Telegraph*: Andrew Gilligan. Gilligan had not been popular on the paper, and he was not to be popular on *Today*. He was very much a print journalist still. BBC correspondents are a recognizable breed, inclined to mute their own individual qualities in the interest of balance, and perpetually concerned about the precise accuracy of what they write. Being one of them myself, I concede that this kind of thing does not necessarily make for buccaneering journalism.

Buccaneering journalism – or rather pro-active, exclusive journalism – was precisely what Rod Liddell wanted, and Andrew Gilligan provided it. He had a knack of getting to significant places and meeting significant people, and obtaining interesting stories in the manner of a Sunday newspaper journalist. Before the invasion of Iraq he cleverly managed to get a visa to Baghdad to cover the war; but he was less talented as an on-the-spot reporter, and his BBC colleagues seemed not to like him very much. 'A pity he's not one of our own,' said one senior journalist of him.

After the war, with the instinct that had brought many exclusives, Gilligan spent a good deal of time investigating the subject of weapons of mass destruction. As we now know, one of his main contacts was Dr David Kelly, a distinguished weapons expert who was prepared to speak off the record to journalists about the wider issues of weapons control and the justification for the war. Like a great many other senior British civil servants, Kelly had his doubts about the way the government, strongly influenced by Alistair Campbell, had used intelligence to shore up its case.

As a result, Gilligan made his famous broadcast for the *Today* programme. If you examine it in the light of what later emerged, most of it turns out to be entirely correct, and without any doubt it was a subject of major public interest. But perhaps because he was reporting live by phone from his Greenwich flat soon after six o'clock in the morning, Gilligan was more careless in his phrasing than he should have been; and he had no evidence for suggesting that the British government had knowingly published evidence it knew to be false. This was an assumption on his part, and he did not make that clear. Alistair Campbell, listening at home to the broadcast, exploded with rage and began his familiar round of threatening phone calls to the BBC, insisting there must be a public apology. At this point, it now seems reasonable to say, the BBC's management should have checked Gilligan's words with some care, made him admit he did not have any reliable source for the allegation, and made an immediate retraction. But Campbell's own violent, often foul-mouthed bullying made that particularly difficult. A public apology would have made it look as though the government controlled the BBC and had brought it to heel.

A more careful journalist would not have made the allegation in the first place; but a wiser, less overbearing and perhaps less exhausted head of Downing Street communications would never have forced the BBC into such a position once the allegation had been made. Campbell's demand for an apology seemed to put the very independence of the BBC into question.

In the following weeks, the way in which Dr Kelly's identity as Gilligan's source was released into the public domain was one of the worst betrayals of trust by a modern British government, and the manner of it led directly to Dr Kelly's decision to take his own life. How any government minister could still remain in office after such a thing had happened to one of his civil servants is hard for those of us who are not politicians to understand; but Geoff Hoon remained secretary of state for defence, even though his position in Whitehall was greatly diminished. Downing Street, in the meantime, announced an inquiry into the affair, and was skilful in choosing the man to conduct it.

From the early 1970s, when he represented British soldiers at the notoriously inept Widgery tribunal into the Bloody Sunday shootings in Derry in 1972 – so inadequate that the entire case had to be reopened thirty years later – Lord Hutton was widely regarded as a supporter of the status quo: unworldly, too, and innocent about the way in which governments behave.

Those of us who had watched his performances at the Widgery tribunal all those years before were not altogether surprised when he made his findings at the end of 2003, merely disappointed that a senior (though retired) judge should have shown himself to be so silly in his findings. Hutton's report seemed to find the BBC guilty of every accusation made against it, while clearing the government almost wholly of any responsibility for Dr Kelly's death.

Some months afterwards, Lord Hutton naively allowed his feelings to be known through a Labour MP. Hutton was astonished, the MP said, that his report should have been regarded as loading all the blame onto the BBC and exonerating the government. He drew attention to various passages in the report which, if anyone had looked at them with sufficient care, did indeed seem intended to redress the balance a little. Yet here too Hutton was woefully naive. If you are charged with judging a matter as sensitive and important as this, you do not mince your words finely and enfold them deep in your text.

The spinners will concentrate on the headline issues, and no one will read the rest of it.

Yet Hutton didn't really do the Blair government much of a service in the longer run. The initial joy at being let off the hook quickly faded, and various senior ministers showed that they were unhappy with the outcome. A more balanced report would, as it turned out, have suited the government rather better; it might also have protected poor Lord Hutton from the widespread contempt which came his way.

As for the BBC, it was devastated by the outcome. People spoke and wrote openly about the need to disband it. Its enemies around the world, from Robert Mugabe in Zimbabwe to Rupert Murdoch's newspapers and television channels, made the greatest play with the BBC's discomfiture. Morale among the BBC's staff was lower than at any time in the previous forty years. It was not a few careless remarks from a very un-BBC contract reporter which had been judged and founding wanting; it was, most people felt, the BBC as an institution

Yet at this moment of crisis the BBC managed to do the right thing. Gavyn Davies, the chairman, having been outspoken in the BBC's defence, immediately resigned. The contrast with Geoff Hoon's behaviour was stark. Davies' deputy, a former Conservative chief whip, Lord Ryder, seemed determined to put the Corporation right as far as the government was concerned, though many people inside and outside the BBC felt that his public apology was abject and went much too far. The director-general, Greg Dyke, had the strong impression that if he too offered his resignation the BBC's Board of Governors, chaired by Ryder after the departure of Gavyn Davies, would not accept it. Not so: when he resigned, the governors agreed to let him go.

So vanished, in a couple of days, the best and most successful chairman/director-general partnership it has been my privilege to work for in thirty-eight years at the BBC. When Andrew Gilligan left the BBC a few days later it was scarcely noticed: the damage his reporting had done still dominated our attention, and the man himself seemed of little importance.

There was more apologizing: far too much, it seemed to some of us. It looked for a time as though there was to be a witch-hunt through the ranks of the editors who had been involved in the episode, and a group of the BBC's senior journalists – John Humphrys, Jeremy Paxman, Andrew Marr, Jeff Randall and I – wrote a crisp letter to Lord Ryder about it.

We were assured that there was no witch-hunt after all: merely an in-house inquiry to find out what had gone wrong. Lord Ryder later announced that he would soon retire from his post as vice-chairman. Slowly, the uncertainty and lack of self-confidence faded. The resignations of Davies and Dyke gave everyone the feeling that the Corporation had acted correctly and honourably and, although they were much missed, the rest of the organization was free to get on with its job. Within a few months the staff began to forget the ordeal they had gone through. As if to demonstrate that it had no designs on the BBC's independence, the government appointed Michael Grade to be the new chairman: a broadcaster's broadcaster, who had been quick to defend the BBC in previous rows with Downing Street.

The government too had changed. At the height of the dispute with the BBC Alistair Campbell announced his departure from Whitehall: nothing to do with the Gilligan affair, he insisted, and some people wondered whether that might actually be true. Directly Campbell was gone, the entire atmosphere in Downing Street was different. The aggression faded, the telephones were quiet, the older, calmer relationship between Number Ten, Whitehall and the media began to re-establish itself.

Yet after Campbell there was no one with the force of character to persuade everyone that Tony Blair had emerged unscathed from the invasion of Iraq. Probably not even Campbell himself could not have done it, because it was patently untrue. Joining President George W. Bush's great enterprise had fatally damaged Tony Blair's reputation for passionate honesty and plain dealing. He would continue as prime minister for some time afterwards; but no one would ever think of him again in quite the way they once had. Perhaps he never thought of himself in that way again, either.

70. HOME

The cemetery outside Tikrit is a depressing place. The brownish-grey earth is blasted to a powder, and the hot wind blows the detritus of the place across the graves, which are little more than lumps of dust and stones. There are no trees to give shade. The people who are buried here were anonymous enough in life; in death their graves are mostly ignored, unknown.

Except, of course, for those which belong to Uday and Qusay Hussein, and Qusay's little son, all killed when the Americans tracked them down. The three graves are in a corner of the cemetery, well away from the rest. One, Uday's, is marked with a little plastic red rose: nothing more. Almost every day people come to see them, though there are fewer visitors now than before. It is not love that brings them, since Uday remains in death one of the most hated men Iraq has produced. Often, of course, the motive is simple curiosity, but there is also an element of respect, even now. The graves represent all that is effectively visible of a once great and terrible dictatorship.

After his ignominious capture in December 2003, scarcely anyone wanted Saddam Hussein back. When the BBC and other news organizations carried out an elaborate and professionally conducted opinion poll in Iraq in March 2004 to mark the first anniversary of the start of the war, only 3.3 per cent of people questioned said they thought Saddam should lead the country again.

As I write this, in the spring of 2004, it seems likely that Saddam will be put on trial relatively soon, and that he will be found guilty and hanged. Maybe that will bring him a certain renewed sympathy from Iraqis and from other Arab and Muslim countries. His body will presumably be laid to rest in the cemetery outside Tikrit, where the people from his tribe and from the village of al-Awja have traditionally been buried. Saddam and his two sons, who shared many of his characteristics, will lie side by side, together with the grandson whose presence gave Saddam so much pleasure.

Properly speaking, none of us should spare Saddam a single sympathetic thought. His was a regime of great wickedness, and the world is a better place for his passing. Whether it was right for one country to march into another and change its regime for something it liked better is an altogether different issue from the personal survival of Saddam Hussein.

Yet we wouldn't be entirely human if we couldn't see the drama of Saddam's rise and fall. The brutalized little boy from al-Awja who rose to brutalize so many others will have been laid to rest in the cemetery which serves the ugly, hot, dusty, mean little village he sprang from: another little heap of grey-brown earth and stones and fine dust, with perhaps a plastic flower to mark it out. Saddam always hated al-Awja. Now it will be his forever.

INDEX

In this index, personal names prefixed by al- or as- are filed under the main component of the name. This does not apply to place names or to the names of corporate bodies.

JOHN SIMPSON

Strange Places, Questionable People

PAN BOOKS

For over thirty years John Simpson, BBC World Affairs Editor, has travelled the world to report on the most significant events of our times.

From being punched in the stomach by Harold Wilson on one of his first days as a reporter, to escaping summary execution in Beirut, flying into Teheran with the returning Ayatollah Khomeini, and narrowly avoiding entrapment by a beautiful Czech secret agent, John Simpson has had an astonishingly eventful career. In 1989 he witnessed the Tiananmen Square massacre, the fall of the Berlin Wall and the collapse of Communism throughout Eastern Europe and only weeks later, in South Africa, the release of Nelson Mandela.

With Simpson's uncanny knack of being in the right place at the right time, this autobiography is a ringside seat at every major event in recent global history.

'So vivid I could feel my heart beating'
Jonathan Mirsky, *Spectator*

'A damn good read . . . He's a first-rate writer and funny with it'
John Humphreys, *Sunday Telegraph*

JOHN SIMPSON

A Mad World, My Masters

Tales from a Traveller's Life

PAN BOOKS

A Mad World, My Masters, John Simpson's second volume of auto-biographical writing, is a celebration of some of the world's wilder places and the unusual characters that inhabit them. Simpson transports his readers on an extraordinary world tour that includes dodging guerrillas at a cocaine market in Colombia, narrowly escaping a murderous Osama bin Laden in Afghanistan and filming undercover in Lebanon with a mad French cameraman.

Simpson's travels uncover small heroes and big villains, spies and secret police everywhere, resourceful fixers and even the occasional icon. A master of storytelling, he recounts some hilarious moments. Discover how it feels to moon the queen, ask an ex-head of state if he is a cannibal and realize that a worldwide scoop may have been ruined by a flatulent Colonel Gadhafi.

JOHN SIMPSON

News From No Man's Land

Reporting the World

PAN BOOKS

On 13 November 2001 John Simpson and a BBC news crew walked into Kabul and the liberation of the Afghan capital was broadcast to a waiting world. It was the end of a sustained campaign against the Taliban, a campaign that Simpson had covered from the beginning, despite appalling difficulties and, often, great danger.

In *News From No Man's Land* John Simpson focuses on how journalists set about finding the stories that make the headlines. Like his previous books, it is rich in anecdote and filled with extraordinary encounters with remarkable individuals. This is quintessential Simpson: utterly absorbing and written with all the care and lucidity of his reporting style.

'A brilliant raconteur'
Spectator

'A wonderful writer, his published work now rivals his television reporting in its clarity, perceptiveness and intelligence . . . Even if he were to pack it in tomorrow, John Simpson would be remembered as one of the greatest foreign correspondents Britain has ever produced'
Scotland on Sunday

CON COUGHLIN

Saddam: The Secret Life

PAN BOOKS

Two weeks before September 11th, Saddam Hussein placed his troops on their highest military alert since the Gulf War. Having provided funding, logistical support and training for Osama bin Laden's al-Qaeda network, the Iraqi dictator prepared to go to war for a second time with the US. In *Saddam: The Secret Life*, Con Coughlin gets right to the heart of one of the most dangerous and murderous dictators of modern times, explaining how an illegitimate child from Tikrit became the West's greatest adversary.

Drawing on an unparalleled network of sources, contacts, and first hand testimonies, Con Coughlin takes us to the centre not only of Saddam's complex and bewildering regime but of the contradictions in his private life: his sponsoring of Islamic fundamentalism, his whisky drinking and womanizing, his reliance on and violent treatment of his family. *Saddam: The Secret Life* is an insightful, penetrating and shocking account one of the world's most dangerous men.

'[an] admirably clear account'
Charles Tripp, *Daily Telegraph*

'Engrossing'
LA Times

OTHER PAN BOOKS
AVAILABLE FROM PAN MACMILLAN

JOHN SIMPSON

STRANGE PLACES, QUESTIONABLE PEOPLE	0 330 35566 X	£7.99
A MAD WORLD, MY MASTERS	0 330 35567 8	£7.99
NEWS FROM NO MAN'S LAND	0 330 48735 3	£7.99

CON COUGHLIN

| SADDAM: THE SECRET LIFE | 0 330 39310 3 | £7.99 |

All Pan Macmillan titles can be ordered from our website,
www.panmacmillan.com, or from your local bookshop
and are also available by post from:

Bookpost, PO Box 29, Douglas, Isle of Man IM99 1BQ
Credit cards accepted. For details:
Telephone: 01624 677237
Fax: 01624 670923
E-mail: bookshop@enterprise.net
www.bookpost.co.uk

Free postage and packing in the United Kingdom

Prices shown above were correct at the time of going to press.
Pan Macmillan reserve the right to show new retail prices on covers
which may differ from those previously advertised in the text
or elsewhere.